Ottoman Brothers

Ottoman Brothers

Muslims, Christians, and Jews in Early Twentieth-Century Palestine

Michelle U. Campos

STANFORD UNIVERSITY PRESS
STANFORD, CALIFORNIA

Stanford University Press
Stanford, California

Printed in the United States of America on acid-free, archival-quality paper

Library of Congress Cataloging-in-Publication Data

Campos, Michelle U. (Michelle Ursula), 1971-
Ottoman brothers : Muslims, Christians, and Jews in early twentieth-century Palestine / Michelle U. Campos.
p. cm.
Includes bibliographical references and index.
ISBN 978-0-8047-7067-5 (cloth : alk. paper)--
ISBN 978-0-8047-7068-2 (pbk. : alk. paper)
1. Cultural pluralism--Palestine--History--20th century. 2. Group identity--Political aspects--Palestine--History--20th century. 3. Citizenship--Palestine--History--20th century. 4. Palestine--Ethnic relations--History--20th century. 5. Palestine--History--1799-1917. 6. Turkey--Politics and government--1909-1918. I. Title.
DS125.C26 2011
305.6095694'09041--dc22 2010033457

Typeset by Bruce Lundquist in 10/12 Sabon

For Tal and Noah

Contents

List of Illustrations and Tables

Figures

Maps

Tables

Acknowledgments

As with any project spanning many years from inception to completion, my book has benefited from the help of numerous institutions and individuals. My debt to them is enormous.

This research project received generous support from: the Fulbright Commission in Israel, the Social Science Research Council, the Palestinian American Research Council, Stanford University (the School of Humanities and Sciences, the Institute of International Studies, and the Taube Center for Jewish Studies), Cornell University (the Department of Near Eastern Studies, the President's Council for Cornell Women, and the Society for the Humanities), and the University of Florida's Department of History. I thank in particular Ross Brann, my former chair at Cornell, and Joe Spillane, my current chair at UF, for their tremendous support for my work, in the form of travel grants, course reductions, and valuable writing time. My research for this book was also greatly facilitated by numerous librarians and archivists in Israel, Palestine, Jordan, Lebanon, Turkey, France, and the United States, and I thank them for their invaluable assistance.

Over the years my work has benefited immensely from the feedback and aid of scholars, colleagues, and friends, including: Butrus Abu Manneh, Iris Agmon, Ida Altman, Joel Beinin, Hanna Berman, Johann Büssow, Linda Butler, Holly Case, Sherman Cochran, Brett de Bary, Louis Fishman, Haim Gerber, Eyal Ginio, Magdi Guirguis, Kim Haines-Eitzen, ʻAwad Halabi, Jessica Harland-Jacobs, Peter Holquist, Avigail Jacobson, Pieter Judson, Erdem Kabadayı, Reşat Kasaba, Dilek Akyalcin Kaya, Vangelis Kechriotis, Sarah Kovner, Gudrun Krämer, Sheryl Kroen, Jacob Landau, Mark LeVine, Joel Migdal, Montasir al-Qaffash, Richard Roberts, Aron Rodrigue, Avi Rubin, Kent Schull, Samir Seikaly, Seteney Shami, Sarah Stein, Salim Tamari, Baki Tezcan, Patricia Woods, and Mahmud Yazbak. My sincere thanks to all of them for their time and generosity, their insights and references, and their gentle criticism. I also thank Israel Gershoni and Charles Kurzman for their close readings of this work and for their enthusiastic support of the project. I am also extremely grateful to my editors at Stanford University Press: Kate Wahl, for believing in this project as well as for her keen eye and valuable feedback, and her very talented assistant, Joa Suorez; and Mariana Raykov, for shepherding it through the various stages of publication with good humor and a great deal of patience and skill.

Spanning debts both professional and personal, my heartfelt thanks go to Shana Bernstein, Shira Robinson, and Celka Straughn for their constructive feedback on this project as well as their overall intellectual and emotional support during the past many (!) years of my life. Thanks also are due to Celka for graciously and reliably procuring various newspapers and pamphlets for me from the Harvard Library over the years.

Finally, it is only fitting that I thank my family. My mother, Rosita Buendia, and my father, Sergio Campos, placed a strong emphasis on the life of the mind and gave us all freedom and support to follow our dreams, even though mine always took me so far from home. My siblings Yvonne, Sandra, Suzette, Adam, and Linda have given moral, material, and logistical support throughout the difficult years of study, research, and writing. Tamir Sorek has read and discussed more versions of this book than I'm sure he cares to remember; he has been a tireless intellectual sounding-board and critic who has strengthened my work immeasurably. I thank him for this, but more importantly, for the rich life outside of the text that we share with our sons.

Ottoman Brothers

Introduction

In the spring of 1909, a young Jewish lawyer by the name of Shlomo Yellin addressed a gathering of Ottoman notables in Beirut. Born and raised in the Old City of Jerusalem, Yellin was the quintessential polyglot Levantine: he spoke Yiddish with his Polish father, Arabic with his Iraqi mother, Hebrew with his Zionist older brother, and Judeo-Spanish with his Sephardi Jewish neighbors; he wrote love letters in English to the schoolgirl niece he later married, and he jotted notes to himself in French. At the same time, the fez- and suit-wearing "Suleiman Effendi" was the perfect Ottoman gentleman: at the prestigious Galatasaray Imperial Lycée in Istanbul, he studied Ottoman Turkish, Arabic, and Persian language, literature, translation, and calligraphy; Ottoman and Islamic history; hygiene, math, science, philosophy, geography, and French literature. After a brief stint at a German university, Yellin graduated from the Ottoman Imperial Law Academy with certification in Islamic law, Ottoman civil and criminal law, and international commercial and maritime law.[1]

On that spring day, Yellin's Ottoman Turkish-speaking audience likely consisted of members of the local branch of the Committee for Union and Progress (CUP; the so-called Young Turks), the underground political party which had carried out the July 1908 Ottoman revolution. Yellin was a member of the Beirut CUP branch, and he later dedicated two pamphlets "in profound admiration" to the movement. Undoubtedly, some members of the audience also belonged to one of several local Freemason lodges to which Yellin had earlier submitted an application for membership while extolling Masonic support for the values of liberty, equality, and fraternity. Whatever their institutional affiliation, what is certain is that Yellin's audience of white-collar *effendi*s, or gentlemen, like himself—lawyers, doctors, businessmen, journalists, school teachers, clerks—were fellow Ottomans who were as committed to and concerned about the future of the "Ottoman nation" as he was.[2]

"The noble Ottoman nation," Yellin told his audience, "is made up of different groups who live together, who for the sake of the homeland [*vatan*] have shaped themselves into one mass." He continued:

> In the Ottoman Empire the different peoples are equal to one another and it is not lawful to divide according to race; the Turkish, Arab, Armenian, and Jewish elements have mixed one with the other, and all of them are connected together, molded into one shape for the holy *vatan*. Each part of the nation took upon itself the name of "Ottoman" as a source of pride and an honorable mark. The responsibility and [illegible] of our holy *vatan* must be our sole aim, and it is necessary to be ready every second and every minute to sacrifice our lives for it. . . . Now we keep [the homeland] deep in our hearts as a basic foundation of our national education. The life of the homeland is bound up with that of the nation."[3]

At the center of Yellin's narrative was the first-person plural—"we Ottomans"—the Ottoman nation united in spirit and in purpose. Yellin's Ottoman nationalism was not distant or official, but rather emphasized an intimate emotional link between individual, collective, and state, reflected in phrases such as "our beloved nation" and "lover of the homeland." His Ottoman nationalism also tapped deeply into religion as inspiration, legitimization, and sacralized form, in many ways becoming a civic religion: he repeatedly invoked the "sacred homeland," and his challenge to his audience to sacrifice themselves for the homeland used terms of martyrdom that were stripped of their traditional Islamic context and reinvested within an Ottoman national framework.[4]

At the same time, Yellin's Ottoman nationalism was tightly linked to the new constitutional regime and nascent notions of Ottoman imperial citizenship. The CUP had succeeded in carrying out a "new conquest" of Istanbul, ushering in a "new era" free of absolutism, where the "holy constitution" linked the individual to the reforming, constitutional state.[5] Also, Yellin viewed Ottoman citizenship as a contract between individual citizens and social groups. In other words, for Yellin and his audience, despite their differences in religion, in ethnicity, and in mother tongue, there was no doubt that they were all believing and practicing Ottomans, connected to their fellow countrymen in the far corners of the empire by territory, law, history, and by the mutual expectations and responsibilities of imperial citizenship.

Situated in the aftermath of the 1908 Ottoman revolution, which briefly transformed the empire from an absolutist state into a type of liberal parliamentary democracy, Shlomo Yellin and his Beirut audience were direct products of and witnesses to the challenges and accomplishments of their beloved empire. The Ottoman state had at various points throughout the previous century implemented numerous important changes and reforms, known as the Tanzimat—revamping the state bureaucracy and legal system; embarking on an ambitious program of building, education, and public works; and promoting loyalty and identification among its diverse population. The fact that Yellin and his companions were educated in modern state institutions resulted in their being literate in numerous languages, including the official language of the state, Ottoman Turkish; fostered a familiarity with fellow subjects of different faiths, ethnicities, and regions; and led to their loyalty to and identification with the state.

At the same time, precisely because of their education, literacy, and travels, they were no doubt aware of the diminished role of the Ottoman Empire in global politics, of its uneven absorption into the world economy, and of the numerous political cross-winds which were blowing in other parts of the world. Thus, even while basking in the glow of revolutionary promise, modern citizens like Yellin and his audience were optimistic but worried about the future of the empire—how it would reform internally, how it would catch up with Europe, and what role the empire might play in a world wracked by revolution, colonialism, and the challenges of a modern age.[6]

This book examines the meaning of liberty, citizenship, and public life in the last Islamic empire. While building on earlier studies of the revolution and the late Ottoman reform tradition, this book is an innovative study of the struggles over the content and contours of imperial citizenship and nationhood on the eve of the end of empire. At the core of the Ottoman revolution is what I call "civic Ottomanism," a grassroots imperial citizenship project that promoted a unified sociopolitical identity of an Ottoman people struggling over the new rights and obligations of revolutionary political membership. By tracing how Muslims, Christians, and Jews became imperial citizens together, I put forward the view of the Ottoman nation, not simply as an "imagined" or discursive imperial community, but as a shared field of social and political interaction and contestation.[7]

This study shifts between the imperial capital in Istanbul, which often set the pace of events and attitudes, and the region of Palestine, hundreds of miles to the south and in some ways a world away, all the while paying attention to developments in other regions and provinces of the empire. Too much of Ottoman history has been written from the vantage point of one corner of the empire alone, often determined along post–World War I nationalist lines. Instead, this study shows how permeable imperial space often was: in addition to soldiers and commodities, people and ideas flowed freely between countryside and city, between province and capital, and between provinces themselves.

With the explosion of the free press in all the languages of the empire, the character and scope of political participation broadened dramatically beyond just the state bureaucracy or provincial notable families, and the new white-collar middle-class of teachers, clerks, and journalists entered into the public arena. Ottoman subjects (*teba'*) claimed their new revolutionary rights and entered into the Ottoman *polis* as imperial citizens (*muwāṭinūn*, Ara.; *vatandaşlar*, Ott. Turk.), marking their substantive transformation from passive beneficiaries or victims of imperial policies to active partners shaping the course of imperial reform.[8] Ottomans throughout the empire received and interpreted the revolutionary language, rhetoric, and symbols disseminated by the dominant political forces, but they *also* produced their own set of meanings and countermeanings, both on the streets and in the press. In developing a view of Ottoman citizenship as a mass social movement that takes into account the desires, strategies, and agency of the empire's new citizens, I explore the ways in which Ottomans took seriously the promise of political change and contributed actively to shaping its meaning.[9]

Ordinary Ottomans, from Salonica to Jerusalem to Baghdad, exercised new political rights and responsibilities, tackled the challenges of ethnic and religious diversity within the body politic, and debated the future of the empire and their role within it. Among the questions that preoccupied them were: Who was an "Ottoman" and what bound the "Ottoman nation" together? What would political liberty, reform, and enfranchisement look like? What did being a "citizen" entail, and how would rights and duties be distributed equally? What role would religion and ethnicity have in the body politic and in the practice of politics in this multiethnic, multireligious, multilingual Islamic empire?

I analyze these public articulations of and engagement with the revolutionary slogans of "liberty, equality, fraternity, and justice" (Chapters 1 and 2). Memoir and newspaper accounts relate that on the streets and in the press, Ottoman Palestinians translated these tropes from the French and Iranian revolutions to their own imperial and local settings, and common citizens employed the spectrum of these ideas for individual and collective purposes. Intellectuals such as the parliamentary representatives from Jerusalem and Beirut, who both published chronicles of the revolutionary thinking, tell us that the Ottoman citizenship project drew on both Western liberal and Islamic notions of liberty, justice, consultation, public good, and accountability. These themes were further developed in the press and other popular media. For example, under the banner of freedom-liberty (*ḥurriyya*, Ara.; *hürriyet*, Ott. Turk.), the revolution served as an inspiration and legitimizing force for the rebellion of peasants against their landlords as well as for the mobilization of Greek-Orthodox Christian, Armenian, and Sephardi Jewish communities in

Jerusalem against their ecclesiastical leaderships in favor of increased representation and "modern" leadership.

The revolutionary slogans of "equality and brotherhood" were premised on an ideology of belonging to a unified Ottoman people-nation. In Palestine as elsewhere throughout the empire, Muslims, Christians, and Jews adopted the viewpoint that the Ottoman nation was comprised of all the ethnic, religious, and linguistic elements of the empire bound together in civic, territorial, and contractual terms. They proclaimed and performed their Ottoman-ness in the streets in public celebrations and on the pages of newspapers in all the languages of the empire: as one proud Ottoman declared in the Jerusalem press, the empire's diverse religious and ethnic groups had entered into the "melting pot of the constitution" and emerged as "pure bullion, the Ottoman nation." At the same time, this civic Ottoman nation was in dialogue with more primordial imaginings based on Romantic notions of blood and soil as well as on religious and ethnic notions of peoplehood.

By illustrating the deep resonance and widespread nature of a professed Ottoman imperial nation, this book challenges entrenched historical narratives about the role of ethnic nationalisms in the breakup of the Ottoman Empire.[10] More broadly, *Ottoman Brothers* suggests an original process of forming universal collective identities in empires. To date, scholars have been uneasy theorizing imperial citizenship and nationhood, instead focusing on presumably inevitable *anti*-imperial nationalisms. According to a view dominant among European diplomats and travel writers in the nineteenth century—a view that was stated in history books until quite recently—multiethnic, multireligious empires like the Ottomans were "prisons of nations" eventually undone by the natural nationalisms of their subject peoples; they were not legitimate nations in and of themselves.[11] Furthermore, as the nation-state emerged as the primary model for European statecraft, "empires" and "nations" were not only depicted as mirror opposites, but in fact their essential opposition was seen as being constitutive.[12]

In other words, by the turn of the twentieth century, empires were considered holdovers of a previous age, ill equipped to meet the modern demands of a changed geopolitical environment—a view that rendered imperial change invisible and loyalty to empire unintelligible. And yet, as a recent volume dedicated to a comparative study of the "end of empire" has argued, the objective distinctions between empire and nation are murky, at best; indeed, "empires" often acted like "nations," and vice versa.[13] Indeed, this process of imagining, articulating, and acting as an imperial collective took a great deal of conceptual, ideological, and even linguistic work, and along the way the Ottoman "imperial-nation" took on forms and discourses that in many ways echoed "traditional" (nation-state) nationalism.[14]

After establishing the centrality of notions of imperial nationhood for the late Ottoman experience, I then trace the myriad ways in which Ottoman Palestinian citizens of all faiths exercised their newly claimed and evolving citizenship rights (Chapters 3 and 4). Ottoman citizens studied and cited the constitution and other revolutionary "sacred texts" that endowed them with political power, and they utilized a variety of tools to exercise and preserve that power. One of those was participation in a months-long, empire-wide boycott against the Austro-Hungarian Empire in response to its October 1908 annexation of the former Ottoman province of Bosnia-Herzegovina. The boycott promoted Ottoman patriotism and the perceived unity of the Ottoman nation, and cemented the popularity of the CUP's local branches as vectors of mass political mobilization. Also, in preparation for the Ottoman parliamentary elections held in the fall of 1908, Ottoman citizens continued their engagement with understanding political representation and rights at the same time that the structural balance between individual and ethno-religious group (*millet*) rights was challenged. Beyond the imperial level, Jerusalemites sought to act out their new claims to imperial citizenship on the urban stage as well, linking together broader discourses about imperial reform and modernization with local visions of progress and cooperation. Locally run institutions like the chamber of commerce and Freemason lodges became important sites for enacting the claims of civic Ottomanism.

And yet, making imperial citizens out of such a heterogeneous population spread out over three continents was not an uncontested process; among the significant challenges of the Ottoman imperial citizenship project were the divergent, indeed sometimes opposed, meanings that it had for the empire's population. Central among those tensions was the one between the universalizing discourse and impulse of civic Ottomanism—the premise that all citizens, irrespective of religion or ethnicity, were partners in the imperial project—and the very real constraints and challenges to this universalism. The last part of this book (Chapters 5–7) examines the various competing "citizenship discourses" that registered uneven application of imperial rights and obligations as well as public allegations of relative privileges and shirked duties. The multilingual press, for example, provided a platform for centripetal *and* centrifugal visions of imperial citizenship, exemplified by the press debate over the mandatory conscription of non-Muslims and the genre of the "open letter."

Because identity and political practice were deeply intertwined, by shifting our analysis to imperial citizenship we can see imperial multiethnicity in a new light—not solely as a significant component of imperial collapse or a predictor of rising nationalisms, but rather as a constitutive force in the struggle over imperial political membership, collective belonging, and identity. As the Ottoman imperial citizenship project incorporated elements of liberal, communitarian, republican, and ethnic models of citizenship, each "citizenship discourse" had distinct visions of the imperial collective, its relationship to other collectivities (religion, ethnic group, local province), and the nature of citizenship rights and duties.[15] The rise of particularistic ethnic, religious, and regional identities and interests—like Zionism, Arabism, and a Palestinian localism—reflected struggles over the contours of imperial citizenship and the boundaries around the "Ottoman nation." In other words, rather than plotting the empire's demise, the prewar Ottoman public by and large was preoccupied with envisioning, claiming, contesting, and implementing what it meant to be an imperial citizen.

In short, by analyzing the diverse Ottoman "citizenship discourses," practices, and identities in play in the years before World War I, this book shows how ethnic and religious minorities both tapped into *and* were excluded from the Ottoman imperial citizenship project. In contrast to the dominant image of increasingly (indeed, inherently) independent and clashing trajectories of Ottoman center and Arab periphery, my project illustrates Arab and Jewish provincials' active participation in and engagement with the imperial state, not their sidestepping or delegitimization of it. Lastly, my relational approach to the social history of Palestine's various religious communities, which illustrates the high degree of interconnectedness and embeddedness of Arabs and Jews at the turn of the century, argues that the Arab-Jewish conflict in Palestine was not immanent, but rather erupted in dialectical tension with the promises and shortcomings of "civic Ottomanism."

RELIGION, ETHNICITY, AND MIXING IN THE OTTOMAN EMPIRE AND PALESTINE

No longer the glorious, expanding state that inspired fear among its rivals and admiration among their intellectuals, by the early twentieth century the Ottoman Empire, long derided in European capitals as "the Sick Man of Europe," had suffered numerous territorial losses, economic contraction, and internal unrest and fragmentation. For a Europe that idealized and normalized the homogeneous nation-state (at the same time, not coincidentally, that it conquered overseas territories and peoples), the Ottoman Empire, home to dozens of religious sects, languages, and ethnic groups, was an anachronism. As G. F. Abbott, a British war correspondent dispatched to Istanbul in early 1909, dryly noted: "The Ottoman nation has been compared, for variety of ingredients, to an omelet. Yet, unless the political epicures are sadly at fault, it lacks the first essential of that dish, for, though stirred and beaten for centuries, the ingredients still refuse to mix."[16] Another foreign correspondent likened Ottoman subjecthood to conscription: "the Greeks, Armenians and Albanians are Turkish subjects because they have to be."[17]

At its base, this sentiment reflected a deterministic understanding of ethnicity where ethnic groups were not only assumed to be fixed and unchanging but were also attributed with political salience. In other words, "Turks," "Arabs," "Bulgars," and "Serbs" were seen as closed demographic groups with inherently competing political interests.[18] As a result, throughout the nineteenth century, the European Great Powers—Austria-Hungary, Great Britain, France, Germany, Italy, and Russia—directly interfered in Ottoman domestic politics, promoting Christian separatism in the southeastern European provinces of the empire (today's Greece, Bulgaria, Romania, the Balkans) where the aim was no less than to "drive the Turk back to Asia."[19] This went hand in hand with outright European occupation of parts of the empire in North Africa, the Caucasus, and central Europe.

For the Ottoman state, however, population diversity was a product of, and a powerful testament to, successful empire building. The eponymous founder of the dynasty, Osman, had consolidated his power in Asia Minor in the late thirteenth century through alliance and intermarriage with local Turkic tribes and Christian principalities. As the empire spread throughout Asia, Europe, and Africa, later sultans continued to integrate their diverse subjects into the state. Among the early Ottoman troops there are examples of Christian *ghazis* (so-called holy warriors) fighting in the sultan's armies, and the Christian youth (*devşirme*) taxed into imperial service, though converted to Islam, rose to important political and military positions in the service of the state. After the conquest of Constantinople, the capital of Byzantium, Sultan "Fatih" Mehmet ("the Conquerer") retained the patriarch of the Greek Orthodox Church and strategically moved Jews into the city to replace the fleeing Byzantines. Decades later, in 1492, when the Spanish monarchs Ferdinand and Isabella expelled Jews and Muslims from the Iberian Peninsula, Sultan Beyazit II famously welcomed the exiles to Ottoman shores.

The point of this recounting is not to argue that the Ottoman Empire was a multicultural paradise, for it surely was not. As an Islamic empire it maintained an "institutionalized difference" between Muslim and non-Muslim subjects which was accentuated—or indeed erupted—in times of crisis.[20] Non-Muslim populations were organized, counted, taxed, legislated, and otherwise "marked" according to their confessional or ethnoconfessional communities. At the same time, however, non-Muslim communities were allowed a tremendous degree of self-governance and autonomy in the realms of communal institutions and religious law, and comparatively speaking, the status of non-Muslims in the Ottoman Empire was far better than that of non-Christians in Europe.[21] There were numerous non-Muslims of high political status in the state, such as the Greek Phanariots or the Armenian *amira* class. Furthermore, economic conditions and contact with European co-religionists increasingly favored the *embourgeoisement* and Westernization of Christian and Jewish communities, particularly in the port cities of the empire, so much so that, on the whole, non-Muslims' socioeconomic position was far more stable and enviable than that of Muslim peasants and workers in the empire.[22]

As a result, it is misleading historically to look at religion as the only, and perhaps even the central, dividing factor in Ottoman history; class and status were clearly no less relevant. Instead, the Ottoman state throughout much of its existence looked upon ethnic and religious diversity among its subject population and state officials in an altogether pragmatic fashion; it did not care about their "identity" per se. As one scholar has written, for most of its history "the Ottoman state was neither seeking to meld together the separate communities nor consciously planting the seeds of further divisions among the subject peoples of the empire."[23]

This political pragmatism, to a certain extent, was born of demographic realities. For the first centuries of its existence, the Ottoman Empire had a majority non-Muslim population, and the dynasty was careful to forge favorable alliances with adjoining Christian principalities. By the sixteenth century, the split between the Muslim population and the non-Muslim population in the empire had flipped to approximately 60-40.[24] On the eve of the end of empire in the early twentieth century, after substantial territorial losses in southeastern Europe bled the empire of many of its Christian subjects, the Ottoman population of almost 21 million was still approximately 25 percent non-Muslim (consisting of about 5.3 million Christians and Jews).[25] In addition to this religious mix, the Ottoman population was even further divided ethnically and linguistically, with Albanians, Arabs, Armenians, Bulgars, Circassians, Greeks, Jews, Kurds, Serbs, Turks, and other groups in residence. Ethnic stereotypes and jokes existed, but for the most part ethnic mixing was just another factor of imperial life until the nineteenth century.[26]

As a result of this demographic reality, in many parts of the Ottoman Empire, in particular in the Balkans, western and eastern Anatolia, Mount Lebanon, and the many mixed cities and towns of the empire,

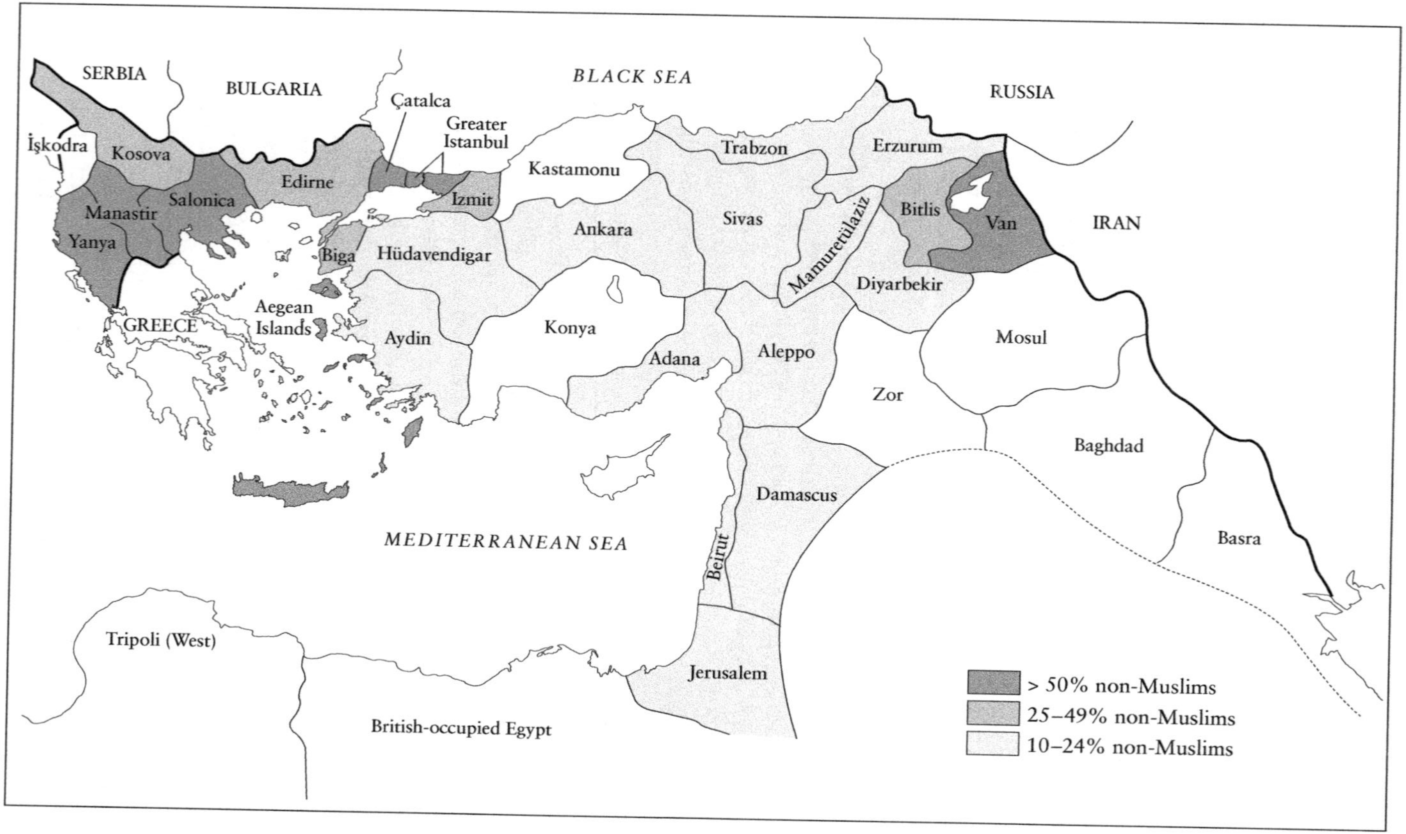

Map I.1. Muslims, Christians, and Jews in the Ottoman Empire, c. 1895. Data from Karpat, *Ottoman Population, 1830–1914: Demographic and Social Characteristics*. Madison: University of Wisconsin Press, 1985.

the various religious and ethnic groups lived together on a daily basis. In 1906–7, the population of the empire's capital and largest city, Istanbul, consisted of about 50 percent Muslims, 20.4 percent Greek Orthodox Christians, 7 percent Armenian Christians, 5.5 percent Jews, and 15 percent European foreigners.[27] Salonica, the third-largest city in the empire, had a population that was 38.9 percent Jewish, 29.1 percent Muslim, and 25.3 percent Greek in the 1913 Greek census, a year *after* thousands of Jews and Muslims had fled the city with the departing Ottoman forces.[28]

In each locale, Muslims, Christians, and Jews developed distinct relationships that were shaped by residential patterns, economic situations, and a wide variety of cultural factors in addition to the policies set in place by the Ottoman state. In these mixed towns and cities, religious and ethnic groups often lived in the same neighborhoods (sometimes even in the same apartment building or courtyard), belonged to the same craft guilds, worked and shopped in the same markets, went into business together, and frequented the same cafés and law courts. The popular tradition of visiting the tombs of holy men and saints further bridged the religious gap and brought Muslims, Christians, and Jews to pray together for divine intercession.[29] In other words, the physical proximity of different religious groups could, and often did, lead to familiarity and even solidarity.[30]

However, proximity also bore the potential for conflict, and times of crisis such as plagues or wars often revealed the fragility of intercommunal relations. A cholera epidemic in Baghdad in 1889–90, for example, set off a wave of Jewish-Muslim clashes in that city. There were also more systemic struggles over scarce resources, and Ottoman subjects of all three religions fought over real estate, competed economically, and occasionally clashed physically.[31] Throughout the mid-nineteenth century there were several intercommunal riots in the Arab provinces of the empire, culminating in the 1860 civil war in Mount Lebanon. In short, the Ottoman record on intercommunal relations was neither one of peaceful coexistence nor one of intractable violence, although elements of both were certainly present. Rather, relations between Muslims, Christians, and Jews were inexorably linked to political, economic, and social factors that stemmed from local, imperial, and global geopolitical concerns.

In many ways, the region of Palestine was a microcosm of the challenges facing the empire at large. Divided between two major administrative seats in Jerusalem, covering the southern half of the country, and Beirut, which administered the northern half, Palestine underwent all of the same transformations that took place in other Ottoman provinces, albeit at its own pace and to a degree determined by local factors. Palestine was very much a part of Ottoman administrative reforms as well as of the economic trends of the nineteenth century—the commercialization of agriculture, the incorporation of province and empire into the world economy, the rise of coastal trade, and the commoditization of land. These economic changes precipitated several important social developments, namely, the emergence of a large landowning class with strong patronage and other ties to rural hinterlands and the rise of minority merchant communities in the cities. Intellectually and ideologically, Palestinians also grappled with the same questions of religious reform, intellectual fermentation, and the pulls of imperial, local, and communal identification and solidarity.

In these ways, then, Palestine was like any other region in the Ottoman Empire, and its history over the nineteenth century assumed familiar Ottoman patterns. At the same time, several factors made the Palestinian experience different from that of other Ottoman provinces and regions. As the site of worldwide religious devotion, Palestine had become an object of heavy international scrutiny and intervention by the turn of the century. Missionaries, pilgrims, and diplomats made their way to the region, many of them staying and putting down roots. With changes to the Ottoman land laws in the 1850s, several groups of Christian religious settlers—Germans, Americans, and Swedes—arrived to purchase land, establish agricultural colonies, and settle among the local population. Most significantly in numerical as well as lasting political terms, Jewish migration to Palestine, which had been a small but steady stream throughout the centuries of Ottoman rule, picked up heavily in the second half of the nineteenth century. Religious European Jews arriving to live and die in the Holy Land, North African Jews fleeing French colonialism, and Yemenite Jews with messianic visions were soon joined by a new kind of Jewish immigrant: the politically motivated settlers of the nascent European Zionist movement. The tensions that arose in Palestine in the last years of the Ottoman Empire between Zionists and their opponents—Arab Muslims and Christians, to be sure, but also fellow Jews and other Ottomans—were reflective of both local and empire-wide problems.

Like the rest of the Ottoman Empire, then, the region of Palestine was also the product of complex demographic and social mixing. By the turn of the twentieth century, Palestine had a population of around 700,000 to 750,000, the great majority of which, around 84 percent, was Muslim Arab. Approximately 72,000 Arab Christians (11 percent of the total population) lived in the two administrative provinces that made up Palestine, concentrated in the cities and towns of Jerusalem, Jaffa, Haifa, and Nazareth, and in the semiurban townlets and villages surrounding them. Finally, there were around 30,000 Ottoman Jews in the region (5 percent of the Ottoman population), as well as up to 30,000 foreign Jews living there temporarily or permanently. Jews lived primarily in the four cities

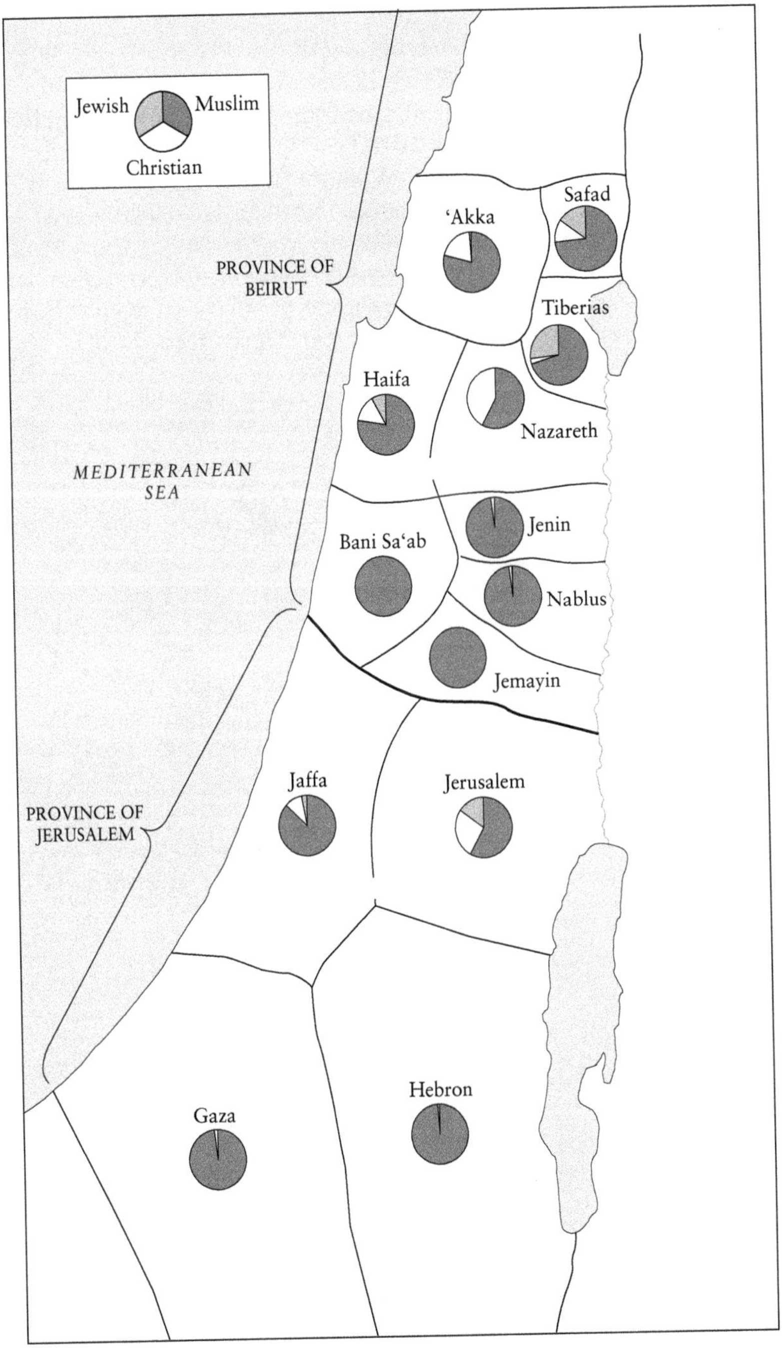

Map I.2. Muslims, Christians, and Jews in Ottoman Palestine, early twentieth century. Data from *McCarthy, The Population of Palestine: Population History and Statistics of the Late Ottoman Period and the Mandate*. New York: Columbia University Press, 1990.

holy to Judaism (Jerusalem, Hebron, Safad, and Tiberias), as well as in the coastal cities of Jaffa and Haifa; in addition, up to 10,000 European Jewish immigrants lived in the almost four dozen Zionist agricultural colonies newly established since 1878.[32]

The two most important cities in southern Palestine, Jerusalem and Jaffa, were also the most heterogeneous: Ottoman Jerusalem was 41 percent Jewish, 34 percent Muslim, and 25 percent Christian—even without accounting for the steady stream of noncitizen pilgrims, travelers, businessmen, and migrants who came to the city that was sacred to the three religions.[33] According to the 1905 Ottoman census records, of the eight

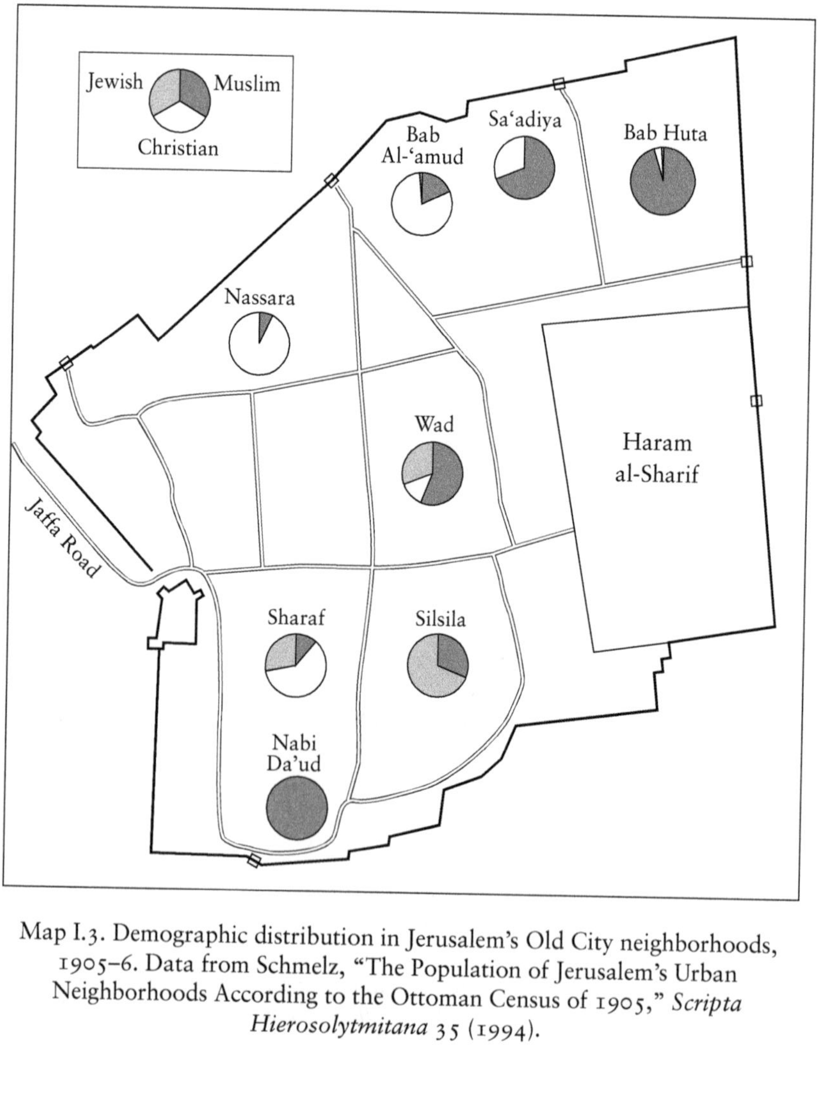

Map I.3. Demographic distribution in Jerusalem's Old City neighborhoods, 1905–6. Data from Schmelz, "The Population of Jerusalem's Urban Neighborhoods According to the Ottoman Census of 1905," *Scripta Hierosolytmitana* 35 (1994).

Figure I.1. Street in the Old City of Jerusalem. The Old City is characterized by narrow, twisting alleyways and unremarkable stone exteriors that shield interior courtyards, the heart of the extended household where women labored and gossiped and children played. Many buildings had tenants belonging to different religions and denominations, making the courtyard a site for intimate intercommunal mixing. Library of Congress, Prints and Photographs Division (LC-DIG-matpc-00851).

neighborhoods within the Old City walls of Jerusalem, only three were religiously homogeneous (defined as at least 80 percent concentration of one religious group), while the remaining five had a substantial mixing (20–45 percent) of members of two or all three religious groups. Not surprisingly, the two most homogeneous neighborhoods included Bab Huta, a 95 percent Muslim neighborhood that bordered the eastern entrance to the Haram al-Sharif–Dome of the Rock Mosque complex, and al-Nassara, a 93 percent Christian neighborhood surrounding the Church of the Holy Sepulcher and the Greek Orthodox Patriarchate.

In contrast to this residential intermixing in the "Old City," the extramural "New City" featured religious separation from the outset, in

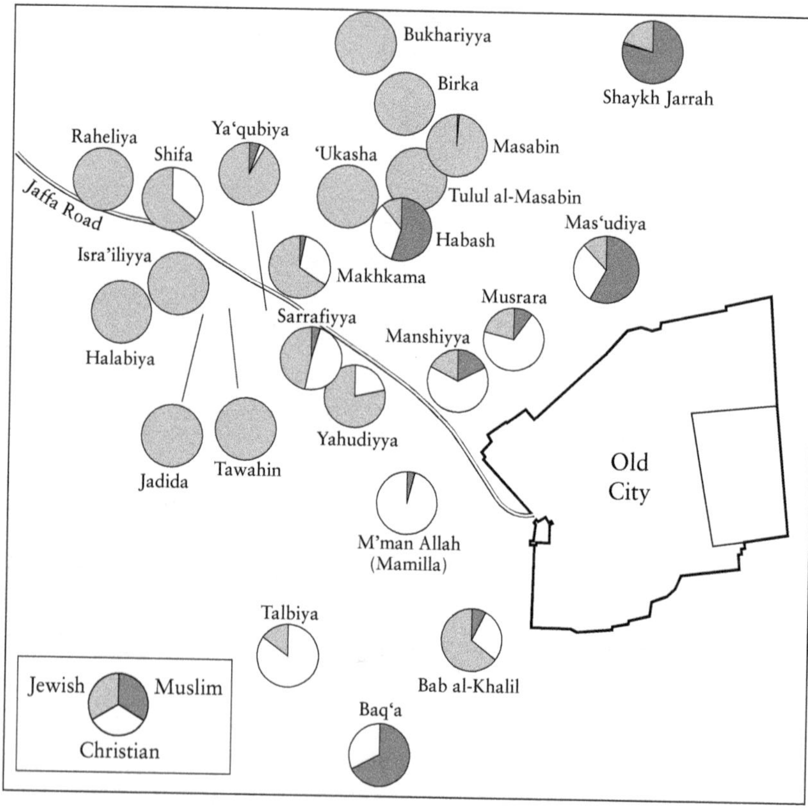

Map I.4. Demographic distribution in Jerusalem's New City neighborhoods, 1905–6. Data from Schmelz, "The Population of Jerusalem's Urban Neighborhoods according to the Ottoman Census of 1905."

many cases as a desired and declared goal. Beginning in the 1850s, Jewish philanthropic societies and Christian religious institutions purchased land and established neighborhoods for their co-religionists' exclusive use, and wealthy Muslim notables established family compounds outside the city walls. As a result, almost half of the extramural neighborhoods were religiously homogenous.[34] Many of these were self-contained, self-supporting neighborhoods, which further limited the residents' contacts with outsiders: the Ashkenazi Jewish neighborhood Me'ah She'arim, for example, had its own synagogues, ritual bath, religious schools, cisterns, grocery store, and guest house.[35] In Jaffa the situation was even more marked.[36]

Figure I.2. Jaffa Road, the main boulevard of extramural Jerusalem (the New City). Extramural Jerusalem offered residents more space, greater cleanliness, and many modern amenities and sensibilities. One long-time Jewish resident of the city, Ita Yellin, remembered: "The matter of having windows facing Jaffa Road was considered precious in those days, because [it] served all of the Jerusalem residents as a pleasurable venue, in place of a public park. On the Sabbath and holidays and when princes visited, this road was filled with thousands of strollers, Arabs, Jews, priests, and tourists of all nationalities." Quoted in Zecharia, *Jerusalem Neighborhoods*, 2. Library of Congress, Prints and Photographs Division (LC-DIG-matpc-06541).

As a result of this spatial mixing, there developed in Jerusalem a local set of norms about communal, ethnic, and religious boundaries and borders. Many memoirs from this period speak of deep ties between Old City Muslim, Christian, and Jewish families and neighbors across religious lines—sharing a courtyard, visiting each other on religious holidays, engaging in a business partnership, or benefiting from a long-term patron-client relationship. Muslim girls learned Judeo-Spanish from their Sephardi Jewish neighbors; Christian and Jewish musicians performed at Muslim weddings and holidays; and all three shared beliefs and traditions about the evil eye, droughts, and visiting the tombs of local saints.[37]

At the same time, religious, economic, and political rivalry appeared from time to time, and the practical aspects of "living together" could be a source of tension. Christians and Jews in particular had fraught intergroup relationships, especially around religious holidays and religious holy sites. Easter-Passover was a particularly dangerous time as Christian Arabs sang anti-Jewish songs on the streets of the city and blood libels accusing Jews of using Christian children's blood for ritual purposes resurfaced periodically.[38] Jews and Muslims, on the whole, did not share the same religious tensions marring their relationships, but economic and political factors played a role in conflicts between these two groups.[39] As a result, the Jewish rabbis in Jerusalem sought to limit the impact of "living together" by the system of *ḥazakah*, whereby one Jew would hold the title to sublet courtyard apartments in a Muslim-owned building. The title holder then was the only one who had to exchange money with a non-Jew, and he also had the discretion of determining to whom the apartments would be rented.[40]

Another factor contributing to the complex picture of intercommunal relations, these memoirs also suggest, was that intraconfessional boundaries could occasionally be as strong as, or at times even stronger than, interconfessional ones. Many memoirs argued that "native" Sephardi and Maghrebi Jews shared cultural, spatial, and everyday practices with their Muslim neighbors that sharply differentiated them from "newcomer" Ashkenazi Jewish co-religionists. In Jerusalem as in many other towns throughout the Ottoman Empire, Sephardi and Ashkenazi Jews spoke different mother tongues, went to different synagogues and schools, lived in different neighborhoods, and usually married within their own ethnic group; they also had different relationships with the Ottoman government and their neighbors.[41] This separation was so complete that in 1867 Ashkenazi Jews in Jerusalem asked the Ottoman government, through the intercession of local Muslim notables, to recognize them as a separate sect (*madhhab*), thereby allowing them autonomy from Sephardi institutional and political hegemony.[42]

Likewise, the Christian community in Palestine was fragmented into sixteen different religious denominations, many of which had their own religious, educational, and legal institutions. Rivalries among the Christian denominations with respect to religious rites and sacred privileges were legendary, and many an Ottoman governor had to intervene to calm tempers and break up fistfights in the Church of the Holy Sepulcher. The daughter of one Ottoman governor who served in Jerusalem at the beginning of the twentieth century recalled that her father had to mediate an argument over unruly choir boys drowning out the other denominations, as well as one about the status of a cushion that one patriarch made for the gatekeeper of the church (they argued that one denomination could not give the cushion to the gatekeeper, as it would privilege that group).[43]

Overall, then, historical Jerusalem was, in the words of one scholar, "one that is fundamentally unrecognizable today, a city of considerable social mobility, of ethnic diversity, and of communal conflict that is tempered by a fair amount of mutual dependence and local solidarities."[44] As a result, rather than seeing Muslims, Christians, and Jews (in the religious sense), or Jews and Arabs (in the ethno-political sense) in isolation from each other inhabiting hermetically sealed separate spaces, this book analyzes the historical relationships between Muslims, Christians, and Jews in Palestine in their shared spaces through the lens of daily life in which communal and civic boundaries were formulated, negotiated, upheld, and transgressed.[45]

Ideas of collective belonging and identity as well as new political practices and expectations were never divorced from the socioeconomic realities of religious and ethnic mixing in Palestine and in the Ottoman Empire at large. Overall, this book reconfigures how we see the Ottoman and Palestinian historical landscapes, showing both the extent to which Muslims, Christians, and Jews had interests in common and worked together for their so-called "shared homeland," as well as the points at which their interests diverged and clashed. By 1914, a process had taken place that succeeded in realigning Muslims, Christians, and Jews, for local, imperial, and geopolitical reasons. This occurred hand in hand with the growth of the Zionist movement, which itself actively sought to segregate indigenous Jews from their neighbors, their environment, and their empire. Ultimately, though, separation in Palestine between Jews and Arabs came about as the *result* of the Zionist-Palestinian conflict—it was not the cause.[46]

CHAPTER ONE

Sacred Liberty

In late July 1908, Muhammad ʿIzzat Darwaza, a twenty-year-old government postal clerk in Nablus, a town in the northern hills of Palestine, transcribed a startling telegram from the governor in Beirut to his local deputy: units of the Ottoman army were marching on the imperial capital in Istanbul, demanding that the sultan reinstate the constitution he had suspended more than three decades earlier. As Nabulsis celebrated with "great joy" over the news, Darwaza joined his fellow clerks in adorning the town post office with banners bearing the revolutionary slogan: "liberty, equality, fraternity, and justice."[1]

Sixty miles to the south in Jerusalem, the young Jewish journalist Gad Frumkin caught wind of the startling news from the wire bulletins that arrived from neighboring Egypt. Trembling with excitement and disbelief, Frumkin went out in search of the government censor to sign off on publication of the unofficial rumors in his father's newspaper, the Hebrew-language *Lily* (*Ḥavaẓelet*). When he could not find the Jewish censor, Frumkin gathered his courage to go to the villa of Ismaʿil "Bey" al-Husayni in the affluent Sheikh Jarrah neighborhood outside the city walls, daring to interrupt the Muslim notable's afternoon siesta only due to the seductive promise of freedom and equality.[2] Frumkin received permission to publish the news, and the following day *Lily* proclaimed exuberantly to its readers: "This is one of the greatest deeds of His Highness the Sultan, May He Be Exalted!" At the same time, printed notices in Arabic were tacked onto the city walls to inform the rest of the city's population about the recent events.[3]

Halfway around the world, in New York, the young Christian expatriate Khalil al-Sakakini read of the granting of the constitution in a local Arabic-language newspaper and considered it an auspicious sign. Like tens of thousands of Ottomans before him, al-Sakakini had left his homeland for less restrictive shores, seeking both liberty and fortune abroad. With the news of the revolution, however, al-Sakakini reconsidered his options and decided to return home to Jerusalem to fulfill his dreams of establishing a progressive school, a newspaper, and youth clubs.[4] It took him a few weeks to tie up his affairs in America and borrow the necessary funds for the long, expensive journey home, but by September al-Sakakini was back in Palestine.

As all three men had perceived, unprecedented and widespread changes were about to take place in Palestine and in the Ottoman Empire as a whole that would deeply affect Muslim, Jew, and Christian alike. Within weeks, their hometowns and their empire were irrevocably altered. As one resident of Jaffa wrote to his friend in Beirut, "one does not recognize any more our Turkey [*sic*], and it sometimes seems as if one lives in a dream."[5] More than any other word, "freedom" or "liberty" (*ḥurriyya*, Ara.; *hürriyet*, Ott. Tur.) captured the hopes and dreams that millions of Ottoman citizens invested in the 1908 revolution. From the elite military officers, civil servants, and intellectuals who had been involved in underground political activity for decades to the millions more whose first political act may not have taken place until after the revolution's announcement, Ottomans empire-wide had complex and often contradictory expectations of what "freedom" would look like.

At the basest level, *ḥurriyya* was a symbol of rupture from the past and the promise of a new era. As was the case in other revolutionary moments, Ottoman *ḥurriyya* was utopian and messianic, serving as a metonym for "righting" the course of history and restoring the Ottoman Empire to a leading political, economic, and cultural role in the world. At the same time, *ḥurriyya* also drew on a specific nineteenth-century discourse of political liberalism that engaged with, and at times stemmed from, Islamic sources of inspiration. Central in this discourse of political liberalism was a reconfiguration of the legitimate role of the sultan, who went from being a sacred ruler (caliph) to being subject to the will of the nation. Surprisingly, *ḥurriyya* also was a potentially sacrilegious discourse, as the boundaries between support for and sanctification of the revolution became increasingly blurred.

But first, we must turn for a moment to the broader empire and wider intellectual currents in order to understand, not only where the revolution came from and why it came about, but also how it was to take the shape and meaning that it did in our corner of the empire, Palestine.

PRELUDE TO REVOLUTION

The fact that newspapers and telegrams played an instrumental role in bringing news of the revolution to these three young men is a significant marker of the extent to which the empire had been transformed by modern technology and the new ideas and habits that inevitably went along with it. By the second half of the nineteenth century, Ottoman cities were connected via telegraph, steamboat, and railroad to the greater empire and to the world beyond. Cities throughout the empire exploded in size as they became magnets for regional rural migrants, foreign immigrants, and international capital. Beirut, for example, went from a fishing town of 6,000 residents to a booming port city of 150,000 to 200,000, the largest on the Eastern Mediterranean coast, in less than one hundred years. The largest, most important Ottoman cities, like Istanbul, Salonica, Izmir, and Beirut had running water, electricity, and intracity tramways, developments which had a revolutionary effect on reshaping the urban landscape, restructuring local notions of time, and altering habits of consumption.[6]

Because of its proximity to Beirut and the status of Jaffa as the second most important port city on the Eastern Mediterranean coast, Palestine was by no means unaware of or unaffected by many of the markers of technological modernization and imperial cosmopolitanism that characterized the rest of the empire. It is true that governors and officers sent from Istanbul or Salonica often thought of Palestine as comparatively backward and provincial, far from the glittering lights and stylish public promenades of the capital, but nevertheless, late Ottoman modernity did arrive in the region to a certain extent.[7] In the 1890s, regular train service between coastal Jaffa and holy Jerusalem began, and within a few years an auxiliary line of the famous Hijaz Railway linked Haifa in northern Palestine with Damascus. Ships from Ottoman ports, neighboring Egypt, and Europe arrived in Jaffa on a regular basis, bringing with them pilgrims, migrants, commodities, and mail.

These technological changes went hand in hand with important intellectual developments; as we saw in the case of Shlomo Yellin and his Beirut audience of gentlemen patriots, the second half of the nineteenth century witnessed unprecedented access to education, public as well as private, which contributed to a rise in literacy, an emerging middle class, and the development of a vibrant public sphere of a multilingual press, civil society organizations, and new ideas about sociability and political involvement. Newspapers, magazines, and books from Cairo, Beirut, Damascus, Istanbul, and other corners of the empire (not to mention from Paris, Berlin, Odessa, and other European publishing centers) made their way into coffeehouses, libraries, and private homes in Palestine.[8] Young men from affluent Palestinian families went to Cairo, Beirut, and Istanbul to continue their studies; many Muslim, Jewish, and Christian families from other parts of the region chose to send their sons to study in boarding schools in the holy city of Jerusalem, bringing with them ideas, contacts, and habits that connected Palestine to the wider empire. In the last years before World War I, public parks for leisurely family strolls and picnics, "moving pictures" (the cinema), competitive soccer matches, and the automobile and airplane all arrived in Palestine to great acclaim and not a little discomfort.[9]

If modernity in Palestine and the Ottoman Empire at the beginning of the twentieth century echoed certain elements of fin-de-siècle Europe, it was out of a spirit of competition more than simple imitation. Generations of Ottoman reformers had seen the empire's relative military and economic decline vis-à-vis Europe as inseparable from the empire's increasing internal corruption and chaos, and in the mid-nineteenth century, reform-minded government officials cooked up an ambitious and broad-ranging program known as the Tanzimat, or Reordering. The reforms aimed at overhauling the empire through centralization and modernization, and within a few decades they had succeeded in bringing about dramatic, if incomplete, changes in the Ottoman military, judiciary, provincial rule, taxation, and land reform.[10]

In addition to bureaucratic reform over the *mechanics* of imperial rule, there emerged as well a sharp critique of the *nature* of imperial rule and of the role of the sultan himself. In the Ottoman and Islamic political traditions, the sultan was considered not only the head of state but also the "deputy of the Prophet," "commander of the faithful," and "shadow of God on earth"; this intertwining of political office with sacred legitimacy had always been a source of loyalty and submission by the sultan-caliph's subjects. Classical Ottoman rule relied on the sultan upholding justice and order, and "complaint registers" monitoring reports from the provinces were an important mechanism in the contract between ruler and ruled.

Nevertheless, by the nineteenth century the Ottoman system had broken down under dynastic absolutism and corruption. The foundational text of the Tanzimat, the 1839 Noble Rescript of the Rose Garden pronounced by the pious and reform-minded Sultan Abdülmecid, argued for the restoration of morality and justice in Ottoman rule as a necessary component of reform. The document echoed earlier classical texts on the proper role of a Muslim ruler which centered on the "public good" (*maṣlaḥa*), and reports from around the empire indicated that the sultan's appeal made a favorable impression on his subjects and was an important component in shoring up domestic support in light of both the expansionist ambitions of the rebellious governor of Egypt, Mehmed Ali, as well as the recent independence of Greece and the European powers' increasing agitation among the empire's Christians.[11]

By the early 1860s and under a new sultan, a group of intellectuals who became known as the Young Ottomans emerged in the capital, turning to Islamic sacred sources and history in calling for further liberal and democratic reforms. Men like Ali Suavi, an intellectual and educator, and Namık Kemal, a poet-playwright who translated Rousseau's *Social Contract* into Ottoman Turkish, preached in mosques (in the case of Suavi) and published opposition newspapers at home and later (in exile) in Europe that rejected sultanic absolutism and instead cited Islamic tradition in support of principles of representation and consultation (*meşveret*, Ott. Tur.; *shūra*, Ara.), sovereignty of the people, equality between ruler and ruled, and notions of justice and inalienable rights.[12] Namık Kemal reminded his fellow Ottomans that "monarchs have no right to govern other than the authorization granted to them by the nation in the form of allegiance," which he equated with the oath of allegiance given to the Prophet's successors in early Islamic history.[13] Both Kemal and Suavi cited Qur'anic verses as well as hadith (oral traditions about the sayings and deeds of the Prophet, Muhammad) to support their positions.

The ideas of the Young Ottomans buttressed reformist government officials like Midhat Pasha, who as grand vizier to the new sultan, Abdülhamid II, was able to achieve the short-term adoption of an Ottoman constitution and establishment of an Ottoman parliament in 1876. For Midhat Pasha, the constitution was nothing short of an Ottoman Magna Carta—intended to be "the curb and limit of arbitrary power and exaction."[14] Instead, even before it was officially promulgated, the constitution was amended by the sultan, who claimed the original version was "incompatible with the habits and aptitudes of the nation." A Russian military assault in April 1878 gave the sultan an excuse to suspend the constitution entirely, disband the parliament, and imprison and exile the reformers who dreamed of turning the empire into a constitutional monarchy. Ali Suavi was killed in an attempt to overthrow the sultan; Namık Kemal died under house arrest in the Aegean islands; and Midhat Pasha was sent to prison in Ta'if on the Arabian Peninsula, where he was strangled by his guards on the order of the sultan.

Despite this severe setback, the ideas of the Ottoman reformists and the ideals of a constitutional, parliamentary government continued to resonate throughout the Ottoman and broader Muslim worlds. Although Abdülhamid II shut down the free press in most of the empire, semi-autonomous Egypt and Lebanon, like the capitals of Europe, served as important centers of political dissidence. Scholars, journalists, and political activists like 'Abdullah al-Nadim, Mustafa Kamil, Wali al-Din Yakan, Francis Fathallah Marrash, and Adib Ishaq published broadly and engaged with meanings of governmental reform, personal liberty, and political legitimacy.[15] The 'Urabi revolution in Egypt in 1881–82 against an impending British occupation and a concessionary palace, and the mass boycotts and emergence of an independent press in Qajar Iran in the 1890s, challenged the political status quo and provided new models for an active political life that drew from both Western liberalism and Islamic tradition.[16]

These ideas of internal reform were linked to the growing awareness by the end of the nineteenth century that the Ottoman Empire was in a precarious geopolitical position. In a period of less than fifty years, the empire lost most of its North African and European provinces to Europe—in the cases of Algeria, Tunisia, and Egypt, through direct military occupation; whereas in the cases of Romania, Serbia, Bulgaria, Bosnia-Herzegovina, and Cyprus, due to unfair treaties imposed upon the empire by the Great Powers. In addition, because of the massive debts it accumulated in the 1856 Crimean War, the empire had been forced to declare bankruptcy and accept a British and French-run Public Debt Administration in 1881, which ensured that Ottoman revenues went first and foremost to servicing its foreign creditors and only later (if at all) to paying for the military, government bureaucracy, public works, and education systems. As a result, Ottomans of the late nineteenth century had every reason to literally fear for the continued existence and well-being of their empire. In the words of one contemporary Turkish historian, the feeling that "the state was slipping from our hands" was palpable among turn-of-the-century Ottoman elites.[17]

By the 1890s, fear of continued European meddling in Ottoman affairs combined with opposition to Hamidian autocracy, inefficiency and corruption crystallized among groups of government bureaucrats, army officers, intellectuals, students, and even estranged princes from the sultan's own family.[18] Ali Fuat, at the time a student at the military academy from a prominent political and military family, expressed the sentiments of his generation aptly:

> Sultan Abdülhamit II, in whose honor we had to shout "Long Live our Padishah" several times a day, gradually lost lustre in our eyes. . . . As we heard that the government worked badly, that corruption was rife, that civil servants and officers did not receive their pay, while secret policemen and courtiers, covered in gold braid, received not only their pay but purses of gold, our confidence in the sultan, which was not strong at the best of times, was totally shaken. We saw that delivered into incompetent hands, the army was losing its effectiveness and prestige. . . . But no one dared to ask "Where are we going? Where are you taking the country?"[19]

Opposition organizations like the Ottoman Consultative Society and the Ottoman Union and minority groups such as the Armenian Dashnak were active in the 1890s, in Istanbul, Cairo, Paris, and even in the Ottoman diaspora in South America. The organizations and activists differed on a number of questions, from the type of empire envisioned (centralized vs. decentralized) to whether or not the path of opposition to the sultan should include requesting European aid or intervention, but in 1902 they agreed to hold the First Congress of Ottoman Opposition Parties in Paris. The following year, an uprising in Macedonia of the Bulgarian nationalist International Macedonian Revolutionary Organization (IMRO) led to the arrival of additional European military and civilian "advisors" in Salonica, the most important city in Ottoman Europe. At the same time, economic crisis throughout 1905–8, sparked by a rising cost of living and declining salaries, dislocation of local workers and industries due to European economic penetration, and agricultural failures, added a new layer of opposition to the government in the form of workers' strikes, grain riots, and tax revolts.[20] These uncertain economic conditions also led to significant unrest in the countryside. For all these reasons, then, by the time the Second Congress of Ottoman Liberals convened in Paris in December 1907, the various opposition movements were unanimous in resolving to overthrow the Ottoman government in order to save the empire.

PALESTINE CELEBRATES *AL-ḤURRIYYA*

The following summer, just as British and Russian diplomats were preparing to meet to "settle" the Balkan problem once and for all (a solution which was certain to include further territorial losses and humiliating limitations on Ottoman sovereignty), Ottoman troops based in Macedonia revolted against the provincial Ottoman authorities, assassinating several of the sultan's most trusted generals in the region. Imperial troops sent from Anatolia failed to crush the rebellion, and on July 23, the Salonica-based Committee for Union and Progress (CUP) unilaterally declared the reinstatement of the 1876 constitution. Afraid of losing control entirely after the rebelling units threatened to march on the capital in Istanbul, the following day Sultan Abdülhamid II restored the constitution, announced elections to a new parliament, and promised widespread political and social reforms including individual freedoms and regulation of all government bodies.

In Salonica, epicenter of the rebelling army units, news of the sultan's "granting of the constitution" immediately resulted in spontaneous mass gatherings at Olympios Square, later renamed "Liberty" (Hürriyet) Square, where the crowd applauded the news and pledged their loyalty to the revolution. News spread quickly to Istanbul, which the young writer Halide Edib Adıvar described as a celebratory sea of red and white, drenched in the colors of the Ottoman flag, and from there to the four corners of the empire and globe.[21] Letters and telegrams arrived from Ottoman subjects-turned-citizens within the empire as well as outside it, such as from British-controlled Sudan and from faraway Brazil and the United States, expressing euphoria and loyalty to the revolution.[22]

In contrast to the immediate reaction seen in Salonica, Istanbul, and other central locales, in more peripheral cities and towns the response was far more cautious, as local residents awaited cues from the local governor and military commander. Such was the case in Harput, a town in eastern Anatolia that had a large and nervous Armenian population. On the Arabian Peninsula, the *sharīf*, the highest religious official in Mecca who was a descendant of the family of the Prophet, and the local governor, who was considered corrupt and oppressive, reportedly ordered that anyone talking about the constitution would be flogged.[23]

Likewise in Jerusalem, almost two weeks passed from the arrival of the first telegrams bearing the news before the local government acted on the notice. The governor of the province, Ekrem Bey, was a former palace secretary who belonged to a distinctly different world than the young soldiers, intellectuals, and officials who had agitated for and carried out the revolution. Unlike them, many of whom were graduates of the modern state military and civil service academies, Ekrem Bey had been trained as a scribe in the sultan's personal office staff, and as such he owed his professional position and livelihood directly to the sultan. And yet, Ekrem Bey was also the son of Namık Kemal, the leading Ottoman liberal thinker who had died under house arrest. Undoubtedly, both position and parentage had taught Ekrem Bey that the secret of political survival lay in conservative caution, and so he apparently did his best to ignore the news of the revolution for as long as he could.

According to a report of the American consul in Jerusalem, the lull ended when "one courageous effendi" initiated a group telegram to the central government, sending its congratulations to the sultan in the aftermath of the announcement of the constitution and at the same time complaining of the governor's refusal to set a date for the public celebration. In short order, the governor "was soon surrounded by a band of Moslems, Christians, and Jews, who, in their turn, encouraged the people to demand their rights."[24] This group of locals complained to CUP headquarters in Salonica about the governor's "unsympathetic attitude," prompting the committee's harsh warning that "any governor or official who put obstacles in the way of the people manifesting their joy were enemies to the liberty of the people and lawless in their actions, and that such were not worthy of being kept in their positions, and that it was for the people to boldly object and oppose such and permit nothing that was against the public peace to continue."[25]

In a letter to his superiors at the Ministry of Interior, however, Ekrem Bey vigorously denied the accusations against him, claiming that when approached by the Jerusalem notables (more than ten days after the news had arrived in Jerusalem), he had hurried to begin making preparations for the celebrations. In Ekrem Bey's mind, he had carried out his official duty fastidiously. "I did not delay in declaring the constitution. I brought the Grand Vizier's telegram for a public reading in an official manner at the government headquarters. I declared. I informed the districts. I brought about its inclusion in the Jerusalem newspapers and I gave details about the manner of its declaration. The duty of a clerk employed by the state was fulfilled."[26] "As for *Kemalzade* [son of Kemal]," he continued, "the joy of his heart was declared out loud to his friends."

In his defense, Ekrem Bey blamed "corrupt villains" in the local CUP branch as well as a local political rival, the deputy-governor of Jaffa.[27] Indeed, the acrimonious relations between Ekrem Bey and the local notables (who he referred to as "insects" on at least one occasion) made such a strong impression upon his young daughter that she remembered their two years in Jerusalem darkly, and even decades later likened Jerusalem to a fire-breathing dragon. In her mind, at least from the perspective of an overworked and unappreciated government official, "there was nothing but gloom, religion and filth. . . . Jerusalem was not an easy city to handle. One had to pacify a thousand hatreds and jealousies."[28]

As a result of the quarrels between the Ottoman governor and leading Jerusalemites, the first ceremony in Palestine to mark the historic moment was not held in Jerusalem, the seat of the provincial government, but rather, in Jaffa, its commercial rival on the coast. On August 6 Ekrem Bey took the two-hour train ride to Jaffa where he was greeted by thousands of new citizens gathered between the government house and the army headquarters with Ottoman flags decorating every building in town.[29] The governor read aloud the imperial decree containing the list of reforms to be implemented while spiritual representatives of the various religious communities accepted the constitution on behalf of their members.

Upon his return to Jerusalem later in the evening, Ekrem Bey announced that an official ceremony would be held that Saturday at noon at the army barracks next to Jaffa Gate; Jerusalemites began preparing for the event by placing Ottoman flags on official buildings as well as houses and stores, and lamps were hung in the streets to light the city at night.[30] However, due to mounting public impatience, spontaneous celebrations broke out the following day, August 7. Immediately after

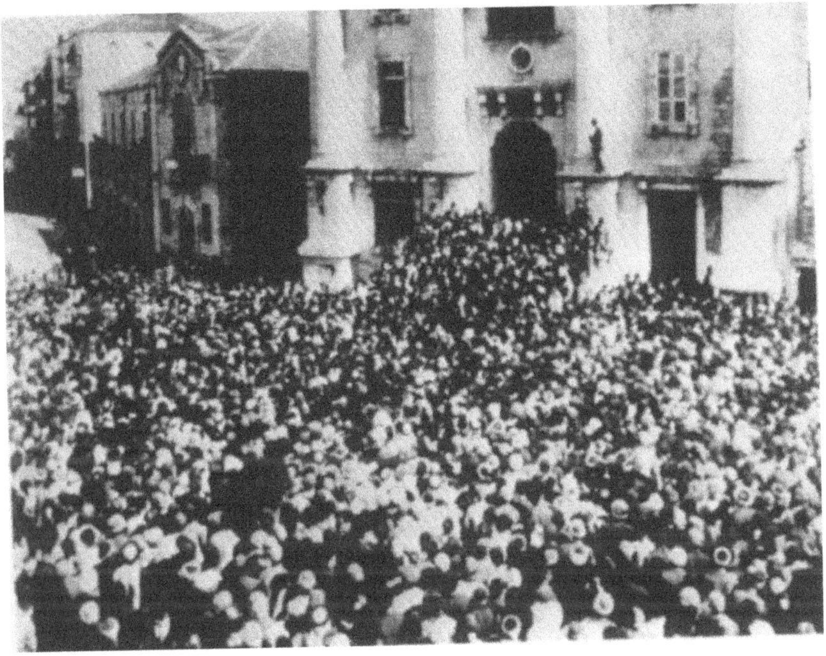

Figure 1.1. Masses gathered in Jaffa for the proclamation of the constitution, August 1908. Jerusalem provincial governor Ekrem Bey read the official proclamation in front of the government building. Wasif Jawhariyya Photograph Collection, Institute for Palestine Studies (Beirut). Reprinted with permission from Walid Khalidi, *Before Their Diaspora: A Photographic History of the Palestinians, 1876–1948*, Institute for Palestine Studies.

noon prayers ended at the Dome of the Rock Mosque, a crowd of about five thousand people set out toward the army barracks, singing, waving flags, dancing with swords, and firing pistols.[31] Upon their arrival, the military commander of Jerusalem, Rıza Bey, "look[ing] upon the crowd with pleasure and honor," sent out Ottoman soldiers and military band members to join in marching through the streets and markets. As one observer noted, "Cries of 'Liberty, equality, fraternity!' [were] heard from thousands of people, and 'love and brotherhood' sang between all the sons of the different communities in Jerusalem." Crowds celebrated in the streets until late into the night.

The following morning, the military band paraded through the markets and streets again, playing military music and the national anthem. Hundreds of people accompanied them through the city, singing, dancing, and shooting pistols, while others sprinkled rose water and tossed

Figure 1.2. Public procession in the Old City of Jerusalem. During the revolutionary celebrations residents standing on the balconies would sprinkle fragrant rosewater on passersby below. Arab Studies Society (Jerusalem).

flowers from the balconies of houses and stores. In addition to government buildings, private houses, stores, and warehouses were decorated with Ottoman flags and flowers, as well as with numerous banners that read, "Long live the sultan! Long live the army! Long live freedom! Liberty, equality, fraternity!"

The crowds began to gather at the appointed spot before noon. According to press accounts, "all types of men were present," characterized by a variety of clothing, religions, parties, and classes; the press focused on the theme of unity among difference, noting that "all went forward with one heart to celebrate freedom!"[32] As the crowd began to file into the courtyard of the army barracks, people squeezed together on the rooftops and adjoining fences—and thousands still remained outside. According to one newspaper correspondent, over forty thousand Muslims, Christians, and Jews had gathered; lemonade, cigarettes, and coffee were distributed gratis in honor of the historic and festive moment.[33]

At 1:30 P.M. the governor and his clerks arrived by carriage, wearing ceremonial black clothing and the same decorative ribbons on their chests as members of the crowd which consisted of three silk ribbons—red in the middle (inscribed, "Long live the sultan! Liberty, equality, brotherhood!"), the two outer ones white (proclaiming, "Long live the Ottoman army!" and "Long live freedom!"). After the crowd parted to let the governor and his entourage through, the governor read the official proclamation reinstating the constitution. The governor, in the words of one account, was:

> seemingly pale and perturbed because of the uncertainty of the reception the populace would give him. The proclamation was read, followed by a speech that had been prepared for the governor, in which he assured all that the time of oppression had ceased and the era of liberty and prosperity had dawned. Little or no enthusiasm was shown except to applaud the reference to liberty. Even the mention of the name of the governor's father [Namık Kemal], a well-known advocate of political freedom, whose books had long ago been destroyed and he himself kept a prisoner until the day of his death, failed to elicit applause.[34]

It is doubtful whether more than several dozen in the audience understood the language of the official proclamation, which was in Ottoman Turkish, but certain key terms derived from Arabic (most significant among them *ḥurriyya*—in Ottoman Turkish *hürriyet*) would have been comprehensible to most of the audience, and indeed served as a pivotal link between the official proclamation and its popular reception. The following speaker, Sa'id al-Husayni, a Jerusalem notable and the new director of education, translated the proclamation into Arabic for the crowd, explaining the concept of "liberty"—which he described as given by the sultan in an act of imperial generosity—as well as the workings of parliament and the parliamentary system. Each time the word *liberty* was pronounced, the crowd cheered in unison, "Hurray!" In a theme that would be repeated often, al-Husayni linked the imminent political changes with the economic revival and social renewal that would surely follow throughout the empire: new schools would open, commerce would flow, the imperial coffers would fill, new railroads would be built, and cars would be purchased, all of which were greeted by the cheers of the crowd. Then 'Abd al-Salam Kamal, the Turkish language editor of the official bilingual newspaper *Noble Jerusalem* (*Kudüs-ü Şerif*/*Al-Quds al-Sharīf*), and Shaykh 'Ali al-Rimawi, the paper's Arabic editor, spoke about freedom of the press.

In many ways, these events followed the proscribed ceremonial rituals not unlike myriad other official imperial ceremonies held on the anniversaries of the sultan's birthday and ascension to the throne or ceremonies to welcome a new governor or provincial official. Government officials had control of the central platform; appropriate homage was paid to the

Figure 1.3. Official ceremony in Jerusalem, August 1908. In attendance were government clerks, foreign consuls, and notables from the Muslim, Jewish, and Christian communities. Wasif Jawhariyya Photograph Collection, Institute for Palestine Studies (Beirut). Reprinted with permission from Walid Khalidi, *Before Their Diaspora: A Photographic History of the Palestinians, 1876–1948*, Institute for Palestine Studies.

sultan; the official Ottoman flag (red with a white crescent) was visible for all; and the usual government clerks, notables, spiritual leaders, and foreign consuls were present. Furthermore, by symbolically accepting the constitution on behalf of their co-religionists, spiritual leaders continued to be used as official intermediaries between the sultan's government and his subjects.[35]

And yet the official ceremonies like this one that took place throughout the empire were only the beginning of the story. For weeks and months during the fall of 1908, in municipal gardens, central squares, and coffeehouses throughout the empire, spontaneous popular gatherings took place that came to represent the transformation of the Ottoman public from prerevolutionary spectators to postrevolutionary participants.[36] These spontaneous celebrations continued in Jerusalem and Jaffa for weeks; to the north in Nablus, ʻIzzat Darwaza, the young postal clerk, reported that his town also hosted celebrations.[37] In scope and tone, the public celebrations in Palestine were strikingly similar to those taking place in other parts of the empire. Damascus, for example, hosted five large celebrations between July 31 and August 12; by the end of September the number had risen to twenty-five, when the CUP and local notables finally called for an end to the celebrations and a return to normalcy.[38] The Jerusalem press faithfully transmitted news of these celebrations taking place throughout the empire, thereby creating a sense of uniform time and experience which enabled residents to feel connected to distant corners of the Ottoman Empire.

Steering away from the official program of the government ceremonies, the celebrations then took on a carnivalesque, populist tone, and people celebrated in an informal manner more congruent with their feelings and local customs. While the Ottoman military band marched through the markets and streets playing patriotic music during the day, towns were alive with songs, drums, and cheers until well past midnight—quite a remarkable phenomenon when one considers that many towns had no electricity and normally only men and women of questionable repute would venture outside after dark. Men stood on each others' shoulders and held mock sword fights, much as they would in popular religious festivals and folk celebrations. Jurji Habib Hanania, editor of the newspaper *Jerusalem* (*Al-Quds*) observed: "Looking at the gathering of the great mass of mankind at the train station one would imagine the days of celebration of the religious festivals which take place each year in Jerusalem among the Muslims and Christians, where thousands gather and the collective voices of the people are raised and their hearts are filled with joy."[39]

Governor Ekrem Bey's own description of the day echoes newspaper descriptions of the broad and popular support for the new revolution, and reveals how he also got caught up in spirit of joyous euphoria.

> The voices of joy in the city of Jerusalem, which has no equal in the world to the contrast of religions, sects, and races in it, were raised to the heavens in a thousand languages and styles. Speeches were given. Hands were shaken. Pleasant tunes were played. . . . For hours one hears—until the furthest points of the city—the cries of "Long live the homeland," "Long live liberty," and "Long live the sultan." At night I invited all the clerks, notables, and residents to my official residence. . . . At night I spoke to the people—and among the people especially the officers—as *Kemalzade*. . . . Tears flowed from the events, and the cries came out so deep from the heart, that there was no other place in the city where liberty was as honored and sanctified to such an extent.[40]

Beyond the celebrations, these public gatherings became important platforms for ordinary Ottomans to learn of, analyze, and debate the many changes that were about to take place. Some changes were already apparent: prisoners had been freed throughout the empire, exiles were returning home, and the notorious censorship had ended. And yet, many components of the revolution were far more ambiguous and uncertain. For over thirty years the Hamidian government had tried to control the power of words and ideas by censoring terms like *despotism*, *republic*, *dynamite*, *rebellion*, *justice*, *independence*, *constitution*, *parliament*, and *liberty*.[41] Now, in this revolutionary moment, Ottomans were free to question the meaning of these long-forbidden terms and ideas. What did "liberty" mean? What was a "constitution" or a "parliament"? What would the role of the sultan-caliph be? And most importantly, how would people's daily lives change, if at all, in this new era?

Local notables and intellectuals, as well as anonymous speakers of all three religions, spoke out in public in a variety of languages. In one report, women and "even a child" took to the pulpit in public demonstrations. It is here, in the demand of common people to take the stage and to discuss and debate the meaning of events surrounding them, that the revolutionary euphoria provided a hint at the deep structural changes that were about to take place. These spontaneous gatherings where previously banned terms and ideas were bandied about freely not only symbolized the end of the sultan's absolutist power, but, more importantly, represented a broader struggle to control the symbolism and language of the revolution, and through that, to define the contours of imperial political culture. In this power vacuum individual Ottomans stepped onto the revolutionary stage and voiced their expectations of the revolution and began to imagine how they would engage and participate in the new era.

SACRED LIBERTY I: A NEW LIFE

Central in the symbolic arsenal of the revolution was the revolutionary slogan of "liberty, equality, fraternity, justice" (translated as *ḥurriyya, musāwā, ikhā', 'adālah*), which echoed both the French revolution and the recent Iranian constitutional revolution of 1906.[42] As we have seen, these slogans were prevalent as a popular cry as well as an emblem reproduced on ribbons, banners, and newspapers. The French historian Lynn Hunt identified the power of words as "revolutionary incantations. . . . Uttered in such a context or included in soon-familiar formulaic expressions, such words bespoke nothing less than adherence to the revolutionary community."[43] In addition to reinforcing loyalty to the revolution by their omnipresence and ritualized repetition, these terms also became central sites of discursive struggles, as Ottomans attempted to come to terms with their new political horizons.

Rather than speaking of a "revolution," most often the press and public referred to "liberty" (*al-ḥurriyya*), such as the "arrival of" *ḥurriyya* or the periods "before" or "after" *ḥurriyya*, and this term more than anything else served as a metonym for the 1908 revolution, encapsulating the aims of the revolutionaries, the dreams of its supporters, and even the fears of its opponents.[44] "Liberty" was not simply a question of political rights, but rather represented a broad, flexible package of competing political, philosophical, social, cultural, and even metaphysical worldviews. For reformist intellectuals, "liberty" had taken on transcendental and spiritual value, captured by the writer Adib Ishaq in the 1880s: "O Liberty, source of all majestic things on earth, we have learned that there is no success without you and no happiness away from you."[45] Likewise, the "love of freedom" (*ḥubb al-ḥurriyya*) marked the consummation of a sacred union

Figure 1.4. A scarlet banner bearing the revolutionary slogans "liberty, equality, fraternity." Subsidiary slogans (in the crescents in the four corners) are "justice, order, homeland, wealth/abundance." Thousands of these banners were sold with the opening of the Ottoman parliament on December 17, 1908. Buxton, *Turkey in Revolution*.

between individual and collective, tied together through the sacral vow of liberty. As the reformist Rafiq al-'Azm wrote, "Whenever I met an Ottoman friend who was known for his love of freedom, whether in Syria or Egypt, we became overwhelmed with emotions, and our eyes burst with tears for the joy that was within us."[46] In other words, *ḥurriyya* was an outlook, an ideology, a personal commitment, an intimate emotional feeling—both historical moment and revolutionary ideal, it was far more than the sum of its parts.

Whatever their political persuasion, Ottomans immediately grasped that their empire was poised to enter a new era.[47] Middle-class, urban, literate Ottomans had internalized the Western critique of their empire as decrepit and sick, and saw in the revolution the possibilities of an imperial renaissance. In an article entitled "The Rebirth of Our Empire," published in one of Jerusalem's Hebrew-language newspapers, the young Jewish journalist Avraham Elmaliach cheered on the revolution as a literal new beginning. "Our homeland has returned to rebirth. A people of 30 million souls awaken to a new life. A whole nation, a huge empire returns to life—a life of freedom!"[48] A Jewish Ottoman patriot in Cairo, Shmuel Ashkenazi, wrote an article for the Judeo-Spanish newspaper *Liberty* (*El Liberal*), in which he forecast that "in place of the Old Turkey [*sic*], ruined and rotten, a New Turkey has emerged, a regenerated Turkey—'Young Turkey.'"[49]

"New versus old" was not the only dichotomy put to use in the revolutionary period; we also see broad usage of "healthy versus sick," "light versus dark," "good versus evil," all meant to mark a dramatic rupture with and inversion of the past. The influential and widely read Cairene Islamic modernist monthly *The Lighthouse* (*Al-Manār*) highlighted the rupture implied by these terms: "The difference between the past and the present is like the difference between night and day, or darkness and light, or justice and injustice, or knowledge and ignorance, or strength and weakness."[50]

At the same time, given that the language of "rebirth," "awakening," and "regeneration" was also a recurrent motif in nineteenth century European nationalism, its use in the Ottoman case reasserted the empire's role at the center of Europe rather than at its margins.[51] Patriotic Ottomans dreamed of restoring the empire's lost position as a leading world power, and saw the revolution as the perfect opportunity for imperial redemption. Such was the vision of the Christian schoolteacher Eftim Mushabbak of Jerusalem, who proclaimed, "This day is the true beginning of the life of the Ottoman nation [*al-umma al-'Uthmāniyya*]. On this day all the nations of the earth will envy us, and on this day the sky and the earth and the angels and the prophets and the gods will bless the free Ottoman nation."[52] A free Ottoman Empire would finally be able to compete again with Europe, hopefully not only catching up with the West economically and technologically but perhaps even surpassing it. A free Ottoman, whose individual and national pride had been restored, would be able to hold his head high in the face of Europeans.[53]

As well, Muslim liberals in the empire saw the revolution as the final answer to those European critics who accused Islam of being a fanatical and backward theocracy. For men like Rashid Rida, the religious scholar from Tripoli who edited *The Lighthouse*, the revolution was a stage for showing the world that Islam and modernity could, in fact, coexist. Not only had Muslim intellectuals and army officers successfully carried out the liberal revolution, but they had done so without extensive bloodshed—a distinct accomplishment in world history. For the empire's non-Muslims, the revolution presented the possibility of finally becoming equal members of the imperial body politic. Earlier imperial proclamations of equality had not substantively altered the existing social, legal, or political hierarchy, but 1908 promised to be different in that regard.

In many ways, then, this "new era" envisioned was a utopian one. In the Ottoman Empire, utopia had a material face, and *ḥurriyya* became a code word for alternately concrete and vague hopes and expectations of technological progress, economic prosperity, and social reform. In order to catch up with Europe in terms of economic, cultural, and technological advances, domestic reform was necessary. A report from an Istanbul-based newspaper correspondent echoed this sentiment: "And suddenly the voice of freedom was raised—and a heavy burden was lifted from every shoulder and a large stone from every heart. We too like all the nations will taste the taste of freedom. Our fate is in our hands, and Turkey [*sic*] will finally enter into the family of European nations and march forward on the road of development."[54]

Political liberty would open the gates for—and indeed was a necessary precondition for—economic, technological, and cultural efflorescence of the empire generally, and of Palestine specifically. We saw in Sa'id al-Husayni's speech that he linked new schools, new cars, and new railroads to the new order. He was not alone. Jurji Habib Hanania had similar expectations linking *ḥurriyya* and material progress: "And now, O gentlemen, now you must raise our situation among the enlightened nations. . . . You must [see to] the agricultural and industrial and commercial advancement in this, your homeland."[55]

This expectation that the empire was entering a new, more promising era was represented in political cartoons in the satiric press and in popular postcards. In the Ottoman satiric press, the European image of the empire represented by the old, hunchbacked, crooked-nosed sultan (the "Sick Man"), had its Ottoman counterpart in depictions that contrasted Abdülhamid II with two of his most illustrious ancestors who represented the golden age of the empire: Osman, the founder of the dynasty, was depicted as the tree of life, whereas Abdülhamid was portrayed as death; likewise, Süleyman the Magnificent, known as "the Law-Giver" in Ottoman Turkish, was contrasted with Abdülhamid as a violator of laws. In other words, Abdülhamid, symbol of the Old Empire, was transformed in Ottoman cartoon space into "a clown, a crow, a monster, a tyrant, a pitiable old man, an obsolete institution, a shade."[56]

Meanwhile, thc New Empire was represented by nineteenth-century liberal intellectuals who had been martyred for their ideals and by the young heroic army officers of the Third Army Brigade who led the revolution. Midhat Pasha, the author of the original constitution who was strangled in his prison exile and therefore served as the original "martyr of liberty," as well as Enver Bey and Niyazi Bey, famous revolutionary army officers, were ubiquitous symbols, the sources of book dedica-

Figure 1.5. Enver Bey and "the dawn of liberty." While the two angels in the foreground herald the arrival of Enver Bey, the revolutionary army officer, the cherubs in sky hold the portrait of Midhat Pasha, the martyred author of the Ottoman constitution. Aflalo, *Regilding the Crescent.*

tions, poems of admiration, postcards, and commemorative kerchiefs, ceramics, and cigarette papers and cases, not to mention the subjects of numerous laudatory reports in the press.[57] The city of Beirut even renamed a street adjacent to Liberty Square after Niyazi Bey.[58] Statesmanlike, vigorous, and representative of virtue, struggle, and hope, these men were the complete opposite of the negative, deathly images of the sultan.

In the postcard shown in Figure 1.5, with the caption "the dawn of liberty," the New Empire is represented by officer Enver Bey, nicknamed by a British observer as "the Garibaldi of Young Turkey," and Midhat Pasha (in the frame), his martyrdom signified by the black ribbon. They are accompanied by cherubic angels, and the heavens smile down on the scene of an empire being led by such honorable men into a sunny future.

In a second postcard, the liberal heroes of the nineteenth century

Figure 1.6. *The Revival of the Ottoman State*. While liberal statesmen support the Ottoman Marianne, it is the heroes of the revolutionary army who succeed in freeing her from her shackles. The banner that the angel holds above reads: liberty, equality, fraternity. Orlando Calumeno Collection and Archives. Used by permission.

(Namık Kemal, Midhat Pasha, Fuat Pasha) support a chained "Lady Ottomania" while the young army heroes Enver and Niyazi take a hammer to her shackles. A crowd approvingly watches in the background, while an angel supervises the event from above, representing the divine blessings being bestowed upon the New Empire. "Lady Ottomania" bears an uncanny resemblance to the French revolutionary Marianne; clearly Ottoman producers and consumers of these images saw themselves as continuing that liberal tradition.

As these images suggest, it was the Ottoman army and the Committee for Union and Progress which were seen as the twin pillars of revolutionary power and promise, the representatives and guardians of liberty. Blow-by-blow accounts of the revolution and its heroes were published in newspapers and on broadsheets and were spread by word of mouth in city cafés and village squares. Niyazi Bey published his own account of those critical weeks, which was quickly translated into Greek, Armenian, Bulgarian, French, and English. When an Arabic translation failed to appear as quickly as the others, one Beiruti newspaper editor complained about the oversight.[59]

The theater was another outlet for the construction and dissemination of revolutionary political culture. The play *How It Came About* (*Nasıl Oldu*), by Kâzim Bey, highlighted the central themes that spoke to the revolution's resonance among the Ottoman populations.[60] The play was performed in the fall in Istanbul as a fundraiser for the winter clothing drive of the Ottoman army, under the patronage of the newly freed half-brother of the sultan, Mehmet Reşat, with two other formerly imprisoned princes in attendance. The protagonist of the play, a young officer named Behalul (*behlül* means "noble" in Ottoman Turkish), belonged to a secret organization of liberals. The motives of the liberal officers clearly stemmed from their sorrow over the impotence of the Ottoman Empire ("once the strongest in the world! . . . and today—the weakest state in Europe!"), and their desire to revive the empire through constitutional parliamentarism.

Behalul manages to escape from the sultan's spies, avaricious men seeking their own promotion rather than the national good, and becomes a lawyer while continuing his mobilization on behalf of the CUP. One day, his luck runs out and he is finally arrested. The brief exchange at his court-martial makes clear that Behalul's loyalty belongs not with the sultan, but with the nation.

INTERROGATOR: How can you be disloyal to the sultan, who has bestowed such benefits on you?

BEHALUL: Ask the spies about benefits—not me! I care nothing for the personality of the Sultan—I am for my country, against the tigers who ravage her. (*Applause.*)

INTERROGATOR: And your precious Committee—what good will that do you?

BEHALUL: It will do everything; it is going to save the Fatherland. (*Renewed applause.*)

At that moment, a revolutionary infantry bursts into the interrogation chamber, setting the prisoners free and arresting the judges, spies, and interrogators. The play ends with the troops taking to the hills to spread the revolution, taking "the solemn oath" and delivering "a speech full of 'liberty,' and 'fraternity for all,' and 'long live the Constitution!'" As the play sought to convince its audience, the army was the true protector of the Ottoman nation, and would usher in a future of divinely-sanctioned prosperity and justice (" . . . and God defend us, God who loves justice!"). Other plays, such as *Those Who Were Sacrificed for Liberty* and *Fighters of Liberty*, reinforced this theme.[61] This intertwining of the CUP, the army, and the nation was also reflected in the fund-raising drive of a local CUP branch in Sidon that wanted to purchase two cruisers for the Ottoman navy to be named in honor of Enver and Niyazi, called "liberators of the homeland and the givers of a constitutional life to the Ottoman people."[62]

The sultan himself was forced to recognize and grudgingly acknowledge the growing influence and prestige of the CUP, which threatened to eclipse his primary position not only within the state but also in the hearts and minds of his "flock." There are reports that he sought to co-opt the rising popularity of the CUP by aligning himself with the organization, either claiming or requesting the office of president, after which he was informed that there was no such position open.[63] The symbolic demotion of the sultan was expressed in various ways in the new revolutionary popular culture. For one, a new liberty anthem was composed that supplanted the sultanic "Hamidiye" march at official ceremonies.[64] In some postcards the sultan's image appeared flanked by Enver and Niyazi Beys, reflecting the sultan's attempt to harness his image to the popularity of the revolutionary officers as well as suggesting the extent to which the sultan's political legitimacy was no longer able to stand on its own. Even more startling, in figure 1.7 we see a postcard of Enver and Niyazi stomping out the skeletal figure of "despotism," alluding to the sultan's aged and decrepit body and foreshadowing the eventual subordination of the sultan to the will of the CUP, the army, and the nation, a sentiment that would be developed in the popular press throughout the fall of 1908.

Figure 1.7. Enver and Niyazi, "the heroes who freed the homeland from despotism." The Ottoman Marianne holds the Ottoman flag in one hand, and the scales of justice in the other. Orlando Calumeno Collection and Archives. Used by permission

SACRED LIBERTY II: FROM OPPRESSION TO CONSULTATION AND JUSTICE

Given that the sultan was not only the political leader of the empire but was also the caliph, or deputy of the Prophet, in guiding the "community of believers," the image of Abdülhamid in the revolutionary satirical press as a comic-grotesque figure representing the "Old Empire" revealed an utter breakdown in sultanic authority.[65] This claimed divinity and infallibility of the sultan was undoubtedly an important factor for some segments of the Ottoman Muslim population, who, as relayed in one account in *The Lighthouse*, saw the "creation of the sultan as replacing the creation of the rest of humanity" and were "ready to go through fire for his life."[66] Furthermore, over the three decades of his rule the sultan had explicitly fostered a public image of himself as a benevolent monarch and paternal figure.[67]

In that sense the Ottoman sultan's divine-paternal-political roles echoed that of the other Eurasian imperial dynasties at the time, the Habsburgs and the Romanovs. The Habsburg dynasty, even as late as under Emperor Franz Joseph (r. 1848–1916), strove to assert "the inherent sacredness of sovereign power" as protectors of the by-then defunct Holy Roman Empire through public displays of imperial piety, such as participation in the Corpus Christi procession and in the Holy Thursday foot-washing ceremony, as well as attendance at religious ceremonies in churches, synagogues, and mosques.[68] Similarly, the Russian Empire depended on inculcating a strong sense of loyalty to the Romanov family, as the heirs to the Byzantine emperors and thus protectors of the Orthodox faith, by means of coronation ceremonies, church holidays, and secular celebrations that comprised a "theater of power" that aimed "to present the ruler as supreme and to vest him or her with sacral qualities." In the 1830s official policy declared the monarch as the embodiment of the nation, and loyalty to the tsars would remain a significant component of Russian imperial identity beyond the turn of the twentieth century.[69]

The emerging political criticism of the Ottoman sultan in the new era would never hold without a corresponding desacralization of his person, made possible by a religious criticism of his performance in office. In the first few months of the revolution, Ottomans wrestled with differing views of the sultan, centering on questions about his responsibility for the "reign of tyranny," his motives for acceding to the demands of the revolutionaries, and the legitimacy and nature of his position. At first, when it was unclear how deep the reforms would be or how long the revolution would last, there was a ritual invocation of the sultan in public demonstrations and to a certain extent in the pages of the press. For example, one enthusiastic report read: "Good news follows good news: the secret police is abolished—Long live the sultan! Newspaper censorship is canceled—Long live the sultan! State prisoners will be released to freedom—Long live the sultan!"[70] Likewise, at a celebration in São Paulo, Brazil, the assembled Ottoman émigrés presented the consul with a petition, two and a half feet long by one and a half feet wide, offering thanks to the sultan for allowing the publication of the Basic Law. These invocations of the sultan might have been sincere, or they simply might have been formulaic, a public performance of sultanic loyalty without a necessary internalization of it.[71]

At the same time, we also read expressions of a conditional status for the sultan due to his role as the "giver of the constitution." As "giver of liberty" or "giver of the constitution," neither the sultan's person nor his office were in and of themselves deserving of loyalty from his erstwhile subjects; rather, Ottoman citizens suspended their criticisms of his past roles to focus on the promised new order.[72] Another formulation described the sultan as simply the tool through which God had acted—"We thank God who inspired our great sultan who revived the nation [*umma*] by giving it the constitution."[73] In this context, the role of the *şeyhülislam* Cemaleddin Effendi, the foremost Muslim official in the empire at the time, in the immediate aftermath of the revolution was paramount; indeed, some reports credited the *şeyhülislam* far more than the sultan. According to various accounts, Cemaleddin was extremely supportive of the new constitutional order and personally conveyed his ruling to Abdülhamid II that the constitution was congruous with Islamic law, the *shari'a*. Public reports cited Cemaleddin as telling the sultan that the day of the announcement of the constitution would be "engraved on the bosom of each *shaykh* and priest, nay each Muslim and Christian, nay each Ottoman and human."[74] It was his personal intervention that reportedly prevented the bloodbath which surely would have resulted had the sultan not acquiesced to the CUP's demands, implicitly countering the claims of the sultan's supporters that the sultan himself was a victim of the intrigues of the palace functionaries and that his own "true" sentiments of liberalism had been stifled during his thirty-three-year reign.[75]

Beyond the temporary and cautious recuperation of status the sultan received by being seen as the "giver of liberty," however, several newspaper reports show that the sultan was a deeply polarizing figure among Ottomans who were celebrating the new era. Indeed, many liberals had good reason to suspect Abdülhamid's commitment to the new regime, for he had long been reviled at home and abroad for his "tyrannical rule."[76] At a popular gathering in Cairo, the assembled crowd decided to send a telegram congratulating the exiled prince Sabaheddin Damad, a known supporter of the opposition parties, as well as the heroes of the Ottoman army, Enver, Nuri, and Niyazi, and finally, the grand vizier. When Rashid Rida, the editor of *The Lighthouse*, suggested that a telegram be sent as well to the sultan thanking him for agreeing to the liberals' demand, his proposal was shot down vigorously.[77]

Another extraordinary account quoted from the newspaper *Al-Muqattam* relays that a crowd at one of the public celebrations in Damascus shouted down a religious figure who tried to begin his speech with the traditional invocation for the sultan; the crowd cried out, "Sit down, sit down, the occasion is neither one of praying for the sultan, nor it is his accession day or his birthday. It is the day of liberty, and death be to anyone who does not cry aloud 'long live liberty'!"[78] Just as potentially subversive, upon his release from prison in Beirut, the Young Ottoman reformer Fuat Pasha found a populace enthusiastic and loyal to the constitution. He reportedly told the crowd that it was necessary to fight for the constitution, "even if the sultan himself" was found to be in opposition—to which the crowd responded in enthusiastic support.[79]

Because of the extensive censorship within the empire, these kinds of criticisms of the sultan were taboo before 1908; afterward, they flooded to the forefront. In public addresses and on the pages of the newly free press, complaints of the sufferings of the past thirty-three years abounded. Father, brother, and son had feared each other, neighbors had informed on one another, and man had to hide his own thoughts from himself.[80] Even the Ottoman chargé d'affairs in New York, Mundji Bey, referred to "the despot who shall not be named" at a celebratory gathering held at Carnegie Hall in early September, where a congratulatory letter from President Theodore Roosevelt was read to the audience. Among the fete's attendees were Ottoman Turks, Greeks, Armenians, and Arabs; according to a press report, the one Armenian speaker who praised the sultan elicited hissing from the audience.[81] Within months, one newspaper editor in Istanbul felt confident enough to publish a poem denouncing the sultan: "So diabolical you are; a greater evil than Satan."[82] Clearly, the divine and protected status of the sultan was dramatically undermined with the revolution.

For Ruhi al-Khalidi, a member of a leading Muslim family in Jerusalem who was serving as Ottoman consul in Bourdeaux at the outbreak of the revolution, the Ottoman dynasty's tyranny itself is what gave birth to the Ottoman revolution.[83] In a series of articles published in the Cairene press in the fall of 1908 around the time he was running for a seat in the Ottoman parliament in his native Jerusalem, al-Khalidi argued that the events of July 1908 were a legitimate revolution ("*inqilāb*") rather than a disobedient revolt ("*thawra*"). While arguing that most Arab writers in practice did not properly differentiate between these two words and phenomena, al-Khalidi maintained that the essential difference between them was vast. Whereas a revolt was "insubordination and a departure from obedience and upholding the legitimate government," "revolution," al-Khalidi explained, "advances the nation a step toward progress and climbs a rung on the ladder of prosperity." At the same time, al-Khalidi explained that a true revolution was not simply a political change but also a revolution of values, customs, thoughts, and language.[84]

Al-Khalidi's essay is important for what it reveals about the political worldview of a Muslim Ottoman intellectual, a long-time critic of the Hamidian regime at the same time that he remained a liberal Ottoman patriot. As well, al-Khalidi's essay reveals the extent to which Ottoman patriotism and Islamic modernism emerged in dialogue with—and in defense against—Western criticisms of the empire and Islam as a whole.

The son of a government official, al-Khalidi received a sound Islamic education at the al-Aqsa Mosque in Jerusalem, but he was also educated in secular subjects at the Alliance Israélite Universelle school in Jerusalem founded by French Jews, as well as at the government Al-Ṣalāḥiyya and Al-Sulṭāniyya schools in Jerusalem and Beirut. Al-Khalidi later went to Istanbul, where his uncle Yusuf Dia al-Khalidi was serving in the first Ottoman parliament, and attached himself to the circle surrounding the pan-Islamist and anticolonial activist Jamal al-Din al-Afghani before both men were exiled from the capital.

As a result of his educational and life experiences, al-Khalidi was steeped in Islamic thought without being apologetic about it, learned in Western thought without being blindly imitative. Thus, al-Khalidi's central justification for revolution against the Ottoman sultan was due to the sultan's failure to live up to the proper Islamic principles of governance, which was rooted in liberalism. In contrast to those critics in Europe who described Islamic governments as oppressive in their essence, al-Khalidi set out to prove that the tyranny that characterized the Hamidian regime came not from Islamic principles, which demand equality and justice, but from a longer legacy of Asiatic despotism. That is to say, political tyranny in the Muslim world was not religious in origin but rather social and historical. As al-Khalidi explained, "Muslim rulers inherited this tyranny from the Persian emperors and Roman Caesars, from the river banks in Babylon and the Egyptian pharaohs, from Ghengis Khan and Tamerlane." In truth, according to al-Khalidi, Islam at its origin opposed tyranny, introduced equality between members of the community of believers, protected individual rights and freedoms, and protected foreigners and minorities in an unprecedented manner. As such, Islam "paved the way for democratic government and located the rule of law with the people, and did not stand in the way of giving freedom in word and deed" (3).

In making this argument, al-Khalidi drew heavily on Islamic history as well as sacred Islamic textual traditions. Al-Khalidi supported his argument with proof texts from the Qur'an and the hadith, in particular Qur'an 3:159 ("for had you been stern and hard of heart they would surely have broken away from you") and 42:38 (". . . whose affairs are settled by mutual consultation").[85] From the hadith, al-Khalidi relied on the examples of pre-Islamic tyranny in Mecca and the final agreement to combat it, which the Prophet, Muhammad, was said to have witnessed personally and looked upon favorably.

According to al-Khalidi, at its origin Islam introduced a new mode of political rule, the caliphate, which was a distinct advance over the monarchical model of the tribes of Israel (Bani Isrā'il) (5). In contrast to the absolute and inherited power of the Hebrew kings, the first four Muslim caliphs were chosen by the people through the practice of consultation (*shūra*). After the fourth caliph, 'Ali, however, when internal rivalries over succession to the caliphate split the Muslim community, the Umayyads turned the caliphate into a hereditary monarchy (660–750 C.E.). From that point on (with one singular exception of the righteous caliph 'Umar bin 'Abd al-'Aziz, r. 717–20, whose son did not inherit the caliphate after his father's death), Muslim rulers became corrupt and self-interested, a situation which continued through most of the Ottoman dynasty, "whose first task was to protect the interests of the dynasty and the great families (of the court)" (6).

As al-Khalidi and other Islamic modernist reformers saw it, the Islamic code of divine law, the *shari'a*, was like a constitution for the people, but because it had been abandoned to tyranny and injustice in the Ottoman Empire, reforms were necessary as an added safeguard to the inherent liberties provided by Islam. For al-Khalidi, the moment of redemption began with the declaration of the Basic Law under Midhat Pasha, and was finally completed with the emergence of the CUP onto the political stage.

Al-Khalidi's narrative of Islamic history is both deeply traditional—echoing the format and some of the assertions of religious scholars—and modernist. His essay reveals the influence of a variety of Islamic modernist thinkers, such as Rashid Rida, the editor of *The Lighthouse*, and, more overtly, the Aleppine scholar 'Abd al-Rahman al-Kawakibi. Less than a decade earlier, al-Kawakibi had published a highly influential book entitled *The Nature of Tyranny*, in which he similarly brought

Qur'anic and hadith examples to criticize the Ottoman ancien régime and advocate political reform, arguing for accountability and for the need of the ruler to serve the people.[86]

While al-Khalidi himself was somewhat elliptical in his criticism of the sultan-caliph, his publisher, Husayn Wasfi Rida, was much more overt about it. Rida blamed Abdülhamid for reintroducing slavery at precisely the moment when the empire seemed poised for reform, by metaphorically and literally drowning the dreams of the reformers in the Bosphorus. Furthermore, Rida blamed the sultan for "fighting against the people" by employing spies and, as is noted in Qur'an 4:77, "filling the people with the fear of men as though it were the fear of God and even more."

At around the same time as al-Khalidi's articles appeared, another commentary on the revolution was published by Suleiman al-Bustani, entitled "Admonition and Remembrance; or, The Ottoman State Before the Constitution and After It."[87] Al-Bustani was a leading intellectual from a prominent Christian Beiruti family, an important contributor to the nineteenth-century "renaissance" in Arabic language and literature, who had translated Homer's *Iliad* into Arabic. Like al-Khalidi, he would be elected to the Ottoman parliament that autumn to represent his hometown. Al-Bustani was also a fervent supporter of the revolution and its promise of liberalism, and he considered constitutionalism as completely congruent with Islam, having roots in the Torah and the New Testament.[88]

The Christian al-Bustani took care to emphasize that constitutional rule would not challenge the religious role of the caliph, but rather would be "representative rule in the new mode where the nation-people [*umma*] rules itself while preserving the rights of the caliphate, wherein the caliphate and constitutional rule support one another" (15). Al-Bustani emphasized the "will of the people-nation [*irādat al-umma*]" in legitimizing representative rule, and his rewriting of Ottoman imperial history to emphasize the long trajectory of political reform in the empire focused on the revolution as the authentic expression of the will of the Ottoman people and as a product of social consensus. His assertions that "the majority of the sons of the land were transformed to be of one opinion" (7), and that "the Ottomans yearned for [freedom]" (22), were meant to place the *umma* as the key actor in history. Thus, without challenging the sacred basis of political rule (the caliphate) or criticizing the sultan directly, al-Bustani clearly shifted the legitimacy of political power from the ruler to the nation, from absolute religious grounds to notions of justice and representative participation.

As prominent intellectuals like al-Khalidi and al-Bustani introduced new measures of sultanic legitimacy, questions remained about the sultan-caliph's loyalty to the new regime. Furthermore, as his role increasingly was questioned in constitutionalist circles, opponents of the revolution took Abdülhamid as their patron and mascot. *The Lighthouse* reported that at one early revolutionary celebration in Cairo, some opposition voices shouted out, "Long live the sultan—down with Young Turkey!"[89] More alarmingly, by October 1908, newspapers reported on the emergence of an anticonstitutional movement in the capital led by lower-level religious functionaries and agitated by the opposition newspaper *Mizan*. According to one account that made its way to the Jerusalem press, Murad Bey, the editor of *Mizan*, reportedly went to the sultan's palace with a note which read: "I lead hundreds who are ready to do what we can to destroy the constitution. If this pleases you we are ready to serve." The paper reported that upon reading it, Abdülhamid responded: "Do you think I am an enemy of the constitution? Even if you were to destroy the entire world I would not do a thing against the constitution, which promised my people happiness and peace."[90] Whether or not the sultan's reported refusal to side with the opposition was believable to the paper's readers was almost beside the point; in the eyes of this newspaper, these types of incidents were occurring daily and were evidence that, as the newspaper article put it, "the constitution is in danger!" Indeed, only a few months later the sultan would prove to be the weakest link of the new constitutional regime.

"SACRED LIBERTY" III: FROM RELIGIOUS LEGITIMACY TO SACRED REVOLUTION

We have already seen that the Ottoman revolution was in many ways a deeply religious revolution, with religious officials and intellectuals interpreting and legitimizing political change in dialogue with religious principles and based on religious sources. Some scholars have argued that after the revolution the official state Islamic hierarchy took a leading role in supporting and propagating the revolutionary principles. As we have seen, this attitude began with the top tier, the *şeyhülislam*, who reportedly stated that "the law of Islam is more liberal than the constitution itself," and that the constitution was "binding upon those who profess Islam."[91] This view trickled down to some extent to the lower levels of the religious establishment. One journalist documented an August 1908 public gathering in the Beyazit mosque in Istanbul where the assembled scholars argued that the Qur'an prescribes constitutional government, and yet another journalist spoke approvingly of the religious scholars of the capital, saying "it is they who have achieved the remarkable feat of convincing themselves and many of their countrymen that the best theoretical sanction for a Constitution is to be found in the Koran, that despotism is a flagrant violation of the teachings of the prophet, and that the true spirit of Islam is in favour of a democratic form of government."[92]

Indeed, preachers such as Jamal al-Din al-Qasimi in Damascus and Shaykh Muhammad Shakir Diab al-Baytuni in Palestine all proselytized on behalf of an Islamic constitutionalism in the mosques and town centers. Pamphlets like *Kuran kerim ve-kanunı asasi* (The Precious Qur'an and the Basic Law) and *Din ve-hürriyet* (Religion and Liberty) brought a series of prooftexts from Islamic sacred sources to legitimize parliamentary constitutionalism and revolution in religious terms. As well, newspapers such as *Path of Righteousness* (*Sirat-i Mustakim*) and *Crescent* (*Hilal*), in Istanbul, *The Lighthouse* in Cairo, and *Ottoman Union* (*Al-Ittiḥād al-ʿUthmānī*) in Beirut also devoted themselves to providing an Islamic framework for the constitutional regime. Finally, CUP chapters in Istanbul and elsewhere distributed less high-brow pamphlets that offered people religious advice and protection from pestilence and other household dangers.[93]

For a deeply religious society and in a state where politics and religion were intertwined, this is quite understandable. At the same time, religion also penetrated the 1908 revolution in unanticipated ways. As the French historian Mona Ozouf has written, "beginning a new life cannot be imagined without faith," resulting in a revolutionary "transfer of sacrality" from old to new.[94] Indeed, the popular iconography around the Ottoman revolution flirted with religious and quasi-messianic images, language, and expectations. *Ḥurriyya* underwent a process of animation, and in surprising ways, *ḥurriyya* was sacralized discursively and ideologically. Far more than a political concept, *ḥurriyya* was treated as a "noble concept," and there was a deep and general reverence expressed toward all things *ḥurriyya*. In some ways, *ḥurriyya* became a new religion that demanded loyalty, love, and personal sacrifice. This connection between religious ardor and the new order (this "blessed era," or *al-ʿaṣr al-mubārak*) was both explicit and implicit. The people's ultimate loyalty was owed to *ḥurriyya* itself; *ḥurriyya* became the most sacred source of authority. Overall, *ḥurriyya* served as a potent symbol in the "world-making" of Ottoman citizenship, providing a sacred source for reformulating the bond between individual and state, as well as between citizens.

Immediately after the revolution, the public watched as the acting governor of Jerusalem demanded from all the government clerks, army officers, and police that they would "swear before God" to uphold the constitution and the laws of the government.[95] Similar vows to the new order were reported from around the Ottoman world. In Damascus, the U.S. consul reported that after the crowds expressed "very liberal opinions," a military officer asked the people to swear "that if tyranny shall reign again, they would overthrow it no matter how dear it might cost them. They solemnly declared that they were ready to sacrifice for liberty their wives, their children and their blood! After this solemn oath three times three cheers were given for Liberty, the Army and the Sultan."[96] In fact, many of the speeches given in the revolutionary celebrations were reported in the press as akin to a religious sermon, often ending in "amen," both pronounced by the speaker and repeated by the audience.

The constitution quickly became the foundational text of the religion of *ḥurriyya*—it was repeatedly referred to as the "precious constitution" (*al-dustūr al-karīm*), the "holy constitution" (*al-dustūr al-muqaddas*)—the sorts of expressions that were often used to describe the sacred books.[97] Jews in the empire also used their own religious imagery, calling the constitution a "new Torah": "Jerusalem has awakened, Jerusalem, with the three religions, the pious and modest, that Jerusalem has awakened to the new Torah which was given to the peoples of Turkey [*sic*]." In the popular celebrations that took place in mid-August in Hebron in southern Palestine, the Jewish youth prepared a flag decorated on one side with the Ten Commandments in gold lettering, and on the other side was the slogan "Long live liberty, fraternity, and equality!" in Hebrew and Arabic in silver lettering, establishing at the least a visual (if not moral) parity between them.[98] On another occasion, the deputy to the Maronite Patriarch in Jerusalem reminded the assembled crowd that "we remembered that we swore an oath on brotherhood and unity, and it will be a sin to break one's oath by stopping at the beginning of the road in the constitutional era."[99]

To a certain extent, these are the contours of the language and culture—Muslim, Christian, and Jew all inhabited a society marked at every level by religious tradition, and the Arabic language itself, as the language of the Qur'an, is laden with religious resonance. In some ways, then, it is natural that religious expression was mobilized for the new order. And yet, the degree to which the revolution and its emblem of *ḥurriyya* were endowed with sacred value at times bordered on sacrilegious. While singing the praises of Macedonia for its leading role in the revolution, the young Palestinian poet Is'af al-Nashashibi declared: "From Macedonia life appeared to us, from Macedonia the light of justice was illuminated. From Macedonia truth began, from Macedonia, from Macedonia, appeared liberty, life of the Ottoman nation. Oh Macedonia . . . *You are our second* ka'ba, *you are our other* qibla."[100]

The *ka'ba*, of course, is the holiest shrine in Islam, the site of the pilgrimage to Mecca. The *qibla* marks the direction of prayer for Muslims toward Mecca. By elevating Macedonia to the status of Mecca, al-Nashashibi not only proclaimed the sacred value of *ḥurriyya*. He also marked off prerevolutionary time (and by extension, antirevolutionary thinking) as the age of ignorance, *jahiliyya*, that references the Arabian Peninsula before the revelations of the Prophet. Furthermore, by intertwining sacred and secular time and space, al-Nashashibi underscored the complex role that religion played in giving shape to a distinct Ottoman nationalism and nation-building project. In other words, in sacralizing the birthplace of the constitution and all that it represented, al-Nashashibi explicitly challenged the sacred sources of sultanic political legitimacy and loyalty, and elevated new parameters for loyalty—to the Ottoman nation and to the Ottoman homeland.

Anthony Smith, the prominent scholar of nationalism, argues that religion and nationalism are more deeply intertwined than earlier scholars have imagined. Rather than seeing nationalism as an essentially secular, modern phenomenon, the functional replacement of religion, and instead of looking at the instrumentalization of religious symbols by nationalists and nationalist movements, Smith underscores the ongoing relevance and symbolic importance of religion in people's lives as the reason for its enduring usage in national movements.[101] Indeed, we will see that Ottoman nationalism tapped into the religious consciousness, symbols, and sacrality of Ottoman citizens in complex and profound ways.[102]

COMMUNAL LIBERTY

The language of liberty, reform, and consultation did not stay focused on the institutions of state, but rather trickled down in remarkable ways. Claiming to have been influenced by the new spirit of *ḥurriyya*, reformists in three religious communities in Jerusalem—the Armenian, Greek Orthodox and Jewish—conducted hard-fought struggles for change within their communities. The three groups demanded liberation from the oppressive rule of the priests and rabbis, participation in the decision-making processes of their congregations, and a new spirit of reform and modernity. Indeed, for many of the Christian and Jewish residents of Palestine, the language of liberty and equality inspired and gave succor to internal efforts to reform and reinvent their communal lives, not only as Ottomans but also as Ottoman Christians and Jews.[103]

The broadest-scale and longest-lasting of the three communal revolts, the "Orthodox renaissance," as the Greek Orthodox struggle for reform was known, began over the principle of representation and power sharing among the elite foreign clergy and the local Arab populace.[104] The Greek Orthodox Patriarchate of Jerusalem was ruled by the Brotherhood of the Holy Sepulcher, a body of celibate monks from Greece who had been educated and trained in Jerusalem, whereas the lower clergy of married Arab priests as well as the local laity were largely excluded from decision making and representation in communal life.[105]

One of the young leaders of the Greek Orthodox revolution was Khalil al-Sakakini, the young schoolteacher discussed earlier, who had recently returned to Jerusalem from America. Together with his old teacher Jurji Zakaria, al-Sakakini put together an informal commission of inquiry to research the needs and rights of the community. As al-Sakakini noted, "though we were freed from the tyranny of the government, we are still under [the tyranny of] the spiritual leadership. . . . My objective . . . is to rip out the Greek yoke [*nīr al-Yūnān*] who have no right to be at the head, neither religiously, nor politically, nor morally."[106]

According to Article 111 of the Ottoman constitution, each religious community was to have an elected council. The Greek Orthodox reformers insisted that the council should include representatives from parishes outside of Jerusalem, a significant demand which in essence called for the unification of the Greek Orthodox Arabs of Palestine. This council would oversee the communal schools, churches, religious endowments, and funds. They also demanded that archbishoprics and provincial religious leaderships be established. Furthermore, the committee demanded that the leading school in Jerusalem admit "national Ottoman Orthodox" students from all the parishes of Palestine and educate them in higher literature and theology so that they would be prepared to enter the priesthood.[107]

Indeed, a significant underlying element of the local Christians' demands was opposition to the Hellenizing aims of the foreign ecclesiastical leadership at the expense of the local indigenous culture, echoing broader complaints against foreign influence and subjugation in the Ottoman Empire as well as a rejection of hated Greece. Out of the twenty-eight Greek Orthodox churches in Jerusalem, only three offered services in Arabic, despite the fact that the Greek Orthodox community in Jerusalem was 85 percent Arabic-speaking and only 15 percent Greek-speaking.[108] Greek Orthodox intellectuals in Jaffa also began proselytizing against "Aryan Christianity" in favor of a purer "Semitic Christianity," sending delegates to the provincial towns to promote this idea. In other words, the Greek Orthodox reformers were careful to paint their communal revolution in national patriotic terms. After several members of the leadership met with the Jerusalem governor, they were greeted on their way home by thousands of co-religionists waving Ottoman flags.[109]

In the dramatic course of events, numerous large-scale demonstrations were held in Jerusalem and Jaffa; protestors occupied churches and monasteries and barricaded themselves, parishioners boycotted the annual Christmas mass at Bethlehem's Church of the Nativity, and the community sent delegations to Istanbul to pursue their claims with the central government. In response, the Holy Synod decided to punish the natives for revolting, cutting off the supply of food to the poor and payment of the communal head tax, and demanding rent payment for communally-owned apartments (which formerly had been rent-free for members of the community).[110]

The Patriarchate requested assistance from the foreign consulates in Jerusalem in pacifying the locals, complaining that the Ottoman government refused to intervene. In fact, the central government at first intervened on behalf of the Greek Orthodox Arabs: the minister of the interior sent a telegram to the Jerusalem governor ordering him to inform the Patriarchate that it would not be able to evict Christian tenants from their apartments until the entire affair was over.[111] At the end of January 1909, a government commission arrived in Jerusalem to investigate the matter, and it was greeted at the train station by hundreds of Jerusalem's assorted residents. A leading member of the Greek Orthodox community, Eftim Mushabbak, gave a rousing speech on behalf of his co-religionists: "Sir, Members of the Committee, all of us standing here, all of us living in this country for generations upon generations, for hundreds and hundreds of years, demand justice, and the rule of law! We want the committee to research and demand everything without prejudice; we demand our rights, to be free in our country and not to be [subject to] the foreign Greeks."[112]

By February, the struggle between the local Arab Greek Orthodox and their ecclesiastical leadership turned into an outright battle, as Greeks and Arabs on both sides were found murdered and Greek shops and passersby were attacked in the city, forcing the army to patrol the streets and leading many shops to shutter their doors.[113] Over the next two years, the Greek Orthodox Arabs of Jerusalem succeeded in securing some concessions, and at the end of 1910 elections for a communal mixed council were finally held.[114]

As Palestinian Christians used the logic and rhetoric of the new political order to secure their own communal rights, this incident reveals the power and appeal of the language and structure of constitutionalism. Additionally, the Greek Orthodox renaissance also sought to link Greek Orthodox Christians throughout Palestine as well as east of the Jordan River in an effort to unite the community. As the leadership of the revolt saw it, this was a substantial victory: "Before the renaissance the life of every Orthodox was a private life, living for himself and taking interest in his own affairs. . . . [Now] . . . the Orthodox has entered a new life which is national life."[115] Finally, the revolt contributed to supporting links between the Greek Orthodox and their Muslim neighbors, planting a seed of local sentiment that sought both to unite and transcend communal boundaries all in the unique "spirit of the times."[116]

The spirit of the Greek Orthodox rebellion spread to other religious communities in Jerusalem, inspiring them to seek similar autonomy and liberty.[117] Reform-minded Sephardi Jews in Jerusalem saw in this an echo of their own internal struggle for change (known as *el pleyto*), and the Jewish press reported on the affair extensively. In the early weeks after the outbreak of the rebellion, the Hebrew newspaper *The Deer* (*Ha-Ẓvi*) editorialized in support of the native Christians' efforts: "This is an important deed in the public life of our country, and not just for the Greek Church but it is first of all a fruit of the constitution, liberty. . . . [We do not know if their claims are just or not, but] we cannot help but feel affinity to anyone who fights for his rights that are important to him."[118]

It was precisely this fear of the spread of the spirit of communal rebellion that worried the Latin Patriarch Camassei, who saw the Greek Orthodox revolt as the beginning of "serious troubles."[119] Other forces would also seek to curtail the boundaries of liberty before it was too late.

THE LIMITS OF LIBERTY

Outside of the main cities, lack of access to information, the personal proclivity of local government officials, and the leadership of important local notables influenced when, how, and along what contours the Ottoman revolution arrived. Over two months after the official announcements of the new constitutional parliamentary regime, the residents of northern Safad (in the Galilee in the province of 'Akka) had "barely heard" of the reforms, and the official celebration mandated by the local deputy governor reportedly did little to move them.[120]

Precious few historical sources document the responses and attitudes of non-elite, nonliterate Ottomans, whether urban workers, villagers, or rural peasants—undoubtedly the majority of the population throughout the empire. Their voicelessness suggests political impotence—the CUP reportedly despised the masses and manipulated them for their own political goals.[121] For some leaders of the CUP, a representative government (parliament) was a necessary evil in order to challenge the negative power of the state, but even then the representatives were considered "agents of the state" rather than "representatives of the people." In this context, the

CUP leader Ahmed Rıza is quoted as saying, "Silly people should not be allowed to enter into politics; however, they have unfortunately even become deputies, and this is a defect of liberty that enables the masses to assume a role in the life and future of the state and nation."[122]

The young novelist Halide Edib Adıvar related an incident that took place in Istanbul immediately after the restoration of the constitution when the CUP leader Dr. Rıza Tevfik encountered a group of Kurdish porters in the mass celebrations: "'Tell us what the constitution means,' the porters had shouted. 'Constitution is such a great thing that those who do not know it are donkeys,' answered the speaker. 'We are donkeys,' roared the porters. 'Your fathers also did not know it. Say that you are the sons of donkeys,' added Rıza Tevfik. 'We are the sons of donkeys,' roared the porters again."[123]

For the lower classes, poorly understood new ideas floated side-by-side with old modes of patronage and political loyalty. The newspaper *Al-Muqattam* quoted a Bani Sakhr tribal chief from the province of Syria: "I do not know what a constitution is, but I swear [allegiance to it]. If the Damascus governor and the deputy governor of this district betray [it], I will betray [it] with them too. If they [carry it out] with faithfulness and uprightness, then I am with them too."[124] For the newspaper's audience, the comment must have underscored the importance of purging officials of the ancien régime from power, particularly in the "backward" margins of the empire which were even more susceptible to manipulation.

As a result, peasants and the uneducated became the objects of careful attention from the middle and upper classes—on the one hand, encouraging their participation in supporting the revolution, while at the same time, ensuring they accepted the boundaries established by their social superiors. The "poor and miserable" peasants were invoked at various public rallies in Jerusalem, and speakers agitated for lowering taxes to lighten the burden of the peasants. In addition, the rights of the peasant took center stage in the claims of government corruption. As one speaker passionately pleaded, "I ask you to lift the tyranny from [the peasants'] shoulders and expel the government despots who plunder his money. Look at the homes of some of the oppressors and see them adorned with the money of the peasant, furnished with silk."[125]

Paternalism was threatened, however, when the peasants', workers', and tribes' interpretations of liberty directly clashed with the interests of other classes. Early workers strikes were ruthlessly put down by the CUP. Reports from northern Palestine of the peasant revolutionaries of Kufr Kana who rebelled against local land tenure and authority structures merited them the label of bandits and thieves. A similar mutiny by peasants against their landlords in the Wadi al-'Ajam district in the province of Syria ended in their submission only after a villager was shot by the gendarme sent by the deputy-governor.[126]

As the months passed many people were to observe bitterly that the "uneducated" seemed to misunderstand *ḥurriyya* to be a license for anarchy and intolerable violations of the social order. The American consul in Haifa frostily noted that "since the proclamation of freedom the natives behave like a lot of ill-treated slaves, who have gained their freedom and do not know how to keep themselves in the limits of law."[127] Another foreign traveler in Istanbul made similar observations:

"Pay the toll?" said a woman crossing the Galata Bridge. "Why should I pay the toll? Have we not liberty now?'" "Is this what you call liberty?" said an Albanian when the Young Turks condemned him to death for shooting a Christian. Persons "falsely representing themselves to be members of the CUP," to use the language of the Grand Vizier, persuaded the people that there would now be no more taxes to pay. A small boy threw a stone at a foreigner driving in a motor-car. The foreigner rebuked him, and received the reply, "It is liberty now!" The foreigner gave him a box on the ear. "All right," said the impartial youngster; "you also have liberty."[128]

In other words, while the 1908 revolution saw the middle classes of the empire fighting for their place on the imperial stage, neither they nor the architects of the revolution intended for the revolution to overturn certain socioeconomic boundaries—a fact marking the limits of *ḥurriyya*.[129]

Changes in gender relations also remained outside the acceptable boundaries of liberty. The linkage between "women's liberation" and "national modernity" was already widely discussed in the Ottoman (as in the Egyptian and Iranian) press starting in the 1890s, and women as mothers of the nation were lauded and idealized in the revolutionary press.[130] However, the changing behavior and public appearance of women in the heady early days of the revolution caused a great deal of social and political concern. Early reports indicate that women appeared unveiled in public for the first time in the days after the revolution and took part in public demonstrations, discussions, and celebrations. One Istanbul press correspondent hailed these women as the symbol of Ottoman freedom and claimed they were received well by the crowd.[131] A visitor from England documented similar occurrences, but also remarked on how short-lived this form of freedom was, calling its end the only "shadow among the sunshine":

They threw off their veils; they came out from behind the closely-latticed windows into streets and public places; they went to the theaters and the cafes; they drove side by side with men in open carriages. The more ardent spirits held an open meeting in Constantinople, at which lady speakers demanded that the century-old shackles should be broken asunder. The thing was too novel to last. After a week or two, remonstrances began. The carriages were stopped, and some of the women roughly handled by the crowd. They felt, instinctively, that they had gone too far; they drew back. The veils reappeared—perhaps not drawn quite so closely as before.[132]

Apparently this phenomenon of unveiling and its backlash spread, because Muslim religious scholars in Damascus agitated against unveiled women there. In Beirut, the Islamic reformist newspaper *Ottoman Union* took a critical tone against Muslim women leaving the house with makeup and adornment, arguing that freedom did not mean the end of relevance of the *shari'a*.[133] *The Lighthouse*, on the other hand, published a translation of an article by a female journalist which had appeared in the Turkish-language newspaper *The Wealth of Knowledge* (*Servet-i Funun*), complaining that Ottoman women were being excluded from the revolution and from public discourse. "The press is concerned with the dress of women," she wrote, "but it forgets men and women have equal obligations. We want to dress our minds, and that is only done by entering schools. Teaching and learning is a service to the homeland, and certainly among us women there are those who are broadminded and know the needs of the nation."[134] Thus, while unveiling crossed into the category of "excessive liberty," Ottoman women would participate in the revolutionary public sphere in other ways, through a vibrant women's press and via numerous women's organizations.

CHAPTER TWO

Brotherhood and Equality

In the view of Ottoman intellectuals, the revolution which brought liberty to the Ottoman Empire on July 24, 1908, put it in the noble company of two other great revolutionary states—America (July 4) and France (July 14). Beyond the obvious symbolism of the numerical symmetry of the three revolutions, Ottoman observers compared themselves favorably to the American and French examples of forging a civic nation. After listening to schoolchildren sing the Ottoman anthem and patriots deliver speeches in Armenian, Turkish, and Arabic for the standing-room-only crowd at a gathering held in an Armenian church in Cairo, Rashid Rida argued that the Ottoman Empire had surpassed even *la France*, the quintessential "civic nation," in its achievements.

> They say that France is the mother of liberty and equality. Yes and no, but the Ottomans are worthier than the French in the glory of equality. France is one nation, one race, one religion, one sect, one language, one civilization, so what is strange in the demands of their wise men for equality between their individuals, after knowing what their government demands and what they owe it and [that] they all agree on its unity?
>
> But we, the Ottomans, have already united from the different nationalities in a way that has not yet happened in any other kingdom. We are different in race, descent, language, religion, sect, education and culture, or, we can say we differ in every thing that people can differ in, but despite that we demand equality and celebrate its granting in a general covenant and in the places of worship and no doubt in this magazine.[1]

For Rida and his audience, the Ottoman Empire was not only de facto an empire of incredible heterogeneity; more important, in its conscious adoption of the political project of equality, it was a multicultural state par excellence, long before the term was coined or even fully imagined in the West. Throughout the revolutionary era, the "Ottoman nation" (*al-umma al-'Uthmāniyya*, Ara.; *millet-i Osmani*, Ott. Tur.) took center stage, both as the subject of popular discourse ("We Ottomans") as well as the object of collective imaginings. Public speakers and the press spoke of the "union of all the Ottomans," "unity of nationality," and "the Ottoman tie." And yet, this outcome was in no way predictable or inevitable. How did individual residents of the empire come to see themselves as "Ottomans"? How did they imagine their relationship to other Ottomans—of different ethnicities, religions, and mother tongues? In other words, how did this Ottoman nation emerge as both a political community and a sociopolitical identity?

FROM COMMUNITY TO NATION

There is a tradition in Islam that considers the Muslim community of believers (*ummat al-Muslimīn*) as one, and ethnic, linguistic, tribal, and class divisions are supposed to be irrelevant in the face of equality of belief. As a result, when Napoleon issued propaganda leaflets appealing to the "Egyptian nation" (*al-umma al-Maṣriyya*) to welcome the French army into Egypt in 1799, he earned the wrath of the Ottoman sultan Selim III, who issued an imperial ferman declaring that the French were plotting to "ruin the Muslim community of believers which is unified in the unity of the lord of the universe."[2] The sultan's anger stemmed from the fact that the term *umma*, which appears throughout the Qur'an, was at the time solely connected to a religiously based principle of peoplehood, making secular claims of collective identity rooted in common territory inconceivable. Within a few short decades, however, two closely related developments unfolded within the Ottoman Empire that would set the stage for the emergence of a territorially based, supra-ethnic, supra-religious identification with the empire, initially as official policy and then as a project broadly adopted by the empire's intellectuals.

First, in the 1820s the Ottoman Empire was faced with a new phenomenon of Greek separatist nationalism, which eventually succeeded in establishing an independent kingdom in the southern and central regions of today's modern Greece. It is true that the eighteenth century had been a period of extreme decentralization throughout the Ottoman Empire, with local potentates arising to carve out spheres of influence far from the watchful eye and effective control of Istanbul, but these Greek nationalists presented a new, ideological challenge to the empire. They had been educated abroad and were deeply influenced by the romantic philo-Hellenism rampant in European capitals at the time, which called on Greek speakers to "awaken" and reclaim the mantle of the cradle of

Western civilization. Indeed, the Western powers' destruction of the Ottoman navy at Navarino proved decisive in the war between Ottoman troops and Greek rebels and ensured Greek independence.

As a result of this staggering development, the Ottoman government turned to create a state ideology known as Ottomanism (*Osmanlılık*), which aimed at promoting universal loyalty to the dynasty and equality under the law for non-Muslims. The architects of state Ottomanism hoped to prevent the spread of new nationalist ideologies among non-Muslim subject populations as well as to neutralize European interventions on their behalf. To that end, the 1839 sultanic decree known as the Noble Rescript of the Rose Garden injected the language of loyalty to "state and people" and "love for the homeland."[3] Less than two decades later, the 1856 Imperial Rescript went one step further in promoting equal discourse among subjects of the empire: from *zimmi* (*dhimmi*, Ara.)—a term rooted in Islamic tradition that referred to non-Muslims who received protection from a Muslim ruler in exchange for loyalty, subservience, and payment of tax—the empire's non-Muslims became "subjects" (*teba'*) like all others.[4] In 1869, the Ottoman Law of Nationality legislated equal status for all Ottoman residents, declaring that "all subjects of the empire are without distinction called Ottomans, irrespective of whatever religion they profess."[5]

The Ottoman law sought to tackle the complex citizenship question for an empire where wars and shifting state boundaries, in- and out-migration, and the politically sensitive presence of foreigners intermixed to create a thorny human landscape. From the outset, the law combined elements of ethnic citizenship (descent, *jus sanguinis*), with elements of civic citizenship, such as territorial criteria (*jus soli*) and a path to naturalization.[6] Unless they were known to be foreign citizens, people resident in Ottoman domains were automatically eligible for Ottoman citizenship. Their offspring were also automatically awarded citizenship, and a child whose Ottoman father took on foreign citizenship still remained an Ottoman. At the same time, the law also specified how foreigners could become Ottoman citizens. An adult immigrant could request citizenship after five years of residence after providing certification that one was not fleeing military service or a lawsuit in one's country of origin. Alternately, if born in Ottoman lands to foreign parents, one could become a citizen three years after entering adulthood.[7]

In either case, whether ascribed at birth or achieved by naturalization, Ottoman citizenship was universal and equal. Legally speaking, no one was any *more* or *less* Ottoman than any other citizen, as citizenship was based on the "normative presumption that . . . rights and obligations are anchored in the individual qua citizen, with no qualifications whatsoever because of his group affiliation."[8] That is to say, according to the law, political membership in the Ottoman nation was as open to a Turkish-speaking Muslim from Cyprus as it was for an Armenian-speaking Christian in Aleppo or a naturalized Arabic-speaking Jewish immigrant from Algeria.

Several contradictory factors seem to have driven the Ottoman citizenship law. On the one hand, the state sought to normalize the status of tens of thousands of Muslim refugees from the Caucasus and southeastern Europe fleeing Russian expansion and separatist nationalisms, respectively.[9] At times, these Muslim migrants were seen as strategic assets to be settled in sensitive (mixed) areas to help bolster the Muslim balance of power, even though this view was a challenge to, if not an outright undermining of, Ottomanist principles. And yet, the Ottoman citizenship law was not broadly pan-Islamic, for at the same time citizenship also aimed to further mark the border between Ottoman and non-Ottoman Muslims, playing a particularly important role in the eastern frontier of the empire with Qajar Iran, where the Ottoman citizenship law penalized Ottoman women who married Iranian men, requiring them to forfeit their citizenship.[10] A similarly tough attitude was taken toward Algerians resident in the empire who sought to marry Ottoman women but refused to forfeit their French nationality or protection. Muslim pilgrims from India, North Africa, or Russia who stayed past the *hajj* were also of deep concern to the Ottoman state.[11] In other words, the Ottoman state did not simply want to expand its Muslim population at any cost, and treated some groups of foreign Muslims with suspicion and distance.

The other important concern of the citizenship law was to formalize the boundaries between foreign citizens resident in the Ottoman Empire, on the one hand, and Ottoman subjects, on the other. The boundary between the two had become blurred by the nineteenth century thanks to the Capitulations, bilateral treaties between the Ottoman Empire and various European countries that were originally intended to give foreign merchants resident in the empire extraterritorial privileges. According to the Capitulations, foreign citizens and protégés were protected from Ottoman law, going instead to the consular courts, and were exempted from Ottoman taxes. By the mid-nineteenth century, however, the Capitulations had spread far beyond their original intent as the European powers recklessly awarded citizenship or protégé status to local Christians, Jews, and to a far lesser extent, select Muslims in an attempt to expand their influence in the empire.

Sometimes these naturalizations were awarded on an individual basis—loyal clerks, administrators, and dragomans (interpreters) were often rewarded for their faithful service to a foreign country. For example, after twelve years of service to the British Consulate in Jaffa as dragoman, vice-consul, and finally proconsul, the Christian Arab Nasri Habib Fiani requested naturalization.[12] On another occasion, the Jewish director of the private Alliance Israélite Universelle school in Haifa requested French citizenship, and the local French consul promised to help his cause.[13]

Much more significant for Ottoman domestic politics than these individual cases, however, was the presence within the empire of large blocs of Christians and, to a lesser extent, Jews yielding foreign citizenship or protection. In the decades after Greek independence from the empire, tens of thousands of Ottoman Greek Orthodox Christians were awarded Hellenic citizenship; the Greek citizenship law required only three years' residence in Greece, a simple requirement for the many Ottoman Greek Orthodox who spent years studying there.[14] As a result, these Ottoman Greek Orthodox subjects would gain Greek citizenship before returning to Ottoman domains wielding the privileges of the Capitulations. In addition, postindependence tens of thousands of Hellenic Greeks immigrated into Ottoman territories, settling in Izmir and along the western Anatolian Aegean coast. Furthermore, immigrant Jews from British-ruled Gibraltar, French-occupied North Africa, and Europe also brought, and in most cases kept, their foreign citizenship with them.

The cumulative impact of these developments was staggering: empire-wide, hundreds of thousands of foreign citizens and protégés lived in permanent or semipermanent residence.[15] In the holy city of Jerusalem, for example, there were at least ten thousand foreign citizens resident among thirty thousand Ottoman subjects.[16] This was magnified exponentially in the empire's larger cities, such as Istanbul, Salonica, and Izmir; in the capital, for example, up to 15 percent of the total population consisted of European foreigners.

In Ottoman cities in particular, the juxtaposition of foreigners and "protected" Ottoman subjects (protégés) alongside regular Ottoman subjects was a consistent source of tensions and conflict. Consulates regularly intervened on behalf of their citizens and protégés with the local police commissioners, governors and deputy governors, mayors, and tax and *tabu* (land title) officials.[17] This consular intervention in many instances encouraged or at least tolerated abuses. For example the American consul in Jerusalem reported in 1908 that resident American citizens were complicit in storing stolen goods, selling rotten meat, and slaughtering animals in the center of crowded quarters in violation of local law, all with virtual impunity.[18] The perceived injustice of the privileges granted to foreigners and their local protégés was such that one Jerusalem newspaper recounted an anecdote of a stray dog that bit passersby, disturbed local road repairs, and posed a public health risk, yet he roamed the streets of Jerusalem freely because he was rumored to be an American citizen![19] Foreign citizens and protégés also benefited from numerous economic privileges that left Ottomans unable to compete since they had to pay higher taxes and fees to the Ottoman government. Even worse, the Ottoman governor was often impotent to act against the resident foreign consuls.

As a result of this state of affairs, the patriotic lawyer Shlomo Yellin argued that the Capitulations had become "criminal" in the eyes of Ottoman citizens.[20] By passing the Ottoman Law of Nationality, the Ottoman state had unsuccessfully attempted to reinforce its claims of proprietorship and to strengthen the bonds of loyalty between the state and its non-Muslims, particularly those whom neighboring rival states would claim as their own.[21] However, because of its relative weakness vis-à-vis its European rivals, the Ottoman Empire was unable to abrogate or limit the terms of the Capitulations until the outbreak of World War I; immediate reinstatement of the Capitulations was one of the Allies' demands in the postwar armistice.

FROM OFFICIAL CITIZENSHIP TO POPULAR NATIONALISM

On one level, the imperial policy of Ottomanism fits in with the noted scholar of nationalism Benedict Anderson's "official imperial nationalisms," what he saw as the response of continental empires like the Austro-Hungarian, Russian, and Ottoman to increasing domestic nationalist threats. In Anderson's view, faced with the rise of ethnic nationalisms in central, eastern, and southern Europe, these official nationalisms were efforts to "stretch . . . the short, tight, skin of the nation over the gigantic body of the empire."[22] Indeed, for Sultan Abdülhamid II, the Ottomanist project was less about fostering any sort of national collective than about protecting the state's paternal interests.

> Henceforth all my subjects will be considered children of the same country, and will be placed under the protection of one law. They will be designated by the name borne by the illustrious race of the Founders of the Empire—a name associated with the glorious annals of a history of six hundred years. I have a firm conviction that from this moment all my subjects will unite their efforts to make the name Osmanlı retain the force and power hitherto surrounding it.[23]

For scholars like the historian Ussama Makdisi, this kind of sentiment is evidence that the broader state reform project known as the Tanzimat was a top-down project par excellence, "imagined by the center, then unilaterally imposed on the periphery." Makdisi argues that the notion of Ottoman citizenship that was envisioned was no more than an "empty vessel to be filled by the center, to be disciplined and then reformed by the authoritarian but supposedly benevolent and modernizing power of the imperial state."[24]

Undoubtedly, in many respects, the state's initial impetus for reform was rooted in self-interest; it viewed its subjects as objects of, rather than partners to, imperial reform. For example, when Sultan Mahmud II pushed for the vernacular language to be used in the official newspaper *Takvim-i Vekayi* (Register of Events), which appeared starting in 1831, he did so in order that all subjects could familiarize themselves with the institutions of the state and the reforms taking place.[25] Likewise, the Imperial Rescript of 1845 argued that new modern schools should be "a means of elevating and enlarging the young Ottoman's intellectual horizon so as to prepare him to comprehend Tanzimat reforms."[26] In other words, the state set the path of reform, and the empire's subjects were left to adapt to it.

And yet, looking at Ottoman reforms in general, and Ottomanism in particular, *only* in terms of the official state project ignores the ways in which Ottoman subjects themselves adopted, finessed, and challenged the state project from the second half of the nineteenth century until the final years of the empire. As one Balkan historian has pointed out, Ottoman subjects learned to "speak Tanzimat," skillfully negotiating the gap between official and subaltern versions of reform and state power.[27] Beyond the Ottoman state's official policy, then, the second critical component of the project of Ottoman nation building lies in the broader social, economic, and cultural changes that took place throughout the nineteenth century that produced a new class of educated professionals and intellectuals, an emerging popular press, and a nascent civil society, all of which played an important role in articulating and disseminating various visions of the imperial collective.

The logic of the Ottoman citizenship legislation and the project of Ottomanism immediately found resonance among intellectuals of the empire. For the Young Ottomans, the "Ottoman nation" was a social contract between the various ethnic and religious groups of the empire, a "union of the peoples [*ittihad-i anasır*]." The leading intellectual Namık Kemal supported a "fusion of the Ottoman peoples [*imtizaj-i akvam*]," but expected that in return for their constitutional rights, non-Muslims would have to show loyalty to the Ottoman homeland and subordinate their religious and ethnic sympathies to their allegiance to the dynasty.[28] They would also, needless to say, be expected to give up their claims on Capitulatory rights as well as their reliance on the intervention of Western powers on their behalf. In Namık Kemal's view, these special privileges for Christians were themselves an injustice to Muslims, reversing the European perception of the source and victims of inequality within the empire.

Another important statesman and reformer, Ahmed Cevdet Pasha, however, doubted that national and patriotic aims could really replace religious ones in the Ottoman Empire. In his words, "Only when we make homeland a theme, only when it has penetrated the people's heads as strongly as in Europe, will it attain the strength of the religious aims."[29] As the organ of the Young Ottoman liberals, the London-based newspaper *Liberty* (*Hürriyet*) played an important role in disseminating new ideas of patriotism and collective belonging. Mustafa Fazıl Pasha, an Ottoman bureaucrat and a copublisher of the paper, argued "it does not matter whether one is Muslim, Catholic, or Greek Orthodox to be able to place the public welfare ahead of private interests. For that it suffices to be a man of progress or a good patriot."[30]

Here it is important to underscore that Ottoman intellectuals did not live in a linguistic or spatial vacuum. The Parisian travel memoirs of the Egyptian scholar-cleric Rifaʿa Rafiʿ al-Tahtawi, which disseminated new notions of patriotism, homeland, and peoplehood, had been published in Arabic in 1834 and translated into Ottoman Turkish in 1840. This work undoubtedly influenced the Young Ottomans, not least of all but perhaps most directly in its revival of a reported hadith that supported the idea of patriotism: "Love of homeland is an article of faith [*ḥubb al-waṭan min al-īmān*]." Kemal's newspaper *Hürriyet* took this as its official slogan, as did at least two Ottomanist newspapers in Beirut in the 1860s and 1870s.[31]

Namık Kemal's landmark play *Vatan yahut Silestre* (Homeland; or, Silestre), which was performed only twice in 1873 and was published as a supplement to the newspaper *Candle* (*Siraj*) before being banned, played a pivotal role in developing a sense of homeland and territorial patriotism. Importantly, Kemal's depiction of the homeland and his casting of its defense as sacred martyrdom reveal a merging of physical and spiritual elements of homeland. As the hero of the play, Islam Bey, tells his beloved, "God created me, the homeland reared me. God nurtured me for the homeland. . . . I feel the bounty of the homeland in my bones. My body [is part] of the homeland's earth, my breath [is part] of the homeland's air. Why was I born if I was not to die for the homeland?"[32] (We will return to this play and the theme of martyrdom shortly.)

It is difficult but not impossible to measure the direct influence of the Young Ottomans on the broader Ottoman intelligentsia. With the establishment of state institutions of higher education in the second half of the nineteenth century and the employment opportunities they provided, increasing numbers of Ottoman intellectuals were at the very least bilingual, with Ottoman Turkish serving as the lingua franca of the empire. Students at the higher academies circulated underground copies of Kemal's and others' works, some of them still in handwritten manuscript form.[33] In addition, works of prominent thinkers were translated into the other major languages of the empire. Kemal, for example, was featured in the prominent biographical dictionary compiled by the Cairo-based Jurji Zeidan, and so at the very least Arab writers were exposed to his works in summary translation if not in the original.

Over the last decades of the nineteenth century, independent newspapers not only in Ottoman Turkish but also in Greek, Armenian, Arabic, Judeo-Spanish (Ladino), and a variety of other languages were critical platforms for promoting patriotism, love of homeland, and a common imperial identity at the same time that they wrestled with what it meant to "be Ottoman."[34] After bloody riots between Muslims and Christians in Mount Lebanon, Aleppo, and Damascus shook the Ottoman and European worlds, the Beiruti Christian journalist-intellectual Butrus al-Bustani argued that the "spirit of the times" demanded a change from religious solidarity (*'uṣba dīniyya*) to national-patriotic solidarity (*'uṣba jinsiyya wa-waṭaniyya*), and he urged his fellow Christians to develop their Ottoman feelings.[35] Already in 1860 he had advocated the development of feelings of mutual solidarity, or "love as members of one family, whose father is the homeland, whose mother is the land, and whose one creator is God." Bustani continued the language of kinship the following decade, promoting a "brotherhood of Turk, Arab, Druze, Jew, Mitwali, Maronite, Orthodox, Protestant, Armenian, Assyrian, and Copt as brothers in the homeland."[36]

As well, Ottoman intellectuals in exile in Egypt, such as the Damascus-born Christian writer Adib Ishaq, further articulated this new imperial collective solidarity. For Ishaq, neither lineage-race nor language-ethnicity were essential to the nation, but rather the nation was rooted in a common nationality, common territory, and a certain collective agreement of belonging to one nation. (Ishaq had the model of the United States in mind.) "The nation," Ishaq wrote,

> for any living being, as well as for a man, is his "people." According to politicians, it is the group that belongs to one nationality and obeys one law. . . . By unity of nationality we mean the agreement of the community to belong to one nationality, under which their children are born and whose name they carry. . . . The "Ottoman nationality" covers all the inhabitants of the Ottoman Empire, in Europe as well as in Asia, whether they be, by origin, Turks, Arabs, or Tartars.[37]

This new nationality demanded sentiments of patriotism (*al-waṭaniyya*) and love for the homeland (*al-waṭan*). In Ishaq's articulation, the *waṭan* was not only the place of origin or family, which was traditionally lauded in Arabic poetry and Qur'anic writings, but it was also the territorial incarnation of the political and social contract of rights and duties, between state and citizen as well as among citizens. Adib Ishaq frequented Cairo's coffeehouses alongside other Ottoman exiles, as well as with Egyptian intellectuals who were also wrestling with reimagining their collective along secular, territorial lines. By the 1870s and 1880s, a notion of the "Egyptian nation" had crystallized among intellectuals and army officers and played a prominent role in the failed 'Urabi revolution and early Egyptian nationalism.[38] As the Egyptian intellectual 'Abdullah al-Nadim famously said, encouraging sentiments of horizontal political belonging: "In whose hand shall I put mine? Put it in the hand of your compatriot."[39] Further afield, in Qajar Iran, notions of patriotism and love of homeland were also developing along nationalist-territorial lines. In describing the recasting of the *millat* from a religious one (*millat-i Shi'a-yi*) to a territorial-national one (*millat-i Irani*), one newspaper editorial proclaimed, "Iranians are of one *millat* [nation], a *millat* that speaks in different dialects and worships God in various ways."[40]

In other words, this process of horizontal imagining and identification was not solely a state project, but rather was adopted and propagated by a wide variety of Ottoman, Egyptian, and Persian intellectuals and the newly educated classes. The relationship of newly named Ottomans to each other was conceived as ties of imperial solidarity and collective identification, the result of both fate and choice. At the same time, however, the imperial collective literally lived in the shadow of other religious, ethnic, regional, and tribal collectives, as the overlapping terms of *ümmet-umma*, *millet-milla*, *kavim-qawm*, and *cins-jins* had to be reconceived in imperial terms.

The linguistic and intellectual-ideological project of coming to terms with new-old meanings and forms of collective identity and loyalty was complex. In official usage such as language in passports and census records, the *millet* was the ethno-religious community, drawn from the list of governmentally recognized sects (Muslim, Rumi, Jewish, Serbian, etc.). And yet, unofficially *millet* was already well on its way from being solely a religious community to also representing the imperial community, *millet-i Osmani*. According to the Muallim Naci dictionary of 1891, *millet* was solely a religious group, whereas a nation should be referred to by either *ümmet* or *kavim*. This was agreed upon by the Ebüzziya Tevfik dictionary of the same year, which argued that "it is absurd to speak of an Ottoman *millet*. Rather it is correct to speak of an Ottoman *ümmet*. Because the different nations and peoples form a single *ümmet* called Ottoman." The 1900 Şemseddin Sami dictionary also argued that it was necessary to correct the mistaken switching of *millet* and *ümmet*, and yet only four years later the Mehmed Salahi dictionary chose *kavm-i osmani* as the most correct rendering of "Ottoman nation."[41]

Clearly, the grammarians were attempting to standardize and correct popular usage of a very murky, but increasingly relevant, concept. However, similar linguistic and conceptual blurring existed in Arabic as references to religious communities alternated between *milla* and *umma* (*al-milla al-Ūrthūdhuksiyya* or *al-umma al-Ūrthūdhuksiyya*, *al-milla al-Isrā'iliyya* and *al-umma al-Isrā'iliyya*), both of which existed alongside the Ottoman nation (*al-umma al-'Uthmāniyya*) that embraced them all. Considered contextually, however, in the Ottoman imperial world one could definitively have more than one collective identity, whether *umma* or *milla*, and there was no inherent contradiction between them.[42]

MOVING TOWARD A "NATIONAL EDUCATION"

As the noted scholar of nationalism Ernest Gellner has argued, the establishment of a state education system is one of the most important characteristics of the modern nation-state.[43] Since national school systems played an important role in promoting a national language, civic loyalty, and horizontal ties of common nationality, the Ottoman Empire would strive to do this and more. Starting with the Ottoman Education Regulation of 1869, which required three years of mandatory education for all male Ottomans, the main aim of the state educational system was to compete with the religious and foreign missionary schools, to promote loyalty to empire and dynasty among the empire's children, and to educate students in secular subjects such as mathematics, geography, and foreign languages, all in the hopes of matching Western accomplishments.[44]

In the thirty-three years of Hamidian rule (1876–1909), the Ottoman state established close to ten thousand new elementary, middle, and high schools throughout the empire as well as prestigious academies in law, medicine, and military science in the capital. Literacy and loyalty were seen as powerfully intertwined in one government report: "The expansion of education will confirm their affinity to religion, fatherland, and patriotism [*milliyet*], and render sincere bonds to our highness the Caliph of the Muslims. But if ignorance continues, it will intensify and aggravate the splitting apart and disintegration." As a result, schools were established in politically sensitive regions like Crete, Cyprus, and Macedonia with the aim of countering the nationalist propaganda of Greek, Bulgarian, and Serbian educators in the empire. In the sensitive eastern border region with Qajar Iran, Sunni religious scholars were sent to combat Shi'i propaganda.[45]

In other areas of the empire like Beirut and Jerusalem, state schools were seen as powerful weapons defending the empire and its youth from the corrupting influence of missionary schools and their Great Power sponsors. For example, the 1898 Beirut Province Yearbook showed a ratio of two-to-one of students in foreign versus Ottoman schools, a statistic the empire would prove unable to reverse by its end less than two decades later.[46] In Palestine the situation was equally dire: by 1912 there were over eleven thousand Christian students enrolled in the more than one hundred schools sponsored by the Russian Imperial Orthodox Palestine Society; at least three thousand Jewish youth were enrolled in the schools of the German-Jewish Ezra society, and almost as many were enrolled in the twelve schools of the French Alliance Israélite Universelle. Several Christian and Jewish British schools also attracted sizable student bodies.[47]

As a result of the dismal state of Ottoman education and its inability to compete with foreign schools, in 1887 the Muslim reformer and scholar Shaykh Muhammad 'Abduh recommended the establishment of a high school in Beirut that would be devoted to the "restoration of faith and love for one's state [*ḥubb al-dawla*]." Four years later, Mihran Boyaciyan, a public servant trainee in government office in Beirut who was also a high school teacher, reported to his superiors the need to further Ottomanize the schools: "Every patriot must shed tears of mourning when he observes foreign intellectual influence prevailing in the name of education." By 1895, the private Muslim Maqāṣid Benevolent Society succeeded in establishing an Ottoman school which would impart "national virtues [*al-akhlāq al-milliyya*]" and religious principles upon its students.[48] A similar Ottoman Islamic patriotic school was established in Jerusalem in 1906, the Rawdat al-Ma'arif school.[49]

The state secondary schools did create a growing cohort of Ottoman subjects who were literate in Ottoman Turkish as well as in their vernacular; who acquired learning in subjects such as geography, sciences, and foreign languages; who discussed and debated current events in informal study circles; and who saw themselves as a vanguard for the empire as a whole.[50] The most prestigious of the Ottoman secondary schools was the Sultani mektebi (later renamed the Galatasaray Lycée), in Istanbul. Founded in 1868, Galatasaray was envisioned as a novel boarding school that would house, feed, and educate Muslim and non-Muslim students together with the aim of promoting Ottomanism; the 341 pupils who enrolled in its first year made up a student body that was 43 percent Muslim, 47 percent Christian, and 10 percent Jewish.[51] Hundreds of important Ottoman civil servants, intellectuals, and members of the free professions passed through the halls of Galatasaray before returning to their home provinces or being sent to other provinces in the service of the state. For those who could not attend the jewel of the crown of Ottoman education, between 1882 and 1894 fifty-one new secondary schools were established throughout the empire, including one in Jerusalem, in central Palestine, and one in ʻAkka, in the north.

Although state secondary education was limited to men, there were state primary schools for girls in addition to *kuttab*, missionary, and *millet* schools for girls. By 1914, at least two thousand girls were studying in private and state schools in Palestine.[52] Beyond the elementary level, upper-class girls often received private tutoring, and by the 1890s there was a vibrant women's press in Ottoman Turkish and Arabic attesting to the high levels of literacy among some women. These modern-educated men and (to a certain extent) women played a significant role in the final decades of the Ottoman Empire, most certainly in ways unanticipated by the Tanzimat architects. As one historian has written, "Those individuals coined new terms of association, formulated novel demands of government, sought to transfer loyalty from the sultan to the state, and debated the interconfessional content of citizenship."[53] In other words, by the eve of the 1908 revolution the state's modern schools were important not only for promoting loyalty to state and giving birth to the Young Turk revolutionaries, but more significantly, for creating a broader reading public that would seize the opportunity of 1908 to push for a more active role in imperial society.

EARLY CHALLENGES TO THE OTTOMANIST PROJECT

From the very beginning, despite the official promulgation of Ottomanism and its adoption by at least some intellectuals throughout the empire, Muslims and non-Muslims alike, Ottomanism nevertheless met with significant challenges from the Ottoman state, its Muslim population, members of the non-Muslim religious hierarchy, and at least some non-Muslims within the empire. More significantly, the project of Ottomanism faced severe structural challenges that limited its spread and adoption.

First, the Ottoman state remained an Islamic state, a fact which sometimes introduced contradictions with the official policy of Ottomanism.

Some state institutions remained off-limits for non-Muslims, such as the professional standing army established in the 1830s, the Victorious Soldiers of Muhammad, which forbade even converts to Islam from serving in its ranks.[54] Although some state offices were open to non-Muslims, particularly in the lower levels of provincial government, others remained completely closed, including those in the Islamic courts, the religious endowments, population registry, and the inspectorate of schools.[55]

As well, Sultan Abdülhamid II in particular went to great lengths to Ottomanize Islam, on the one hand, and to Islamicize the empire, on the other, at the same time that he pursued a policy of pan-Islamism. From establishing schools to educate the tribal Bedouins and integrate them into orthodox Islamic practices and the Ottoman state, to sending missionary preachers to regions which were susceptible to Shi'ism, to promoting the Hijaz Railroad among the Muslims in British-ruled India, the policies of Abdülhamid II certainly reinforced the Islamic character of the state at precisely the moment when Ottomanism, which purported to be neutral to the religion of all Ottoman citizens, was ascendant.[56]

On the more popular level, the policy of declared equality among religions was, at least to some Muslims, a religious heresy. For a believing Muslim who took as a matter of faith that Islam was the final message of God among man which superseded both Judaism and Christianity, how could Muslims and non-Muslims be equal? Indeed, in 1859, the Kuleli conspiracy was hatched by one leading religious figure, Shaykh Ahmed, who preached that the 1839 and 1856 reform edicts, which offered Christians equality with Muslims, were contraventions of Islamic law.[57]

In addition to the complex, often unsupportive attitude of the Ottoman state and Muslim religious sentiments, however, the Ottoman historian Roderic Davison attributed a much larger role for the failure of the early equality edicts to the Christians of the empire themselves. In his words, "the program of equality between Christian and Muslim in the empire remained largely unrealized not because of bad faith on the part of leading Ottoman statesmen but because many of the Christians wanted it to fail."[58] As he pointed out, non-Muslim religious leaders would have much to lose both financially and politically in a setting of actualized Ottomanism. In that context, Davison reported that after the 1839 reform decree was read to the assembled notables and then returned into its red satin pouch, the Greek Orthodox patriarch proclaimed, "*Inshallah*—God grant that it not be taken out of this bag again."

In addition to the Greek Orthodox patriarch's resistance to Ottomanism, another major challenge involved the unwillingness of many of the empire's Christians and Jews to partake of the emancipation bargain—

equal rights in exchange for equal obligations, or in other words, Ottomanism instead of Capitulations. In fact, despite the 1869 Nationality Law—which in theory recognized Greek Orthodox with dual citizenship as being Greek when in the Hellenic kingdom but as being Ottoman while in the empire—nonetheless many Greek Orthodox dual citizens continued to wave their Greek passports in order to avoid taxation, at least until the 1897 Greek-Ottoman war abrogated Greek Capitulatory rights entirely.[59] Truth be told, given their privileged state of affairs, what non-Muslim with foreign citizenship or protégé status in his right mind would willingly give it up?

In addition, by the mid-nineteenth century there were already nuclei of separatist nationalist movements in the southeastern European provinces of the empire and on the island of Crete. In Davison's view, the Ottomanist project emerged too late to forge any loyalty and patriotism in those parts of the empire. Indeed, those southeastern provinces were taken from the empire in the Treaty of Berlin, which was seen as evidence by some of the Young Ottomans of the ongoing inequality in Muslim-Christian and Ottoman-European relations. In other words, the possibilities of actual implemented Ottomanism as well as Ottomans' support of it shrank in direct relation to the intervention of Europe on behalf of Ottoman Christians.

Finally, despite the formal application of the term *Ottoman* to all citizens of the empire regardless of religion, ethnicity, or mother tongue, nonetheless there remained an assumption among some intellectuals that Ottoman meant "Muslim" and even "Turk." Commanders of the Victorious Soldiers of Muhammad saw the "sons of the Turks" as the most reliable soldiering class even as compared to other Muslim ethnic groups.[60] As well, despite the empire's historically famed equal-opportunity in government service where converts throughout the empire had risen to become grand vizier, thirty-four of the last thirty-nine grand viziers were Anatolian or Rumelian Muslims whose mother tongue was Turkish. In line with these state policies which increasingly revealed a preferential attitude toward Turks and Muslims, Osman Nuri Pasha, a former governor to the Hijaz and Yemen, likened the empire to a tree whose trunk of roots was made up of the Turks, whereas the boughs and branches were the other peoples of the empire.[61] Liberal intellectuals were not immune to this sentiment, either; when asked on a train in Europe in 1889 if he was Jewish, the highly respected writer Ahmed Midhat Effendi responded: "No, sir. I am not Jewish, I am Ottoman. [In fact] I am the purest Ottoman, I am Turkish and Muslim."[62] Clearly Ottomanism still had a great deal of work left to do at the turn of the twentieth century.

THE THEATRICALITY OF REVOLUTIONARY BROTHERHOOD

With the 1908 revolution, this simmering issue of the empire's religious and ethnic diversity came to the fore in the most visceral and immediate way by means of the literal visibility of the empire's various religious and ethnic groups, creating a certain theatrical production of revolutionary brotherhood. Just as the revolutionary trope of "liberty" tapped into a longstanding critique of the Hamidian regime in particular as well as new ways of thinking about political legitimacy and rule more broadly, so too did the revolutionary slogans of "equality and brotherhood" reveal much about the Ottoman social reality on the eve of revolution, as much a criticism of the existing state of interreligious relations as an ideal for the future.

Four central themes emerged from contemporary reports of the revolutionary celebrations: the rhetoric of unanimous, consensual participation of all Ottomans; symbolic peace, reconciliation, and mutual regard between groups in the form of kissing, hugging, and shaking hands; the redrawing of spatial and territorial boundaries; and the promotion of a new language of kinship, solidarity, and affiliation—in other words, the emergence of a new discourse of the Ottoman nation.

The union being celebrated among Ottomans took place against the backdrop of former hostilities and conflicts, often cast as being products of the previous regime. "Everyone felt what freedom is, and how much they [had] suffered!" one Hebrew newspaper editorialized.[63] A similar thought was expressed in an Arabic newspaper that declared "as we were equal in oppression, so we were equal in demanding equality and the constitution . . . the oppression of tyranny was on the head of the Muslim and Christian, on the Turk and Arab and Armenian and Kurd and Albanian and Greek."[64]

Public figures such as Suleiman al-Bustani, the Christian parliamentary candidate in Beirut, explicitly blamed the Hamidian government for its politics of division and sectarianism (*siyāsat al-tafrīq*), took to task tyrannical religious leaders for serving the government, and called on Muslims and non-Muslims alike to overcome their historic prejudices.[65] In addition to general discussion of past mutual hostility and suspicion, the Armenian massacres of the 1890s took prominent place in the litany of examples of Hamidian-orchestrated sectarianism. At a general celebration held in honor of the constitution at an Armenian church in Cairo, where men and women of all religions were in attendance, Dr. Sharaf al-Din, a Muslim who had long been active in liberal secret societies, blamed the old regime for the "calamitous events," but also recalled the good relations that had previously existed between Muslims and their Armenian neighbors who would leave their children, wives, and belongings in the other's care when called away for military service or travel.[66] Furthermore, the speaker claimed, one of the first acts carried out by the Young Turks after the revolution was a pilgrimage to the graves of those Armenians who had "fallen victims to the tyrants."

In other words, past conflicts between Ottoman religious and ethnic groups were blamed on the sultan or other manipulating parties (the European powers, nationalist propagandists, religious extremists), rather than reflecting any essential or structural limitation afflicting the Ottoman nation. Instead, revolutionary discourse saw Ottomans of all stripes as displaying their true character and true commitments in the days of revolutionary euphoria. The ubiquitous phrase *irrespective of* (*'ala ikhtilāf*, in Arabic) was used as a way of leveling participation among all Ottomans "irrespective of" religion, sect, ethnicity, or status, and reinforcing the idea of a united Ottoman people in all its diversity. "If you had seen them on the day of the constitution," al-Bustani waxed lyrically, "the imam and the priest and the rabbi—all were united with tears of joy."[67]

Symbolically, this reconciliation played itself out in spontaneous and ritualized physical expressions between members of historically antagonistic or alienated groups—hugs, kisses, and handshaking all represented the peaceful settling of old scores as well as the intimate commitment to the new era. This reconciliation took place at the highest levels, with the famous hug between the *şeyhülislam* and the Greek-Orthodox patriarch in Istanbul, and spread down through the common crowds in the empire's mixed towns and cities. Rashid Rida cited the *şeyhülislam*'s behavior as the model for his own, after he hugged Armenian priests at a public event at an Armenian church in Cairo, to the applause of the crowd.[68] Another article approvingly noted that "the Muslim shook hands with the Christian, and the Kurd reconciled with the Armenian, and the Turk hugged the Arab."[69]

From Istanbul we have the following report from a Jewish correspondent:

> The joy of the masses is quiet, celebratory. Not a drop of blood, not one tear. The joy is genuine, internal. There is not a single shadow of hatred or jealousy. And Armenian hugs Greek. Both of them hug the Bulgarian. And taking part are the Turk, citizen of Istanbul, and his brother the Jew, and they all dance out of joy. . . . And so it is in the houses of prayer and the mosques—we are all brothers: as Jews, as Turks, as Greeks we will live in peace and tranquility and we will work for our land and for our sultan![70]

In Aleppo, it was reported that "Moslems, Christians and Jews mingled together, with brotherly feeling, and strong men of all sects wept with joy."[71] From Beirut, the American consul reported:

> Perhaps the most significant feature of the general rejoicing has been and is the dropping of religious animosities and prejudices. . . . Hence, we now observe, in the streets of Beirut, the Maronite priest four times kiss the Moslem Sheikh and the Moslem Sheikh respond by four times kissing the Maronite priest. Moslems and Christians publicly embrace each other, protesting that henceforth they are brethren, that there are Christians, Moslems, Jews, Mitwalehs [Shi'ites] etc., no more, only loyal Ottoman subjects standing shoulder to shoulder prepared to fight for the liberties granted by the Sultan, long live the Sultan![72]

This spirit of interpersonal reconciliation spread across physical space in the empire, as public displays of literally crossing communal boundaries were reported throughout the empire. A local consular official in Jerusalem observed:

> Bands of Moslem young men went into the Greek quarter, where they were entertained, they then bringing back numbers of the Christian young men into the Moslem quarter, where they rejoiced together, the Moslems then escorting the Greeks through the sacred Mosque of Omar grounds, into which, hitherto, no Christian could enter except by official permission and accompanied by a soldier. The Christians also brought many Jews from their quarter and entertained them, and then took them through the Church of the Holy Sepulcher, to pass in front of which even was heretofore as much as a Jew's life would be worth.[73]

However, this emergent "brotherhood" of the revolution, while celebrated, was neither obvious nor unchallenged by the structural limitations of local relationships, which varied from region to city to neighborhood to household. In Hebron, a majority Muslim town with only a tiny Jewish community and no Christian community of which to speak, the newspaper correspondent Menashe Mani, the child of a Jewish family from Baghdad with deep roots in Hebron, reminds us that intercommunal relations were often a fragile thing.[74]

> Just a few days earlier Jews were afraid to host Arabs in their courtyards, but now they are brothers and there is a feeling that something unites them. Some power lifted the wall that divides the people, and they are brothers, all sons of one land, all sons of one government. The public love of the Jews grew—Muslim youth danced in front of the Jews and honored them; Jews could not believe it. All was wonderful until a woman cried about her son being taken to the army—woman, be quiet and do not worry, and anyway is this not everyone's duty?[75]

Other reports from throughout Palestine and the empire highlighted joint celebrations and accounts of mutual hospitality. In coastal Jaffa, which had a sizeable Christian and much smaller Jewish population, Shaykh Salim al-Ya'qubi, who had studied at the famed Al-Azhar Mosque in Cairo, gave a very emotional speech denouncing differences between Muslims, Jews, and Christians.[76] The crowd responded enthusiastically, followed by emotional support from Christian and Jewish representatives. Later, a private citizen named Salim Salahi sponsored a three-day fete in Jaffa at his own expense, inviting all the notables from the three religions; he also placed an announcement in Hebrew on the doors of the synagogues inviting Jewish religious figures. In honor of the event, his home was decorated; tables covered with food were set up in the street; and lemonade, scented water, and cigarettes were freely distributed. There were also speeches in Arabic, Turkish, and French, and a band played to entertain the guests.[77]

In Jaffa, the Jewish community held a general celebration to which government officials and members of other religious communities were invited. In Jerusalem, the Greek Orthodox Christian Arab and the Armenian Christian communities also hosted celebrations at which they opened up the extensive gated grounds of the Patriarchate to the public and distributed free refreshments.[78] These celebrations marked the community's first steps into the Ottoman public sphere as an equal of its neighbors; by hosting the entire city, the community honored the rest of the populace, while in turn, by attending, the rest of the population honored the host community.

These rituals of revolutionary brotherhood led to expressions of a new discourse of the Ottoman nation. *Ottoman* became a term of self-identity; rather than referring solely to "them"—namely the bureaucratic ruling class—for the empire's many ethnic and religious groups Ottoman now referred to the first person plural: "we" and "us." This first-person plural sentiment was already articulated in the first days by Mendel Kremer, the Jaffa-based correspondent for the Hebrew paper *The Observation* (*Ha-Hashkafa*) and an Ottomanized Jew: "Without a big mess or spilling of blood, *our people* had achieved the dearest thing possible"—a representative government.[79] As Kremer's articulation alluded, this imperial collective was to a great extent civic and recalled its base in political membership and citizenship rights. Phrases like "fellow citizens" (*vatandaşlar/muwāṭinīn*), "Ottoman compatriots" (*muwāṭinīn 'Uthmānīyīn*), "all Ottomans," and "dear voter(s)" were bandied around in speeches and articles as underscoring the core link between Ottomans.

At the same time, despite the fact that there was little pretense of an actual shared genealogical background that linked all Ottomans together, one of the cornerstones of primordial or ethnic nationalism, the "Ottoman nation" was nonetheless discursively reformulated as a "family."[80] The discursive formulation of an Ottoman family had existed before: the Greek Orthodox Constantin Adosside (1817–95) wrote an Ottoman language textbook for use among Greek Orthodox youth in which he used the expression "the great Ottoman family."[81] However, the language of family and the corresponding implications of ties of kinship and mutual affection and obligation became much more widespread during the revolutionary era. In the words of one Jerusalemite, Avraham Elmaliach, in the euphoric first weeks "everyone felt they were brothers from birth, everyone danced together, everyone walked together arm in arm."[82] Public speakers and newspapers alike appealed to their "Ottoman brotherhood" or "dear Ottoman brothers."

In part, this bond of kinship and brotherhood was seen as having been born of the revolution, literally through the constitution and through the bonds of imperial citizenship. As one Jewish celebrant in Jerusalem, David Yellin (the older brother of Shlomo Yellin), noted, "Today we have reached that which was far and made familiar that which was strange, and justice comprises all of the Ottomans without difference to their rites or religions, and has turned them into one people henceforth in its progress and advancement."[83] Months later, Yellin further elaborated the citizenship-kinship formulation of Ottoman brotherhood:

> Thank God that tyranny and its men fell. Its replacement is unity and its beauty which caused the whole nation of the homeland to be brothers in one endeavor—the success of the homeland and its people and the pride of membership in one family: the Ottoman family. And who among us does not remember how the fire of brotherhood was kindled suddenly in the hearts of all the Ottomans, and how the whole nation experienced in one stroke the holy feeling—the feeling of unity to endeavor for the good of the country (and it is their country, all of them) and the success of the state (and it is their state without exception).[84]

This Ottoman brotherhood was born of and suckled by constitutionalism, and as a result syncretistic phrases like "brother voter" combined civic Ottoman duties (voting) with the primordial language of kinship (brother). While brothers and families share blood running through their veins, the Ottoman civic brotherhood was born of the metaphorical mixing of its peoples. As the Muslim lawyer Ragheb al-Imam stated in Jerusalem, "The Ottoman races who were of different nations entered through the melting pot of the constitution [*būdaqat al-dustūr*] and came out as one bullion of pure gold which is Ottomanism, which unites the hearts of the *umma* and brings together their souls."[85] In this metaphor of the melting pot, al-Imam was echoing Rashid Rida, who had declared months earlier that "all the groups (of the empire) mixed in the melting pot of the basic law and became one bullion of gold which cannot be counterfeited and which does not rust."[86]

Ottoman brotherhood went even further to incorporate the classic nineteenth-century nationalist elements of blood, soil, and homeland, all of which would help overcome the superficial differences of religion, ethnic group, and language. The *waṭan*—homeland—emerged as a central trope in the revolutionary period, directly building on the sentiments of loyalty and patriotism that had begun to emerge decades earlier. The iconic works of Namık Kemal were republished several times in the years 1908–10. As the Cairene monthly *The Crescent* (*Al-Hilāl*) reminded its readers, "If the people know the meaning of *waṭan* in its true meaning, the greatest responsibility goes to Kemal Bey alone. Because [before him] everyone considered his *waṭan* the region where he was born, but Kemal Bey told them that the *waṭan* is the whole of the lands where their flag flutters and where their army defends and where their hearts beat."[87]

In the fall of 1908, performances of Kemal's famous play *Vatan yahut Silestre* were held throughout the empire.[88] According to newspaper accounts reporting on a Beirut performance in October, there had been much popular demand for his "story of the homeland." The performance took place in the military courtyard with over two thousand Beirutis in attendance, including notables, intellectuals, and the army, as well as foreign consuls. The newspaper report stated that the climax of the performance came at the end of the play, when a soldier-actor visited the grave of the playwright Namık Kemal, the "nightingale" and "martyr" of liberty. Upon opening the tomb, Kemal emerged wearing a white shroud, and was "carried in the glory of liberty" by the soldiers present before returning to his grave and his now-peaceful, eternal rest.[89]

The connection that Kemal had forged between homeland and patriot, or land and body, went through martyrdom. The "Homeland Poem" (*Vatan şiiri*), performed in the play and sung in chorus by the cast, illustrates this well:

> Wounds are medals on the brave's body
> The grave [martyrdom] is the soldier's highest rank;
> The earth is the same, above and underneath;
> March, you brave ones, to defend the homeland.[90]

This emphasis on the intimate union of territory and individual-collective—blood and soil—is particularly resonant for observers of modern nationalism. In the words of the theorist Anthony Smith, "The cult of the glorious dead gives the most tangible expression to the idea of the nation as a sacred communion of the dead, the living and the yet unborn. But, more important, the cult of the glorious dead, and the rites and ceremonies of national commemoration that accompany it, are themselves seen and felt as sacred components of the nation, intrinsic to its 'sacred communion' of history and destiny."[91] Indeed, martyrdom became a prominent theme of the Ottoman revolution, not only retroactively describing Kemal, Midhat Pasha, and the other early liberals, but applying as well as to the soldiers and others who fell as "martyrs" in the cause of liberty throughout the events of 1908–9 and after.

In the fall of 1908 prayer services and commemorative ceremonies honoring the martyrs of liberty were held in mosques, churches, and synagogues throughout the empire. For example a ceremony was held in the Red Armenian Church in Pera (Istanbul), to which members of the Young Turk central committee were invited; the priests led a procession to the accompaniment of the Ottoman military band which played the Armenian national anthem.[92] Another Armenian church in Cairo held a ceremony in tribute to the "Ottoman martyrs of liberty [*shuhadā' al-ḥurriyya al-'Uthmānīyīn*]." Schoolchildren sang the Ottoman anthem and speeches were given in Armenian, Turkish, and Arabic for the standing-room-only crowd.[93] Another service in memory of the "martyrs of liberty" was organized by the Committee of the Union of Ottoman Women and held at the Yeni Cami (New Mosque) in Istanbul.[94]

Later, the approximately seventy men who fell in the brief April 1909 anticonstitutional coup were rendered martyrs. The body of one of the members of parliament killed by the rioters, Muhammad Arslan, a notable Druze from Lattakia whose family demanded that his body be returned to Lebanon, was left unwashed by order of Shaykh Abdullah at the Gülhane hospital. The *shaykh* reportedly exclaimed: "For it is the body of a martyr and his blood is 'lotion' enough!"[95] The remaining martyrs were buried in a collective grave in Istanbul in Şişli, which happened to be a mixed neighborhood with numerous churches, synagogues, and Christian and Jewish cemeteries. In the patriotic state burial service, CUP leaders emphasized that Muslims and Christians were lying side by side, a daring assertion that the law of patriotism and Ottomanism trumped religious law.[96] Later, a national monument was established on the site, called Abide-i hürriyet (Monument of Liberty), on which we see engraved: "the tomb of the martyrs of liberty [*maqbarat-ı shuhada hürriyeti*]." This became the single most important site for Ottoman (and later early Turkish republican) constitutional and patriotic ideals, the location of the "national holiday" (*iyd-i milli*) ceremonies for almost a quarter of a century, as well as the site of various military parades and ceremonies.[97]

Figure 2.1. Abide-i hürriyet, the Monument of Liberty, Şişli, Istanbul. Ottoman soldiers killed in the spring 1909 counterrevolution while defending the constitutional regime were buried here in an elaborate state ceremony, and the site served as the central monument in Ottoman and early Turkish republican patriotic commemoration. Personal photograph of Dr. Kent F. Schull, assistant professor of history, University of Memphis. Used by permission.

Prime value was placed on this sentiment of self-sacrifice for the homeland in the press and in the revolutionary public sphere, a sentiment that would be pressed into constant service from 1911 onward as the Ottoman Empire engaged in three major wars before its final military enterprise, the First World War. Ottoman soldiers who fell in battle in Libya (1911), the Balkans (1912–13), and the First World War (1914–18) were accorded martyr status, both rhetorically and in terms of survivor benefits. Importantly, though, for many observers this martyrdom remained linked to the Ottoman citizenship project. Reuven Qattan, the Jewish poet from Izmir, expressed the value of national sacrifice in his two-part article "Our Line of Conduct: To Die and Kill for Liberty." According to Qattan, the Ottoman government should know that "among its most sacred duties is to defend the natural rights of the nation, liberty and the constitution, and not to allow anything to touch these inviolable things. The nation prefers to kill the diseased dog. The nation prefers to die than to lose liberty."[98]

INSTITUTIONALIZING OTTOMANISM

The political model of revolutionary brotherhood was a fulfillment of Namık Kemal's emancipation trade-off that he had offered decades earlier: in exchange for full equal rights in the Ottoman nation, non-Muslims were to give up their unique privileges and take on the duties of other Ottoman citizens. In other words, the theater of revolutionary brotherhood was premised on the expectation that all Ottomans would share not only rights but also obligations, and that all communities—being recast as Ottoman first and foremost—would work for the public good in a republican spirit of shared citizenship. This was presciently expressed by one public speaker who proclaimed that "from now on we will no longer hear another 'Armenian,' 'Muslim,' 'Hebrew,' or 'Christian,' but rather 'Ottoman'! We're all brothers! We all need to work for the good of the homeland, and we hope that it will [in fact] be good."[99] Along those lines, a similar sentiment was expressed in *The Lighthouse* newspaper: "On this day the Ottomans showed that they are an *umma* which has rights over its state, and their unity will bring it utility, and upon them are obligations and commitments to their government, and they have a law that treats them equally in its dealings, and they have a nationality that unites them irrespective of lineage, language, sect, and religion."[100]

Thus, to a great extent the "Ottoman *umma*" was premised on the underlying principle of civic nationhood, bounded by the legal borders of the Ottoman Empire, united in the mutual rights and obligations of Ottoman citizenship. This was explicitly articulated in the political program of the CUP, translated and republished widely in the Arabic press, which stated in Article 9: "Each person will enjoy complete liberty and equality irrespective of his race and sect, and is expected of the same things as each Ottoman irrespective of race and sect."[101] More specifically, the CUP charged that "all the Ottoman subjects are equal before the law and have the right to government positions, and each individual who fulfills the conditions of competence will serve in the government according to his worth and competence just as the non-Muslim subjects will serve in the army."

In other national projects, in particular in territorial nations, two important state-led institutions historically have played a central role in forging the nation—schools and the army.[102] Likewise, these two institutions were seen as critical to the success of the Ottomanization project. We have already seen that from the mid-nineteenth century there was an emergent discourse that saw schools as central to creating Ottoman patriots; in the postrevolutionary period, the schools once again became a focus of national attention. In the CUP's view, Ottomanization would be facilitated through the teaching of the Ottoman Turkish language, the official language of the state.[103] From 1894, Ottoman Turkish language teaching was mandatory in all schools of the empire, including private and *millet* schools, but the practical application of this requirement varied widely. It seems that most schools taught the minimum required hours, since Ottoman Turkish had to compete against vernacular languages, sacred languages (including Arabic, Hebrew, and Greek), and international languages like French, English, and German as the language of instruction in foreign-sponsored schools. As a result, unless they continued on to higher education in a state school, few Ottoman schoolchildren attained functional literacy in Ottoman Turkish.

This seems to be corroborated by notices in the press advertising private adult education evening classes in Ottoman Turkish. However, these courses generally were undersubscribed; one program in Jerusalem in 1897 only succeeded in recruiting three students.[104] It seems that in practice given the rare occasions on which knowledge of Ottoman Turkish was required, most people simply preferred to hire the translation services of knowledgeable professionals such as Nissim Effendi, an Izmiri Jew who worked out of the store of Mercado Habib, the Baghdadi Jew who prepared documents in Arabic across from the saray (government building).[105]

After the revolution these night schools proliferated and were joined by civil society organizations whose aims were to support language education and other citizenship efforts.[106] For communal leaders the knowledge of Ottoman Turkish was considered a real asset, in particular as it was a requirement for election to the Ottoman parliament; in addition, it was important in facilitating interpersonal exchange with local Ottoman officials. For that reason Albert Antébi argued that knowledge of Ottoman Turkish should be a prerequisite for candidates to the office of chief rabbi, and he repeatedly publicly promoted candidates who knew Ottoman Turkish and denigrated those who did not.[107]

Beyond the language question, intellectuals and journalists focused on the school system's potential role in carrying out Ottomanization in the broadest sense. Aside from the famous Galatasaray Lycée and the prestigious military, medicine, law, and civil service imperial academies, state institutions primarily educated Muslim students, whereas Christian and Jewish students by and large attended their own confessional or foreign-run schools. For example in 1907 the Schneller School, a German-sponsored Lutheran institution in Jerusalem, enrolled ninety boys (including eleven Muslims) and fifty-nine girls (including nine Muslims) in kindergarten; the day school, however, included only four Muslims (out of 108 total), and the boarding school had only five non-

Christians out of 264 male students.[108] It is true that some Muslim notable families in Jerusalem sent their sons to the St. George Anglican School and their daughters to the Evelina de Rothschild School, hoping to give them the perceived benefits of a Western education, but this was not an extensive practice at the time.

For their part, the Jewish schools in Jerusalem were divided into traditional theological schools (the *ḥeder/meldar* and Talmud Torah), philanthropic schools established by European Jews, and new nationalist-Zionist schools with a Hebraic agenda. The school of the Hilfsverein der deutschen Juden (Ezra), a school with philanthropic origins and a German-language curriculum, enrolled only one Muslim student.[109] Even in the case of the famed schools of the French-Jewish Alliance Israélite Universelle, which had educated notable figures in the CUP in other parts of the empire, the schools in Palestine had a mixed record. The vocational school in Jerusalem included 10 Muslim apprentices in addition to 128 Jewish apprentices, but the AIU's agricultural school, Mikveh Israel, enrolled only four non-Jewish students between 1900 and 1908, each of whom remained only a year, and another four Muslim students from 1908 to 1915. In fact the strikingly low enrollment of Muslim students became a sticking point between the director of the AIU's Jerusalem school, Albert Antébi, and the governor of the province, Subhi Bey, who made it clear to Antébi that he wanted to see equal numbers of Jewish and Muslim students in the AIU schools.[110] Needless to say, the new Hebraist schools, which by 1913 had grown to sixty institutions with thirty-six hundred students, had no intention of enrolling non-Jewish students.[111]

Given this state of affairs, Ottoman intellectuals attributed an important role to education in the revolutionary era. In the view of Husayn Wasfi Rida, "national schools" were needed to operationalize liberty: "We need national schools that will ignore differences and personal attributes, and [instead] will raise its students with the same spirit, whose aims are elevation of the interests of the homeland and the protection of liberty."[112] However, the state school system was severely handicapped, structurally speaking, largely as a result of severe underfunding. In 1913, for example, the Beirut province spent only 2.95 percent of its budget on education, a fact prompting Salim 'Ali Salam, a member of the Ottoman parliament representing Beirut, to call for new taxes to finance investment in the educational system. As a result of this systemic underfunding, in Beirut and Jerusalem three times as many students studied in private schools as in state schools.[113]

One Palestinian educator, Khalil al-Sakakini, took matters into his own hands and established the Patriotic Constitutional School (Al-madrasa al-dustūriyya al-waṭaniyya) in Jerusalem in 1909, a private school that he saw as a model for reform-minded Ottomans. He envisioned a school that would cater to the city's youth of the three religions and imbibe in them the spirit of the constitution and of the liberal empire.[114] Combining Ottoman patriotism with modern notions of pedagogy, the Constitutional School set out to "honor the student and to support his spirit." To that end, the school did away with punishment, prizes, and grades; set aside regular class time for sports, nature, and music; and focused on "strengthening the brain" rather than simply filling it with details.[115]

Al-Sakakini also sought to undermine the traditional hierarchy of teacher and student and encouraged his staff to participate in games and activities with their charges. He himself seems to have taken this informal mentor role seriously; he regularly held salons and discussion circles at his home, often reading aloud from his journals to his students as a way of encouraging them to think and write about their experiences in an authentic and independent voice.[116]

Figure 2.2. Al-madrasa al-dustūriyya al-waṭaniyya, the Patriotic Constitutional School, Jerusalem. The school director, Khalil al-Sakakini, is seated on the left. Note that the pullovers of the younger schoolchildren feature the Ottoman flag, while the older pupils wear the Ottoman tarbush. Wasif Jawhariyya Photograph Collection, Institute for Palestine Studies (Beirut). Reprinted with permission from Walid Khalidi, *Before Their Diaspora: A Photographic History of the Palestinians, 1876–1948*, Institute for Palestine Studies.

Visitors to the Constitutional School were uniformly impressed by its mission and its modern appearance. The first three guests of honor after its opening were Hafiz al-Sa'id, Ruhi al-Khalidi, and Faid Allah (Faidi) al-'Alami, two parliamentarians and the mayor of Jerusalem, respectively. Al-Sa'id thanked the school for the "national service" it was rendering while al-Khalidi praised the school's "new methods and organization." Other visitors were more emotional and verbose in their responses. One guest shared his feelings of deep joy upon seeing the modern pedagogical methods and the energy and devotion of the teaching staff; another visitor argued that there was no true progress outside of education, and yet another praised the school's noble aims in cultivating the youth in the spirit of liberty and self-reliance and true brotherhood. Two visitors from Qalqiliya praised the honorable "national beginning" and "blessed renaissance" that the school represented, and prayed for its success in the cause of advancing and elevating the *umma* by educating the men of the future.[117]

In addition to the efforts of the Constitutional School, other private schools played important roles in Ottomanizing their student body. Newspaper reports indicate that schoolchildren often sang the liberty anthem or read patriotic poems at official events, and in general youth were targeted for special attention by the state, the CUP, and interested intellectuals empire-wide. Several children's and youth newspapers and magazines were published throughout the period before the First World War, which included patriotic anthems and parables.[118]

In addition to the schools, imperial attention turned to the army as a potential arm for Ottomanizing the population. When mandatory universal conscription was announced in 1909 in the Ottoman parliament, ending non-Muslims' exemption from conscription in exchange for paying the *bedel-i askerî* tax, it was seen as integral to the literal mixing of the peoples of the empire.[119] Universal conscription was talked about as a tool of social engineering, a universalizing experience that would unite the empire's polyglot communities. As one foreign journalist characterized the attitude dominant in the capital at the time, "the barracks are to complete the assimilation begun by the schools."[120]

In the prevailing euphoria of the early revolutionary days, when the Ottoman military was praised for its role in bringing liberty and while the Ottoman public was still eager to participate in the benefits and responsibilities of citizenship, universal conscription took its place among the slogans of a changing empire. One event participant, the Christian Jerusalemite Shibli Nauphal, described this as a necessary step for true equality: "Equality is the aim of justice and its true foundation, and if the Ottoman peoples will not be equal and mix their blood on the soil of the homeland in defense of it, then equality will not come about, and we will not have glory but through broadening the military and defense of the land."[121]

Indeed, various groups and individuals proclaimed their willingness to serve in the Ottoman army. One Armenian member of parliament, Krikor Zohrab, proclaimed that given that "military service for the various elements of the nation is the fundamental condition of safeguarding civil equality under the constitution," the Armenian community was committed to "serv[ing] the Motherland as citizen-soldiers."[122] Likewise, the Sephardi Jewish press in Jerusalem trumpeted, "We the Jews were always loyal to our homeland and to our enlightened government, and it is incumbent upon us to fulfill our holy duty especially according to the laws . . . [and] to give the last drop of blood for the good of the homeland."[123] Another newspaper editorialized that "all Ottomans, Muslims, and non-Muslims, should enter under the Ottoman flag."[124]

For its part, the CUP saw universal conscription as the final test of the empire's non-Muslim communities' commitment to Ottomanism. While the legitimate concerns of non-Muslims (such as issues relating to religious practice) would have to be addressed, they could not claim to be Ottoman citizens without contributing to the national effort. The pro-CUP newspaper *Tanin* (*Dawn*) argued:

> Is it to be conceived that, under a constitutional government, any section of the nation is going to refuse to submit to the decision of the National Assembly? Apart from such an absurdity, it is a simple fact that Greeks, Bulgars and Armenians are all anxious to bear their share of the defence of the Ottoman fatherland, and consequently, in spite of such objections as may be made, the institution of military service for all creeds may be regarded as an accomplished fact.[125]

However, as we will see in Chapter Four, the issue of military conscription quickly became a source of rivalry and contention in the Ottoman Empire—a marker of the limits and boundaries of Ottomanization. Likewise, education reform would also pit the centralizing impulses of the CUP against the protectionist impulses and cultural preferences of non-Muslim and non-Turkish communities.

CHALLENGES TO "EQUALITY AND BROTHERHOOD"

In addition to the difficulties of institutionalizing Ottomanism, from the outset it faced additional significant challenges. Neither Muslims nor non-Muslims were homogeneous, monolithic groups, and there were to be found numerous advocates of Ottomanism and Ottomanization as well as opponents to it. We have seen already that some Muslim public speakers objected to the equality of Muslims and non-Muslims, although they seemed to occupy a much smaller space in the press—perhaps more a testament to the orientation of the intellectual classes rather than a pure public referendum.[126]

Other public expressions, although in theory supportive of equality, nonetheless revealed internal inconsistencies and the difficulty of internalizing a true notion of equal citizenship. For example, at the same time that Rashid Rida extolled the beauty of equal brotherhood, his language was layered with terms resonant of Islamic history that placed non-Muslims in the empire back in the role of "tolerated guest" rather than "fellow citizen." In one article in which he fiercely defended the record of Muslim liberals, Rida wrote:

> After the victory of the constitution they were the ones who agreed to Ottomanism with the Armenians and other Christians, and they were the ones who raised their voices everywhere that we will not cause the religion to divide us and our Ottoman brothers but rather we will be with them as Islam commands us in the famous saying "for them that which is for us, and upon them that which is upon us."[127]

At first glance this expression might sound like a notion of republican citizenship—shared rights and duties irrespective of religion. However, this famous saying reportedly originated with the Caliph 'Umar bin al-Khattab, who is remembered in Islamic history for normalizing relations between Muslims and non-Muslims under the so-called "Pact of 'Umar." By returning non-Muslims to their position as "people of the book," the article explains, the superior role of Islam in the empire is preserved. This is made clearer later in the article, where Rida denounces those liberals who "exceeded the boundaries" of brotherhood and equality by offering to convert the Aya Sofia Mosque (formerly the Hagia Sophia Byzantine church) into the future parliament: as he reminds his readers, many still remembered the conquest of Constantinople as one of the glories of Islam. In other words, even among people who had struggled for liberty and theoretically supported equality and brotherhood, Ottoman equality threatened some Ottoman Muslims' sense of history, divine will, and sacred revelation.

Likewise, the "cost" of equality and brotherhood was not far from the minds of non-Muslims. Like his predecessor during the Tanzimat's first attempts to reform the status of non-Muslims, the Greek-Orthodox patriarch was the most visible—and worrying—example of unwillingness to fulfill the emancipation bargain by giving up the special privileges provided non-Muslims under the Capitulations. One foreign correspondent, admittedly no friend of the Greeks, commented about the Greeks in the empire that

> their idea of Ottoman citizenship, so far as themselves were concerned, was to avoid all the obligations of that citizenship, while enjoying all the rights conferred by it and retaining all their special privileges intact. . . . The Moslems have had to give up their special rights, but the Greeks refused to surrender a single one of their privileges for the sake of Ottoman unity. The Greeks chatter about liberty, equality, and fraternity, but their aim is to secure to themselves advantages over the other Christian peoples.[128]

The response of the CUP, through its cheerleader *Tanin*, was quite clear. After receiving legal equality, the right to vote for and serve in parliament, and above all after being welcomed as full members in the Ottoman nation, non-Muslims who clung to their privileges had no place in the new era.

> They [non-Muslims] surely are guilty of an injustice if, still dissatisfied, they also continue to claim their former privileges. For the aim of the constitution is to establish equality for all. To exact more is not right. We will never force our Greek countrymen to renounce their privileges, but we will say to them that the time of inequalities is over and if they want to live with us as brothers, we will open our arms wide and also our hearts. If, on the other hand, they also insist on maintaining the exceptional conditions of other times, they must still be *rayas* in our eyes, for surely we cannot grant them more than we ourselves enjoy, or the Arabs, or the Albanians![129]

In addition to a certain unwillingness to give up their special privileges, there also was a latent concern and fear about the transgressive potential of "brotherhood" and what this would mean for communal solidarity and existence. In the play *How It Came About*, discussed in Chapter One, the hero of the play, Behalul, falls in love with a Greek Orthodox Christian girl, Victoria. The actors proudly proclaim that "the love of a Greek and a Turk will be a symbol of the union of all the Ottoman peoples!" And yet, several scenes later, Victoria converts to Islam and renames herself Hope (Umit), after which she and Behalul finally wed.[130] According to Islamic law, however, a Muslim male is permitted to marry a Christian or Jewish female without requiring her conversion and without compromising the religion of the future children of such a union, who would automatically take their father's religion. So the question remains, why did the playwright call for Victoria's conversion? What did this symbolic act suggest for the real possibilities of the "union of the Ottoman peoples"?

Perhaps not coincidentally, in the fall of 1908, the story of an actual Muslim-Turkish–Greek-Christian romance in Istanbul shook the empire, making its way through the press even to faraway Jerusalem. In this case it was a Greek doctor, Teodori, who fell in love with a Muslim neighbor girl, Badriyya. According to the news report, Teodori went to Badriyya's father to ask for her hand in marriage, but the father flew into a rage, yelling to his neighbors that his daughter was leaving Islam. After a mob assembled, the police were summoned to escort the star-crossed lovers to the police station. However on their journey the couple and their police escort were intercepted by the mob, which beat Teodori to death and (possibly) fatally injured Badriyya. Of course the sad tale of the Ottoman Romeo and Juliet was complicated by the fact that Islamic law does *not* permit the marriage of Muslim women to non-Muslim men, an important difference from our fictional lovers Behalul and Victoria-Hope. Teodori's funeral reportedly drew three thousand Greeks, and while the CUP declared it would prosecute the perpetrators, tensions in the capital ran high after that.[131] According to the newspaper report, the lynching was incited by two conservative Muslim leaders in the capital who were battling against the constitutional regime.

In the aftermath of Teodori and Badriyya, the trope of intercommunal sexual transgression became a persistent subtext throughout the constitutional period of the fearful side of Ottoman brotherhood. For example, Armenians were inflamed by rumors of an Armenian girl being kidnapped and married to a Turk, and the Jewish press frequently decried rumors of Jewish women entering into relations with Arab Muslim or Christian men. After one such report, a Jerusalem newspaper cried out to its readers for help: "Help us save this woman! Three more Jews are ready to convert [after her]!"[132]

In addition to these conflicts sparked by passion, there were also interreligious and interethnic tensions of a more long-term, structural basis that would prove in some cases stronger than an ideological or political commitment to brotherhood. The Beirut newspaper *Ottoman Union* related in the fall of 1908 that the "pillars of corruption" had led to Muslim-Christian clashes in the northern Palestinian town of Shefa-'Amr; afraid of the riots spreading, the governor chided the villagers in a letter "reminding them of the meaning of the constitution and of liberty."[133]

Far more significant than the scuffle in this Palestinian village, however, was the series of anti-Armenian riots that spread from the fall of 1908 through the spring of 1909 in eastern Anatolia. Kurdish-Armenian relations in eastern Anatolia had long been uneasy, going back to at least the 1890s and ongoing land disputes between the two communities. Unrest began in October 1908, when news of Kurdish attacks against Armenians in the village of Viranşehir was published in the press throughout the empire.[134] After several months, reports were published that a local Muslim religious leader in eastern Anatolia was calling for attacks on Armenians, and he was soon arrested. In the spring of 1909, however, against the backdrop of the failed anticonstitutional coup and the deposition of the sultan, tensions in Anatolia finally erupted: locals were reportedly incensed by rumors of mosque desecrations and rapes, and by fears that the Armenians wanted to restore the ancient Armenian kingdom of Cicilia in Anatolia. In violence that lasted several weeks and decimated the town of Adana and several villages, between ten thousand and twenty thousand Armenians were killed.[135]

The massacres shook the empire to its core: less than a year after the revolution and within weeks after the triumph of the constitutionalists over their opponents in the capital, the bonds of Ottoman brotherhood were tested to their breaking point. The public response was one of shock—newspapers in Jerusalem collected funds for the Armenian victims of the massacre and watched the response of the government closely.[136] The most moving tribute was made by Halide Edib (Adıvar), a young Muslim writer for the Turkish-language press in Istanbul. She attributed the massacres to the spirit of the past, but also called on the CUP to apply justice and to ensure that such an atrocity never occurred again:

> My poor Armenian brethren, you are the greatest victims of the Hamidian regime. The fiery joy of my soul for our reestablished liberty turns to ice in the face of your darkened, desolate lands, the sad fate of your homeless, motherless little ones! Our national joy stalls in the dust with shame before this awful tragedy. . . . The ruins of Adana! O vast, bloody grave of my countrymen, you are a humiliation, not only to the Turks who caused it, but to the whole human race.
>
> O great Ottoman nation . . . Ottoman race . . . [we] must wipe out the blood of our Armenian brethren, that reddens the hands of our people.[137]

In the aftermath of the massacres, the CUP-aligned Armenian leadership like member of parliament Krikor Zohrab had to contend with Armenian nationalists who wanted them to break off ties with the CUP at the same time that they pushed the CUP for further aid to the Armenians. In negotiations between the Armenian Revolutionary Federation (Dashnak) and the CUP, it was agreed that Armenian guards would be posted in Armenian villages and that local reforms would be implemented to help calm matters on the ground. However, in an address to the Armenian National Assembly, Krikor Zohrab revealed that Muslim-Armenian relations had taken a serious hit. "You should know, compatriots, that the famed revolution of the Ottoman Constitution is still far from accomplishing its entire work. Indeed that circumstance where the Muslim element, full of hatred, resumes their criminal oppression, is a sign that the Turk has not matured enough for constitutional order."[138]

Despite Krikor Zohrab's own apparent ethnic and religious prejudices and the pressures he and other ARF leaders faced from the Armenian National Assembly as well as from their Armenian co-religionists, a joint decision was reached by the CUP headquarters and the ARF-Constantinople Responsible Body that stated that "considering that saving the sacred Ottoman fatherland from separation and division is an objective of the two organizations' joint cooperation, they will work to practically dispel within public opinion the false story inherited from the despotic regime that the Armenians strive for independence."[139] With that, Ottoman brotherhood and equality were put back on course, at least for the time being.

CHAPTER THREE

Of Boycotts and Ballots

In its first edition which appeared in late September 1908, the Beirut newspaper *Ottoman Union* published an "open letter to every esteemed Ottoman." This open letter appeared exactly two months after the announcement of the restoration of the constitution—by which time many cities and towns throughout the empire, Beirut included, had witnessed numerous mass rallies, celebrations, and an unprecedented, persistent level of public engagement. The editor of the paper, Shaykh Ahmad Husayn Tabbara, sought to prepare his readers for "the day after" the constitution once the heady days of revolutionary celebrations had died down. Tabbara lectured his readers:

> This is not a time of laziness and ignorance, but of hard work and wisdom. . . . It is not enough to show our joy and proclaim "long live the constitution," but rather it demands from us great efforts. . . . The revolution is just one phase, and if we do not study these rights or laws and work for these deeds, then [the constitution will be in name only]. On its own, the constitution will not advance the nation from backwardness to progress suddenly, nor will it bring it to progress from decay at once, but rather it points the nation on the path of goodness and away from the path of damage and harm.
>
> O, intellectuals, know that the nation is decayed in its knowledge, poor in its commerce, backward in its industry, ignorant in its agriculture, and many of its sons especially in the interior have not comprehended the meaning of the constitution until now.[1]

By cautioning his fellow citizens not to assume that the hard work of liberty had been achieved with the mere announcement of the constitution, Tabbara sought to convince his readers that they, too, were each personally and collectively responsible for political change and for the empire's general progress. This view of Ottoman citizenship as an *active* citizenship was expressed in various ways over the fall of 1908 with the establishment of numerous political and civil society organizations, the holding of parliamentary elections, and the publication of countless newspaper editorials that reveal a great deal about people's ideas, expectations, and hopes for an Ottoman imperial citizenship. This citizenship was premised on a strong Ottoman patriotism and drew on republican citizenship and historic Islamic notions like the "public good" and "general benefit."

"PRACTICING" CITIZENSHIP

The sultan's tyrannical reign had been propped up by hundreds if not thousands of government officials and spies, and "liberty" included a sense that justice would put in their place the men who had spied on, punished, and impoverished the Ottoman people. In various Ottoman cities and towns throughout the empire, ordinary citizens were emboldened to petition the state to dismiss local officials known to be corrupt, whether through formal channels such as petitions and telegrams or through informal channels such as demonstrations and vigilante justice. The press in some cases aided and even provoked this watchdog phenomenon; for example, several early issues of *Ottoman Union* featured letters either denouncing or defending particular individuals who were accused of belonging to the ancien régime.[2]

Heads of the gendarme and police lost their positions in Beirut and Damascus, and in the latter city another forty military and administrative officials reportedly were purged from their positions.[3] According to postal clerk 'Izzat Darwaza, emboldened by telegraphs reporting the "will of the nation [*irādat al-umma*]" in other neighboring cities like Jerusalem, 'Akka, and Beirut, in Nablus the "people's anger [*ghaḍab al-nās*]" erupted and they informed on clerks who had been corrupt and demanded their dismissal.[4] The military commander of Nablus, a notable religious scholar, and other leading men all known to be spies for the sultan were brought down in the revolutionary era.

In Jerusalem, despite former governor Ekrem Bey's systematic purges against local officials which had resulted in the firing of forty-five corrupt officials in his two-year tenure, various Jerusalemites nonetheless called for further purges of those officials who were, in their words, "accustomed to tyranny in the nation and [did] not place importance on the reforms of the people."[5] At a public demonstration, Shaykh Muhammad Shakir Diab al-Baytuni threatened the region's clerks: "We will learn which of them is wicked and who among them is good, because most of them were raised in the culture of cunning swindlers."[6] This was considered a vital step, and al-Baytuni called for "purifying the homeland [*taṭhīr al-waṭan*]" of the despots.

Simultaneous to these grassroots purges, within days after the announcement of the restoration of the constitution public education efforts were taking place on the streets and in the press. Public lectures on the constitution were held throughout the empire by individuals and nascent institutions established to support the revolution's aims. For example, in early October the Beirut Ottoman Union Society announced that two lawyers, 'Abd al-Ghani Badran and Jean Naqqash, would give public lectures on the Basic Law at the society's club. "All liberal Ottomans" from the various sects were invited to attend the lectures and join the society.[7] A few days later, the Beirut CUP branch announced that it too would hold a public meeting with speeches about the "beloved homeland and its holy laws."[8] Similar traces of public education talks survive in Nablus, where Ibrahim al-Qasim 'Abd al-Hadi "would speak to the public in the courtyard of the government house in a language close to the masses . . . in a simple style explaining the meaning of the constitution and the banishment of its announcement [in 1878] and its appearance, and that which was granted of liberty and brotherhood and equality and justice."[9] In Jerusalem, Yitzhak Levi gave a lecture at the Jewish cultural club Beit ha-'Am (House of the People/Nation), analyzing various relevant articles of the constitution.[10]

In addition to public talks taking place in various cities around the empire, numerous newspapers published translations of the constitution, making the document accessible to citizens empire-wide regardless of mother tongue.[11] *The Lighthouse* told its readers it was publishing sections of the constitution "so that the Ottomans will contemplate it and know their worth and that they are not servants to their rulers."[12] Other newspapers published queries from their readers about the new laws and new political system. For example, the Cairene newspaper *The Crescent*, which had wide distribution in the Arab Eastern Mediterranean, published the following letter from reader Muhammad Hasan al-'Amari. "Al-'Amari: People talk about the constitution that the Ottoman liberals attained and we understand that [the empire] moved from tyranny to liberty, but we do not understand the shape of a constitutional government, and we have heard that the Easterners [are not compatible with constitutionalism]. Also, what is the role of the Basic Law and the parliament?"[13]

The Crescent responded with a long explanation of comparative political history: In a tyrannical government like that which had previously ruled in the East, the ruler makes the laws over his people, and he is the highest authority and can rule the people as he wishes; also, men of government implement the laws over the people. In contrast, constitutional government constrains absolute power. It is guided by the constitution, which is a handbook on how to compose government, what the traits of its members should be, and how to govern. The most important difference, *The Crescent* emphasized to its readers, is that constitutional government is based on "the will of the nation," and the nation itself elects who will represent it in the government. Furthermore, *The Crescent* argued that there was no inherent reason why Easterners could not adopt constitutionalism—they simply needed to familiarize themselves with it.

To that end, numerous political and civil society organizations were established in the fall of 1908 to support the constitution. In fact, the establishment of universal civic organizations was seen as a vital step to supporting Ottomanism. The journalist Husayn Wasfi Rida pleaded with his countrymen: "It is not permissible that [an organization] be for only some of the people, neither Muslims nor Christians nor Jews, neither in aims nor design, but it must be purely Ottoman. . . . You are Ottomans, O brothers, therefore your associations must be Ottoman."[14] As Rida argued, only by establishing organizations held together by civic rather than religious bonds would Ottomans succeed in "operationalizing liberty."

We have already seen the existence of an Ottoman Unity Society in Beirut that held public lectures on the constitution. A branch of the society was established in Tripoli that was aimed at "support[ing] the Basic Law and defend[ing] its laws and serv[ing] its general benefit"—in other words, "service to the beloved homeland."[15] Reports of other organizations sprouted throughout the empire after the revolution, such as Ottoman Brotherhood (Uhuvvet-i Osmaniye).[16] However, far beyond these local societies in terms of both spread and importance were the local branches of the Committee for Union and Progress.

THE "SACRED COMMITTEE": THE LOCAL BRANCHES OF THE CUP

Because of the relative ease with which it succeeded in restoring the constitution, the CUP had burst onto the imperial stage as the heroic "savior" of the Ottoman Empire, attaining widespread popularity and a significant degree of public legitimacy virtually overnight. Popularly referred to as the "sacred committee [*cemiyet-i mukaddese*]," the CUP had local branches popping up in the empire's cities and towns almost immediately. According to one report, by the end of 1909 there were over 360 CUP branches and 850,000 members spread throughout the empire.[17] In Palestine, CUP branches were established in the important cities of Jaffa, Jerusalem, Nablus, and 'Akka, but also in the smaller towns of Safad, Tiberias, Haifa, and Gaza. Over the next several years these provincial branches became significant political actors, injecting previously apolitical social classes into political life, mobilizing a mass street boycott of a major European power, and pointing to new modes of political participation.

Some of the provincial branches grew out of existing underground cells, whereas others were newly constituted by local initiative, comprised of members who were unknown and in many cases unaccountable to the central committee. For the first few years after the revolution, while the CUP remained an unofficial (shadow) actor in central government politics, CUP headquarters in Salonica had limited control over the provincial branches, their internal organization, membership, or activities. Indeed, until 1910 there were reported cases of branches attempting to overrule local government officials and of imposters issuing forged announcements and imposing fake taxes on the local populace, and as a result, the central CUP preferred to rely on loyal army officers rather than the branches to carry out its program.[18]

Members of these new provincial CUP branches most certainly had various motivations—ranging from revolutionary euphoria, to sincere ideological affinity, to naked political opportunism. Many branches probably started like the one in Nablus, where local postal clerks swept up in revolutionary excitement simply declared the post office as the Nablus chapter of the CUP.[19] The branch in nearby Safad was founded by the youth of the town of all three religions explicitly to "defend the laws and rights granted by the constitution."[20] Further east in Mesopotamia, however, CUP branches belonging to rival notable families in Mosul betrayed more Machiavellian motives—the CUP was a rising power in a changing empire, and it is reasonable to believe that a not insignificant percentage of its new members were simply jumping on the bandwagon.[21]

A closer look at two Palestinian CUP branches, those of Jerusalem and Jaffa, reveals that the membership was religiously diverse and drew largely from the younger members of traditional notable families as well as the white-collar middle class, many of whom had a real ideological commitment to both the liberal revolution and Ottoman patriotism. The Jerusalem branch, reportedly numbering 140 members, elected a ten-member leadership committee which consisted of five Muslims, four Christians, and one Jew.[22] The Muslim members of the leadership included one Turkish-speaking army officer stationed in Jerusalem, Celal, as well as younger members of the influential al-Husayni, Jarallah, and al-Nashashibi families. Other Muslim members of the branch included Shaykh 'Ali al-Rimawi, the Arabic-language editor of the official provincial government newspaper *Noble Jerusalem* (*Al-Quds al-Sharīf/Kudüs-ü Şerif*), and Is'af al-Nashashibi, the well-known young poet and public speaker from a notable family.[23]

The Christian members of the leadership council included men such as Jurji Habib Hanania, editor of the newspaper *Jerusalem*, and schoolteachers Eftim Mushabbak and Jurji Zakaria; the educational reformer Khalil al-Sakakini was also briefly a member of the branch. Albert Antébi, the sole Jewish member of the leadership, was a French-educated powerbroker between the local communities, Ottoman administration, and foreign Jewish organizations; in fact he tied for the highest number of votes in internal elections for chairman. Other Jewish members of the branch included the Hebraist schoolteacher David Yellin, the lawyer Malchiel Mani from Hebron, the young journalist Gad Frumkin, and Gad's brother Zalman Frumkin. The presence of Jewish members in the CUP was not without controversy, however; at least two other Jewish candidates were denied membership in the local branch because they refused to renounce their ties to the Zionist movement.[24]

The Jaffa CUP was larger and more active than the Jerusalem branch, reportedly twice its size in May 1909. Its leadership committee consisted of three army officers; the customs director Ali Rıza Bey; members of large Muslim land-owning families like Yusuf 'Ashur; the Christian railroad employee Yusuf al-'Issa; white-collar Christian clerks like Anton Jellat and Nasri Talamas; and the Jewish entrepreneur and land speculator Musa (Moshe) Matalon.[25] In Gaza, a primarily Muslim city, members of the local CUP branch included leading notables and landowners, current and former government officials, and religious scholars.[26]

In their demographic makeup, the provincial CUP branches were very similar to branches of Freemasonry lodges, and indeed, there is a heavily documented relationship between the two institutions in the late Ottoman Empire, explored further in Chapter Five. Similar to the Freemasons, the CUP branches combined elements of a secret society and a cultural club: members had to be recommended by two existing members in order to be considered; they underwent secret initiation rites; and once initiated, they carried around a membership card. As well, CUP branch dues worked on a sliding scale similar to the Freemasons: workers paid 2 percent of their monthly salary, whereas the upper classes paid 2 percent of their annual income.[27]

The Christian schoolteacher Khalil al-Sakakini provided us with an account of his initiation into the Jerusalem CUP branch, further underscoring the influence of Masonry on the CUP. As he recorded in his diaries, soon after his return to Jerusalem from New York he was invited to join the Jerusalem branch, a rare honor since reportedly men were being turned away at the branch headquarters every day. As part of his initiation, al-Sakakini was led by members Hanna Yasmina, Shaykh

Tawfiq al-Tanbaqqa, and Jurji Jid'un to a secret location where he was greeted by CUP members. There they blindfolded him, placed his right hand on the New Testament (since he was Christian) and his left hand on a pistol, and said to him: "By this [the Bible] swear and by this [the pistol] defend." They read the CUP pledge to him, which he repeated. In his words, he swore "to protect the constitution, to work for the advancement of the homeland, to do what the society requested of him and to protect its secrets, and to defend the homeland and constitution until death."[28]

This dramatic initiation was meant to underscore that the association was a closed brotherhood. However, the CUP was also involved in more open activities involving the broader population. Soon after its establishment, the Jerusalem CUP branch rented out a large building with a garden for its activities and the use of its members, hinting at the central role that sociability must have played in branch life. For example, to support its activities, the Jaffa CUP put on several fundraising plays open to the wider populace. The CUP urged the city's better classes to come "purify [their] morals" and welcome a spirit of "exertive patriotism [*al-waṭaniyya al-ḥamāsa*]," while supporting the CUP. By 1910, a "sister" society, the Society of Ottoman Women for the Greatness of the Homeland, was founded in Salonica, reportedly to support the navy and publish a women's journal, and affiliated branches of the religious scholars (*ulama*) and trades were established as well. In July 1909 a Society for the Protection of Animals was established in Jerusalem under the patronage of the local CUP.[29]

In terms of their main activities, the branches carried out administrative and political functions. The provincial lodges played active roles in purging the local administration of corrupt and repressive officials, even in some cases directly taking over the local government; they reported on local affairs to the central CUP in Salonica; and monitored the parliamentary elections.[30] In addition, the Palestinian branches distinguished themselves in particular ways. The Jerusalem CUP branch served as a high court for complaints from other lodges. The CUP in Gaza reportedly opened an agricultural school along the lines of the AIU's Mikveh Israel school, hired a Jewish teacher from Be'er Tuvia, and began importing seeds from France; the local committee in Gaza reportedly wanted to open a factory as well. In addition, the northern Palestinian and Beirut branches played a growing role in organizing local opposition to the Zionist movement in the country.[31] The most visible political accomplishment of the Palestinian CUP branches, however, was the successful mobilization of a massive, months-long boycott of a major European power.

BOYCOTT 1908: OTTOMANISM AND ITS CONFRONTATION WITH THE WEST

In early October 1908, two announcements from southeastern Europe shook the Ottoman Empire to its core: first, Bulgaria's declaration of independence on October 5, and on the following day, the Austro-Hungarian annexation of Bosnia-Herzegovina. Both Bulgaria and Bosnia-Herzegovina were former Ottoman provinces, and both had been pawns in the European grab for Ottoman territories which resulted in the 1878 Treaty of Berlin. Although the European powers—and especially Russia, as the self-proclaimed protector of Orthodox Christians—had pressed for autonomy on behalf of the region's Christians, in the aftermath of the treaty conflict continued between the Ottoman army and nationalist militias on both sides of the empire's borders.

The announcement of Bulgarian independence came on the heels of months of rising tensions between Bulgaria and the Ottoman Empire, but the annexation of Bosnia-Herzegovina came as a complete surprise. In the aftermath of the annexation news, the Ottoman government appealed to the "family of nations" to come to its defense, but Germany supported the Austro-Hungarian move, Russia quietly acquiesced, and France and Britain refused to get involved.[32] News of the annexation hit the Ottoman populace especially hard; it was a reminder of the humiliations and territorial losses the empire had suffered throughout the nineteenth century and a crushing blow to the revolutionary dream of standing as equals with the European powers. In the aftermath, public boycotts against Austrian goods, ships, and commerce quickly spread throughout the Ottoman Empire, a grassroots expression of Ottoman patriotism and mass political mobilization.

The Ottoman boycott drew on two legacies in the developing world: first, as an expression of nationalism and anticolonialism, and second, as a "weapon of the weak" to protest against the unequal fortunes of the nonindustrial, peripheral East and the industrial, colonizing West. Similar boycotts in protest against European economic and political penetration had been carried out in China, Japan, and Qajar Iran in the two decades prior. As in these other countries, the Ottoman boycott was a mass social movement, carried out by tens of thousands of participants, pushed forward by dozens of boycott committees and organizations, and sustained by the Ottoman press.[33] A closer look at the boycott in Jaffa illustrates ways in which the Ottoman public became politically mobilized, but also reveals interesting insights into a local Ottoman nationalism that drew on elements of Ottoman patriotism, Islamism, and the legacy of conflict with Europe.

The spark which ignited the boycott came from two newspaper articles published in Istanbul in *Servet-i Funun* and *Tanin*, both pro-CUP organs, which called on the Ottoman public to boycott Austria-Hungary. *Tanin*'s article urged citizens to boycott Austrian goods based "on . . . love of country, calling on Ottoman patriots to avenge constitutional Turkey [*sic*], betrayed at the very moment it needed Western 'sympathy and encouragement.'"[34] The next day, mass demonstrations of several thousand strong protesting the annexation took place in Istanbul in front of the Ministry of War and in Salonica's main square. Within days, merchants had canceled orders of Austrian goods, consumers were being harassed outside of Austrian shops, and placards urged people not to shop at the listed stores.

A brief telegram from the Beirut Ottoman Commercial Committee informed Jaffa merchants of the outbreak of the boycott and called for their participation. In the committee's narration, the merchants led the boycott with the unanimous consent of the local population.[35] A meeting was held at the residence of the Jerusalem governor together in attendance with the mufti and his son, the head scribe and translator of the Greek Orthodox monastery, and the chief rabbi, to discuss the immanent boycott declaration.[36] By October 12, leaders from Jaffa and Jerusalem decided to boycott Austrian ships arriving in Palestine. The decision was not without significant risk: Jaffa at the time was the second largest port on the Ottoman Syrian coast, after Beirut, and as such was the province's economic center of foreign trade. In 1908 alone, 14.5 million francs in imports entered Jaffa port, with 12.5 million francs leaving as exports. Furthermore, Austria-Hungary was Jaffa's fourth largest trading partner and held a sizeable trading surplus with the port city.[37] The economic costs of cutting ties with Austria-Hungary were potentially enormous, especially given the recent economic troubles of 1907–8.

The Jaffa-based Ottoman Commercial Committee issued the following decree to the "sons of the homeland" invoking the help of God as well as appealing to public opinion and observance to uphold Ottoman unity and promote Ottoman national interests. "We must prevent the sale of every piece of Austrian merchandise and clothing . . . ; we must work with all our Ottoman capital, our businesses, and we hope that we will preserve that which is demanded of us by our heart, our homeland, our honor, and our conscience, and God is great and lofty and he is vigilant over the masses."[38]

Simultaneously, Jerusalem mayor Husayn Hashem al-Husayni issued a public flyer announcing the boycott to the local populace in similar terms, demanding compliance with the boycott as a sign of loyalty and patriotism to the Ottoman nation. In his words: "There is no doubt that whoever does other than this will expose himself as betraying the homeland, civilization, and Islam."[39]

In response to these calls, the first public actions against local vestiges of Austria-Hungary's existence took effect on October 13, upon the arrival of a ship of the Österreichischen Lloyd Company to Jaffa's coastline. Because of the poor condition of the Jaffa port that did not allow large ships to actually dock at the harbor, instead ships dropped anchor offshore and small boats were hired to ferry goods and passengers to land. These port boatmen played a critical role in the Jaffa boycott, for without them, there was no possibility of reaching the shore. They refused to allow the government health commissioners onboard to disinfect the ship and refused to unload the ship's mail for the Austrian postal service. According to German consular reports, the quar-

Figure 3.1. Off the coast of Jaffa. Since the port was not deep enough to accommodate large vessels, ships dropped anchor off the coast and relied on small rowboats to carry goods and passengers to shore. These boatmen were integral to the success of the patriotic Ottoman boycott against the Austro-Hungarian Empire in the fall of 1908. Library of Congress, Prints and Photographs Division (LC-DIG-matpc-06513).

antine boat was attacked, its officials beaten, and disinfection tools destroyed.[40]

The same morning of these tense events at the port, massive popular unrest and near rioting spread in the town and the incoming mail delivery and local office of the Austrian post were attacked. According to the report of the postal director to the Austrian Consulate, a crowd gathered at the post office incited by ringleaders and "fanatical" Muslim clerics.[41] They forced themselves inside "with insulting cries," attacked the postal clerk Tawfiq Lorenzo, threatened the other clerks, and forced the clerks outside while demanding they shut down the post office. Egged on by the cries of the assembled crowd, the rioters pulled the mailbox from the wall, threw it in the mud, and trampled it underfoot. The postal wagon was attacked and partially destroyed before it was thrown into the sea, and the sign of the post office would have been removed and destroyed but for the efforts of the post office director.

The Austrian and German reports surrounding the boycott were damning, describing fanatical mobs pushed into a frenzy by zealous and diabolical clerics, aided and abetted by incompetent and perhaps complicit local officials and police. The Austrians further claimed that the demonstrations against them were far from spontaneous, but rather were conceived of by the central headquarters of the CUP, which they characterized as both authoritarian and "fanatically Eastern." As well, the Austro-Hungarian consul in Jaffa emphasized the coercive nature of the boycott, alleging that the boatmen had been threatened that their boats would be destroyed if they assisted the Austrian ship.[42]

By seeking to portray the boycott and mass mobilization as the machinations of a few fanatics, the Austro-Hungarian representatives sought to undermine the legitimacy of the boycott. In the eyes of European observers, instead of being a possibly legitimate form of political protest against the foreign policy of Austria-Hungary, the boycott was instead another sign of the backwardness of the empire and another front in the timeless clash of Western and Eastern civilizations. They reported that the crowds invoked Islamic and strongly anti-Western sentiments: "*dīn Muhammad qām bi al-sayf*"—the religion of Muhammad rose up by the sword; "*Allah yanṣur al-sulṭān*"—God will make the sultan victorious; and "*Allah yahlik al-kuffār*"—God will destroy the infidels.

Without doubt, popular anger tapped into a longer historical consciousness of European-Ottoman and Christian-Islamic clashes and tensions. On the popular level, encroaching Western powers were visible daily in the Capitulation system, the brashness of many foreign consuls and residents, and the recurring visits of Western warships along the Ottoman coast that constantly threatened to undermine Ottoman sovereignty once and for all. In the aftermath of the July revolution, then, further concessions to the West were too much to bear, at least not silently. One newspaper confirmed that participants in a Jaffa demonstration waved "sacred flags."[43]

However, it is inaccurate to see this boycott as a purely Muslim versus Christian conflict; rather, Islamic discourse was rallied alongside Ottoman patriotism. Importantly, Muslims were not the only participants in the imperial boycott, and in many locations Christians and Jews were also active as organizers, mobilizers, and participants. When the mass demonstrations spread inland to Jerusalem, they were led by the Mufti Taher al-Husayni, but he was joined by Jewish, Greek Orthodox, and Armenian representatives who were elected to serve alongside him on a boycott committee.[44]

In mid-November 1908, the Greek Orthodox community of Jaffa organized a play entitled *Salah al-Din al-Ayyubi*, where all the major European powers were represented, the Austro-Hungarian monarch represented by a "poor Polish Jew" who was the butt of the jokes of the play. In attendance were Jaffa's honorable Christian families, who shouted, "Down with Austria!" at the appearance of the emperor-Jew.[45] Salah al-Din al-Ayyubi, known as Saladin in the West, had pushed back the Christian crusaders from Egypt and liberated Palestine after almost one hundred years of Crusader rule in which thousands of local Muslims, Jews, and Christians had been killed. For this he is considered a great hero in Islamic and Arab history, a symbol of Islamic and Arab liberation from Western aggression as well as of Islamic tolerance, for unlike the Crusaders, Salah al-Din did not massacre non-Muslims but rather allowed them to live alongside their neighbors.

Due to both a shared language and social proximity, many Christian Arabs were steeped in Islamic civilization, history, and tradition, so the turn of Jaffa's Greek Orthodox community to the legacy of Salah al-Din is not unusual in and of itself.[46] However, the fact that the Greek Orthodox community in Jaffa was so supportive of the boycott—indeed several of the local CUP organizers themselves were Greek Orthodox—is significant in another respect. Some historians have seen the boycott as highlighting the divergent interests of non-Muslims, overrepresented in the commercial and merchant classes, and Muslims, underrepresented in those areas. As the Ottoman historian Donald Quataert has written, the boycott "exposed the fragile position of Ottoman Christians, living in a Muslim society but dependent on the Western economy. By highlighting the different interests of the non-Muslim and Muslim merchant communities, it hastened the disappearance of Christians from the commercial and industrial life of the Ottoman Empire."[47]

To be sure, the boycott was the first step heralding a broader turn toward creating an Ottoman "national economy" (*milli iktisat*), but one important component of that was overcoming the Ottoman Empire's uneven economic position as a consumer of European finished products while providing only raw materials for export. To that end the Ottoman press encouraged the entire Ottoman population to buy nationally produced goods at the same time that it encouraged the government and the capitalist classes to build up a national industry.[48] The Izmir-based Greek Orthodox newspaper *Amaltheia* was one of the most vocal proponents of economic protectionism, taking a hard-line view that Ottoman citizens should only purchase Ottoman-made goods, even if that meant forgoing products for which there was no local equivalent.[49] Certainly few parties were interested in allowing the economic boycott to introduce cracks in Ottoman unity, and there is some evidence that the local CUP leadership tried to moderate the public cries of the crowds.[50] There is no evidence, however, that Christian Ottomans were targeted by the crowds, but rather they were given an opportunity to display their Ottoman patriotism and commitment to the imperial public good.

In the meantime, the Austrian ship had been kept waiting off the shores of Jaffa for several days; the crowds reportedly threatened to bomb and attack the ship if it was allowed to land and unload its passengers or goods. Instead, the ship was rerouted to either Beirut or Cyprus and the mass demonstrations ended. Immediately afterward, the Ottoman governor sent forty gendarmes and three infantry companies from Jerusalem to Jaffa to keep order. A passing European warship was also believed to have a "salutary" and "calming" effect on the public's mood, at least according to the German Consulate; arguably the effect would have been more akin to "intimidating" from the Ottoman perspective.[51]

The boycott continued, however, and within a few days it had spread to target Austro-Hungarian shops and goods already on store shelves.[52] By the beginning of November, the Jaffa boycott widened to target German ships and goods as well, based on the claim that Austrian goods were being shipped on German boats and sold under false German labels. A flyer that survived from the period, signed by "Zealous Ottoman Patriot ['Uthmānī waṭani ghayūr]," made this claim, linking the boycott, Ottoman patriotism, religion, and the force of society in marking and protecting social and political boundaries. The flyer was addressed to and written by those who identified themselves with the Ottoman nation; the flyer's exhortations were based on Ottoman national feelings; and the people were elevated to the level of legitimate enforcer of nationalism.

Now we hear that the Austrian goods are coming by way of German ships via Germany. [Those of you partaking of this], if you do not fear Allah then at least be ashamed before the people and be embarrassed that . . . it will be said that even the poor people are greater than you . . . and are more patriotic than you.

No. No. God forbid, we do not believe that . . . there are people in the world who are released from human feelings and are greedy for profits from the port customs. . . . Likewise we do not believe that there are merchants who use this national zeal in order to raise the price of their goods. So, sons of the homeland, shame on us for hearing such a thing as these deeds, and we must point a finger publicly at the man who does them, and fathers must show their children while saying, "There goes the man who sold his patriotism out of his desire to fill his coffers," and he will earn the anger of Allah and the contempt of the people.[53]

In this appeal we hear the echo of a republican understanding of citizenship, where every individual has to contribute to the public good. Indeed, the Ottoman press was rife with discussions of "national honor and public spirit" (*hamiyyet*, Ott. Tur.; *ḥamiyya*, Ara.)—those who displayed it were praised (*hamiyyetli*), those who lacked it were disparaged (*hamiyyetsiz*).[54] For the "Zealous Ottoman Patriot," those middle-class merchants and shopkeepers who refused to stop importing Austro-Hungarian goods or who exploited their countrymen through price gouging were most decidedly lacking in public spirit and national honor, not to mention that they were acting against the public good and religious morals.

Though the German Consulate became aware of the threats on its ships and appealed to the Jaffa deputy governor to keep order and ensure that the port stevedores did not refuse to unload German ships, in mid-November a German ship called *Galata* was attacked when it tried to dock in Jaffa. When the ship arrived simultaneously with another ship, the port workers unloaded the ships' goods for a few hours in the morning. Around three in the afternoon a rumor circulated that Austro-Hungarian goods were to be found among the German ship's cargo, and the angry boatmen began tossing the cargo into the sea. Although the German consul immediately went to secure the aid of the deputy governor, the latter "stood quietly and let them do it," according to the bitter complaints of the consul; the local demonstrators threw 998 packages of commercial goods into the sea as well as an unspecified number of packages sent as a gift by the German kaiser for the German-Catholic hospice in Jerusalem.[55] Only the intervention of the newly elected member of parliament Hafiz al-Sa'id persuaded the boatmen to stop throwing the cargo overboard, and he even succeeded in convincing them to fish out several cases of cargo from the sea.

The German consul pressed for a full investigation, and eventually six leaders and fifteen perpetrators of the attack were either arrested or went into hiding. Among the men accused of participation were leading figures of the local CUP, such as army officer Ihsan Effendi, Muslim landowner Yusuf 'Ashur, and the Christian railroad employee Yusuf al-'Issa. In addition, the deputy governor Rüşdi Bey was relieved of his duties, the police commissioner Mehmet Fevzi was also fired, and the customs official was threatened with dismissal.[56]

Yet again, the Austro-Hungarian and German consuls blamed the "terrorism" perpetrated by the locals on the CUP. The Jerusalem governor Subhi Bey and the foreign affairs secretary of the province, Bishara Effendi, reportedly opposed the boycott as they believed it would eventually harm local and Ottoman imperial interests, but they too proved ineffective in squashing the local developments. Government officials in Istanbul also tried unsuccessfully to end the boycott, but their inability to do so was a result both of the power of the CUP to stand as an independent political force and of grassroots fervor. Indeed, in early December 1908, the visit of two envoys of the CUP's central committee to the Syrian port towns led to a renewal of the boycott in Haifa although Austro-Hungarian goods had begun to be unloaded there. In Beirut, the boycott had been dying down as well due to the intervention of the local governor but was renewed upon orders from Salonica and Istanbul, causing "heavy damage" to Austro-Hungarian exports.[57]

At the same time, there was also a clear, strong grassroots component to the boycott. Certainly, continued news of the situation in Bosnia-Herzegovina, where Muslim homes were occupied and mosques were turned into churches and barns, helped to reignite public outrage; in addition, Bosnian refugees flooded into the empire, organizing themselves and publishing their own flyers in support of the boycott. By early December, the boycott syndicate in Istanbul had over fifteen thousand members. In Palestine, newspaper reports commented on the population's identification with the boycott, which "the nation [had] declared."[58] In Jerusalem and Jaffa, the wearing of the white tarbush, produced locally in the empire, rather than the red tarbush, imported from the Austro-Hungarian Empire, was greeted as a patriotic act. As well, one Hebrew newspaper reported that in addition to the nightly demonstrations being held in Jerusalem, where hundreds of residents marched through the streets holding torches and singing nationalist songs, a group of five hundred young men showed up at the governor's residence ready "to spill their blood for liberty," and asked to be sent to the front to battle Austria-Hungary.[59] 'Izzat Darwaza's memoirs indicate that there was strong public support for the boycott also in Nablus, where popular honorific poems (*qaṣīda*s) were written in support of the boycott, indicating a deep cultural and emotional support that could not have been purely orchestrated. In fact, boycott fever spread even to British-occupied Egypt, where the press and local stores were mobilized on behalf of the patriotic Ottoman nation.[60]

Then, abruptly and without much fanfare, on February 27, 1909, a telegram arrived in Jaffa from Istanbul and Beirut stating that the Ottoman boycott against the Austro-Hungarian Empire was over. The Ottoman government had succeeded in forcing Austria-Hungary to agree to a large financial settlement as compensation for the loss of Bosnia-Herzegovina. The economic pressure of the boycott on Austria-Hungary had been significant: as of December 1908 the boycott had cost Austria-Hungary 20–25 million Kronen in lost revenues, and other shipping lines even refused to load Austrian goods for fear of reprisals or landing difficulties at Ottoman ports. The Austrian fez factories and sugar industry were hit hard, but the largest casualty of the boycott of Austria was the Österreichischen Lloyd shipping line, which in four months had seen twenty-nine ships blocked from landing in Jaffa port alone, at a loss of seventy-five thousand francs.[61]

Despite the heavy damage inflicted upon Austria-Hungary by the boycott, the Ottoman imperial and local Palestinian economies suffered greatly from the boycott. Imperial tax revenues declined dramatically and customs revenues declined by almost one-third. In Palestine, due to the delays and losses in shipping, local banks as well as the Jaffa customs house faced a severe downturn. Banks were unable to collect on shipping statements, as most customers refused to pay until they received their goods. In early December 1908, less than halfway through the boycott, local banks had unpaid shipping statements worth 42,715 francs, and the local customs house was even harder hit with 53,571 francs of unredeemed shipping statements.[62]

In addition, local merchants were hard-hit by dramatic cost increases in the absence of Austro-Hungarian goods. The export-heavy orange industry in particular suffered, as the boycott began at the start of the fall harvest season. Packing paper and packing crates for the oranges, previously purchased from the Austro-Hungarian Empire, had to be purchased at almost triple the price from Germany and Italy. The price of sugar doubled as consumers turned to French, English, and Egyptian sugar; paper, ready-to-wear clothing, glass, and the ubiquitous red tarbush, all middle- and upper-class urban consumer goods, were similarly affected. The one sector that seemed to benefit financially was Jaffa's boatmen, who successfully demanded higher prices for their services; boatmen in other port cities were also successful in pushing for higher wages through the boycott months.[63]

And yet, while the boycott of Austria-Hungary took a heavy toll on the Ottoman and Palestinian economies, it was considered a successful example of popular participation in the political process. The Ottoman nation had discovered a powerful new weapon that it would put to use again. Similar boycotts were waged in 1910 against Greece following its annexation of Crete, in 1911 against Italy following its attack on Ottoman Libya, and in 1912–13 on Greece again as a result of its war over the Balkans.

THE FIRST PARLIAMENTARY ELECTIONS, FALL 1908

If the boycott against Austria-Hungary represented an informal, grassroots entry into the political arena, elections to the new Ottoman parliament presented a formal opportunity for provincial Ottomans to influence imperial administration and policy in the capital. Unlike the first parliament in 1877–78, whose members were appointed by the provincial councils, the new members would be elected by the broader (adult male, taxpaying) population. The 1908 elections marked a new beginning for Ottoman civic-political life. The opening of the parliament in December 1908 was a national holiday, and as we will see, reflected local expectations of "representative government" in the new era. At the same time, however, the parliamentary elections also highlighted the tensions inherent in the new Ottomanist project as the empire's various ethnic and religious groups struggled to find their place in the body politic.

The Sectarian Prism I: Voting Rights

The tension between the electoral system and the expectations of Ottomans was first played out in terms of political enfranchisement. From the outset, confusion and lack of information characterized the election process, particularly concerning the voting status of individuals as well as the electoral (and thus political) power of the various ethnoreligious communities. Among the central issues in the election was the gap between the liberal basis of electoral politics formally adopted—one man, one vote—and the persistence of the legacy of a confessional political system in which the ethno-religious community (*millet*) was the central actor. With regard to demographics, enfranchisement, campaigning, and negotiations, the *millet* took a leading role in the entire electoral process, eclipsing the individual citizen as a political actor. Thus even in this first act of constituting the civic Ottoman corpus, and although celebrating their voting rights as Ottoman citizens, ethnic and religious groups still sought to play a role in the political life of the empire.

According to the electoral system adopted, parliamentary elections were to be a two-tier process. In the first stage, Ottoman taxpaying males with the right to vote would select second-tier electors (one elector per five hundred voters in the first stage); the second-tier electors would in turn vote for members of parliament (one MP per fifty thousand males).[64] Based on the official Ottoman census records, it was determined that the Jerusalem province had the right to 180 electors who would, in turn, choose three members of parliament.[65] The northern Palestinian provinces administered by Beirut would also elect two members of parliament.

Ottoman citizens shared a basic inexperience with electoral politics, suffered from haphazard record keeping in the Ottoman registers, and were either enthusiastically optimistic or deeply suspicious of political change. In the cities, an elections inspection commission was established consisting of notable leaders from the community who would meet with the religious leaders and neighborhood *mukhtars* to facilitate the process. In Jerusalem the city council invited all the neighborhood and confessional *mukhtars* to a meeting to explain the rules and order of the upcoming elections. Election lists and voting procedures were to be announced by criers in the markets and neighborhoods and conveyed by the spiritual heads and *mukhtars* in addition to being posted in houses of worship and on the streets and published in the newspapers. Citizens were given the opportunity to file a correction or appeal with the elections commission.[66]

According to the electoral law, any taxpaying Ottoman male citizen over the age of twenty-five was eligible to vote in the parliamentary elections; this necessarily excluded foreign citizens (pilgrims, merchants, non-Ottomanized immigrants), foreign protégés, and stateless persons, as well as women. While tying electoral rights to citizenship was a logical requirement and certainly the basis of modern liberal politics even today, nonetheless in the early twentieth-century Ottoman Empire the result was the effective and disproportionate disenfranchisement of large numbers of non-Muslims from the voting rolls.

In Palestine, for example, a large percentage of the foreign-born Jewish community was disqualified from receiving voting rights in the election, as many of them had arrived under three-month pilgrim visas and simply settled in the country. Thus while the 1905 Ottoman census counted 13,441 Jews with Ottoman citizenship resident in Jerusalem, the Zionist Palestine Office estimated there were up to 45,000 to 50,000 Jews actually living in the city, mostly foreign citizens, while the U.S. Consulate in Jerusalem estimated their numbers reached 60,000.[67] In other words, although Jews constituted a plurality of the population in Jerusalem (41.3 percent of the city's Ottoman citizens and a majority once total non-Ottoman residents were taken into account), their absolute voting numbers as well as their relative voting power were drastically reduced once non-Ottomans were discounted.

In recognition of the huge gap between the number of Jews with Ottoman citizenship and the total number of Jews living in Jerusalem, immediately after the announcement of upcoming elections voices within the Palestinian Jewish communities as well as international Jewish communities repeatedly called on foreign Jews living in Palestine to renounce their foreign citizenship and to adopt Ottoman citizenship, a step which would bolster the political power of the local Jewish community.[68] The newspaper editor and noted Hebrew linguist Eli'ezer Ben-Yehuda, himself an immigrant from Russia who had taken on Ottoman citizenship, repeatedly called on his readers: "Jews, become Ottomans!" This formal drive for Jewish Ottomanization (known as *hit'atmenut*) would become timelier and much more pressing in the early months of the First World War, but in 1908 the campaign was ad hoc and informal and therefore had little time or chance to succeed.

The second demographic blow to the non-Muslim communities in terms of the parliamentary elections concerned the taxpayer requirements of the Ottoman election law. Compared to other liberal parliamentary democracies at the time, the taxpaying requirement was completely in line with international norms, but nonetheless, its implementation—and the specific determination of what constituted a "taxpayer"—would have a disproportionate impact on the empire's non-Muslims. Early reports claimed that those who paid the mandatory military exemption tax for non-Muslims (*bedel-i askerî*) or the mandatory work-service tax (*'amaliyya*) would be included.[69] Since it was imposed collectively upon the non-Muslim communities, the military tax had a high degree of compliance and therefore would have resulted in the highest number of non-Muslims participating in the elections. It was also rumored that those paying the tax on the free liberal professions and crafts (*temettü*) would qualify for voting rights; this also would result in a high non-Muslim enfranchisement, given their overrepresentation in the white-collar liberal professions. In the end, however, it was decided that only those who paid property tax (*vergi*) on a home or store registered in their name would be eligible to vote.[70]

Empire-wide, this definition of taxpayer disenfranchised workers, agricultural laborers, nomads, and others. Because the Old City of Jerusalem was exempt from *vergi* tax, the Cabinet decided on September 16, 1908, that Jerusalemites who possessed real estate could vote. However, while recovering the rights of Jerusalem property owners in general, this restriction severely curtailed the voting rights of non-Muslim Jerusalemites in particular, since many of them rented apartments from landlords or from religious communal bodies. Christians in the Old City of Jerusalem rented out apartments owned by the Greek Orthodox and Armenian patriarchates, for example, and the Sephardi Jewish custom of subletting apartments limited their numbers as well.[71]

In short, relatively few Jews and Christians in late Ottoman Jerusalem were property owners. To give an example of the radical effect of basing electoral rights on property taxes rather than on the military-exemption taxes, according to one newspaper report, whereas Jerusalem had approximately ten thousand *bedel*-paying citizens, less than four thousand *vergi*-paying citizens were eventually given the right to vote. For the Jewish community of Jerusalem, the net decrease went from four thousand *bedel*-paying Jews to eleven hundred *vergi*-paying Jews.[72] The Jewish Ben-Yehuda family protested the decision in their newspaper *The Observation*, saying that the definition of taxes should be "defined by justice, not by law"; in their view, a just definition would include both the *'amaliyya* and the *bedel*, either of which would enable more Jewish citizens to take part in the election. Another Jewish merchant in Jaffa from the Matalon family suggested that all the Jewish *temettü* payers should protest the decision.[73]

As we can see in Table 3.1, Jews and Christians were the most negatively affected by the election rules and their voting numbers were diminished quite dramatically. Despite the fact that Christians and Jews together formed the majority of the Jerusalem Ottoman population (21,519, or 66 percent), due to property restrictions they were the minority in the 1908 elections. Of the approximately four thousand Jerusalem voters eligible to participate in the 1908 elections, the majority

Table 3.1. Jerusalem voters, 1908. Data from *Ha-Hashkafa*, August 19, 1908; *Ha-Hashkafa*, September 26, 1908; *Ha-Po'el ha-Ẓa'ir*, September 1908.

	Total	*Christians*	*Jews*	*Muslims*	*Notes*
Ottoman males	15,124	4,096	6,277	4,751	
% of male population		27.1%	41.5%	31.4%	
Right to vote	3,924	600	1,100	2,300	
% of electorate		15%	28%	58.6%	
Enfranchisement	**26%**	**14.6%**	**17.5%**	**48.4%**	This does not account for the division between men over and under age 25.

(approximately twenty-three hundred, 58.6 percent) were Muslims, followed by eleven hundred Jews (28 percent) and six hundred Christians (15 percent). In other words, there was a significant overrepresentation of Jerusalem's Muslim Ottoman citizens as voters and a notable underrepresentation of the city's Christian and Jewish citizen voters.[74]

The numbers are even starker when we consider the relative rate of enfranchisement: nearly half of all Muslim Ottoman men in Jerusalem had the right to vote in the elections, compared to 17.5 percent of Jerusalem's Ottoman Jews and only 14.6 percent of Jerusalem's Ottoman Christians. Although the statistics available to us for areas outside of Jerusalem are even less complete, in Jaffa, only 112 Jews and 800 Christians (3 percent and 23 percent, respectively, out of 3,463 total voters) had the right to vote.[75]

At the same time, the overall enfranchisement of Jerusalem's Ottoman citizens (8.3 percent of all Ottoman citizens, or 26 percent of Ottoman males in the city) placed this corner of the empire, at least, on par with its European contemporaries. In the 1890s, for example, about 7 percent of Austro-Hungarian urban citizens had the right to vote; after Italy's electoral reform of 1881, 6.9 percent of the population was qualified to vote.[76]

Although we do not have comprehensive population or voting data for the other districts in the province, looking at the statistics from the larger Jerusalem district in Table 3.2, we see that with the exception of Bethlehem, which had a large Christian population, the other electoral

Table 3.2. Jerusalem region electoral districts, 1908. Data from *Ha-Hashkafa*, September 26, 1908; *Ḥavaẓelet*, October 19, 1908.

Place	*Ottoman males*	*Enfranchisement*	*1st-level voters*	*2nd level*	*Notes*
Jerusalem	14,807	26.5%	3,924	6	
Surrounding villages	11,518	39%	4,500		
Bethlehem	8,290	27.5%	2,284		Including 49 villages.
Masafa	4,499	38%	1,712		In the *Salname* this district is listed as Safa; including 22 villages.
'Abawin	7,088	41%	2,934		Including 24 villages.
Jericho	293	45%	133		Including 20 villages.
SUBTOTAL	46,495	33%	15,487	26	

districts had relatively high levels of voter enfranchisement. Overall, almost a third of Ottoman males in the Jerusalem province had the right to vote in 1908.

Candidate Platforms

In addition to the nuts-and-bolts procedural aspects of the election, newspapers attempted to educate the Ottoman populace about the historic election's broader legislative and political aspects. Among the central concerns was the type of men to be elected to the parliament and the work that they proposed to carry out there, and as a result the press provided candidates with a platform to reach their would-be constituents, and provided other leading intellectuals and organizations the opportunity to publicly endorse or challenge candidates.

The press sought to identify those men who were representative of the new spirit of the times, in other words, liberals committed to the constitutional revolution, or, conversely, to warn readers of men who opposed the constitution. For example, a "Proud Damascene" revealed that at a public meeting of the Liberals' (Aḥrār) party in the city, most of the candidates were "men of the old government and partisans of tyranny," including men who had been denounced by the populace after the revolution. As well, he noted that the *Al-Shām* newspaper had published a list of the leaders of the 'Ilmiyya (Scholars') party, "which included men without knowledge or learning." There also were reports that in Nablus a party of anticonstitutional conservatives was organizing to participate in the elections.[77] And yet, Proud Damascene remained optimistic: "Dear reader, do not think the general elections will go like this—thank God the past gave useful lessons to the people."

Given this backdrop, the CUP selected candidates for its list in regions throughout the empire. In Beirut it endorsed Suleiman al-Bustani with a clear warning to the populace: "We must not take those who do not comprehend the meaning of personal liberty and freedom of deed and freedom of sentiment and thought and behavior." Likewise, one individual endorser, Zakaria Nasuli, urged his compatriots to vote wisely: "Every thinker should ask and consult on what reform is. It is a matter of the advanced nations and we the Ottomans will have a bright future and a happy era, God willing."[78] Other candidates declared their political identification with the new regime publicly, like Jurji Hurfush, who declared that "my feelings have long been 'liberty, equality, and fraternity,' and my sect has always been 'the love of homeland is an article of faith.'" Nasuli invoked this patriotic hadith and praised individuals who saw "homeland as a sacred word."[79]

Since they were to be "deputies of the nation," press editorials and candidate platforms supported the idea that the parliament needed men who were committed to public service. The empire needed men who understood the "public good [*al-maṣlaḥa al-ʿāmma*]," and who were committed to the "benefit of the state and the nation" and the "holy service to the nation and the beloved homeland" rather than to their own greedy interests.[80] The contemporary Ottoman discussion of "public good" utilized a term, *maṣlaḥa*, with a long tradition in Islamic civilization. As we will see, while at times this was a creative overlapping of multiple systems of meanings, at other times it would introduce new tensions to the electoral process.

In addition to notions of public service, candidates' professional experience, their familiarity with the laws and administration of the empire, and their knowledge of languages were all highlighted. For example, Suleiman al-Bustani was publicly praised by his friend Rafiq al-ʿAzm as "the best from among the men of the homeland who will represent the people." *Ottoman Union*'s editor emphasized al-Bustani's multidisciplinary knowledge as well as his mastery of Turkish, Arabic, Greek (both ancient and modern), English, French, German, and Italian.[81]

And yet, perhaps in reaction to the image of the Renaissance man as the gold standard for the Ottoman parliament, another candidate cautioned that the electorate needed to maintain realistic expectations. "Yes, the representatives should be of the highest morals and intelligence, with vast knowledge about the country and its condition and laws, liberal in his thinking and known for promoting the general interest over private interest. [But] some people expect the representative to be not a human but a king, attributing him with such traits as are only to be found [in fairy tales]."[82] Real patriots, liberal and experienced, should be chosen, not idealized. However, in contrast to the dynamic discussion taking place in some cities and provinces, other regions dispensed with the first-tier elections entirely, instead designating notables or tribal chiefs and further revealing the very real limits of reform and active citizenship in the early months after the revolution.[83]

In terms of the imagined work of the parliament, the platform of Salim al-Jaza'iri, running for a seat in Damascus, is illuminating. Al-Jaza'iri promised reforms along three lines: liberal political reforms, administrative restructuring, and economic and infrastructure development. In terms of political reforms, al-Jaza'iri committed himself to freedom of speech, action, and press, amending unjust clauses in the Ottoman law books (which he left tantalizingly vague), and reforming the military conscription laws "to be fair to the whole nation." Administratively, al-Jaza'iri proposed revamping the Ottoman military "so that it can defend the honor of the nation and homeland," eliminating unnecessary governmental positions and returning their salary to the treasury, and reforming the municipalities, provincial councils, police and gendarme "in accordance with the principles of the civilized countries."[84]

Al-Jaza'iri's economic and infrastructure development platform was much more extensive. He called for tax cuts to promote commerce and agriculture; redistribution of land "based on fairness and equality" between landowners and peasants according to cadastral surveys; promotion of river commerce; protection of domestic industry and promotion of exports; reformation of banking laws based on equality; promotion of trade via railroads and the sea; reformation of the imperial currency; standardization of weights and measures; reformation of the postal service; establishment of tribal schools "to enlighten their thought, to increase their numbers in civilization, and to settle them eventually"; and establishment of agricultural and vocational schools in every province. (Despite his ambitious and detailed platform, however, al-Jaza'iri failed in his parliamentary bid that fall.)

In Jerusalem, according to French consular reports, over one hundred men stood for election in the first tier, including twenty Christians and Jews. Alongside members of the city's leading Muslim families, including at least six members of the al-Khalidi family ('Uthman Zaki, Jamal al-Din, Jamil, Shawkat, Nazif, and Ruhi), three members of the al-Husayni family (Husayn Hashem, Kamil, and Sa'id), Rajib al-'Alami, and 'Uthman al-Nashashibi, candidates included members of the city's middle class—like Jewish schoolteacher David Yellin, Jewish bank official Yitzhak Levi, the Greek-Orthodox Dr. Photios, and the Roman Catholic lawyer Nejib Abousouan. In addition, apparently there was a political organization of peasants from the villages outside of Jerusalem.[85]

Unfortunately very little material survives about the election campaign of any of the Jerusalem candidates. Reports do indicate that the elections featured several elements of a modern political campaign, with stump speeches on the campaign trail and backroom negotiations for support. Khalil al-Sakakini mentioned in his memoirs a visit by two (unsuccessful) parliamentary candidates, Jamil and Nazif al-Khalidi, to discuss their platform and ask for support. Another report from the Ramle district indicated that political candidates went from village to village to attract electoral support.[86]

The Sectarian Prism II: The Millet in the Voting Booth

Empire-wide, voting took place over several weeks. One foreign traveler noted that the night before the election in Istanbul, town criers went throughout the city's neighborhoods accompanied by drummers reminding voters that "it was their duty as good citizens of a free country to go on the morrow to the appointed places and drop their voting papers in the ballot boxes."[87] Various other sources describe the day of the elections in festive terms: processions were led by units of the Ottoman military band playing patriotic songs with infantry troops lending a dignified aura; after them were carriages draped with Ottoman flags transporting the voting urn and public officials; and religious leaders, citizens, and schoolchildren marched alongside en route to the voting site. In one Istanbul district, Muslim, Greek, and Armenian schoolgirls dressed in white and adorned with flowers stood next to the voting urn to "protect" it with their unity and purity.[88]

Voting took place in the courtyards of select neighborhood mosques, churches, and schools, likely chosen because they could accommodate sizable crowds. Local elections commission members sat close by to verify the voters' eligibility. In some locales, there were complaints about eligible voters being turned away deliberately, and these accusations took a sectarian turn. For example, in Istanbul, one foreign observer reported that Greeks complained that "they were treated like ticket-of-leave men

Figure 3.2. Voting at Galatasaray Imperial Lycée (Istanbul), 1908. A Muslim shaykh and Greek Orthodox and Armenian priests are at the center table; also present are government clerks and members of the local elections commission, who were responsible for checking voter eligibility, and soldiers to maintain order. Orlando Calumeno Collection and Archives. Used by permission.

Figure 3.3. The opening of the Chamber of Deputies, December 1908. Delegates' clothing signified their background and status, whether the robe and turban of the Muslim religious scholars (ulema), the suit and tarbush of the "gentlemen effendis", or the robe and headdress of the Arab tribal leaders. Orlando Calumeno Collection and Archives. Used by permission.

reporting themselves to the police. They were subjected to endless cross-examinations as to their age, business, and qualifications, the accuracy of their replies was disputed, and the validity of their certificates was denied. So, under one pretext or another, many of them were excluded from the polls."[89] In contrast, another foreign observer who was admittedly unsympathetic to the Greek community accused them of committing voter fraud by using the documents of dead men or émigrés, or of voting more than once. He also accused the Greeks of adding unnecessary drama to the elections, causing riots in Izmir and Istanbul at the behest of the Greek government in Athens. "It was noticeable that when a man of another race was not permitted to register his vote on account of some irregularity in his papers or other disqualification, he went away quietly, whereas the Greeks in like circumstances stayed to protest and bluster until they formed crowds of disappointed voters who blocked the way to the urns, and by so doing considerably delayed the course of the election."[90]

In the Jerusalem district, voting took place over several weeks in October 1908. The city of Jerusalem had six electoral districts, based more or less according to adjacent neighborhoods, and voting sites were located in each of the districts. After two weeks, the winners of Jerusalem's first round of elections, who would become second-level electors, were announced, consisting of four Muslims and two Jews: Shawkat al-Khalidi, Ishaq Abu Sa'ud, Taher 'Umar, Jamil al-Husayni, David Yellin, and Yitzhak Levi.[91] Many first-level voters—if they bothered to show up at the polls at all—had displayed confessional loyalty at the voting booths. Indeed, surviving fliers from several Jewish electoral districts indicate that Jews were expected to support other Jews; members of the Jewish community were alarmed by the possibility that the deep rivalry between two leading Jewish politicians, Yitzhak Levi and Albert Antébi, could split the Jewish vote. Such appears to be the case in a heavily Christian district where Jurji Zakaria and Todor Yanko split the votes between them.[92] For their part, the Christians displayed the weakest political weight and unity, and not a single Christian candidate made it to the second round. Even in districts that were evenly split demographically between Muslims and Christians, the Muslim candidates succeeded in winning.

In other words, as we see in Table 3.3, despite their absolute demographic majority in only one district of Jerusalem (1), the city's Muslims yielded disproportionate electoral weight in three other districts (2, 3, and 5), displacing Christian majorities in one district (2) and a Jewish majority in two other districts (3 and 5). Stated differently, in districts 2 and 4 an apparent Christian demographic lead did not correspond to electoral weight; likewise for the Jews in districts 3 and 5.

At the second level, it became even clearer that without establishing alliances with more powerful candidates, non-Muslim candidates had little chance of influence; as a result, negotiations and agreements across communal lines became more important. One member of the Jaffa Jewish community noted that while the Jews from Jaffa and the surrounding Jewish colonies supported Levi's candidacy, their numbers were too insignificant in the current electoral system. "The chances for the election of a Jewish delegate are quite minimal, according to the present mode of election and taking into account the small number of the Jewish voters, meanwhile we must unite forces for a Jewish candidate and seek to prevent a splitting of the Jewish vote."[93] In order to help Levi's chances, Yellin dropped out of active consideration (his Ottoman Turkish was also considered not good enough), but Levi's long-time political rival, Albert Antébi, stubbornly refused to mobilize support on Levi's behalf. As well, it seems that some votes were bought by the Zionist movement for their preferred candidate, although they turned out to be inconsequential in the final count.[94]

Numerous accusations and complaints briefly swirled around the election. 'Uthman al-Nashashibi, one of the top three vote earners in Jerusalem, was accused of securing false votes and thus was disqualified from

Table 3.3. Jerusalem electoral districts level-1 results, 1908. Elections data from *Ḥavaẓelet*, October 21, 1908; *Ha-Ẓvi*, October 9, 1908; *Ha-Po'el ha-ẓa'ir*, September 1908. Census data from Schmelz, "The Population of Jerusalem's Urban Neighborhoods According to the Ottoman Census of 1905." District divisions partly from Arnon, "Mifkedei ha-ukhlusiya bi-Yerushalayim be-shalhei ha-tkufah ha-'Otomanit."

District	*Candidates*[1]	*Neighborhoods*	*No. voters*	*Ottoman citizens in district*	*Christian %*	*Jewish %*	*Muslim %*
1	Rajib al- 'Alami (M)	Bab Huta, Sa'adia, al-Wad	716	8,445	14	14	71
2	'Uthman Zaki al-Khalidi (M); Israel Dov Frumkin (J)	Bab al-'Amud, Nassara	789	3,836	83	1.3	15.4
3	Jurji Zakaria (C); Todor Yanko (C); Jamal al-Din al-Khalidi (M); Haim Aharon Valero (J)	Silsila, Sharaf, Sidna Da'ud, Bak'a, Bab al-Khalil	687	8,313	16.5	53.9	29.6
4	Tanyus Effendi (C); Muhammad Nimr (M); Yitzhak Levi (J); Albert Antébi (J); Shahabi	Talbiyah, Mamila, Manshiyya, Even Israel (Sarafiyya); Mas'udiya, Musrara	525	2,992	60.7	19.6	19.6
5	Rahamim Mizrachi (J); Jamal al-Khalidi (M)	Y'aqubiyya, Isra'iliyya, Shaykh Jarrah, Halabiyya, Tawahin, Raheliyya	599	5,193	1.9	76	22.1
6	David Yellin (J); Jiryis Bador (C); Musa Shafiq (M)	Mahane Yehuda, Me'ah She'arim (Tal-lul al-Massaben), Bukhariya, Beit Israel (Massaben), Birka, Shifa, Habash, Ju-deida, 'Ukasha	586	3,729	9.9	84.5	5.5

1 In order to declare candidacy one needed the signed support of 100 voters. Other candidates included : Jurji Zakaria, Todor Yanko, Nejuib Azoury, Nazif al-Khalidi, Jamil al-Khalidi, Neguib Abousouan, Husayn Salim al-Husayni, Dr. Photios, 'Uthman al-Nashashibi, Shawkat al-Khalidi, Yishaq Abu Sa'ud, Taher 'Umar, Kamil al-Husayni, Ruhi al-Khalidi, and Sa'id al-Husayni. Akram Musallam, ed., *Yawmiyaat Khalil al-Sakakini*; Consulate General of France in Palestine (G. Gueyrand) to the Directorate of Political and Commercial Affairs, Subdirectorate of the Levant, October 8, 1908. MAEF, film 132.

the election. Another complaint was registered that the temporary deputy governor in Gaza, Hafiz Bey, had pressured voters in his district to elect him to the parliament.[95] In addition, a ministorm erupted when one Jewish newspaper, *The Deer* (also of the Ben-Yehuda family), published a negative report in its Arabic-French supplement about Sa'id al-Husayni, calling him an anti-Semite and a fanatic. The article reportedly "caused indignation among the voters and peasants"; complaints were lodged against the paper by al-Nashashibi, and two additional influential families demanded right of reply in the local Greek newspaper. The Jewish newspaper was forced to publish a retraction on October 23, where the correspondent Mendel Kremer wrote that "Sa'id Effendi has only ever been kind to us [the Jews], and he will be an honorable representative in the parliament." In fact, an internal report of the Zionist organization had concluded that while al-Husayni was an enemy of Zionism and of the immigration of foreign Jews to Palestine, he was no "Judenfeind" and had respect for Ottoman Jews.[96]

In the end, election results for the Jerusalem province were in favor of two Jerusalem notables and one Jaffan notable, all Muslims, all members of the Palestinian urban elite who had traditionally been involved in Ottoman government and Islamic religious offices: Ruhi al-Khalidi (with sixty second-tier electoral votes total); Sa'id al-Husayni (with fifty-nine electoral votes); and Hafiz al-Sa'id (with forty-seven total electoral votes).[97] With the exception of Hafiz al-Sa'id, the Palestinian representatives were relatively young, in their thirties and early forties, following the trend established by the Arab provinces in the 1876 parliament to send younger members of prominent local families.[98] All three had been government officials, but al-Khalidi, the former Ottoman consul in Bordeaux, France, was the only one of the three considered a "true liberal" ideologically in tune with the spirit of the revolution. Al-Husayni had been head of the education division in the Jerusalem provincial government, and al-Sa'id had served in various provincial offices throughout Palestine. In northern Palestine, two religious scholars were elected: Shaykh Ahmad al-Khammash of Nablus and Shaykh As'ad Shuqayri of 'Akka.[99]

The election results provide further evidence for the very deep ties between urban centers and their outlying hinterlands, as well as for the resilience of patronage networks fashioned by urban notables and rural leaderships. As one historian notes, "Ordinary voters deferred to community leaders who would presumably better judge the interests of the community." Furthermore, the two-tier system itself "preserved and reinforced patronage relationships and precluded the election of candidates truly representative of the common people."[100] In other words, while self-made individuals like lawyers, doctors, and journalists could and did

Figure 3.4. Jerusalem MP Ruhi al-Khalidi. Khalidi, the former Ottoman consul in Bordeaux, France, argued that Islam required political liberalism. From *Osmanlı mebûsları.*

run for election, oftentimes in the end those who were elected had the backing of family connections and strong social and political networks, in addition to years of government service, behind them.

The Sectarian Prism III: Ethnic Politics

Despite the Ottomanist moment represented by the parliamentary elections, it is clear that some individuals and groups within the empire expected the parliament to be a platform, not simply for broader Ottoman reforms, but more important, for the airing of communal agendas. This was expressed by one Zionist correspondent for the Jerusalem Jewish newspaper *The Deer*, Ya'kov Friman, who argued:

> The people, through its representatives, can turn to the government and demand the reforms needed for the country's material and spiritual elevation. Not only that, but each nation that lives in the empire can send its representatives to parliament to demand its rights living in a united empire. . . . The more complete freedom will give each of the peoples room to develop in its own communities and according to its inclination. Political unity of the peoples of Ottomania does not mean assimilation: it does not mean to forget one's future and turn into someone else. This is harmful to the nation and does not contribute to the public good.[101]

A similar view seems to have existed within the Greek Orthodox community, many of whom (including the patriarch) had pressed for proportional representation. In fact, unhappy with the elections results, thousands of Greeks protested the opening of the parliament demanding that the elections be voided in areas where Greeks were not elected; reflecting the lingering arrogance born of the Capitulations, one Greek who was arrested argued, "I am entitled to vote not because I am a citizen, but because I am a Greek."[102]

For those segments of the Ottoman population and for some European observers, the parliamentary results were worrying evidence of the Turkish, Muslim orientation of the new government. Of the parliament's 260 members, 214 (82 percent) were Muslims, 43 (16.5 percent) were Christians, and 4 were Jews. Ethnically, native Turkish speakers comprised 46 percent of the parliament (119 members), followed by Arabic-speakers at 28 percent of the parliament (72 members), as well as smaller numbers of Greek, Albanian, Kurdish, Serbian, Bulgarian, and Romanian speakers.[103] A visiting French deputy complained about the overall underrepresentation of Greeks and Armenians, starkest in the province of Edirne, which did not have a single non-Muslim among its nine elected representatives despite a sizable non-Muslim population.[104]

As the historian Hasan Kayalı has noted in a different region of the empire, "particularly after 1908, electoral politics animated and politicized protonationalist movements among the Muslims, while it also crystallized competing multiethnic agendas."[105] While it is undoubtedly true that certain segments of the Ottoman population in some parts of the empire saw the elections as an opportunity for ethnic self-determination, we should be careful not to assign too much causal influence to the ethnic fragmentation of the empire. In 1908, it is clear, the special path viewed for the Arab provinces, more distant from imperial rule in Istanbul, was a question of decentralization rather than ethnic self-determination. MP Ruhi al-Khalidi said as much in his departure speech; after thanking the crowd for their support of the "holy homeland and freedom," al-Khalidi laid out the broad-based reforms to be carried out through the parliament, first and foremost to lighten the "imperial burden" in the provinces in favor of decentralization. The desired reforms according to al-Khalidi included implementing an ambitious public works program, bringing running water, planting trees, increasing life expectancy, opening roads and train lines, expanding the educational system, forming new commercial agreements, and establishing a people's bank—all of which are administrative and infrastructure policy issues rather than a question of identity politics or self-determination.[106]

Indeed, residents had very specific expectations that their representatives would bring utility and good works to the province. The editor of *Jerusalem*, Jurji Habib Hanania, appealed to his new representatives:

> And now, oh gentlemen . . . yes you will be in the parliament not only as representatives of Jerusalem but rather as representatives of the entire Ottoman nation. I want to remind you in the name of our beloved city Jerusalem, . . . do not forget that the future of Jerusalem demands [much] from you two and we depend on you to teach the people our duties.[107]

At the same time, as we have seen, the 1908 election did carry with it an element of communal rivalry. After the experience of the first elections, it was apparent that the Jewish and Christian communities were ill-prepared to exercise their political rights.[108] Christians and Jews were electorally weak due to the low numbers of Ottoman citizens as well as the low number of property taxpayers in both groups, they were disorganized and factionalized communally, and they were unwilling or unable to successfully build alliances across communal lines. In Levi's final analysis of the case of the Palestinian Jewish communities, "If we had known our own weaknesses and admitted them, then it would have been only half as bad, because we would have tried to team up with the other peoples. However we are convinced of the fact that Palestine comes to us as our birth right and we are the worse for it!"[109]

The Hebrew newspaper *The Deer* saw the elections from the outset as a zero-sum game, referring to them on one occasion as "the war between the nations." This would seem to be born out by a brief note in *The Deer*'s report of the public farewell, which differed in significant ways from that which appeared in *Jerusalem*. In contrast to the Ottomanist, universalist portrait depicted by *Jerusalem*, *The Deer* emphasized that the majority of those gathered were Muslims and that there was a distinctly pro-Arab sentiment in the air.[110] According to the paper, 'Abd al-Salam Kamal had called on the newly elected members of parliament to defend the Arabs' rights, followed by David Yellin, who spoke of the corresponding demands of the Jewish community. Afterward, the crowd fired pistols, waved swords, and cheered for "the Arabs."

Whether or not *The Deer*'s account is accurate is almost immaterial, for it reflects the ways in which the elections marked the entrance of a sanctioned sectarian element into postrevolutionary Ottoman politics that directly challenged the civic Ottomanist project. Rather than solely relying on their geographically designated representatives, non-Muslim groups imposed a neo-*millet* structure onto the parliament through which they sought help from members of parliament and senators belonging to their own ethno-religious groups. For example, the Jews of Palestine repeatedly appealed to the four Jewish members of parliament on various issues of particularistic Jewish interest, despite the fact that these representatives were from Salonica, Izmir, Istanbul, and Baghdad.[111] In addition to the Jewish members of parliament, the chief rabbi was another central address the Jews turned to for aid in dealing with the authorities, further illustrative of a neo-*millet*–civic hybridity.[112]

KHALIDI, HUSAYNI AND SA'ID GO TO ISTANBUL

Despite these serious issues, the election controversies were quickly put to rest and the three southern Palestinian members of parliament were given elaborate populist sendoffs that celebrated the unity of Jerusalem's electorate in November 1908. Indeed, although the 1908 Ottoman parliamentary election left much to be desired in terms of absolute democratic as well as relative sectarian enfranchisement, it still marked a milestone in achieving local rights and reaffirming participation in the imperial endeavor. As one historian has written about emerging elections in nineteenth-century Latin America, "the rhetoric of representation displayed around the elections also had symbolic and ideological effects that contributed to the circulation and reformulation of republican and democratic ideas on citizenship among the population."[113]

In the Ottoman Empire, the most significant feature of republican citizenship was the entrenchment of the nation as the leading political actor. The revolutionary atmosphere of *ḥurriyya* had succeeded in overthrowing the supreme authority of the sultan, on the one hand, and the political passivity of the nation, on the other. According to the Ottoman electorate, the members of parliament were their agents, their representatives, with a mission to act on behalf of the nation, to fulfill the hopes and promises of the revolution itself. At the Jerusalem celebration sending off al-Khalidi and al-Husayni, David Yellin, himself a failed candidate for parliament, addressed the crowd ("O Ottoman citizens!") and new representatives: "O elected ones, you were selected from among the candidates, not only because you promised to bring reform to the province, which others did as well, but of those who are men of thoughts and men of deeds, it is our fortune that you are of the latter. We collectively hope that your love for the homeland and your famous readiness will enable us to gain together . . . the improvements necessary for our holy land."[114]

Yellin closed his speech with a play on the names of the representatives: "we collectively hope that 'Ruhi' will revive our spirits. And 'Sa'id' will make us happy. And 'Hafiz' will protect our rights. Long live the delegates and long live the homeland and long live the constitution and the basic law!"

This understanding of the role of the deputies to act on behalf of the will of the nation was reiterated by newly elected MP Ruhi al-Khalidi: "We are going to aid the Ottoman nation irrespective of its differences in religions and languages for this is the rule of law and this law belongs to the nation. . . . Laws and regulations are an expression of the will of the nation [*irādat al-umma*], which is [carried out] by means of its representatives according to the rule of law." Al-Khalidi went on to explain how the parliament would operate, what the role of the political parties would be, and how the liberals' first mission should be to reform the Basic Law so that the sultan and his reactionary cronies would not be able to dissolve the parliament or harass its work, as they had the first parliament in 1877–78. "Even if [the reactionaries] give an order and tell them 'Get out, O gentlemen, from this council,' [the liberals] will answer with one voice and a rushing heart: 'We entered this council by the will of the nation, and we will not leave it except through the force of arms.'"[115]

Khalidi's invocation of the "will of the nation [*irādat al-umma*]" was significant.[116] Not only does it reinforce seeing the new Ottoman citizenry as supportive of the revolution and seizing it as their own, but it also indicates the bonds of reciprocity articulated between the citizenry (electorate) and its elected officials. Government appointees may not have a direct loyalty to the people, but the elected representatives must. Their office and their legitimacy come directly from the people. This contract was reiterated by the second MP, Sa'id al-Husayni, who stated briefly: "I am certain that you are following and expecting from us that great deeds and services will come back to you and to us for the good and to protect you and us from every harm, so have full confidence in us and we will remain in your good opinions, God willing."[117]

Beyond Jerusalem, the broader Arabic press took a similar stance. *The Crescent* congratulated the newly elected representatives, saying: "We congratulate the honorable representatives for they were bestowed with the trust of the nation in their learning and the loyalty of their Ottomanism, and they show the goodness of the sons of the homeland and it is no wonder that the nation ties its hopes in them and entrusts them with its political and administrative affairs."[118]

The day of the opening of the parliament was a national holiday empire-wide. City officials were instructed to fire a 101-cannon salute, to give government employees the day off, and to aid the populace in decorating the streets and buildings for the festivities.[119] In Jerusalem and Jaffa, houses and stores were decorated with flags, people wandered the streets shouting in support of liberty, and an official ceremony was held in the military courtyard with speeches from notable locals. The Jerusalem celebration was organized by the mayor, Faidi al-'Alami. The ceremony opened with an invocation by the military imam, then a long speech by a young officer in which he recounted Midhat Pasha's efforts to write the constitution as well as the army's efforts to restore it. Speeches were given by the poet Is'af al-Nashashibi and Yusuf al-Mu'allam, the deputy to the Maronite patriarch, both of whom emphasized the need to fight against religious fanaticism and to promote brotherhood in the Ottoman nation.

Another speaker, Eftim Mushabbak, proclaimed that the parliament represented not only the nation's first step but, indeed, its very rebirth. His sentiments bordered on the utopian, again reiterating the tropes of stark dichotomy between pre- and post-1908 articulated in the revolutionary period.

> On the 11th of Tammuz a light shone upon us not from the sky [but from] the capital of the empire—the light of the holy constitution, grantor of justice and freedom and brotherhood and equality. . . . Today . . . all our faith has come true and all our hope has been justified. . . . This day is the true beginning of the life of the Ottoman nation. On this day all the nations of the earth will envy us, and on this day the sky and the earth and the angels and the prophets and the gods will

bless the free Ottoman nation. . . . On this day hearts rejoice together, liberal sons of the Ottoman nation and their souls are invigorated.[120]

For their part, the people also had a responsibility in the new political order. Mushabbak informed his compatriots that they would no longer be allowed to be passive beneficiaries or inactive bystanders, but had to take an active and informed role in the country's future.

Today the mute has begun to speak and the deaf hears and even the blind sees. Before the day ends the Ottoman nation must open its eyes and ears and look in its entirety toward that beloved, venerable council to hear and see what is published from it and about it. Today the Ottoman nation together must increase the readers of newspapers so they can know what the representatives are doing and what happens in the parliament.[121]

The ceremony was an orchestrated demonstration of the unity through diversity of the Ottoman nation. We have already seen that Muslims, Christians, and Jews addressed the crowd. As well, ethno-linguistic diversity was given a platform: Ithnasa Effendi Bendazi, the editor of the Greek-language newspaper *The Palestine Herald* (*Bashīr Filasṭīn*), also spoke in Greek; after him, several Armenian schoolchildren gave rousing, patriotic speeches in Turkish and Arabic, as did a Jewish student from Aleppo. As another newspaper proclaimed, "Everyone from all the elements of the empire is drenched in love of the homeland and drinks from it."[122]

In fact, the spirit of national unity was so strong that the American consul in Beirut reported to his superiors:

It struck me as very evident that the sentiments which inspired the extraordinary demonstrations, during the last week of July, in honor of the Constitution, still burn within the hearts of the Ottomans, and that the process of emancipation has suffered but slight interruption during the intervening months of meditation. Mohammedans, Christians and Jews still fraternize, and the misgivings of the cynic or of the chicken-hearted have not proved well founded.[123]

Rashid Rida, who spoke at three different events in his native Lebanon marking the opening of the parliament, also conveyed the sense that this was a seminal moment in strengthening the bonds of the Ottoman nation. Furthermore, the active citizenship that was represented by the opening of the parliament bolstered the ideas of an imperial public good and shared interest of the Ottomans. At the general celebration in Beirut's central square, in what was his most rhetorical and optimistic speech of the three, Rida informed his countrymen:

Today you became a nation, and how beautiful is that expression in my mouth, how dear to my heart, yes on this day it is correct to apply the phrase "nation" to you. . . . On this day the Muslim and the Christian and the Jew and others will celebrate, and the Turk and the Arab and the Albanian and Greek and Kurd and Armenian will celebrate. And the Ottomans in the Ottoman lands as well as those in foreign lands will celebrate, they will celebrate gathered in mixing together because it is a holiday for the whole nation. Look at this celebration, where the political rulers and administrators and *qadi* and army officers and others from the government are mixed with Islamic scholars and Christian priests and the rest of the trades of the nation, from agriculture to industry and merchants, workers, and school students.[124]

For Rida, as for Mushabbak and countless other Ottomans, the opening of the parliament was a signal that the Ottoman nation had become "a ruler of itself [*ḥākima li-nafsiha*]": the nation, not the sultan, not the grand vizier, certainly not the members of parliament themselves, is "the highest authority."[125] In his speeches to the Ottoman Club and the CUP branch, Rida addressed the fears of liberals and reformers in the empire that the revolutionary reforms would prove short-lived. Rida argued that in contrast to the period of the first parliament, which was a pliant body, the nation was now better educated, more informed, and had the army and the CUP to help defend the constitution.

This idea of the nation as the source of legitimacy and loyalty would be taken up by the sultan's critics, who refused to view liberty as being "given by the sultan," for that would mean it was granted rather than earned, conditional rather than contractual. Is'af al-Nashashibi, the young poet, gave an eloquent speech at the Jerusalem celebrations in December 1908 in which he sought to overturn the notion that *ḥurriyya* had been given or granted; rather, al-Nashashibi proclaimed that liberty was both man's natural state *and* the hard-won birthright of the Ottoman people. While it had been withheld from the people in the past, now the nation would not allow such a thing to happen again: "O Ottomans, O Patriots. . . . Ottomania sold her soul in order to buy our lives. Great were her deeds, and [God] have mercy on their spilled blood, as the precious from among our heroes were killed. Know that [the first man] was created free, and he lived free, and he died free. And you see that Allah is more just than that mankind should carry two heavy burdens—the burden of life and its evils, and the burden of tyranny and its misery."[126]

Likewise the Izmir-based Jewish poet Reuven Qattan echoed the claims that the nation was not awarded liberty out of good will, but rather it had conquered liberty at the same time that liberty was also a sacred, natural right of mankind.[127] In other words, if liberty was both God-given and man-won, the sultan—who was, after all, "flesh and blood just like you"—had a dwindling and diminished role in the New Era.[128]

THE FAILED COUP OF 1909 AND THE "LOVE OF LIBERTY"

Only months after the opening of the parliament and despite the fact that Rashid Rida had assured his compatriots that any danger to the constitutional regime would come from outside the empire, not from within, an anticonstitutional coup was carried out by lower-level soldiers and religious students. Shots were fired in the parliament building, representatives were assassinated, newspaper offices were ransacked, and the leading liberals of the capital briefly went into hiding and exile.

In response, tens of thousands of Ottomans empire-wide took to the streets crying, "The constitution is in danger!"[129] In Jerusalem and Jaffa, thousands gathered to demonstrate in front of the government buildings, satisfied only once the senior government officials emerged to swear on the Qur'an that they would "remain true" to the constitution. The local customs officer threatened to stop sending customs taxes to the capital until the new regime promised to uphold the constitution, while another account noted that Palestinians marched to the tax office themselves and declared they would not send in their taxes until the constitutional government was restored. Residents sent telegrams to the relevant offices in the capital, organized into local militias, and threw their full support behind the activities of the CUP seeking to return to power.[130]

In less than two weeks, the segments of the army that were loyal to the CUP succeeded in crushing the coup and took control of the capital again. The local press response was ecstatic: "The era of despotism was escaped, and liberty and progress face Turkey [*sic*] now," crowed the Judeo-Spanish paper *Liberty*. The newspaper reports described the scenes of popular joy that recalled the early celebrations after the revolution itself—music, festivities, and all-around admiration for the CUP, "which for the second time managed to save the Ottoman people." *Jerusalem* triumphantly declared: "Now we have seen that the love of freedom [*ḥubb al-ḥurriyya*] is like a great flood flattening the mountains and shaking the earth, and nothing in the world can stop it on its way."[131]

Once the dust of the so-called March Events had settled, the sultan was held personally responsible.[132] Several newspapers called on Abdülhamid to resign voluntarily; when he did not, he was deposed. Previous sultans had been deposed throughout Ottoman history, and Abdülhamid II himself ascended the throne on the heels of the deposition of his uncle. However, what was significant about his own dethronement was the way in which ideas about political legitimacy were intertwined with constitutional rule. Decades earlier the anti-colonial pan-Islamist activist Jamal al-Din al-Afghani had warned the Ottoman sultan and the Qajar shah that their days were numbered in a constitutional regime. "The nation, crowning him on that oath, tells him that the crown will stay on his head as long as he loyally upholds the constitution. If he should break his oath and betray the constitution of the nation either his head would lose the crown or his crown would lose the head."[133] In the spring of 1909 that threat was actualized with the blessings of the religious establishment.

The *şeyhülislam*'s religious ruling (*fetva emine*) which approved the deposing of Abdülhamid incorporated religious and civic models of legitimacy, bringing in the notions of just rule and public good as well as the will of the people:

QUESTION: What should be done with a Commander of the Faithful who has suppressed books and important dispositions of the Sheriat law; who forbids the reading of and burns such books; who wastes public money for improper purposes; who, without legal authority, kills, imprisons, and tortures his subjects, and commits other tyrannical acts; who, after he has bound himself by oath to amend, violates such oath, and persists in sowing discord, so as to disturb the public peace, thus occasioning bloodshed? From various provinces the news comes that the population has deposed him; and it is shewn that to maintain him is manifestly dangerous, and his deposition advantageous. Under such conditions is it permissible for the actual governing body to decide as seems best upon his abdication or deposition?

RULING: It is permissible [*olur*].[134]

As well, much of the Ottoman popular press fully supported the deposition of the sultan. The Islamic reformist newspapers *The Lighthouse* and *Crescent* (*Hilal*) approved of the *fetva-emine* on the grounds that Abdülhamid II, as an unjust ruler, had not ruled according to Islamic principles. *The Lighthouse* fully supported the *fetva* and gave its own extensive textual support for the decision, and *Crescent* opined: "Let each true Mussulman [*sic*] rest convinced that, in virtue of the Sheriat and the holy laws of the Koran, Abd-ul-Hamid can never have been the real Caliph of the Believers. All those that can see in Abd-ul-Hamid the real Caliph are quite ignorant of the laws of the Sheriat or else act in opposition to them."[135]

When the sultan's half-brother Mehmet Reşat (also known as Muhammad V) was installed as sultan in April 1909, the office of the sultan was transformed into yet another element fully subject to the nation itself. In his formal remarks upon ascending the throne, the sultan reportedly addressed his fellow citizens, saying that he hoped to work for the nation's success and happiness, and that "since the nation has already chosen me today," he would serve it faithfully.[136] In fact, by that point, a mere nine months after the revolution, that was more or less the understanding shared by many of his fellow citizens. In terms that would have been unprecedented before, David Yellin pronounced the new sultan "is not the one who grants freedom to the nation (as if *ḥurriyya* is a thing to be bought or granted), but it is the nation who granted the sultan its voluntary compliance."[137]

Part-invitation, part-warning, the newspaper *Sabah* in Istanbul informed the new sultan of the duties of a constitutional monarch: "The constitution forbids absolutism and the arbitrary will of the sovereign. But it does not prevent him from working for the greatness of his nation. He is *millet babasi*, "the father of the nation," and it behooves him to act as one. The despot governs through fear, the constitutional monarch governs through affection. It is his duty to earn the affection of the nation which is master of his destinies."[138] This radical view had taken divergent notions of "liberty" to challenge the sultan's legitimacy, one important step in the transformation of the relationship between Ottoman citizens and their government.

CHAPTER FOUR

The Mouthpiece of the People

There is perhaps no greater marker of the power and importance of the press in the Ottoman revolution than the fact that during the spring 1909 counterrevolutionary coup—essentially ten days of rioting in Istanbul by low-level soldiers and *softajis* (religious seminary students) who were reportedly paid off with gold from the sultan's coffers—the offices of two newspapers, the official CUP organ *Şura-yı Ümmet* and the pro-CUP *Tanin*, were ransacked and destroyed. One journalist who published regularly in *Tanin*, the noted female author Halide Edib Adıvar, described days spent in hiding until her daring nocturnal escape on a steamer bound for Alexandria.[1]

In the capital and in the provinces, the multilingual press had become a central site for an emergent revolutionary public sphere whose primary task was the deeply public process of endowing Ottomanness with meaning. Rather than passively recording events or words or simply transmitting information and knowledge, newspapers played a much more productive role in constituting and articulating the public imperial self. Newspaper editors had very strong ideas that they conveyed to their readers with missionary zeal. The Beirut-based newspaper *Ottoman Union*, for example, saw itself as the mouthpiece *of* the people, reflecting their "authentic" wishes and desires, at the same time that it took it upon itself to be a mouthpiece *to* the people, educating and enlightening them to the requirements of a changing world.[2] In other words, the press would serve as the handmaiden of the revolution, carrying out its aims of reforming and reviving the Ottoman Empire by showing its readers—the Ottoman public—what it meant to "be Ottoman" at a time of rapidly changing political and social realities.[3]

In order to accomplish this, first and foremost the press consciously took upon itself the task of promoting Ottoman unity and citizenship practices across ethnic, religious, and linguistic boundaries. As *Ottoman*

Union stated in that same article, "The Ottoman state is comprised of many groups and it is incumbent upon us to strive to publish newspapers composed of the elite of the groups present in the Ottoman lands until true synthesis [*al-tā'līf al-ḥaqīqī*] and true devotion are attained, and until the editors will possess the trust of the people and their consent." We have also seen, in the previous chapter, that the press played a self-appointed role in educating Ottomans to their new political and social roles as imperial citizens.

Newspapers appeared in Ottoman Turkish, Arabic, Greek, Armenian, Ladino, Bulgarian, and Hebrew, to name just a few of the languages of the empire. However, these newspapers did not represent autonomous publics: some readers were undoubtedly multilingual and had access to newspapers in several languages, and many newspapers translated articles that had appeared in other local languages for the benefit of their broader readership. These translations could be simply informative or aimed at serving the Ottomanist vision, but they just as easily could promote intercommunal rivalry. As we will see in the Palestinian press, complaints about the relative standing or privileges of another community found their way to a large number of readers and listeners through the press. As a result, the press in this period served not only to help "imagine" the community in universally inclusive imperial terms, but also increasingly in exclusionary sectarian and ethnic terms. Stated differently, at the same time that the press was a vehicle for creating and underscoring new forms of centripetal solidarity, it *also* became a new platform for expressions of centrifugal tensions and rivalries.

MAKING NEW READERS

Even before the advent of the press, Ottoman residents had access to numerous sources of information as well as sites for public discourse, whether it be the neighborhood crier or written announcements posted on city walls and squares, formal announcements in mosques, synagogues, and churches, or informal gossip in coffeehouses, markets, and social gatherings.[4] By the second half of the nineteenth century, the emergence of a semi-independent press, the rise in education, new civil-society institutions, and the role of the city in creating an urban citizenry all contributed to the undeniable existence of a vibrant public sphere of discourse and debate in many corners of the empire.[5] The first independent newspaper in Ottoman Turkish had appeared in 1860; by 1876 a total of forty-seven papers were being published in Istanbul alone—thirteen in Ottoman Turkish, nine in Armenian and Greek each, seven in French, three in Bulgarian, two in Hebrew and English each, one in German, and one in Arabic.[6]

It is impossible to overstate the impact of this first wave of press and publishing on the intellectual and social life of the Ottoman Empire. We have already seen in Chapter One the important role that early newspapers played as a platform for the opposition of the Young Ottomans. Newspapers like *Vakit* and *Istikbal* published daring commentaries on the sovereignty of the people and the contingency of the sultan, and the emerging satirical press also contributed to fostering debate and political criticism, at least until the 1864 and 1867 press laws clamped down on this sort of journalism and forced it abroad. Despite growing government censorship, the early newspapers seem to have enjoyed vast popularity; one estimate places the circulation figures for the important paper *Tasvir-i Efkar* at twenty thousand. More important to the circulation of ideas than individual subscribers, however, were the dozens of bookshops and "reading rooms" (*kiraathaneler*) in Istanbul, where educated men could access and discuss the latest publications.[7]

This vibrant life of the mind was not limited to the imperial capital alone. Salonica, Izmir, and Beirut were also important centers for publishing, and the circulation of journals as well as books was widespread. Literate Palestinian men also tapped into these broader imperial and regional currents; as partial evidence, one scholar has counted over one hundred letters to the editor from Palestine to two different Cairene newspapers in the last decade of the nineteenth century alone. These readers accessed the press and other publications either by subscription or, much more likely, through important urban institutions like the Khalidi Library or the library of the Al-Aqsa Mosque in Jerusalem, both of which had holdings of dozens of regional newspapers and magazines, and thousands of books. At the same time, even the *shaykh* of the tiny Palestinian village of Yarka, Marzuq Ma'addi, had subscriptions to at least four different newspapers in the 1880s and 1890s, underscoring the fact that the press was not solely an urban, elite phenomenon.[8]

And yet, due to the strict limitations of the Hamidian regime on public life (censorship, limitations on public gatherings and organization) as well as the political impotence of the average Ottoman subject, the connection of the Ottoman public sphere to political action was highly constricted. In other words, Ottomans could read about events taking place around their empire and the world, but they could do little about it—in contrast to the situation in contemporary Egypt and Qajar Iran, where the press was an important platform for political mobilization.[9] With the revolution of 1908, however, the Ottoman public sphere was radically transformed both in scale and in scope.

Figure 4.1. The Khalidi Library, Jerusalem. The library's collection before World War I consisted of dozens of newspapers, hundreds of manuscripts, and over forty-five hundred printed books, including a thousand in European languages. The library's guidelines banned talking and smoking cigarettes or *nargileh* inside the library. Library of Congress, Prints and Photographs Division, (LC-DIG-matpc-06804).

With the news that the constitution was being restored and that the strict censorship laws were being lifted, the press in the Ottoman Empire virtually exploded: one scholar has characterized the journalistic reaction to the revolution throughout the empire as "immediate and powerful, like the rush of a great river upon the collapse of a large dam."[10] Indeed, over two hundred new publications appeared in Istanbul alone in the year after the revolution. A similar wave of new journals overtook the rest of the empire's important provinces and urban centers: in the provinces that comprise today's Iraq, whereas before the revolution only official newspapers were published in the provincial centers of Baghdad, Basra, and Mosul, after the revolution over seventy political, literary, and caricature newspapers entered the marketplace; in Aleppo, at least twenty-three new newspapers and journals appeared in the four years following the revolution.[11] Likewise, within the half-year following the revolution, at least sixteen new Arabic newspapers emerged in Palestine, and by World War I, another eighteen Arabic newspapers had been established.[12] In addition to the booming Arabic press, several new Hebrew-language newspapers began appearing as well as three Ladino newspapers and at least one Greek newspaper.

Indeed, the lively public discussions we have seen in earlier chapters were facilitated by these new outlets, and a new audience was drawn to the press via the coffeehouses and the streets. Rather than simply being the private domain of urban elites, the late Ottoman press appealed to members of the new middle class, workers, women, children, and the rural populations.[13] According to a European visitor in Istanbul in those early months: "Every one was reading them—the very cabbies, waiting on the box of their broken-down little victorias, were drinking in the new learning—the knowledge of good and evil, of politics, of the things outside, of chancelleries, Parliaments, democratic movements, of the strife of nations, of their armies, their railways, their restless commerce, of all manners of strange amusements."[14] A German archaeologist observed a similar proliferation of the newspaper on his 1914 trip to Syria and Palestine, where he saw "people eagerly reading newspapers in the streets, the railway stations, the houses and shops."[15]

Above all, however, the new revolutionary press emerged out of the *effendiyya* strata; precisely those Muslims, Christians, and Jews who had been educated in the preceding decades under new conditions were attuned to the changes taking place throughout the empire, hungry for new outlets of information and expression. A fascinating survey conducted in the coffeehouses of Istanbul in 1913 by an Ottoman youth studying political science at Columbia University reinforces this assessment: slightly over half of the 120 café-readers he interviewed were graduates of the new university programs in law, medicine, commerce, or military sciences, and another 20 percent were graduates of state high schools or lyceum. Most (113 of 120) bought and read newspapers on a regular basis, and many (72 out of 120) read two or more newspapers *per day* in addition to weekly and monthly periodicals. Overall, the Columbia student concluded that there was deep interest, high expectations, and a widespread influence of the press.[16]

In Istanbul and the larger cities, circulation rates for the most popular newspapers could run in the tens of thousands.[17] In far less populous Palestine, however, it seems that the more popular newspapers had up to two thousand subscribers, with smaller newspapers having only three hundred to five hundred subscribers.[18] With local annual subscription rates between forty to seventy *kuruş* for an Arabic newspaper and around thirty *kuruş* for a Hebrew paper, they were certainly within the means of the salaried and independent middle classes. However, seeing how the average day laborer earned at best eight *kuruş* per day, it is unlikely that many workers could afford newspapers on other than the most sporadic basis.[19]

Subscription rates tell only part of the story, however, as newspapers were often read out loud, passed from hand to hand, or borrowed in coffeehouses, reading rooms, and libraries. According to the Columbia student, for example, each purchased Istanbul newspaper went through five to fifteen readers on average, as the original purchaser would share it with family members, neighbors, and friends before sending it to relatives in the provinces.[20] In Palestine, there is evidence of this newspaper sharing as well as other steps taken in an effort to engage financially modest, nonurban, and nonliterate groups of people. A proposal was recorded in the fall of 1908 to establish regular institutionalized reading nights, where an "educated Arab" would read the newspaper in a central location for the benefit of the masses that could not read. We also have records of bookshops and libraries that either lent or rented out reading materials, including a new "readers' library" by means of which readers could pay a small fee for access to the latest news, and patrons at cafés could catch up on reading newspapers while sipping their tea or coffee or smoking a *nargileh*. Lastly, the newspaper *Palestine* (*Filasṭīn*) sent free copies to each village in the region with a population over one hundred.[21]

Thus, with a conscious awareness that their readership was both changing and expanding, these newspapers went about shaping the revolutionary Ottoman public sphere. As one contemporary journalist and press observer noted, the Arabic press was uniform in expressing the belief that saw the revolution as "bringing redemption to the Ottoman people in the Ottoman lands, without difference to religion and nationality."[22] The Arabic press was not alone in this sentiment, for the Judeo-Spanish newspaper *Liberty* (*El Liberal*) hailed in its opening column, ". . . this day in which all the people of the empire trill with joy, this day that finally marks the beginning of a new life for all Ottomans."[23] Many other newspapers in Palestine explicitly emphasized their sympathy with the new political reality, such as *Progress* (*Al-Taraqqi*), Equity (*Al-Inṣāf*), Success (*Al-Najāḥ*), *Liberty* (*Al-Ḥurriyya*), *Constitution* (*Al-Dustūr*), *Voice of Ottomanism* (*Ṣawt al-ʿUthmāniyya*), and *Liberty* (*Ha-Ḥerut*; a Sephardi newspaper, which had a Ladino version, *El Liberal*).[24] And, as shown in Figure 4.2, the masthead of the newspaper *Jerusalem* proudly illustrated its embrace of the revolutionary principles of "liberty, equality, fraternity" in the stars—*ḥurriyya, musāwā, ikhā'*.

In this, the press was simultaneously echoing popular excitement in the aftermath of the revolution and placing itself at the forefront

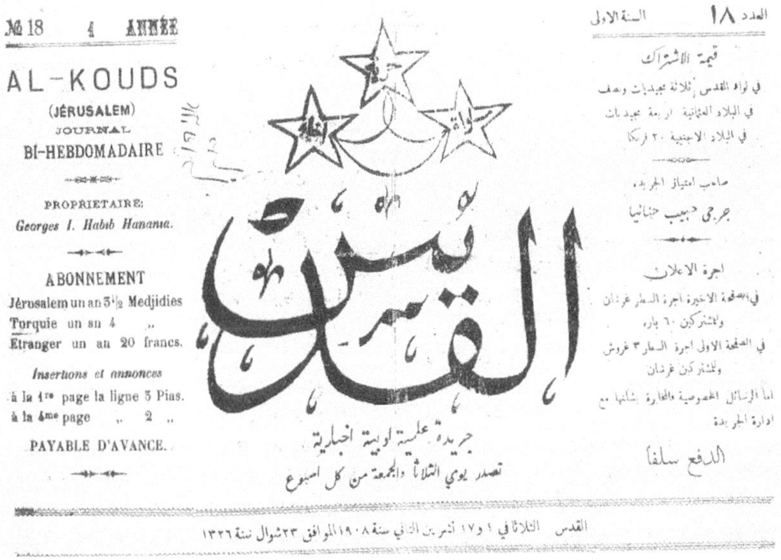

№ 18 1 ANNÉE

AL-KOUDS

(JÉRUSALEM)

JOURNAL

BI-HEBDOMADAIRE

PROPRIETAIRE:

Georges I. Habib Hanania.

ABONNEMENT

Jérusalem un an 3½ Medjidies

Turquie un an 4 „

Etranger un an 20 francs.

Insertions et annonces

à la 1re page la ligne 3 Pias.

à la 4me page „ 2 „

PAYABLE D'AVANCE.

القدس

جريدة علمية ادبية اخبارية

تصدر يومي الثلاثا والجمعة من كل اسبوع

العدد ١٨ السنة الاولى

قيمة الاشتراك

في لواء القدس ثلاثة مجيديات ونصف

في البلاد العثمانية اربعة مجيديات

في البلاد الاجنبية ٢٠ فرنكا

صاحب امتياز الجريدة

جرجي حبيب حنانيا

اجرة الاعلان

في الصفحة الاخيرة اجرة السطر غرشان

وللمشتركين ٦٠ باره

في الصفحة الاولى اجرة السطر ٣ غروش

وللمشتركين غرشان

اما الرسائل الخصوصية فالمخابرة بشانها مع ادارة الجريدة

الدفع سلفا

القدس الثلاثا في ٤ و١٧ تشرين الثاني سنة ١٩٠٨ الموافق ٢٣ شوال سنة ١٣٢٦

Figure 4.2. Masthead of *Al-Quds* newspaper. Calling itself a "scientific, literary, and informative newspaper", *Al-Quds* was a strong advocate of the Ottoman revolution, a fact it underscored visually for its readers with the revolution's slogan of "liberty, equality, fraternity," encased in the stars of the masthead. Central Zionist Archives (Jerusalem).

of the Ottomanist and Ottomanizing program.[25] In order to prepare the citizenry for the new era, the press took it upon itself to serve as a link between the citizenry and the transforming state in two important ways: first, by strengthening Ottomanism and sentiments of belonging to empire; and second, by solidifying imperial citizenship. First, newspapers actively helped shape an imperial identification among their readers, publishing reports on the history of the Osman dynasty, for example, or of the Ottoman liberals from the mid-nineteenth century to the revolution. As well, the press served as an intermediary between the state and the populace, and we have seen that the multilingual press published important new laws; transmitted directives from the central and local governments; informed citizens how to carry out normal business with government offices; and reported on the functioning of the various regional and local councils.[26]

In addition to underscoring this vertical relationship between the reader and the Ottoman state, the press simultaneously played an important role in forging horizontal ties between Ottomans. Strengthening ties across city, region, and empire, the press also served as a bridge between languages, communities, and reading publics. Often through regular columns, the press relayed news from the capital in Istanbul, neighboring provinces and cities in the empire, and events from faraway corners of the Ottoman world.[27] In the Palestinian press, for example, there were regular reports of famine in Anatolia; the Bedouin revolts in Kerak; updates on secret societies in Crete, Albania, the Hawran, and Yemen; the Armenian massacres; and of course the wars in Tripoli and the Balkans. Thanks to this coverage as well as to the modern wire services, the Palestinian press and public were tapped in to the major occurrences around the empire and world, and Palestinians thus were able to envision their future in the empire in "real time" conjunction with the empire's changing contours.

Informing readers about events and attitudes in other corners of the empire and among their compatriots also had the purpose of psychologically and imaginatively linking Palestinians to the broader Ottoman world.[28] For example the Hebrew newspaper *Liberty* (*Ha-Ḥerut*) displayed a great deal of sympathy and understanding toward the Bedouin revolt in Syria, arguing that the government was taking away the Bedouins' livelihood (protection money from the pilgrimage caravans), conscripting their sons into the army, and demanding their sedentarization and taxation, all without offering them any benefits in return. The paper also criticized the CUP's treatment of the revolts in the Hawran and Albania, already accusing them of Turkification policies inappropriate to the empire's heterogeneity.[29]

The press's spatial elements were not only imperial, however. The Palestinian press also contributed to a geography of locality, as newspapers featured columns on local news (*akhbār maḥaliyya*), published reports from correspondents in other Palestinian cities, and featured stories on towns and villages throughout Palestine, from Gaza in the south to 'Akka in the north. For example, *The Crier* (*Al-Munādī*) newspaper based in Jerusalem regularly carried news from southern Palestinian cities like Lydda, Ramallah, Bethlehem, and Gaza. (We will see later that the press contributed greatly to an emerging Palestinian local identity in ideological ways as well.)

Without ignoring the local aspects of the press's import, it is important nevertheless to underscore that many newspapers openly declared to their readers their commitment to contributing to the efflorescence of a civic identity in the empire. In the words of one publisher, Jurji Habib Hanania of *Jerusalem*: "Circumstances require the establishment of a press that will plant the seeds of brotherhood and work all together for equality whose aims are service to the homeland, not to take advantage in the differences of another."[30] And *Progress* (*Al-Taraqqi*), a "progressive constitutional newspaper" founded in Jaffa in September 1908, declared that it aimed to: serve the group, homeland, and humanity; enlighten minds; prepare the people for economic changes while limiting the negative effects of those changes; and support principles of brotherhood, justice, and equality.[31]

MAKING CRITICAL CITIZENS

Much of the press took upon itself the role of promoting citizenship as an active, critical endeavor. Such was the approach of *Ottoman Union*:

> We said in our last article that it is required of every free Ottoman to show his ignorant brother the benefits of the constitution. . . . The best speakers in these days are the newspapers, and the newspapers are the ears of the needs and necessities after the constitution. It is true that the establishment of the newspapers was one of the most important of that work which is required of us after the constitution, but which newspapers do I want? Free newspapers whose aims are the reform of the self, not commerce and not literature as is the case in most of the newspapers today.[32]

For *Palestine*, distributing the paper to villagers was a vital fulfillment of its self-appointed role as both informer and educator. As villagers learned of events taking place throughout the empire, which would serve to help underscore the process of "imagining themselves as Ottoman," at the same time the peasants would learn of their political rights as new citizens.[33]

Indeed, we have seen the press as playing a central role in transmitting information about voting rights and procedures, publishing candidate platforms and endorsements, and setting expectations for the parliamentary elections of 1908. It continued its work in rendering the constitutional government visible and legible to its readers by publishing regular reports of parliamentary proceedings from Istanbul as well as reporting on the sessions of the provincial administrative and general councils. The demand for governmental transparency and accountability to the people was so strong that one newspaper called for total transparency, demanding the protocols and weekly blotter of the police commission, the balance sheets of the city council, and all incoming and outgoing orders of the provincial government, "so that the people can know what belongs to him and what is incumbent upon him."[34] Criticisms were repeatedly expressed against newspapers that were seen as towing the government line, such as *Noble Jerusalem*, the official newspaper of the province. The paper was forced to defend itself against these public charges, arguing that "our paper does not slander and does not take sides, never. Our job is [simply] to convey announcements from the government orders to its people."[35]

A central tool of the constitutional press's public engagement with government officials and councils was the "open letter," known as *kitāb maftūḥ* in the Arabic press and *mikhtav patuaḥ* in the Hebrew press. Through the open letter, newspaper editors and private citizens alike addressed their elected and appointed officials, demanding answers, suggesting policy changes, and even, in some cases, rendering accusations and ridicule public. For example, in the summer of 1911 the newspaper *Palestine* addressed a public letter to MP Ruhi al-Khalidi in the aftermath of a storm off the coast of Jaffa which, in addition to destroying several houses and buildings in town, cost Jaffan merchants some fifty thousand cases of oranges. *Palestine* complained that Jaffa had asked the government for a new port for years while its requests had gone unheeded. At once soliciting the MP's opinion on the matter ("What is your opinion of this, Khalidi? Do you have a suggestion for the government?"), the open letter also made clear that Khalidi would be held accountable for meeting or failing to meet the city's needs: "Now it is upon you, our honored representative," to continue the struggle Jaffa's new port.[36] Interviewed for the article, Khalidi responded meekly, blaming his earlier inattention to the port issue on the ongoing war against the Italian invasion of Libya, but nonetheless promising to "bring to fruition the trust of our dear nation."

The Jerusalem newspaper *The Crier* excelled in the open letter, publishing dozens of them in its short fourteen-month run. Most frequently, these open letters addressed the governor, the general council, and the city council, but the paper also published open letters addressed to the general prosecutor in various Palestinian towns as well as the Jerusalem police commission. In some cases, the open letter provoked a public response by the official or council. Such was the case when former MP Hafiz al-Sa'id responded on the front page of *The Crier*. Likewise, the Jerusalem police department felt compelled to publicly respond to *The Crier*'s charges against it and defend its record.[37]

The Haifa-based newspaper *The Carmel* (*Al-Karmil*) also regularly took government officials to task on its pages, criticizing the new deputy governor in 'Ajloun for failing to understand constitutional rule, attacking various local officials including the MP from 'Akka, Shaykh As'ad Shuqayri, the deputy governor of Tiberias, and the former governor of Jerusalem for facilitating Zionism contrary to standard legal procedures and the interest of the Ottoman state, and decrying the corruption of both local officials and notable families.[38] After a particularly scathing run of articles criticizing the provincial government for failing to provide adequate public security, the deputy governor of Nazareth, Amin 'Abd al-Hadi, wrote back insisting that the editor of *The Carmel*, Nejuib Nassar, must have confused the boundaries of Nazareth with those of neighboring Jenin, for in his district only three donkeys had been stolen since he had entered office whereas seventy murders had been committed in Jenin in the past three months alone. 'Abd al-Hadi demanded that Nassar publish his letter along with a correction "in a prominent place on the front page," in accordance with article 21 of the new press laws. In a follow-up letter, 'Abd al-Hadi chided the paper saying that it served no good public purpose if he had to constantly write in to correct the paper's mistakes. In response, Nassar defended his paper's claim, saying that many crimes were not reported to government officials because people did not expect them to be investigated, but he also expressed a hope that all government officials would take the newspaper as seriously as 'Abd al-Hadi did.[39]

And yet, there were nonetheless limits on the freedom of the press to challenge the authorities; on more than one occasion newspapers were closed down, editors sued, jailed, or fined, or other penalties were imposed. One of the earliest cases of this happened when *The Deer* published a rather inflammatory article entitled "We Demand Police!"[40] The article decried the lack of public security and complained that Jerusalem had only sixteen policemen while Rome, which was only five times the size of Jerusalem, had four thousand police. In light of this oversight, the author of the article, Itamar Ben-Avi, demanded a police brigade to be made up of Jews and Christians. Despite the fact that the lack of security in Palestine was well reported in the press, the Ben-Avi article crossed an unwritten line and was seen as unacceptable agitation against the government. The article was translated into Arabic and Ottoman Turkish by order of the police, and after being taken to court, *The Deer* was shut down for three weeks.[41]

The open letter also became a format used to address readers—a conscious act of creating, naming, and enlisting a particular group under a chosen banner. In many cases this was imperial: for example, *Ottoman Union* and other papers frequently published open letters to "all Ottomans," "brother Ottomans," and "fellow citizens." Still other letters addressed a provincial public, such as the letters in *The Crier* "to the Palestinians." Other letters reinforced the city as a shared civic unit, with letters to "Jerusalemites."[42] These various audiences can be seen as concentric circles of overlapping affiliation: one was never simply a Jaffan or a Palestinian or an Ottoman or a Christian—one was all at the same time, even when the content or tone of the open letter might highlight the tensions between these various commitments.

As another example of this contextual identification of group-ness and "we"-ness, the Sephardi Jewish newspaper *Liberty* used the Hebrew word *umah* (nation, people) to refer alternately to a number of overlapping groups: the ethnolinguistic (Sephardim), ethnoreligious (Jews locally and/or globally), civic-regional (people of Palestine), and civic-imperial (Ottoman nation). Similarly, in Ladino the words *nacion* and *pueblo* modified various communities, as in Arabic *umma* (nation-people) and *waṭan* (homeland) were at various times local and imperial, confessional or communal. In other words, the "voice of the people" in reality reflected many voices, and many peoples.

INTERCOMMUNAL RIVALRY I: THE PRESS AS A PLATFORM FOR COMMUNAL RIGHTS

The multilingual press of the late Ottoman Empire expressed a keen awareness of the different elements of the empire and their shifting roles in the new political order. Often this came in the form of short notices that underscored the mutual participation of different communities in the Ottomanist project. For example, in the fall of 1908, the Hebrew paper *The Deer* published a notice that the Armenian organization ARF had publicly declared that there were forty thousand Armenians ready to give their lives to defend the empire against external aggression and internal anticonstitutionalists; likewise, the ARF claimed, if the government was short on cash the Armenians were prepared to raise two million Ottoman liras for its benefit. *The Deer* noted that as a result the Ottoman Turkish press was unanimous in praising the "loyal Armenians."[43] In another incident during the Balkan war, the newspaper *The Crier* alerted its readers to the fact that Jewish religious leaders and scholars in town had asked Jewish workers and shop owners to close down during a prayer service in the synagogue for the victory of the empire over its enemies; *The Crier* publicly thanked the Jewish community for the gesture and for the patriotic sentiments.[44]

In that same vein, many newspapers published regular appeals for donations to the Ottoman military fund. Listing people's names with the amount of their donations gave papers the opportunity to publicly praise patriotic activities, but also introduced an element of competitiveness among the city's readers. For example, when *Success* newspaper published a short notice from the head of the Ottoman fleet committee publicly thanking the Greek patriarch and priests for their sizable contributions to the fund and praising their "patriotic devotion [*ḥamiyya waṭaniyya*]," he closed his note with an expression of confidence that this would inspire the other religious institutions and officials of Jerusalem to show their own patriotic devotion in a similar manner. In another case in early 1910, in addition to acknowledging 'Uthman al-Nashashibi for his sizable donation to the Ottoman navy, *Liberty* also took care to identify the four Jewish donors whose cumulative contributions matched al-Nashashibi's. In this context, we can understand that when *Liberty* informed its readers about a benefit performance of Shakespeare's works in Arabic by a Jewish theatrical group in Damascus, the proceeds of which would go to the Ottoman military, it did so not simply as a piece of news about Damascene cultural life but also to highlight a collective Jewish contribution to the patriotic effort.[45]

In other words, press notices about other communities and stories translated from other languages of the empire could be innocently informative, competitive in a friendly way, or provocatively challenging. The Ottoman constitutional parliamentary system was important not only for "Ottomania" as a whole but indeed for each of its ethnic, religious, and linguistic groups. In the rapidly changing environment of the post-revolution empire, the ethno-religious groups in the empire worriedly and hurriedly worked to mobilize and strategize to ensure that their community was not left behind in the new political and social order. In fact, the need to preserve (or enlarge) the community's position in a rapidly changing hierarchy made rivalry between communities a significant undercurrent of Ottomanist discourse. Rights and privileges were measured not only against absolute standards of Ottomanist civic identity, but also, more important, against those enjoyed by the other ethnic and religious groups of the empire.

Thus, newspaper reports about the constitution and new political rights often had the subtext of "keeping up with the Joneses." For example, only weeks after the revolution, Avraham Elmaliach, a young Jewish journalist who would later edit both the Ladino and Hebrew *Liberty* newspapers, published an homage to the revolution while at the same time indicating that the new freedom of press would serve as a yardstick, not only to measure the renaissance of the Ottoman Empire, but also to ensure the Jewish role within it. As he wrote in "Rebirth of Our Empire": "Our homeland has returned to rebirth . . . Freedom is the dearest thing to mankind, and therefore our brothers the Jewish people, residents of Turkey [*sic*], will endeavor through the freedoms given to us to bring closer all that is good and useful for our homeland . . . [Thanks to the freedom of the press,] we will demand our rights from their hands and they will know that there is an eye that sees and an ear that hears."[46]

Indeed, the emergence of a free and flourishing press encompassed the dual imperative that Elmaliach articulated of "an eye that sees and an ear that hears"—on the one hand, the press was a transparent source of knowledge and information that would bolster citizenship claims; on the other hand, however, the press could also facilitate or even empower competing claims and demands.

This struggle in Palestine ranged from the petty to the weighty. For example, invitations to the official celebrations on the one-year anniversary of the ascension to the throne of the new sultan Mehmet Reşat took on a distinctly political weight. The Jewish community of Jerusalem publicly complained that only three Jews had received invitations to the celebration, whereas Christians ("who are one-third the size of the Jewish community") had received forty-three invitations. After complaining to one of the local government officials, the Jews were allowed to submit a list of Jewish notables to be invited.[47] In another example, more significant because of its political implications, after reading that the Greek Patriarchate insisted on proportional representation during the 1914 parliamentary election cycle and was allegedly promised a number of representatives equal to the Armenians, the Jaffa chief rabbi, Ben-Zion 'Uziel, wrote to a colleague that "this awakens my ambitions too to have our voices also heard as Jews and for us to also demand . . . to send representatives according to our numbers."[48]

In the winter of 1909, the Ladino newspaper *Paradise* published a series of articles on the newly appointed Jewish representative to the administrative council, Rabbi Lieb Dayan. Dayan, who was put forth by the Ashkenazi community, knew neither Ottoman Turkish nor Arabic, which thus rendered him completely ineffective, the paper complained. Moreover, his boorish mannerisms made him a laughingstock in the council meetings. Instead, the paper urged, the Jews needed another representative on the council who would fight to defend Jewish rights as well as someone who would "redeem the Jews' honor" that Dayan had sullied in front of the city's other groups. The paper also demanded a second representative on the council "like the other peoples." Indeed, several other newspaper articles as well as leading Jews who were called on to intervene with the government emphasized that two major Christian denominations in Jerusalem had two representatives each on the administrative council (one religious, one lay member), whereas the Jews only had one total. Later that spring, after the city's Jews had failed to earn another seat on the administrative council, *Paradise* wondered out loud if the Jews were to blame for failing to awaken enough to demand their rights or if the government was to blame for failing to wake them.[49]

When the press was not sufficiently loud in its proactive defense of Jewish claims, *Paradise* turned to a new private organization called the Society of Ottoman Jews (SOJ; Agudat ha-Yehudim he-'Otomanim). The society proclaimed it would carry out propaganda in the press, civic education such as Ottoman Turkish and Arabic evening classes and translations of Ottoman laws, lobbying government officials, establishment of a free legal defense project, and citizenship (Ottomanization) drives. Viewed differently, its most frequent efforts were centered on ensuring that the Jews received their fair share in the new Ottoman polity. According to newspaper reports, the SOJ was quite active in Jerusalem in the half-year after the revolution, and its meetings at the Yohanan Ben-Zakkai and Ohel Moshe synagogues regularly drew hundreds of Jews.[50]

From the surviving Ladino and Hebrew press we see that individuals or groups in the Jewish community often appealed to the SOJ to intervene to correct injustices or to defend the Jewish community. In the aftermath of the arrest and improper sentencing of a Jewish baker, the Sephardi Jewish lawyer Malchiel Mani, of Hebron, was commissioned by the SOJ to "defend the interests of the Jewish public of our city without anyone having to pay a cent," in order to protect the Jewish community from injustices which happen every day because "people do not know the laws."[51] In a flyer made up by the SOJ asking for donations to establish this legal aid unit, they appealed to the sense of uncertainty and vulnerability that underlay the transition to the constitutional period. "Which of you, dear brothers, does not feel the need for a Jewish lawyer in Jerusalem?" they asked, citing the growth of the Jewish community in Jerusalem, and as a result, the rise in complaints against them. As the SOJ told its members, "we suffer here because there is no one with strength and talent to demand a trial, there is no one to defend our souls and property and prosecute our insults and fight for our honor, in every instance."[52]

In this atmosphere of increasing rivalry over every community's civic status born in the uncertain aftermath of attempted mandated equality, even favors shown to certain communities appeared to reflect the inalienable rights of the emerging Ottoman body politic. Under the headline banner of "Honor de los judios!" *Paradise* recounted an incident in March 1909 where the SOJ intervened to demand an Ottoman military band performance for the Jewish holiday of Purim since the band had performed for a previous Christian holiday. The reason for this demand, as the author wrote, was "so that we will not be considered less than the Christians, we who are many more than they in the city. . . . Forward, brothers, a little bit of force and everything can be accomplished. In order to save our honor before everything!"[53]

In another instance, when several poor Jews who could not pay the military exemption tax were mistreated by Ottoman soldiers, the leaders of the society complained to military headquarters and the soldiers subsequently "made sweet" to the men. However, the SOJ's countless efforts to get the "red note" canceled did not meet with success for several years.[54] Along with the chief rabbi in Istanbul, Haim Nahum, it also unsuccessfully petitioned to change a tradition that prevented Jews from walking down the street adjoining the Holy Sepulcher in Jerusalem or from ascending more than five steps at the Cave of the Patriarchs in Hebron. In another incident, where three Jewish vagrants were sentenced to three weeks in prison, the intervention of the SOJ on their behalf caused the president of the tribunal to increase the sentence to three months, in response to "the creation of this Jewish society formed to intimidate us."[55]

By that point, the SOJ was identified with the Zionist movement, and as a result by 1910 it lost the bulk of its membership, its legitimacy within the non-Zionist Jewish community, and the good favor of the local government. Albert Antébi dismissed the organization, saying "this Jewish Ottoman Palestinian society is incapable of naturalizing a single Jew or of delivering a single prisoner, but it has engendered anti-Semitism."[56] In a scathing editorial published in the Hebrew newspaper *Liberty*, "'Otomani" blamed the organization for "mix[ing] us up with haters of the Muslims," and declared, "Thus in the name of many of the Ottoman Jews I hereby notify the SOJ that it has no right and justice to speak in the name of all the Jewish Ottoman people in Jerusalem." By the summer of 1910 the SOJ finally was declared illegal.[57]

With the rapid fall of the SOJ, the Jewish press returned to other channels for pressing for their rights "like the other Ottomans."[58] The Ladino and Hebrew newspapers frequently published open letters to the Chief Rabbi of the empire, Haim Nahum, as well as to the four Jewish members of the Ottoman parliament, calling for their intervention with the government. More often, however, the pages of the press themselves increasingly monitored and documented the failures of Ottomanism.

INTERCOMMUNAL RIVALRY II: THE PRESS AS BAROMETER OF OTTOMANISM

The historian Palmira Brummett's fascinating study of the Istanbul satirical press captures the role played by that medium in documenting the gap between the aspirations of the new regime and its shortcomings. She argues that, in contrast to the earnest treatment of the revolutionary era one found in the "serious press," the satirical newspaper *Kalem*, for example, depicted a "vision of revolutionary chaos and parliamentary malaise."[59] Other satirical papers expressed repeated disillusionment with the new regime. In a similar function, if far more earnest in tone, throughout the revolutionary period the press in Palestine became a platform for depicting and decrying "violations" or shortcomings of reform, and usually were followed by calls for mobilization to the powers-that-be, whether to local Ottoman officials or to the imperial government in the capital via chosen intermediaries. For example, one scholar who was familiar with the Jaffa-based newspaper *The News* (*Al-Akhbār*) characterized its concerns as "the deeds and misdeeds of the government officials, freedom and actions against it, and the failure of reforms."[60] Other newspapers would carry out similar functions.

Within a few months of the revolution, the press was documenting abuses and persistent elements of the ancien régime. The Judeo-Spanish press bewailed the return to "the times before liberty."[61] In essence, the Ottoman Jewish community in Palestine measured the success of liberty and the Ottoman revolution by its own standing vis-à-vis the other religious communities. In 1909, complaints began to appear quite loudly in the Jerusalem press about the limited impact of the revolution in bringing about the betterment of the Jewish community. By the fall of 1909, two incidents rattled the Jewish community in Jerusalem and called into question the basic premises of Ottomanism.

In October, a Jew visiting Hebron for the Jewish festival of Sukkot was reported murdered after he mistakenly climbed past the fifth step of the Cave of the Patriarchs, traditionally forbidden to Jews. The event caused outrage among Jewish journalists as proof of how the Jews had yet to benefit from real liberty. It is unclear whether this is a true story, however, since a government commission sent to investigate the disappearance and murder of the Jew was told by the Hebron chief rabbi, Suleiman Mani, that no such thing had taken place. Nonetheless, *Liberty* insisted that the man had been killed and scorned the chief rabbi for not taking the opportunity to demand that the prohibition on Jewish entry to the cave be lifted.[62]

Around the same time, an incident emerged involving a drunken homeless Jew by the name of Shlomo who insulted the police and subsequently was arrested and beaten by them and Arab passersby in the Old City of Jerusalem. The police said Shlomo had insulted Islam, and by the time he arrived at the jail one of his eyes was swollen shut. The Sephardi press responded in outrage:

> After all this, there are people who think that there is liberty for all, there are those who say that all have the rights of equality, those who notify us that we live with our neighbors in brotherhood . . . this is intolerable! When the constitution was proclaimed in Turkey [*sic*] and the word *ḥurriyya* rang out, our joy was great, very great, thinking that we would finally . . . be able to breathe a pure and free air . . . [but] our situation has gotten worse! Yes! Worse! Before our lives were secure, our interests were not trampled and our dignity was not trespassed; while

now they insult us, they mistreat us, they trample us daily, and they look to calumny us always under the name of "liberty"![63]

That same day, a stinging critique was published in *Liberty*, "Such is Brotherhood and Equality," complaining about elements of discrimination against Jews as well as demanding full equality as promised by the new order:

Everyone says to give it time and our situation will improve. Enough! A year and a half have passed from the giving of equality to all the peoples without difference in religion or race. Fifteen months since the words freedom, equality, and brotherhood had high hopes, but every good change passes us by . . . our situation gets worse by the day, just because we are "Jews." . . . Why don't we raise our voices and demand a lawsuit?

If we are good enough to pay taxes and burdens, to go to the army and spill our blood for our homeland, then we should also enjoy the rights of the government. . . . All of us cannot remain silent—we must demand from the government an investigation, a trial. If everything is done and the government defends us, so our lives are secure from the accusing masses, and we know that freedom, equality, and brotherhood that were given to us were not just empty words, but according to law and deed.[64]

Liberty's anger had been cumulative, and it also reflected a broader dissatisfaction with the post-Hamidian order that had fallen far short of expectations in numerous ways. Jews were not the only ones who were affected or concerned by the growing lack of security in the land and the frightful inability of the local government to impose order. In fact, this lack of security (the rise of robberies, assault, murder, and rape) was a recurrent theme in the Palestinian press, as we saw in the complaints in *The Carmel*, as well as elsewhere.[65]

As the Jewish community was not alone in its dissatisfaction with the shortcomings of the new era, the press offers us a window onto the development and expression of growing intercommunal rivalry. Rather than expressing age-old hatreds, the intercommunal rivalry of the constitutional period was cast in an Ottomanist lens. Tensions between communities found their expression in the pages of their newspapers, particularly around the new rights and responsibilities of citizenship and relative privileges. The language of a shared citizenship and nationhood was juxtaposed next to the much more complicated reality, where both Muslims and non-Muslims alike resented their own forced contribution to changing the status quo while questioning their neighbors' lack of willingness to do so.

A perfect illustration of this is the case of universal military conscription. Until 1909, only Muslims were subjected to conscription in the Ottoman army, and military service was considered a heavy burden.

Healthy young men were taken for years to battle malnourishment, disease, late or missing paychecks, and appalling conditions in remote corners of the empire. Back home, families were deprived of healthy wage earners and working hands, uncertain about the fate of their departed sons.[66] For their part, Jewish and Christian male subjects of the empire were expected to pay the military exemption tax. This tax was charged on a communal, not individual, level: each *millet* was taxed a lump sum based on the reported number of men in the community; in turn, the communal leadership would settle accounts with their members, heavily subsidizing the poor. While the *bedel* (or *'askariyya*, as it was known in Arabic) was also considered a heavy financial burden, there is no doubt that it was preferable to military service.

However, in the prevailing euphoria of the postrevolutionary period, when the Ottoman military was praised for its role in the revolution and in bringing *ḥurriyya*, and while the Ottoman public was eager to participate in the benefits as well as responsibilities of citizenship, universal conscription took its place among the slogans of a changing empire. Universal conscription was talked about as a tool of social engineering, a policy that would Ottomanize and homogenize the empire's polyglot communities. Public discourse embraced universal conscription as sharing the burdens of defending the empire as well as putting an end to the myriad privileges enjoyed by the non-Muslim communities of the empire.

For many non-Muslims and particularly for the Ottoman Jewish communities, support for universal conscription became a measure of support for Ottomanism, for the empire, and for the responsible participation of non-Muslims in the new Ottoman body politic. It was considered an honorable contribution to the Ottoman nation, not only a duty but a privilege for all Ottoman citizens.[67] In short order, however, military service became another yardstick by which to measure the relative Ottomanist contribution of each ethno-religious community. In many respects military conscription became a new source of intercommunal rivalry more than of integration.

However, at the same time that universal conscription was praised as properly "Ottomanist," the Ottoman government itself was wary of universal conscription and its impact on the sectarian and ethnic status quo of the empire. Among the official bodies there was a real reluctance to arm and train suspect minorities of the empire, particularly the Orthodox and Armenian communities.[68] As well, the issue of conscription threatened to reawaken the conflict over electoral representation. In one parliamentary debate, when it was demanded that non-Muslims be conscripted at a ratio consistent with their population, Greek representatives retorted that proportional representation had not been adopted in the parliament so should not be adopted in the army, either.[69]

After several months of debate in the Ottoman parliament, the parliament finally voted in favor of universal conscription in May 1909.[70] However, pragmatic considerations intervened to limit the appeal and practicality of conscription: the Ottoman budget simply could not absorb the cost of training and maintaining thousands of new soldiers from the non-Muslim communities. In July, the parliament reopened debate on the issue, as the loss of the *bedel* tax from the non-Muslim citizens posed a serious fiscal challenge to the empire. Bringing in over one million Turkish lira annually, the *bedel* was an important regular source of revenue for imperial coffers. In the Jerusalem province alone, the 1907–8 *bedel* amounted to 5.7 percent of total local revenues (12,416 Turkish lira); by fiscal year 1909–10, it had grown to 9 percent of local revenues, a not insignificant chunk for the cash-strapped empire.[71]

Due to the political and economic ramifications of universal conscription, the first non-Muslim recruits did not head out to the field until 1910; even then, the parliament continued to debate various aspects of military service. In addition to the question of non-Muslim conscription, the parliamentarians debated exemptions for religious scholars and students and for descendants of the Prophet and Ottoman princes, and questioned military reforms and the broader role of military service in social engineering. One parliamentarian, Bertakis Effendi, criticized the law on interesting grounds: religious scholars should not be exempt from service because in the days of freedom and equality it is impossible to separate the shepherd from his flock; soldiers should be educated while in service so that they return home as better men; and the empire should be divided into three regions based on climate so that soldiers do not have to suffer from radical changes. Previously, the *sharif*s and *sayyid*s, purportedly descendants of the family of the Prophet, were exempt from conscription. The governor of Mecca responded to the parliament that Muhammad himself had been a military man, and hence, no exemptions should be granted for them. Also, MPs Sidqi Bey and Basfi Bey argued that "equality" had no meaning if the Ottoman princes were not subject to the draft.[72]

In part because of the lack of a clear policy emanating from Istanbul, the conscription issue was the source of much confusion and misinformation, and as a result the local press became an important intermediary for the people. The Jewish press published numerous articles and notices about the new law, exemption regulations, dates of medical exams, call-up notices, and procedures.[73] In order to preempt any intercommunal conflicts, the government established local induction and appeals committees consisting of the governor, local military commander, head of military conscription, population registry (*nüfus*) clerks, and religious heads and lay leaders placed there, "so that no injustice is done and all is carried out according to law."[74] One member of the military induction committee, Albert Antébi, wrote that it was important to "fight for equality with the Muslims in terms of exemption rights." Nevertheless, the conscription process was messy and inefficient, and led to frequent public complaints of unfairness, inefficiency, and exploitation.[75]

Because of their shared interests in negotiating the new reality, initially there was a degree of tentative cooperation between Jews and Christians in Palestine and in the empire at large around the conscription issue. As early as May 1909 the Roman Catholic *millet* in Jerusalem invited Jewish leaders to participate in a community discussion of army service. In late 1909 a joint committee of sixteen Jews and Christians was established to deal with military matters, most pressingly the updating of census registers; joint appeals were sent from Jerusalem, and Jewish and Christian members of parliament together lobbied the Ministry of War.[76] Furthermore, non-Muslim religious leaders pushed for separate units, local service in Jerusalem, and other concessions that would ameliorate the new demands. For example, Haim Nahum, the chief rabbi of the empire, was actively involved in trying to minimize the impact of conscription on the Jewish community by securing kosher food for Jewish soldiers, establishing religious holidays as leave time, and arranging the assignment of Jewish soldiers to regions with an existing Jewish community. Ultimately the Ministry of War rejected the demand for separate units out of hand as being counter to the spirit of the conscription law, and Jewish and Christian soldiers were not awarded any special privileges.[77]

While at first loudly declaring Jewish excitement at serving the homeland, once the popular image of the romantic heroism of the Ottoman military wore off, many non-Muslim youth showed themselves unwilling to join an institution that posed certain health and financial risks. The press therefore played a dual function as platform for promoting military service as a duty of citizenship and trumpeting the community's loyalty to the empire, while at the same time pleading with Jewish youth not to emigrate or otherwise escape military service, thereby revealing the limits of that loyalty. In May 1909, for example, *Liberty* proclaimed that "we the Jews were always loyal to our homeland and to our enlightened government, and it is incumbent upon us to fulfill our holy duty especially according to the laws." Although new beginnings are difficult, the paper continued, particularly since the majority of Jewish young men did not know Arabic and Ottoman Turkish, it was incumbent upon Jews to "give the last drop of their blood for the good of the homeland."[78]

The Jewish press thus explicitly reinforced the link between the Ottoman citizenship project and the duty to serve in the military. On the eve of the first conscriptions, the press exhorted young men to think of the Ottoman *patria* and Ottoman *umma*: "Brothers! Don't be lazy, it is incumbent upon us to carry weapons and fight with our bodies for our dear homeland, because its peace is also peace for us."[79] One article by Nissim Behar reminded his readers that since they all had celebrated with the coming of freedom, they must serve as free citizens in their free land. "And we the Ottoman Jews especially will fulfill of course with strength of heart and great joy our duties to the homeland, with our blood, a duty that we could not fulfill until now because of the former lawlessness."[80] Patriotic articles were published that praised Jewish volunteers to the Ottoman army, Jewish war heroes from the spring 1909 countercoup, and even heroic Jews in uniform throughout the world. In that context, several articles reminded readers that Jews had served in the Russian army, despite the fact that they had no civil rights in Russia, making service in the army of a constitutional Ottoman Empire all the more reasonable and obligatory.[81]

In February 1910, the first non-Muslims were finally inducted into the army in Istanbul, and the Palestinian Jewish press seized the opportunity to adopt the "Jewish pioneers" as an example to the local youth. As one newspaper remarked, the "capital was full of emotion" as people from all walks of life came to see the nearly one thousand non-Muslim conscripts performing their "duty for the homeland."[82] Furthermore, through their induction the Jewish and Christian youth embodied equality in deed and not just in words. That Friday evening, for the first time, the press noted, Christian, Jewish, and Muslim soldiers sat and ate together, fulfilling the revolution's promises of brotherhood, equality, and a united Ottoman nation (though the paper did note that each ate from his own utensils, implying that the Jewish soldiers' dietary restrictions were not compromised). Later, reports were published of a patriotic organization in Damascus visiting over fifty Jewish soldiers wounded in the fighting in the Hawran.[83]

With the passage of time, though, the Jewish press in Palestine had to acknowledge the growing resistance on the part of Jewish youth to voluntarily don the Ottoman uniform. The September 1909 rolls of eligible non-Muslim men in the Jerusalem area yielded 1,953 names, which included almost 600 Jews. However, from the periodic reports in the press, we know that by the time the actual call-ups came around, a significant percentage of the summoned youth never showed up; of those who did, large numbers requested exemptions or paid the optional exemption tax, and others flashed their foreign citizenship to get out of military service.[84] Even while the first call-ups and inspections were taking place, an advertisement placed in a local newspaper urged all Ashkenazi, Sephardi, Maghrebi, and Yemeni Jewish young men who stood to be drafted to go to the house of one Shlomo Eliach to get advice on what could be done to better "their depressing situation." In fact, dozens of Jewish and Christian youth were leaving Palestine weekly, with hundreds leaving Greater Syria. The Ottoman government's threats against the émigrés did little to stem the tide. One article argued in their defense that the departing youth should not be blamed for not having received a patriotic education, which would have encouraged them to stay and enlist.[85]

Against this backdrop, by the spring of 1910, the tentative Christian-Jewish cooperation on conscription matters had given way to public rivalry. In the same issue that lauded the brotherhood and patriotism of the Istanbul recruits, the Hebrew *Liberty* published an article translated from the Christian-Arab newspaper *Equity*, which accused the Jerusalem Jewish community of lying to the local medical inspection committee in order to win exemptions from military service. In response, the Jewish newspaper voiced outrage, citing the deep loyalty and commitment of the Jewish community to the empire and, significantly, relying on the newly granted laws and rights of the constitutionalist regime to redeem them. "'Otomani" (Ottoman) urged the Jewish community to sue the Arab paper according to articles 17 and 19 of the new press laws. As he wrote, "I call on every Jew who in his heart has feelings of patriotism and honor that it is a holy duty laid down upon them to prosecute the editor of this paper to either show the truth of his words or to punish him according to the law for the honor of the Jews." *Liberty*'s editor seconded this recommendation and dismissed the Arab editor who was, in his opinion, jealous of the Jewish community's advances in commerce, industry, and education. "The government knows its Jews well because they are loyal to it, not less than the Christians and perhaps much more than them."[86]

At the same time, Mendel Kremer, a *mukhtar* of Ashkenazi Jews in Jerusalem, went to the head of the military inspection committee to complain about the Christian paper's libelous accusations; the official reportedly denied the Christian press's allegation of Jewish shirking. The editor of *Liberty* then demanded that official steps be taken through the SOJ to sue the editor for libel. At that point, the Christian editor of *Equity* apologized and promised to retract his statements in the next issue if the Jewish community did not sue him. Partially placated, the Jewish *Liberty* insisted that if the other editor fulfilled his promise, they would forgive him, but "if not, we will demand a lawsuit so that all our haters and enemies will hear, and know that there is an eye that sees and an ear that hears, and the Jews will go to court over everything."[87] Several days later, *Liberty* reported that *Equity* had in fact retracted its former accusations in a short note to its readers, stating, "By the way, the notice we published that some Jewish youth put tobacco in their eyes to fool the doctors is a falsehood."[88] In response, the Jewish newspaper editors wrote that while they were uncertain whether the Arab editor had "seen the truth" or simply feared punishment, they were pleased that he had considered their demands for a retraction.

In addition to its formal retraction, *Equity* published a lead article praising the Jewish population of the empire, sections of which were translated and republished in *Liberty* for its readers. If the article struck the Jewish editors as overly florid or sarcastic they did not let on:

> All the peoples in the great Ottoman Empire received the constitution like a man thirsty for water and on the faces of all we saw the joy and brotherhood and equality. But more than all the people of Turkey [*sic*] the Israelite nation excelled in its amazing celebrations, and more than once we saw our Jewish brothers in the markets and streets with the flag of freedom in their hands, and their homes were decorated with lights and lamps at the gate of each Jewish house and window decorated wonderfully, and the joy on their faces called for equality and brotherhood. But that was not enough for them, and when the non-Muslim youth were called to inspection before the military committee, they marched young and old to the tents outside the military fortress with joy and excitement due to the constitution that made them equal to the rest of their brothers in the empire. And it is a miracle that all the Jewish youth who said they were sick at the first inspection were in fact proven at the second inspection in front of doctors to be sick, and they were exempted. And the Jews like the rest of their brothers thanked God for creating them Ottomans.[89]

By the time the first Jewish and Christian youth from Jerusalem were conscripted in the fall of 1910, the difficulties between them were temporarily put to rest. The induction of the seventeen Christian and eleven Jewish youth was depicted as the ideal Ottomanist moment—three thousand Jerusalemites went to the train station for their departure, the military commander gave a speech about their "duty to the homeland," the military band played patriotic songs, and the cries of the parents, brothers, and children of the departing soldiers rose up to the heavens as one. One local Jewish paper waxed lyrical: "And you, dear soldiers! Be strong and courageous and be loyal sons to our land and our dear homeland, struggle for the good of the state in peace because her peace is also peace for you. Be loyal to our religion and our holy Torah and be with your Ottoman brothers in brotherhood and friendship so that your names will be blessed and Jerusalem will boast about you!"[90] In fact, the soldiers' names were published in the local paper, as sources of pride, alongside the names of those who chose to pay the *bedel* instead, as objects of shame.

Once Jews had been inducted into the Ottoman army, the Jewish community began a new wave of activity and mobilization on their behalf. The community established ad hoc committees to take up donations to support poor soldiers and their families and to provide clothing and kosher food for soldiers stationed in Jerusalem.[91] The press continued to publish articles about Jewish soldiers in the Ottoman army, as an example to local Jews and as proof of Jewish Ottomanism.[92] Throughout 1911–13, the conflict against the Bedouin of the Hawran and Kerak as well as the wars in Libya and the Balkans increased the need for soldiers in the Ottoman army and the pressure on non-Muslim communities to prove their loyalty to the empire. In particular, the Christian communities were under pressure to prove that the remaining Christians would be loyal Ottoman citizens. For Jewish citizens in Palestine, the suspicions against Christians provided an excellent opportunity to highlight their own loyalty. The Jewish press stepped up its own pressure on the communal leadership to provide Ottoman Turkish language lessons for Jewish youth so they would be able to advance in the military. Furthermore, public criticisms of the youth who fled military service grew, since the high attrition rate "does not give honor to the Jewish community."[93]

At the time of the Balkan wars, the Jewish press advocated that Jews volunteer for the army, "for the good of the homeland, the love of which is deep in their hearts!"[94] Reports in the Ottoman Turkish-language press that the empire's Jews were not contributing to the war effort elicited a strongly worded rebuttal in the Hebrew press. As a further measure, the chief rabbi issued a circular to the Jewish communities of the empire:

> My dear brothers! Our dear and beloved homeland stands in danger. The enemies who launched a war against our land want to defile her honor! In the face of such a situation the whole Ottoman nation is rising without difference to race or religion like one person to defend her holy homeland, her honor and her sons. . . . In these difficult moments in which our beloved homeland finds herself, there is upon us, especially, a sacred responsibility to show our government how much we are in her debt with gratitude, how much we give her without limit, and every one of us will help save the honor of her nation and her land.[95]

The chief rabbi's circular underscores the very fragile position of non-Muslims by 1912–13, a situation that renewed tensions between them and revealed the very real strains under which the Ottomanist project was suffering. Locally, an unnamed Christian newspaper defamed a Jewish doctor in Jaffa who had volunteered to serve as a military physician, saying that he had volunteered purely for personal financial gain. In his defense, "Ottoman Jew/Yehudi 'Otomani," from Jaffa, blamed "the usual Christian jealousy," claiming that the Christians had done this "at a time when their doctors are fleeing to Egypt." "Certainly Dr. Moyal will take them to court," the anonymous writer confidently proclaimed.[96]

INTERCOMMUNAL RIVALRY III: ANTI-SEMITISM, ANTI-ZIONISM, AND THE PRESS WARS IN PALESTINE

Indeed, throughout the years 1910–14, Muslims, Christians, and Jews used the Ottoman censor and court system extensively as an arbitrator as they sought legitimacy from the government that their activities were, unlike those of their opponents, compatible with Ottomanism. In addition to the issue of military service, there were dozens of mutual recriminations in the Ottoman press between Jewish, Christian, and Muslim writers, editors, and ordinary citizens who accused each other of libel or defamation on the individual, communal, and imperial level. Lawsuits generally involved accusations of printing falsehoods, of slander, and of dividing the Ottoman nation.[97]

For example, *Liberty*'s editor, Haim Ben-'Atar, was taken to court in late 1912 after publishing two short articles: one stating that the Italians were bringing running water to Tripoli after their invasion, and the other claiming that the Italian, Austrian, and Russian governments had plans to conquer additional Ottoman territories. The judge who questioned Ben-'Atar asked why he was publishing "false news that stirs up the spirit of the people." In response, Ben-'Atar argued that his paper "fulfills its obligation as an Ottoman newspaper devoted to homeland and the good of the government," and that he had published those translated articles only to show what the European press was writing about the empire.[98] Two months later *Liberty* noted that its editor was appearing in court for the fourth time that month. Similar altercations with the government censor took other newspaper editors to court.

More than any single other issue, however, Zionism stood at the center of the "press wars" in Palestine, drawing not only numerous lawsuits, but also an unprecedented public dialogue between newspapers. As the extensive research of historian Rashid Khalidi has shown, at least six hundred anti-Zionist articles were published in ten leading Arabic newspapers between 1908 and 1914.[99] These articles espoused opposition to Jewish immigration (as a demographic threat), land purchases (as a territorial threat), and the Zionist ideology of establishing an independent Jewish homeland (as an ideological and political threat). The importance of these articles in the consolidation of a collective Palestinian consciousness has been analyzed elsewhere, but it is also important to note that the press wars over Zionism were frequently depicted as an intercommunal clash in Ottomanist terms. Criticisms from Christian or Muslim newspapers were, according to the Jews, nothing less than attempts to divide the Ottoman nation. Likewise, for Christian and Muslim critics, Zionism itself was counter to the integrity of the Ottoman state no less than it was a danger to Palestinians.

Already in the spring of 1909, two Ladino newspapers in Jerusalem published an account of an article which had appeared in the Jaffa newspaper *Al-Asmʿaī*, in which Isʿaf al-Nashashibi, the young Ottomanist poet, had reportedly "dishonored the Jews." Al-Nashashibi's original articles are missing, but it seems that in addition to publishing an offensive cartoon and anecdote about a Jew in the desert, al-Nashashibi complained about Palestinian Jews' indifference toward the broader cultural renaissance that was taking place among Jerusalem's Muslim and Christian intellectuals.

> They [the Jews] should help in reviving this [Arabic] language after its destruction . . . since they [want to] attach their hearts to ours in this land. And I expect that they will rid their hearts of those empty aspirations like the question of Zionism or governing Palestine, since this is a hope which will be very difficult to execute. If the Jews want to live a good life with us, they should trample these hopes under their feet, and they should unite with us in respecting this beautiful language which their grandfathers enriched so much in Spain. . . . They should imitate our brothers the Christians, who are founding schools and teaching this beautiful language.[100]

The Ladino newspapers took offense and immediately demanded that the Jewish community establish an Arabic-language newspaper to "clos[e] the mouths of these terrible adversaries." In addition to defending the Jews against attacks, the envisioned newspaper would also "show how much good our brothers bring to their *patria* and how great is the part that the Jews take in the economic development of Palestine."[101] Indeed, almost immediately, the Jewish writers Shimʿon and Esther Moyal, fluent in Arabic, issued flyers responding to *Al-Asmʿaī*'s attacks.[102]

Interviewed weeks later by *Liberty*, Dr. Moyal argued that the Jewish community needed to respond to these attacks in the Arabic press before they spread. Indeed, he feared, it may already be too late. A later article in *Liberty* cried out, "Danger!" to its readers, pointing out that after the establishment of "our beloved constitution," the Arabic press began printing anti-Semitic articles. "Only he who has read . . . only he can feel the enormity of the terrible things which will come to pass in the future to the people of Israel, in the land of Israel, if we do not hurry to preempt them."[103]

Moyal was not the first to propose a Jewish newspaper in Arabic, although he would be the strongest proponent of this plan and the one to eventually accomplish the task. Even before the Nashashibi incident, Albert Antébi had proposed the establishment of a bilingual Arabic-French newspaper that would be moderate, a supporter of the sultanate and the constitution, as well as a defender of regional and municipal economic interests—"openly Ottoman-national." The newspaper would be run by Jews, however it would identify with general (not Jewish chauvinistic) interests. According to Antébi's vision, "by identifying the Jewish interests with those general to the area, we will ensure our colonization project an era of prosperity that the diffusion of *baksheesh* [bribery] does not."[104] When his correspondent revealed that he was not interested and proposed that the Zionists pay for such a paper instead, Antébi responded that the Zionists would provoke a Muslim, nationalist, and anti-Semitic response; all the separatists, Antébi warned, whether Macedonian, Albanian, or Zionist, would be crushed with the same vigor. Instead, he argued, "the future is with patriotic, Ottoman liberalism, enlightened, active and devoted. All our Jews—and the [Zionist] colonists especially—must embrace it without delay or reserve."[105]

Despite Antébis's efforts, in the years before World War I the main thrust of the Jewish press in Palestine would be to cope with anti-Zionism in the local press. More than any other newspaper, the Sephardi-edited and -run *Liberty* stood out in its efforts to monitor the Arabic press and alert its Jewish readership to Arab opposition to Zionism.[106] It translated articles from Arabic language newspapers, devoted numerous columns to the topic, and included news "from the field." It was also a frequent instigator of using legal recourse and political pressure to moderate the local critics of Zionism, as its numerous letters to the chief rabbi of the empire attest. Around the same time, *Liberty* turned its attention to alleged anti-Jewish reports in the Ottoman Turkish and Greek press. It bemoaned, "The days of joy and delight have passed, the days of noisy parades have changed, the voices of 'Long live liberty, brotherhood, equality!' have vanished, and here and there began to be heard voices of incitement against the Jews."[107] As the paper wrote, "we hope that the constitutional Ottoman government will see all those who lecture like this and forbid the publication of these kinds of articles whose whole aim is to create an anti-Semitic movement in our free country which needs only more unity."[108]

Moyal had warned the editors of *Liberty* that a new newspaper published up north, *The Carmel*, was already agitating against the Zionist colonies in the Galilee.[109] Over the next several years, the most intense battles were fought between *The Carmel* and representatives of the Jewish community and Zionist movement, characterized by a cycle of complaints against the paper, after which *The Carmel* might be forced to shut down for one- to two-month periods. For example, in the fall of 1909, Chief Rabbi Haim Nahum filed an official complaint with the Ottoman Ministry of Interior about the paper, and in late October, *Liberty* notified its readers that *The Carmel* had ceased publication for unknown reasons. In early February, *Liberty* notified its readers that *The Carmel* had resumed publication, but just one week later, Haim Nahum again requested that the paper be shut down, since "it was at the root of distance and disturbances among the peoples in the country."[110]

Members of the Haifa Jewish community supported the chief rabbi's lawsuits, arguing that *The Carmel*'s true aim was "of course to destroy our value in the eyes of our surrounding neighbors and to awaken the anger of the masses against us."[111] Additional newspaper articles accused *The Carmel* of turning the Ottoman Turkish press and public opinion in Istanbul against the Jews, as well as of corrupting other Arabic newspapers. As *Liberty* darkly noted, "Slowly the seed of hatred from *The Carmel* bore fruit not only in Haifa but also in Damascus, Beirut, Sidon, 'Akka (Acre), and all the cities of Syria."[112]

In June 1910, however, Neguib Nassar successfully defended *The Carmel* against the chief rabbi's latest lawsuit, arguing that the paper was founded to protect human rights, Ottoman unity and assimilation of its peoples, and to warn the government of the ambitions of foreign residents. The aims of the Jews, according to *The Carmel*, could only damage the advancement of Ottomania and its success.[113] The general prosecutor agreed that *The Carmel* was anti-Zionist, but maintained that this was a legitimate political position that was Ottomanist in sentiment, rather than anti-Jewish, as the chief rabbi and *The Carmel*'s critics maintained. For its part, *Liberty* angrily reported that Nassar was cheered on by the assembled (and, in its view, anti-Semitic) audience.

In addition to *The Carmel*, the Jaffa-based newspaper *Palestine* was shut down several times, once after the governor declared that it "sows discord among the elements of the country." After another such lawsuit, this time launched at the initiative of the Ministry of Interior, *The Carmel* came to the defense of its southern ally, arguing that "*Palestine* is among the newspapers that serve the state and the homeland in loyalty and devotion." Two months later, after additional incitement by *Liberty* against *Palestine*, *The Carmel* opined that it was odd that *Liberty*, "a Zionist paper that advocates foreign government in the heart of the Ottoman Empire," should cast aspersion on *Palestine*, "a paper which serves the government and defends its existence and unity and social and economic success." The press wars continued; on another occasion, in April 1913, the government shut down *Palestine* for "dividing between the races." The following year, *Palestine* successfully defended itself against another lawsuit when the court found that an article it published fell within the purview of free speech, given that it targeted Zionists and foreign Jews, not Ottoman Jews.[114]

In other words, in addition to expressing rivalry in the public sphere, the press was also a site for battles over Ottomanism itself. The legal proceedings against the Palestinian press centered on a discourse of "public good" and the "unity" or "utility" of the nation. The Hebrew *Liberty* explained its role in the press wars in these terms:

> If we attack *Palestine* or *The Carmel* or any other paper that plants hatred and animosity between the nations and especially between the Jews and the Muslims who always lived in complete brotherhood and traditional friendship . . . no one can find in this any chutzpah since our war is a holy and exalted war. . . . How can *The Carmel* claim that their brother [*Palestine*] is loyal and faithful to the state? Is placing thorns of accusation on an entire people who bring life to the state and its residents [really] defending on behalf of the government? Is slander against the Jews who are truly loyal to the beloved homeland and for whom no sacrifice is too burdensome for the good and wholeness (of the homeland), is that fighting on behalf of unity of the peoples? No and no! . . . The duty of the government is to protect the honor of the quiet and peaceful peoples truly loyal to it in their innocent hearts, and to control those who plant the seeds of hatred.[115]

To a certain degree, then, the press was used as a deliberate tool by both Jews and Christians to divide the other from their Muslim compatriots. For example, in the midst of the wars in the Balkans, *Liberty* encouraged the press to work to "strengthen the good ties" between Muslims and Jews that had emerged as a result of the war which had cast doubt on the loyalty of the empire's Christians. Within days, however, *Liberty* complained that the Christian-run *Palestine* had published "another lie" that local Jews were agitating against the Muslim Rumelian refugees. "Our Muslims here should think about the aim of these lies," the paper warned.[116] Indeed, as we will see in the concluding chapter, the press was a significant factor in the reorganization of communal alliances in Palestine.

For its part, the Jewish press conflated anti-Zionism with anti-Semitism and, as we will see in Chapter Six, never engaged with the substance of the criticisms aired in the Palestinian Arab press, despite working hard to fight against them. By early 1912, Shim'on Moyal organized a public meeting in the Jewish community to discuss the anti-Zionist press. *Liberty*'s Jaffa correspondent "Ben-Emeti" reported on the meeting in some detail, and remarked that despite the fact that the meeting was set for noon on a work day (and not on Shabbat or in the evening), there was a significant gathering that showed up at the main synagogue, Kehilat

Ya'kov. He remarked that though many public officials did not come, "those whose hearts ache at the awful situation found among his people in his land came."[117]

In his invitation to the meeting, Moyal indicated how he and others like him were able to reconcile their positions as both supportive of Zionism and seeking rapprochement with their Arab neighbors: "Our Hebrew national ambitions do not oppose [the Arabs'] own ambitions and we have the ability to work with energy and a devoted spirit for the shared homeland [*ha-moledet ha-meshutefet*] and for the foundational level of the Ottoman people under whose umbrella we live, at the same time that we desire to be a special Jewish nation concerned with its own language, its own style, its own past, its own future, and its own customs." While several leading Ashkenazi members of the Jewish community expressed opposition to placing any importance at all on the Arabic press, Moyal insisted, saying, "We must organize and present ourselves before the masses, to [show them] our ambitions for the good of the homeland."[118]

Together with Nissim Malul, the Moyals established the Society for Arabic Publishing (ḥevrat hadpasa he-'aravit) in Jaffa, selling shares in order to establish a printing press to "disseminate the news of how the Jews have worked for the good of the homeland" and to "[defend] against our enemies."[119] The society published numerous telegrams and articles as flyers, but its role was controversial within the Jewish community. For example, on December 27, 1912, *Liberty* published a notice about a meeting between the leaders of the Zionist colonies and the Ottoman government to determine their taxes due. *Palestine* issued an article that argued the colonies should be taxed for the income of the ha-Carmel ha-Mizrahi wine company. According to *Liberty*, the society "immediately mobilized and issued a flyer that said it was unfair [to tax them] because there was no connection between the private company and the colony farmers." This article was printed and distributed in the city about an hour after the emergence of the *Palestine* article and the two were practically sold side by side. According to the correspondent, however, "the absurd thing is that the owners of the newspaper *Palestine* say . . . that they write their poisonous articles only because Dr. Moyal and Dr. Malul answer them, and they are angry because those two Jewish writers purport to being deputies of the Jewish people in its entirety! . . . It's a shame we did not disappoint them."[120]

Around the same time, the Moyals, Malul, and a dozen other Sephardi men and women organized themselves in a group called The Shield (Ha-Magen), in order to consolidate efforts to defend the Jews from press attacks as well as to foster understanding between Arabs and Jews. Other known members of the group included sons of the most prominent Sephardi families—David Moyal, Yoshu'a Elkayam, Yosef Amzalek, David Hivan, Yosef Eliyahu Chelouche and Ya'kov Chelouche, Avraham Elmaliach, Moshe Matalon, and Nissim Malul, as well as two women, Esther Moyal and Farha (Simha) Chelouche (a Moyal cousin).[121] Many of these men and women had been educated in Arab schools and universities in Beirut and Cairo, and their weekly meetings at the home office of David Moyal were conducted in Arabic.

In the sole surviving copy of The Shield's founding manifesto, entitled "To the Hebrew Nation in the Lands of Its Dispersion," Secretary Avraham Elmaliach laid out the organization's aims and tactics.[122] Although the text begins with a traditional laudatory summary of Zionist pioneer accomplishments in Palestine, what emerges is a fascinating document that clearly links their activities with a distinct Ottomanist and Palestinianist shared civic vision. When Elmaliach wrote of the Zionists as "bringing industry and culture and commerce" to Palestine, he meant that they did so for the "betterment of the *shared homeland* [h*a-moledet ha-meshutefet*], materially and spiritually." "Here, finally," Elmaliach wrote, "we have arrived at the moment when we can work together with our brothers . . . for the development of their land and our land [*arẓam ve-arẓenu*]." Most explicitly, Elmaliach pressed the Arabs and Jews to work together for *moledetam u-moledetenu*—their homeland and ours. The Shield's vision was not one of exclusive ownership or rights to Palestine. Rather, it used the very evocative Hebrew of the Zionist movement to declare joint ownership and responsibility between Jews and Arabs, a fact that would earn them the opprobrium of a wide segment of the local Ashkenazi Zionist community.[123]

Elmaliach outlined the aims of the association—mainly, "to defend through all legal and kosher means our status in the land." The Shield, according to its manifesto, was to concern itself with both internal and external concerns. Internally, The Shield "would endeavor to strengthen the bond between the Jews and the rest of the residents of the land and the government." To this end, it intended to launch a press campaign that would translate the Arabic, Ottoman Turkish, and foreign-language publications that appeared in the Ottoman Empire and send them to every major Jewish and Hebrew publication "so that the sons of our people will know what is written about them, between the good and the bad." The association also called on "the guardians of Israel" to respond to anti-Zionist and anti-Semitic articles with their own submissions to the non-Jewish press. Furthermore, The Shield intended to influence the existing Arabic and Ottoman Turkish press, to increase their subscribers and readers and to improve their content and style. Finally, The Shield vowed that it "would not let pass quietly any hateful article, big or small, in order that such a silence would be considered a message from our side." All of these activities, of course, reflect a very defensive program of public relations, and also reflect the degree to which the press, far from its Ottomanist origins, had become a battlefield in an emerging sectarian-nationalist struggle in Palestine.

CHAPTER FIVE

Shared Urban Spaces

In the fall of 1908, an extraordinary public exchange took place between Yitzhak Levi, a private Jewish citizen and then-candidate for Ottoman parliament, and the new governor of Jerusalem Subhi Bey. In an open letter published in the Hebrew press, Levi challenged the new governor, raising questions about the role of a "constitutional pasha" and the contours of projected progress for the provincial corners of the empire.[1] Levi's letter began by emphasizing a sharp break between the new constitutional regime and the old Hamidian state; previous governors had been more interested in their own financial gain and in stunting local progress, Levi claimed, while at the same time being praised in the official state press as "servants of the nation." In contrast, the constitutional era demanded a new relationship between the state's functionaries and its citizenry. In this new era, according to Levi, the chief utility of the imperial government would be in advancing local development and progress. "Your Honor is the chief functionary of the Jerusalem district but also its chief servant, and it is incumbent upon Your Honor before everything else . . . not to place any obstacle in the way of this movement in propelling the country towards the path of progress and civilization."

Levi proposed a series of economic and political reforms for Jerusalem which would result in a complete overhaul of administration in the province, and placed it on the governor's shoulders.

> We are thirsty for progress and ameliorations since we have been deprived for thirty-two years from this pleasure, and we have lost the most beautiful years of our youth under the pressure of that tyrannous government . . . You do not have to take a glance around you to see what you have to do. The cities and the rural areas are in the saddest state. With the exception of a very few areas, agriculture and animal husbandry are almost abandoned everywhere. Industry and trade are hardly developed. The urban and rural administration leaves much to be desired. The legislation is full of obstacles. The courts system and justice are far too blind in this

country. Your sphere of activity is thus immense; there is enough to fill the most beautiful career of a civil servant, if you want to devote yourself to it seriously.

Most important, Levi demanded an increased role for the local population in provincial administration: "Before anything, Excellency, remember this well: it is clear that if the people were nothing to date, it is decided [they will] be everything in the future." Levi was speaking as a former Ottoman government employee, but also as a newly empowered imperial citizen.

Subhi Bey's response, which was published separately as a trilingual French-Arabic-Ottoman Turkish pamphlet, was an unprecedented public act of incorporating the city's leading citizens into the discussion and indeed, of forging a partnership between the expanding citizenry and the local government.[2] While consultative bodies had been established in the provinces following the 1867 Vilayets Law, the reality was more of tolerance of local involvement rather than real partnership, and the locals saw political-administrative involvement more as a "privilege" rather than a "right." Given the changing revolutionary mandate as well as the hostile circumstances under which Ekrem Bey, Subhi Bey's predecessor, had left Jerusalem, it was all the more critical for the new governor to propose partnership rather than conflict.

He clearly saw his role as central to the modernization of the province, including its adherence to the revolutionary, constitutional regime. In addition to outlining the various broader issues of local development and reform, the governor also listed the meetings he had held in his first week on the job, and he informed his readers of the various investigative and consultative commissions he had established with local bureaucrats and civic leaders. Among other things, Subhi Bey had received complaints and requests from the population, created a commission to examine the agricultural needs of the province, initiated the establishment of a chamber of commerce for the city, commissioned a research study for routing water to Jerusalem from the Arroube spring, met with the Jaffa-Jerusalem railroad company about transportation issues, and asked the municipality to study the construction of sewers in the city.

Subhi Bey had a busy first week indeed. More noteworthy than his schedule, however, was that, by translating, publishing, and disseminating the exchange between himself and Citizen Levi, Subhi Bey committed himself to the principles of transparency and accountability. This was implicit in the pamphlet's preface addressed to the reader, wherein the anonymous, pro-government publisher wrote:

This letter program is of the utmost importance for all the inhabitants of our province because it develops in a concise way all the reforms and improvements which His Excellency Subhi Bey will apply in the course of his administration. This letter is a *precious guarantee* for all of us, because it allows us to expect that henceforth the government understands the gravity of [the situation]. . . .

In addition, we urgently ask of all our fellow citizens [*muwāṭinaynā*] to facilitate the difficult task of our governor while providing him with all the . . . forces available to this country—then, one will see marvelous results emerging from all sides. *The collaboration of the people and the government* is the path of the future.

By appealing to his fellow citizens, irrespective of religion or ethnicity, the publisher of the pamphlet privileged the civic identification of the people of Jerusalem, casting it as a source of legitimacy and incorporation. This chapter further explores the city as an important site for revolutionary discourses and practices of imperial citizenship. After the 1908 revolution, throughout the empire middle-class citizens began to take on a new, public role, no longer content to defer to the central or local governments, or to the traditional urban notables of the provinces. Active in institutions such as local chambers of commerce and Freemasonry lodges, the urban residents of Jerusalem shared interests and values—local development and infrastructure, "modernization and progress," and good government. These institutions aided in the Ottomanization of the city in several ways: as sites of interconfessional sociability and cooperation, through their commitment to the revolutionary ideals of reform, democratization, and a modern vision of progress, and under the banner of Ottoman imperial patriotism. At the same time, however, they reflected and confronted the extant and budding cultural and political conflicts of the time.

URBAN CITIZENSHIP IN JERUSALEM

Jerusalemites were not entirely unfamiliar with the idea that members of the local population had a role to play in local governance. In fact, this had been a feature of the nineteenth-century Ottoman reform project, the Tanzimat, and from the issuance of the 1864 and 1871 Vilayets Laws, local councils had been established in Palestine—the administrative council, general council, and municipal councils.[3] Of the three, the administrative council was the most important for the province as a whole. It was authorized to deliberate and decide on public works, agriculture, finance, tax collection, police, land registry, and extraregional matters. It also could approve municipal budgets and had quasi-judicial powers over issues of landholding, such as overseeing the legality of land transfers and issuing land title deeds.[4] The general council met twice every year for forty-day sessions in which it deliberated on budget matters. Members of the administrative and general councils were appointed by the governor, who normally tapped members of prominent families as well as representatives from the various religious communities.[5] In the Jerusalem province, there was a history of regular, though by no means equal, Christian and Jewish representation on these provincial councils.

Beyond these provincial councils that implemented imperial policies, it was the municipal council which oversaw the day-to-day needs of the empire's residents. The first municipal government in Palestine was established in the 1860s in Jerusalem; half a century later at the end of Ottoman rule, there were twenty-two city councils active throughout the country.[6] Taxpaying city dwellers voted for the ten members of the city council, who also had to be property owners themselves, establishing an important precedent for urban citizenship practices.[7]

Little is known about the activities of the other municipalities, but the Jerusalem municipality's responsibilities were extensive: administration (budget, population registration, supervision of markets and cafés, monitoring currency use in the markets); law and order (overseeing the police force); health and sanitation (establishing a municipal hospital and pharmacy; cleaning streets and sewage on a regular basis); and construction, building planning and supervision (issuing permits; land expropriation for municipal use).[8] The municipal government also carried out social welfare programs such as supporting the poor and homeless, as well as supporting families unexpectedly blessed (and challenged) with the birth of twins.[9]

Out of all of the municipality's concerns, health and sanitation seemed to provide the greatest source of worry for the city council at the turn of the twentieth century. Cleanliness in public spaces was imperative for maintaining public health and preventing the spread of disease. This was particularly true for the Old City of Jerusalem, with its close quarters, mixed commercial and residential spaces, and narrow, winding alleys, but this concern for public health also led to the city council expanding its jurisdiction to the new extramural neighborhoods in 1902.[10] A few years later, in February 1905, the municipality more than doubled its cleaning budget, hiring al-Hajj Muhammad Khalaf, from the village of 'Ayn Karam, to bring twenty beasts of burden and the necessary tools for street cleanup. The city also planned to purchase sixty-six additional brooms, twenty-two baskets, and to hire an additional twenty workers for the job.[11] In addition to its cleanup efforts, the Jerusalem municipality, like other cities in the Ottoman Empire, employed a doctor and staffed a medical clinic; in 1912, the municipality opened a municipal hospital in the city to compete with the various private (usually European and Christian) hospitals in town.

The municipality did not run the city on its own, but relied on recruiting residents in the city. In fact, members of the urban republic were tapped to serve on a variety of city committees, such as the city's military reserve, guard duty and security, police reform, and elections committees, as well as to help supervise the above-mentioned cleanup project on the neighborhood level.[12] Furthermore, neighborhood and confessional "headmen" (known as *mukhtar*s) fulfilled important functions in mediating between the provincial government, the municipality, the *shari'a* court, and town residents. It also seems that there were elected councils in various neighborhoods, with ex officio religious leaders as well as four to five elected residents.[13]

With the 1908 revolution, an important new tool emerged in the practice of urban citizenship: the newspaper. As we saw in the last chapter, the Ottoman revolutionary press far surpassed its predecessors in scope and aims, and played a central role in outlining and debating the shape and content of Ottoman imperial citizenship. At the same time, by legitimating the city as a shared unit and in exhorting readers to participate in urban life in a responsible manner, the press was vital in shaping a conscious and engaged urban citizenry.

In addition to reporting on the work of municipal authorities or publishing municipal announcements, among the various subjects for press coverage were security, reports on the government's new urban antivagrancy measures, and public health measures.[14] For example, the municipality reminded the town's residents that throwing trash in the street was a public health risk and a traffic hazard, not to mention being illegal; it urged them to make use of "special containers" which would be picked up by the municipality. On other occasions, readers were warned to take precautions against cholera by purifying and washing their wells; informed of an outbreak of spinal meningitis and other epidemics; warned about rabid dogs; and cautioned against the sale of bad meat and dead fish.[15] At times and for good measure, appeals from the religious authorities would be published to strengthen the authority of the municipality and press.[16]

The press also served a role in the commercial life of the city, announcing the arrival of ships to Jaffa port, printing advertisements from various private businesses, publishing prices of staple goods, economic reports, new coins in use in the markets, and other related announcements.[17] In addition, the press contributed to the cultural life of the city by posting announcements of upcoming cultural events and announcements of the establishment of various institutions or associations, in addition to the more extensive coverage that certain organizations or events merited.[18]

Significantly, these news items went beyond the level of mere public service announcements; they were part of the press's active involvement in articulating the contours of a shared, modern city and its citizenry, in prodding the citizenry to participate or think of an event or issue in a particular way. In this vein the office of the *mukhtar* was praised as being useful, and irresponsible or inexcusable (in other words, anticivic) behavior was publicly reprimanded, such as when the Jewish neighborhood Me'ah She'arim was scolded in the pages of the press for refusing to pay for street-cleaning services.[19]

As well, press coverage of other Ottoman and world cities contributed to the local vision of the city. Comparisons were made, differences were pointed out, and lessons were drawn from others. For example, one newspaper editor wrote that "it should be hoped that Jerusalem will learn from its smaller and younger sister," Jaffa, since even though Jerusalem was cleaner than Jaffa, there were still areas with cats and dogs roaming freely among the trash and sewage.[20] Another article informed Jerusalemites about the municipal reforms under way in Galilean Safad, where, among other things, the deputy governor had ordered work to begin the project of bringing running water to the city and had appointed a citizens' committee to oversee the matter.[21] The unfamiliar thus was rendered familiar and possible, and knowledge of precedent elsewhere was intended to empower locals. Such was the case when readers in Jaffa and Jerusalem turned their eyes to the other provincial capitals in the empire, demanding a local health council "like that of other cities in Turkey [*sic*]" as well as improved infrastructure (port, railroad).[22]

The press also became an important voice in providing public praise or pressure on the municipal council, and the council, like governor Subhi Bey before, had little choice but to respond to the press in public. In the summer of 1909, for example, *Jerusalem* newspaper praised the Jerusalem City Council for banning peasant women selling crates of vegetables from sitting on the steps at the entrance to alleyways, as they blocked the path of residents. The paper then took the opportunity to pressure the municipality to close down the open market adjacent to Jaffa Gate, as it was an eyesore for the tourists who flocked to that part of the city. In response, the city council ordered that the market close down at seven in the morning, when tourists tended to wake up, after which the vegetable market would relocate to a side street.[23] In another case, a reader of *Palestine* newspaper complained that the Jaffa City Council needed to act against the smoke-filled cafés in town which posed a public health hazard. A few months later *Palestine* again complained that its request to the city council to regulate the meat market had been ignored, and a week after that, it requested that the city council lower the price of meat for the city's poor.[24] Other newspaper articles demanded more firefighters, policemen, and additional services for the city.[25]

Many of these complaints focused on a "modern" vision of the city as the literate, urban middle classes of Palestine demanded cleaner cities and more municipal services, and saw themselves in the eyes of Western visitors.[26] Other complaints, however, were directed at the city council for being a vestige of the ancien régime—corrupt, inefficient, prone to cronyism, and certainly not representative of the people. The Hebrew newspaper *Liberty* complained that one of the newly elected Jewish City Council members, Rahamim Mizrachi, wanted to fire a beloved municipal clerk and hire his sister's son in his place. "We won't let him!" warned the paper.[27] As well, in the summer of 1912 *The Crier* newspaper in Jerusalem reported that a municipal inspector who happened to be a member of the mayor's extended family had kicked a peasant woman in the market. The paper warned, "The inspectors should know that they serve the nation and the peasants as one. It is their duty to lighten the burden of the labors of the sellers and to guide them in the order of law."[28]

In fact, *The Crier* engaged in all-out war against the Jerusalem municipality and frequently published criticisms of the mayor, Husayn Hashem al-Husayni, and the council as a whole. *The Crier* accused the mayor of deliberately delaying new elections in 1912 in an attempt to hold on to power. "Certainly the members will not remain the same if there are new elections," *The Crier* declared confidently.[29] As we will see, this coincided with the beginning of sectarian struggles within Jerusalem.

MUNICIPAL MODERNITY

One of the important expectations of the revolution was its vision of progress and development. Along those lines, the Jerusalem municipality actively promoted local development and progress along a particular model of a modern, urban city, envisioned as a city with running water, electricity and telephones, modern urban transport, and other visible public works. In the summer of 1910, Jewish city councilman David Yellin undertook a fact-finding trip to research municipal services in European cities. Their motivation, according to his letter of introduction sent by Mayor Husayn Hashem al-Husayni, was simply because "after the proclamation of the constitution in Turkey [*sic*], our town of Jerusalem has tried to organize itself and to bring itself to the level of *modern requirements*."[30]

In this endeavor, as in previous projects of local development, the municipality worked closely with (and also sometimes against) other institutions, individuals, and government bodies to promote and successfully execute the modernization of the city. The various actors' plans for the city were part of the revolutionary project, aspiring to transcommunal "civic Ottomanism," Ottoman economic nationalism, and a certain degree of mimicry of European modernity.

Perhaps the most important organization for bourgeois activity in promoting local development was the local Chamber of Commerce, Industry, and Agriculture, established in Jerusalem and Jaffa.[31] The chamber solicited the participation of all sectors of the commercial classes so that already in its first months, it had fifty-nine registered voting members. These members ranged from large landowners, import-export merchants, shopkeepers, moneychangers, and other local businessmen; in addition foreign consuls were represented in the chamber. While membership dues were on a progressive sliding scale, the minimum was still a sizable sum that only the reasonably successful could afford.[32] As evidenced by the list of the chambers' officers, it is clear that Jews and Christians played a prominent role in the commercial life of Jerusalem and Jaffa, respectively.[33]

As a semiofficial Ottoman institution, the chamber served a variety of commercial, legal, and networking functions. Among its central responsibilities were sending weekly statistical reports to the chamber of commerce in Istanbul (which was part of the Ministry of Commerce), registering merchants and businesses in a commercial directory, and serving as liaison between local consulates, merchants abroad, and local businessmen. The chamber had some legal power in that it conducted bookkeeping and certification, legalization, and registration of notes, contracts, bills, and so on, for a fee. It also had legal status in the commercial and *shar'ia* courts.[34] Significantly, the chamber seemed to have a real role in the administration and decision making of the province; it sometimes filled in for the governor in administrative decision making when he was away, and relevant Ottoman officials such as the imperial agricultural inspector were awarded with positions in the chamber.[35]

Most important, the chamber represented the interests of Palestine's middle- and upper-class business community, and often served as a lobbying arm between private business and the Ottoman government or European vendors. For example, in 1909 the chamber successfully lobbied the Ministry of Agriculture to send them twenty-five hundred doses of serum to combat bovine pests. On a separate occasion, when the Ministry of Religious Endowments decided to regulate the deforestation of olive and mulberry trees in Palestine, the chamber ordered a reforestation project analysis. The chamber also advocated on behalf of Palestine's vintners, who were being charged a high tax rate (76 percent) for the sale of alcoholic spirits. More successful, however, was the lobbying drive to establish a mixed commercial court in Palestine, which finally came into being by 1910.[36]

The chamber's real ambitions, however, lay with the promotion of public works and infrastructure development in Palestine. While Palestine already had an intercity railway line between Jerusalem and Jaffa, it lacked public transport that would connect the rest of the country, as well as intracity local transport such as electric tramways in Jerusalem to connect the New and Old Cities as well as the outlying villages and towns. It also lacked running water, sewage, electricity, telephones, and other amenities of modern urban life.[37]

Until then, Jerusalem had been dependent on rainwater that was stored in the city's numerous public and private cisterns as well as springwater that fed into a number of natural pools and ancient wells around the city; the city's Roman-era aqueduct system had been repaired as recently as the 1890s. However, by the turn of the twentieth century these natural and traditional sources proved insufficient for the growing city, and it was forced to rely on a private market of water purchased from water carriers who transported it from springs and wells outside the city limits.[38]

For Jerusalem's leading citizens, infrastructure development, commercial growth, and political liberty were intimately intertwined. As the chamber stated: "Air, water, and heat are the basic elements of the life of man and of beast . . . we deplore the debased situation . . . which obliges the municipality to import water by wagon during the years of drought. . . . It is incumbent upon a constitutional regime to reform the oversights of nature and to render healthy water and lively heat accessible to all the poor."[39]

In fact, one of the first steps taken by the new governor, Subhi Bey, we will recall, was to appoint a local committee to study the question of bringing running water to Jerusalem. That committee, which consisted of a combination of important local officials and regular citizens, including one Christian and one Jew, issued its reports with the understanding that running water was important, not only for the hygiene and public health of the city, but also for the city's dignity as well as its image in the eyes of its European residents and visitors.[40] In making its report, the committee thought in clear civic terms as well as commercial ones. Given that in the past forty years the population of Jerusalem had more than doubled and that an additional ten thousand to fifteen thousand immigrants were expected in the following ten to fifteen years, it was imperative that Jerusalem's water needs be addressed as an element of urban growth. As well, the committee was not blind to the fact that the city drew poorer religious pilgrims and migrants more often than affluent ones, and therefore the affordability and availability of water for all of the city's residents and visitors was a central concern. Free water distributed to the city's public fountains was a necessary component of urban development as well as a respectful continuation of the Islamic charitable practice of building these fountains.

The committee outlined the technical aspects of bringing running water to Jerusalem, siding with an 1891 report by the city's then-engineer, Franghia Bey, which had identified a spring outside of Jerusalem as the best source from which to build canals to the city. The committee then raised the question of financing for the project, given that the municipality could not afford such an investment. The committee recommended that a private Ottoman investment society be founded to undertake the project, that the administrative council transfer funds to the city council

Figure 5.1. Traditional public water fountain in the Old City of Jerusalem. Throughout the Islamic world, public fountains provided city residents with water for drinking, cooking, and sacred ablutions. In Jerusalem the water supply came from wells, rainwater collected in cisterns and natural pools, and water brought by water carriers from natural springs outside the city. Library of Congress, Prints and Photographs Division (LC-DIG-matpc-06598).

for a research study, and that the eventual water project be organized along the lines of a religious endowment where its revenues would continue to benefit the city in perpetuity. The committee's recommendations signaled a local critique against the standard way that Ottoman development in public works had taken place throughout the nineteenth century—via European concessionaires whose investment in the empire's ports, railroads, and cities were first and foremost commercial ventures. In contrast, Jerusalem's leading members envisioned its development as lying in the hands of fellow Ottomans who had a stake in the project's success for the good of the city's residents, not simply for their own pocketbooks.

To that end, in late 1908 the chamber of commerce in Jerusalem established an investment society, the Commercial Society of Palestine (Société commerciale de Palestine; Bank Filasṭīn al-Tijārī; SCP) as an effort to mobilize private, local capital and investment.[41] At a time when most of the empire's finances and public works concessions were in the hands of foreign banks and firms, the chamber of commerce was committing itself to a national Ottoman economic policy, a spirit which was certainly aided by the ongoing boycott against Austro-Hungarian goods explored in Chapter Three. In fact, when the SCP was finally legalized by the Ottoman government in the summer of 1909, one of the conditions on the imperial *ferman* was that they employ "as far as possible" Ottomans with diplomas from Ottoman upper schools.[42]

Although the French Consulate claimed that the idea behind the SCP was spearheaded by "Christians of diverse rites," the SCP was a mixed society. Leading members included the chamber of commerce president, Hajj Yusuf Wafa, Isma'il al-Husayni, Albert Antébi, and Selim Ayoub. Jerusalem's two parliamentarians were also rumored to be leading forces behind the society's founding.[43] The SCP was a shareholders' bank, and it raised money from leading merchants, members of the chamber of commerce, and through the sale of smaller-scale shares to local Palestinians. Out of the six thousand individual shares sold by January 1909, five thousand had been sold to Muslims and Christians, while Jews purchased the remaining thousand. Another report stated that the largest group of shareholders was the investors affiliated with Hajj Yusuf Wafa (who owned two thousand shares); Isma'il al-Husayni and mayor Husayn Hashem al-Husayni (two thousand shares); Antébi, Tagger, and Abuchedid (two thousand shares); and Ayoub, Batatu, Jean, and Homsi G (two thousand shares).[44]

The society's objectives were banking operations and financial, commercial, industrial, and agricultural affairs. More specifically, the SCP set out to engage in five major areas in finance and commerce: applying for and securing concessions of public works in Palestine and the empire, in transportation, electricity and water; undertaking all agricultural and financial enterprises; financing industry; offering discounts on commercial matters, such as advances on titles, merchandise, and precious metals, current accounts, deposits of accounts, and so on; and securing titles for its enterprises or those of other concessionary societies.[45]

By September 1909, the bank had officially opened its doors to customers; Selim Ayoub, a Christian, was its branch director, with Yeroham Elyashar, a Sephardi Jew, as assistant director. Little is known of the bank's day-to-day activities, although it reportedly was engaged in mortgage loans, real estate investment advising, credit lines, and foreign currency and stocks. In addition it seems to have pursued commercial interests as a broker between foreign and local business. In 1912, for example, the SCP expressed interest in purchasing American-made mowers, plows, and harvesting machines for sale in the Jerusalem region. The SCP was also a dues-paying institutional member of the American Chamber of Commerce for the Levant.[46]

The jewel of its investment activities, without a doubt, was the pursuit of public works concessions in Palestine. Because the society was composed of highly influential individuals, it very early on enjoyed a strong relationship with the local Ottoman governor, who "promised it would have preference over all other entrepreneurs in all governmental enterprises." Because of the governor's assurances and because of its political commitment to economic nationalism, the founders of the SCP thought they would have a distinct advantage in soliciting the public works concessions in Jerusalem.[47]

Therefore, the SCP submitted a proposal to provide running water for Jerusalem via a canal from the al-Arroub springs twenty-one miles south of the city. According to the terms of its proposal, it would provide water free of charge to all of Jerusalem's residents, irrespective of confession or nationality, up to a certain limit; water would also be distributed freely to the city's public fountains. Beyond that stated limit, the SCP would charge for additional water use. The SCP also agreed to local and central government oversight, submission to the Ottoman courts, and responsibility vis-à-vis the populace. Their proposal was approved by the provincial administrative council on May 1, 1909.[48] The chamber of commerce praised the progress on the water project, arguing that it was necessary for economic development, political emancipation, and intellectual regeneration.

Soon thereafter, however, negotiations broke down. The SCP had proposed a tax on tanneries in Jerusalem in order to subsidize the water concession and ensure that the bank would be able to fully amortize the loan. However, MP Sa'id al-Husayni informed them that the Ministry of the Interior intended to tax the sale of meat in Jerusalem instead, a step which was vigorously opposed by the mayor, Faidi al-'Alami as well as Wafa, speaking on behalf of the chamber of commerce. Without warning, the mayor promptly signed a separate agreement with a German concessionaire to provide running water from 'Ayn Faraḥ, another spring, located eleven miles north of Jerusalem, undercutting the SCP as well as acting against the decision and authority of the administrative council.

The SCP protested vigorously, and its objections, voiced through the chamber of commerce, were phrased in national and reformist terms. The chamber expressed surprise that a deal had been hastily and secretly achieved between al-'Alami and the concessionaire Franck, in contrast to the extended and very public negotiations the SCP had carried out. The chamber argued that it would carry out "its imperative duty to translate public opinion and to present the general interest, despite all opposition and against all constraints. This is the essence of the principle of a constitutional government and its raison d'être, and its guarantee is the public discussion of everything that deals with the life of the nation."[49]

The chamber criticized the municipality's contract with Franck on technical terms, arguing that the chosen spring was located at an inhospitable elevation. More important, however, the financial terms of the contract were suspect. On the one hand, the contract avoided the tax on either meat or tanneries, but on the other hand, the contract would allow the Franck firm to charge high prices for the sale of water to the city's residents. In contrast to the SCP's proposal to sell water that exceeded the free quota at fifty cents per cubic meter, the Franck contract would charge residents 1.25 francs per cubic meter. The chamber opined: "Here is the antidemocratic side of the matter. The sacrifice of the vital interests of the masses for the egoism of the rich should be banned in a constitutional government."[50]

Moreover, whereas the SCP was a "local and Ottoman" project that would look after local and Ottoman interests, the other party was a European concessionaire who was apparently interested in the project solely as economic exploitation. The double standard applied was apparent: "Why was it not imposed on M. Frank as it was on the Commercial Bank to favor the industry and commerce of the country? Is this unimportant now?" The chamber demanded a public referendum to decide which plan Jerusalem would accept.

In its own direct appeal to the governor, the SCP reaffirmed its hope that its "status of being a local and indigenous bank [would result in its] preference."[51] Indeed, this was an important point for Jerusalem's investors and merchants, as was further evidenced in a public exchange in a French commercial newspaper that took place the following year. The paper, *La Vérité*, published an article praising the new director of the Jerusalem branch of the Ottoman Imperial Bank, which, despite its name, was in fact owned by French and British investors. According to *La Vérité*, director Fenech was an instrumental force in pushing forward public works in Jerusalem. The article elicited the angry response of "JD," a reader from Jerusalem intimately familiar with the SCP and the water concession, who argued that Fenech "is unknown" in Jerusalem and that *La Vérité* was ignoring the dozens of local figures—from the governor and parliamentary deputies to the municipality, chamber of commerce, and SCP—who had been involved in the Jerusalem public works project, not to mention the numerous local studies that had been undertaken in recent years to address the problem of bringing running water to Jerusalem.

La Vérité's editors responded by sarcastically noting that "even Pontius Pilate had studied the [water] issue," but that was a far cry from having the technical know-how and financial capacity to undertake such a project, which apparently only European capitalists did. "JD" wrote back one more time, arguing more clearly for a national economic policy.

> Constitutional Turkey [*sic*] and its [finance] minister, Cavit Bey, are rightly searching to emancipate our democracy from the financial oligarchy which pressured it [under] the old regime. It favors the development of independent national groups constituted of small savings. In this it follows the example of republican France. All our wishes are with the efforts of Cavit Bey in his battle against these powerful groups, because the independence of a nation resides foremost in its financial independence.[52]

However, for all its talk of being a local, national society, the truth is that the SCP was unable to raise enough capital in Palestine, forcing it to turn to the Anglo-Palestine Bank, a Zionist bank based in London with branches in Jerusalem and Jaffa, to secure its operations, which the bank did via the sizable collateral put up by the SCP board's leading members.[53] As well, the SCP was involved in secret negotiations with the Zionist movement to raise additional, significant sums of capital. In one meeting, Antébi proposed that the Zionist movement purchase up to half of the SCP's shares. The director of the movement's Palestine office, Dr. Arthur Ruppin, was intrigued by the possibility. First, there was undeniable political significance to being involved in public works in Palestine. As Ruppin put it to skeptical officials in Europe, "This will strengthen our position here so that Jewish interests cannot be ignored."[54] In addition, by becoming large shareholders the Zionist movement could ensure that people "of our beliefs" would sit on the board. However, Ruppin's desires on that score were disappointed when he was informed that non-Ottomans could not serve on the board of the SCP, and given that they could not be assured of a sympathetic majority on the board, the Zionist leadership decided against formalizing ties.[55]

Despite the collapse of talks with Zionist officials, it was clear to everyone involved that the sensitive issue of foreign financing and shareholding in the SCP should be discreet. As Ruppin delicately conveyed to another European Jewish organization, the Palestine Industrial Syndicate, "We kindly note that the recruitment of European capital should be entirely quiet and should happen without the involvement of the press. If the government felt that European capitalists stand behind the Ottoman society, it could spoil the whole thing."[56] Indeed, later attempts by the Zionist movement to secure a public works concession to modernize the natural baths in Tiberias and to mine the salt of the Dead Sea were severely criticized in the Arabic press on national patriotic grounds.[57]

As well, despite the enthusiasm displayed by some Zionist officials in Palestine for the project, the rumored cooperation also elicited Jewish opposition. One of the Yiddish newspapers in New York published a story about the establishment of an "Arab bank" led by Antébi and demanded an investigation by Z. D. Levontin, the director of the Jerusalem branch of the Anglo-Palestine Bank, presumably based on the assumption that cooperation of a Jewish, Zionist institution with an Arab bank bordered on treason, despite the fact that Antébi and other Sephardi Jews were involved in the project. In turn, Levontin responded that he hoped it would help Jewish-Arab relations. "We can and need to walk hand-in-hand with our neighbors the Arabs, residents of the land, in all matters relating to the flowering of our country, and it saddens me to see articles such as those that cause a rift between the residents of the land and the good leadership."[58]

In the end, the lobbying efforts of the SCP, aided by the Jerusalem Administrative Council and Chamber of Commerce as well as by influential Jewish figures in Istanbul, led to the collapse of the Franck concession. The Public Works Ministry in the capital objected to any local initiative in this matter, and took over the granting of concessions in Jerusalem. In the fall of 1911, the SCP hired a German engineer to study the issue further, hoping that the subsequent report would bolster its own renewed concessionary bid.[59] However in early 1914, the concession to bring water, electric tramways, and electricity to Jerusalem was awarded to an Ottoman Greek Orthodox developer, Euripide Mavrommatis, who was tied to a French banking firm. The SCP, which had failed in its own bid for the concession, succeeded in reserving 40 percent of the capital shares of the concession for "sons of the homeland."[60]

However, only months after Mavrommatis was granted the Jerusalem concession, the First World War broke out, and all plans for development in Jerusalem were shelved. It would be the British, not the Ottomans, who would be seen as "bringing modernity" to Jerusalem, in the form of running water, electricity, and telephone lines. And yet, the story of the SCP and its efforts to promote local development is inseparable from its politically Ottomanist mandate of uniting the Muslims, Jews, and Christians of Jerusalem as a force for local progress and development.

This shared civic commitment was evidenced in the proposed tramway lines for Jerusalem, as the six proposed lines took into account the interests of the Muslim, Jewish, and Christian resident communities as well as the needs of the city's many pilgrims and tourists. The tramway would have linked the Old City and the New City, secular spaces (the Schneller School, the municipal hospital) and spiritual spaces (Mount of Olives, Saint Croix), commercial markets and residential neighborhoods. The tramway also would have linked Jerusalem with some of its neighboring villages, Christian Bethlehem to the south and Muslim Shaykh Badr to the west.[61]

Figure 5.2. Train station in Jerusalem. The two-hour trip to Jaffa was considered a small luxury, and people of more modest means took the arduous overnight journey by wagon or carriage. In the years before World War I plans were drawn up by the Jerusalem City Council to construct a light rail (tramway) that would service outlying villages. Library of Congress, Prints and Photographs Division (LC-DIG-matpc-07472).

A similar apolitical civic spirit emerged in the proposed tramway lines for Jaffa that also targeted areas of importance to the city's Muslim, Christian, and Jewish communities. The hub of the tramway was to be the government house and the two lines were to pass through major neighborhoods ('Ajami, Manshiyya), stop at important religious sites (the tomb of Shaykh Ibrahim al-'Ajami), hit important commercial centers (markets, the import office, the German bank, the tobacco concession office), pass by two public fountains, and link the city with neighboring villages (Muslim Yazur and the new "Hebrew" suburb of Tel Aviv).[62]

The partnership between Jerusalem's business and civic leaders to promote the city's modern development could not have occurred against a blank slate, and in fact, it built upon a good deal of economic and commercial partnerships that existed between Muslims, Christians, and Jews in this period. For example, in the autobiography of Yosef Eliyahu Chelouche, a young Jew of North African provenance in Jaffa who was a prominent builder and merchant at the time, we learn that he partnered with Jurji 'Abdelnour, a Christian, and Khalil Damiati, a Muslim, to import wood from Rhodes; he also named numerous other individuals with whom he and his relatives were engaged in business, political, and personal exchanges.[63]

Rather than looking at these economic relationships (business partnerships, loans, sales and rentals, etc.) as transactions limited in time and space, I instead view these economic ties as important evidence of strong, ongoing social networks. Indeed, Chelouche's memoir is a testimony to the extensive network of relations that he, his father, uncle, and brother maintained with their Muslim and Christian neighbors. More poignant, Chelouche gratefully and painstakingly recounted each individual who aided him and his family during World War I, highlighting their place in his extended social network, whether it was a former business partner who lent them money, grain, and camels or a former employee who became a military prison guard and in turn aided his one-time patron. These relationships were based on trust, respect, and the common belief in a social system that rewarded both. For example, Chelouche mentions that his uncle Avraham Haim Chelouche famously conducted business with Bedouin tribal nomads from Bi'r al-Saba' (today's Be'er Sheva') and Muslims from Gaza without counting his receipts, trusting them to tell him the correct amount they owed and paid.

In most cases, these relationships took place in informal settings—the *diwan* (sitting room), the market, the neighborhood. By the turn of the twentieth century, however, new social institutions such as Freemason lodges had emerged as an institutionalized setting for social interaction and the creation of new social ties of solidarity.

BROTHER BUILDERS

From the mid-nineteenth century, Freemasonry provided a fertile philosophical and organizational ground for Ottoman liberal thinkers and reformers. Incorporating a belief in a Supreme Being, secretive rituals, and modern Enlightenment ideals, Freemasonry offered its members a progressive philosophical and social outlook, an important economic and social network, ties to the West, and a potential arm for political organizing. According to one historian of Ottoman Masonry, "By the end of the [nineteenth] century, there was hardly a city or town of importance without at least one lodge."[64]

While the British model of Freemasonry was more conservative in bent and generally was supportive of the religious and political status quo, the French tradition of Freemasonry which became more prominent throughout the Middle East emphasized liberal, philosophical positions and encouraged political engagement and critique, including support for revolution. In Egypt Freemasonry provided an outlet for political and social organization in the aftermath of British colonization, and Masons played a prominent role in the 1882 'Urabi revolution.[65] Indeed, the prominent Islamic anticolonial activist Jamal al-Din al-Afghani consciously linked a desired political reform with his Masonic activities: "The first thing that enticed me to work in the building of the free was a solemn, impressive slogan: Liberty, Equality, Fraternity—whose objective seemed to be the good of mankind, the demolition of the edifices and the erection of the monuments of absolute justice. Hence I took Freemasonry to mean a drive for work, self-respect and disdain for life in the cause of fighting injustice."[66]

We recall, of course, that al-Afghani had numerous protégés and disciples throughout the Ottoman world, especially in Istanbul and Cairo, and as a result, Freemasonry emerged to be one of the most important organizations during the Hamidian period. A number of leading Young Turks were active Masons before 1908, possibly because of the immunity from police scrutiny that the foreign lodges offered.[67] After 1908, far from its origins as a closeted secret society pursued by the state and its secret police, Freemasonry was legitimized and institutionalized as part of the new sociopolitical order. In 1909, the long-defunct "Supreme Council" of the Scottish rite of Masonry within the Ottoman Empire was reconstituted under the leadership of Minister of Finance Cavit Bey, MP Emmanuel Carasso, MP Dr. Rıza Tevfiq, and other luminaries of the CUP. Also that year, the Grand Orient Ottoman (GOO; sometimes called the Grand Orient de la Turquie) was established as

Figure 5.3. Diploma of the Grand Orient Ottoman. Bibliothèque Nationale (Paris), Manuscripts Division (Richelieu), FM54768.

the umbrella mother lodge of the empire, and Ottoman Minister of the Interior Talat Pasha was elected grand master. In establishing the GOO, the leadership sought to establish an autonomous Masonry in the spirit of political and national emancipation as well as to form a core of constitutional liberals who would be able to stand up to the reactionaries still found throughout the empire.[68]

With this kind of institutional support, it is no wonder that Freemasonry flourished openly in the empire in the revolutionary era. Between 1909 and 1910, at least seven new lodges were established or old ones revived from dormancy in Istanbul alone; most of them had names that linked them to the new spirit of liberty and progress: Les vrais amis de l'Union et Progrès, La Veritas, La Patrie, La Renaissance, Shefak (L'Aurore). In Salonica, Masonic lodges multiplied so much that another historian has characterized it as "proliferation that was likely to emerge, shortly, in a true Masonic colonization of the Ottoman Empire."[69] In Jaffa, the existing lodge, Barkai, exploded numerically, and in the following years several new lodges were established in Jaffa and Jerusalem.[70]

As a stark illustration of the rapid growth of Freemasonry in Palestine, in contrast to the 57 known Palestinian Masons who were active in the seventeen years before the July 1908 revolution, in the seven years after it, another 131 young men were initiated as Masons. Surely at least some of the men newly drawn to Freemasonry joined out of philosophical affinity. One surviving application for admission to a Beirut Masonic lodge describes the aspirant's motivation precisely in this way: "The Freemasonry order is an order that has rendered great services to humanity throughout the centuries and always raised high the banner of equality, fraternity, and liberty. It is an order that seeks to bring together mankind and to better it. I would also like to be part of such an order, to take part in benevolence and the useful works of your order."[71]

In the catechism for the first degree, the apprentice initiate was asked to reiterate the philosophical aims of Freemasonry in numerous ways:

QUESTION: What is a Freemason?

RESPONSE: He is a free man of good qualities, who prefers above all justice and truth, and who banishes prejudice and vulgarity, is equally friend of rich and poor, if they are virtuous.

QUESTION: What is Freemasonry?

RESPONSE: Freemasonry is an institution whose aim is to establish justice in humanity and for brotherhood to reign.

QUESTION: Why do you desire to be a Freemason?

RESPONSE: Because I am in darkness and I desire enlightenment.

QUESTION: What does a lodge do?

RESPONSE: It combats tyranny, ignorance, prejudice, and errors; it glorifies law, justice, truth, and reason.[72]

New members swore to abide by these principles as well as to promote mutual aid, public service, and Masonic loyalty, on pain of excommunication.

At the same time, it is also likely that at least some of the new Masons joined out of more worldly considerations, taking into account the close relationship between the Young Turks and the Masonic movement which gave it a crucial stamp of approval as well as a certain cachet. Indeed, several longstanding Masons expressed unease at the rapid proliferation of the movement in the revolutionary era. At least one Salonican lodge affiliated with the Grand Orient de France (GODF) objected to the establishment of the GOO on Masonic grounds, complaining to Paris, "among the reasons which push to me to place obstacles at the development of this new Masonic power is that I noted, alas, that the lodges subjected to its influence completely neglect the regulations of the Masonic statutes and regulations with regard to the recruitment of the members and blindly are subjects to the instructions of parties which work with another collective aim." Within weeks, however, Mason de Botton's reservations had dissipated, and he wrote to the GODF to ask them to do all that was "humanly and Masonically possible" to recognize the GOO.[73] Nonetheless unease continued, and another Mason complained later that "each [new initiate] wanted to become a Mason like the leaders of the new order. Those who entered a lodge by conviction were not very numerous."[74]

While we cannot know the motivation of each new (or, for that matter, old) Mason for certain, we do see a pattern of less intensive Masonic involvement on the part of these new initiates. A large percentage of the post-1908 initiates remained at the lowest Masonic level, that of apprentice, suggesting either insufficient Masonic fervor or insufficient preparation for promotion.

However, whether their motivations were ideological, political, personal, or a combination of all three, it is clear that new members were entering into one of the rare sites of institutionalized interconfessional, interethnic, and international sociability available in the Ottoman Empire.[75] The historian Paul Dumont gives as an early example the 1869 membership count of the Salonican lodge L'Union d'Orient: 143 brothers, among them 53 Muslims. As well, the "Prométhée" lodge in Janina was a mixed Greek-Muslim-Armenian-Jewish lodge until the 1897 Greco-Turkish war closed its doors.[76] In Palestine, of the 157 known

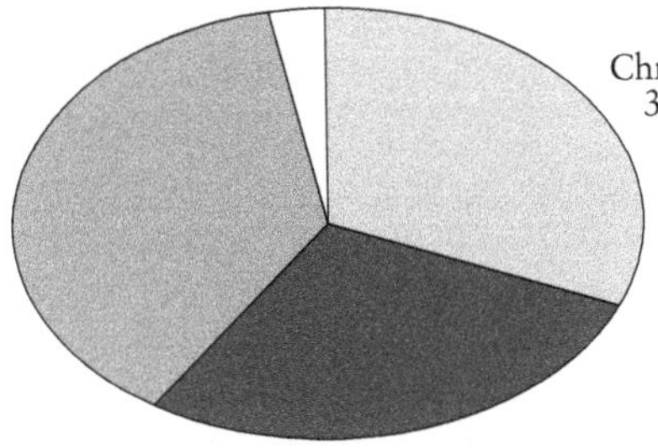

Figure 5.4. Freemasons in Palestine, 1906–15. Data from Centre de Documentation du Grand Orient de France, Paris, boxes 1126–27; and Tidhar, *Barkai: Album ha-yovel.*

members and affiliates of the main Masonic lodge from 1906 to 1915, 45 percent were Muslim, 33 percent were Christian, and 22 percent were Jews.

This is startling, considering that much of the anti-Masonic literature in the Middle East, historically as well as at present, denounces Masonry as the purview of the "minority" Jewish and Christian and foreigner European communities. The high participation of Muslims from Palestine and other parts of the Ottoman Empire in Masonic activity contradicts this charge, although it is still true that there was quite a significant overrepresentation of Jews and Christians in the lodges—roughly double their presence in the wider population.

The membership records of Barkai lodge in Jaffa also show quite starkly that the appeal of Freemasonry to Palestine's Muslims rose concurrent with the 1908 revolution. Originally founded in 1891 by Jews and Christians as Le port du Temple de Salomon and reconstituted in 1906 under French tutelage, Barkai emerged as the most important Masonic lodge in southern Palestine, a center for leading members of the political, intellectual, and economic elite of the province. At the beginning of 1908, Barkai had only three Muslim members out of thirty-seven total members; by the end of 1908, another fourteen Muslims had joined the lodge along with six Jews and Christians, marking the first time that new Muslim enlistment in the lodge exceeded that of the other two communities. In the six years following, new Muslim recruits exceeded both Christian and Jewish recruits every year; in most years the Muslim initiates exceeded new Jewish and Christian members combined.

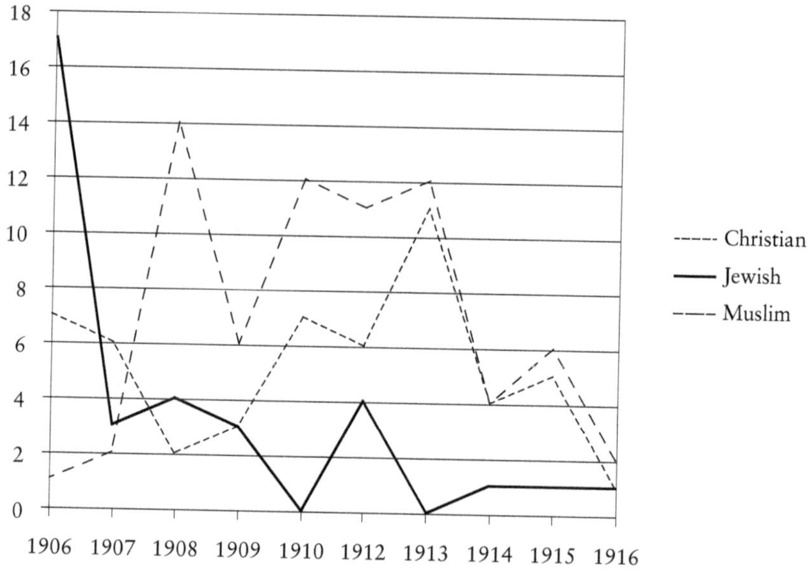

Figure 5.5. Barkai lodge, new members by religion. Data from Centre de Documentation du Grand Orient de France, Paris, boxes 1126–27; and Tidhar, *Barkai: Album ha-yovel.*

Beyond serving as a "neutral" meeting ground for members of different religions, Masonic lodges also served as vehicles for internal solidarity and social cohesion across various middle-strata and elite groups.[77] By and large, the lodges did not attract the older, established leaders of each community, but rather the "new generation" on the rise. Most Palestinian Freemasons in this period joined in their mid-twenties to mid-thirties (the average age was 31.8 years old at time of pledging), although they were sometimes younger (especially with family legacies) and sometimes older. These were the same men who supported the CUP, and later, the various decentralization and nationalist parties.

The members of Palestine's Masonic lodges were largely of the newly mobile middle classes of the liberal professions as well as younger members of the traditional notable families.[78] Fully one-fourth were government employees: fifteen lawyers and judges, seventeen administrative officials at both the provincial and municipal levels, and a dozen members of the military and police. Another third worked in commerce, banking, and accounting. The rest of the members were teachers, doctors, pharmacists, lawyers, and white-collar clerks.

Notable Muslim Masons included members of the ʻArafat, Abu Ghazaleh, Abu Khadra', al-Bitar, al-Dajani, al-Khalidi, al-Nashashibi, and al-Nusseibi families, most of whom fulfilled important state functions.[79] The Christian Masons were members of the growing middle classes, primarily employed in commerce and the liberal professions, from the Burdqush, al-ʻIssa, Khoury, Mantura, Sleim, Soulban, and Tamari families. Among the Jewish members, the Ashkenazim were largely colonists who had arrived in the 1880s and 1890s to live on the early Zionist agricultural settlements, adopting Ottoman citizenship upon arrival. The Sephardi and Maghrebi Jews, on the other hand, were younger members of economically and communally established families: Amzalek, Elyashar, Mani, Moyal, Panijel, Taranto, and Valero.[80]

Thus there was a certain degree of what one scholar has called the "democratic sociability" of the Freemasonry movement.[81] The radical innovation of a single organization that would voluntarily encompass—and equalize—Khalidis and Nashashibis as well as Burdqushes, Manis, and other young men from less illustrious families cannot be overlooked. At the same time, however, Freemasonry had the effect of reaffirming class lines. These men shared similar modes of modern education, exposure to foreign languages and Western ideas, a relatively high level of economic independence, and a growing sociopolitical weight in their province and the empire as a whole.[82]

To a certain extent, this group was preselected and self-perpetuating. In order to be accepted into a lodge, a prospective candidate had to secure the sponsorship of two lodge members in good standing. These recommendations often came from relatives (older brothers, cousins, uncles, sometimes fathers); in fact fully 32 percent of all Freemasons in Palestine had family members who were also member Masons, highest among Christians and Muslims.[83] As well, educational and professional ties also proved significant. Among the members of Barkai lodge were at least six recent graduates of the American University in Beirut in addition to many who had studied in the various professional schools in Istanbul.[84] Nine employees of the Jaffa and Jerusalem branches of the Ottoman Imperial Bank were brother Masons. Notably, only one Palestinian Mason was born in a village, and only one Mason was a religious functionary (in the Greek Orthodox Church). In this sense, then, Masonic lodges served as social networks for the growing middle class and governmental urban elites.

Because of this demographic and professional profile, networking played a huge role in Masonic appeal and cachet.[85] Inter-Masonic commercial relationships were frequent, and it was not uncommon for businessmen to request letters of introduction with a Masonic stamp of approval. Such a letter was obtained by Yosef Eliyahu Chelouche, who was not himself a Mason, from then-Venerable of the Barkai lodge Iskandar Fiuni (Alexander Fiani) in preparation for a business meeting with a Greek contact in Egypt.[86] Furthermore, a significant number (22 percent) of Freemasons in Palestine belonged to other Masonic lodges, whether locally or abroad, indicating the extent to which Freemasonry itself served as an overlapping affiliation network.

Masonic Activities

In the winter of 1913, a shocking case of "Masonic treason" rocked Palestinian Freemasonry: an Italian doctor named Salvatore Garcea had penetrated the Moriah Masonic lodge in Jerusalem and reported its activities both to the anti-Masonic French consul and to the heads of various religious communities. As a result of the exposé, seven or eight members faced "complete ruin."[87] This context of religious persecution of Masons as well as the loss of the Barkai lodge archives during World War I make it difficult to retrace the full scope of Masonic activities in the late Ottoman world.[88]

Nonetheless we do know that the Palestinian lodges' regular activities focused on philanthropy, mutual aid, and lay education. Lodge banquets were held to raise funds for the Ottoman army's winter clothing drive, for example. Lodge leaders regularly intervened on behalf of members, such as helping Anis Jaber, who was rendered destitute in September 1908. The lodge also lobbied on behalf of members with the Paris GODF headquarters, urging their assistance in one member's bid to be hired as director of the Rothschild Hospital in Jerusalem. In two cases of wrongful dismissal of Masons from the Jaffa-Jerusalem Railroad and the Messageries Maritimes at the Jaffa port, however, the GODF in Paris refused to intervene on the pretext that the economic importance of Jaffa to France overruled brotherly obligations.[89]

Beyond that, we can only wonder at what sort of Masonic activity was implied when members spoke of their missionary-like activities of "contributing to the diffusion of Masonic ideas in this Ottoman Empire which is our fatherland, which greatly needs to take as a starting point our motto to ensure the well-being of its children." In this context, Barkai requested that it be allowed to affiliate itself with the Grand Orient Ottoman in order to coordinate Masonic activities empire-wide.[90]

Barkai's appeal for permission to affiliate itself with the new GOO, however, was not made simply out of Masonic brotherhood; rather, it also was seeking protection and alliance with the potentially powerful umbrella organization. Because of its close ties with leading members of the new government and ruling party, the GOO was an important friend to have and to turn to, a fact not lost on Palestine's Masons who were under attack by a newly elected parliamentarian, apparently an avowed enemy of Freemasonry.[91]

Eventually, in 1910, the GODF did establish "fraternal relations" with the GOO and authorized its members to fraternize with the Ottoman organization.[92] As a result, in June 1910, several members of Barkai lodge decided to revive the defunct Temple of Solomon lodge in Jerusalem under the aegis of the GOO; eventually, twenty-two members of Barkai joined the new GOO lodge. Within a couple of years, however, the Temple of Solomon would undergo an internal split that divided Palestinian Freemasonry along political and sectarian lines.

Brother Against Brother

Virtually nothing is known of the Temple of Solomon lodge until March 1913, when a faction of the lodge broke off and formed its own provisional lodge demanding "symbolic and constitutional acceptance" by the GODF.[93] The new lodge, named Moriah, immediately requested catechism books, proposed a lodge seal, began searching for a garden as lodge headquarters, and set strict guidelines for admission to the lodge: only those with "irreproachable reputations" and decent French need apply.

According to its new Venerable, the task of the Masons of Moriah would be to defend the ideas of freedom and justice, particularly in Jerusalem, where clericalism and fanaticism were strongly against Masonic work. Avraham Abushadid, newly elected speaker of the lodge, urged his fellow Masons to ensure that "mutual tolerance, respect of others and yourself, and absolute freedom of conscience are not words in vain."[94] According to Abushadid, in the East "the word 'freedom' is replaced by 'servility' and 'fanaticism,' while 'equality' and 'fraternity' are vocabulary replaced by the synonyms of superstition and hypocrisy."

Through their Masonic mission, Abushadid envisioned a renaissance of the Ottoman people: "This new star which comes from our East, continues to shine with an increasingly sharp glare, and our path is clear. . . . The day will come when its luminous clarity will disperse all darkness, and the base of this shaking humanity will collapse and one will see then, all the nations, all the races, all the religions will be erased and disappear, and to make place for a rising generation, young people, free, fraternizing and sacrificing a whole glorious past, for a new era of peace, truth and justice."[95]

However, despite this claim of "erasing lines" between peoples, the split within the Temple of Solomon lodge had been a cultural and political one between two separate factions—one Arabic speaking, largely

Muslim and Christian; and the other French-speaking, largely Jewish and foreign. Of the eight known Temple of Solomon members who defected to form Moriah, five of them were Jewish, one Christian, and two were foreign Frenchmen. If before the split Temple of Solomon had been a relatively mixed lodge, with 40 percent Muslim, 33 percent Jewish, and 18.5 percent Christian members, postsplit Moriah had only one Muslim member. The "natives" of Temple of Solomon accused the "foreigners" of being, among other things, Zionists, while they were accused in turn of being "xenophobes."[96]

In the face of this growing schism between Freemasons in Jerusalem, the Temple of Solomon requested that the Jaffa-based lodge, Barkai, appeal to the GODF to deny Moriah's request for recognition.[97] According to Barkai Venerable Cesar 'Araktinji, the presence of two competing Masonic lodges in Jerusalem would cause discord. His request was politely denied by the GODF, which had long wanted a lodge in Jerusalem. "Tell our Freemason brothers of the lodge of the Temple of Solomon that they should not look at [Moriah] as a rival lodge, but rather a new hearth working also to realize our ideals of justice and brotherhood."[98]

Not to be dissuaded, 'Araktinji again appealed to the GODF, stating that the founders of Moriah had acted improperly in founding a lodge on their own. He also asserted that language problems had been one of the catalysts to the defection, since many of the Temple of Solomon members did not know French, and several of the defectors apparently did not know Arabic.[99] Furthermore, most of the Temple of Solomon members had been initiated under the GODF order through Barkai, and as a result, the GODF owed them special consideration. Finally, according to 'Araktinji, the main instigator of the defections, the French banker Henri Frigere, had promoted personal animosity among Jerusalem's Freemasons, and in order to mend the growing rifts in Palestinian Freemasonry, 'Araktinji demanded that he be transferred elsewhere in the empire.[100]

In their defense, the founders of the Moriah lodge wrote again to the GODF, this time indicting not only the members of Temple of Solomon from whom they split, but also the Jaffa-based lodge Barkai and all "indigenous" Freemasons. According to Moriah,

> The indigenous Turkish and Arab element is still unable to understand and appreciate the superior principles of Masonry, and in consequence, of practicing them. For the majority, Freemasonry is probably only an instrument of protection and occult recommendation [?], and for others an instrument of local and political influence. The work of the lodges consists primarily of [illegible text] . . . and recommendations, not always unfortunately, for just causes and in favor of innocent Freemasons. The rest does not exist and cannot exist because the indigenous know

only despotism, from which they suffer for long centuries, and their instruction is very undeveloped, and is not prepared to work with a disinterested aim for humanity and justice.[101]

This situation, according to Moriah, had caused a deadlock in lodge work, since the "indigenous" lodge members reportedly vetoed suggestions of the second faction. Naturally this letter also reveals a racist and patronizing attitude not unfamiliar in colonial Masonic circles: "natives" could not be expected to truly understand Masonic principles as "Europeans" did. Furthermore, while proposing universalism on the one hand, Masonic lodges in practice expounded a very Eurocentric—and in the case of the GODF, Francophone—view of the modern liberal man. The irony, of course, is that only Ottomans who were already exposed to and open to European language, ideology, or manners sought out membership in European lodges. Members of a certain class and cultural milieu sought fraternity and legitimacy in this very European institution, precisely because of all it represented—cosmopolitanism, liberalism, modernity, and acculturation to a changed global setting. Regardless of whether or not they *already were* all these things, Ottoman Masons certainly *aspired* to be them.

Yet, revealing an inherent tension in the modernizing class's orientation toward Europe, the core indigenous Temple of Solomon lodge members were suspicious of the two Frenchmen (Frigere and Drouillard) and their influence over the other defectors. Frigere reported that the Temple of Solomon leadership "persuaded the other Freemasons that our lodge [Moriah] was created with the aim of facilitating the descent of the French into Palestine . . . and other stupid stories, which can appear ridiculous by far, but which were not, considering the particular situation of Turkey [*sic*], without a rather pressing danger."[102] Of course, during this period the Ottoman Empire had recently fought several wars, one against Italy over its annexation of an Ottoman province (Libya), and the other against Greece and Bulgaria over the Ottoman regions of the Balkans—both of which it lost. Furthermore, longstanding local resentments against the privileges accorded foreigners in the empire under the Capitulations as well as the arrogance of European consuls who repeatedly demanded passing warships to intimidate and control the local population also weighed into the equation. As a result, anti-European suspicions and sentiment were understandably running particularly high.

Interestingly, by the next year the local Masons' depiction of the split had changed slightly. Barkai Venerable 'Araktinji wrote to the GODF complaining that the Moriah lodge had been based on a failed bid for leadership of the Temple of Solomon lodge (in other words, a petty personal political struggle), and that moreover, it harbored Zionists, a fact which had hardened the position of its external opponents and brought about its own internal critics. "We have gone twice to Jerusalem to appease the hatred and reconcile the brother members of both lodges and we have succeeded only slightly. . . . Our brothers in Jerusalem are the high functionaries of the government, they are the notables (though well-educated, nonfanatics) who fear being viewed derisively in the eyes of their compatriots and [therefore] prefer to move away from their Freemason brothers, the Zionists."[103]

According to 'Araktinji, the members of Temple of Solomon would have liked to have joined a GODF-sponsored lodge in Jerusalem had Moriah not undercut them. He recommended again that the GODF withhold its support for Moriah and arrange for the professional transfer of Frigere, which would eventually open the way for reform and reconciliation between the Jerusalem lodges. In 'Araktinji's optimistic view, "the balance at the time of the elections will be right and our brother Zionists will be more useful in secrecy and more content though the majority of the lodge would be notable natives and senior officials of the government, at least the name of the lodge ceases being a Zionist lodge and will be respected more in the eyes of the population of Jerusalem."[104]

As for Moriah, in addition to the opposition it had raised among fellow Masons, it also faced a great deal of persecution by the local "clerics," especially the French among them. For this the lodge blamed the French consul and vice-consul in Jerusalem, along with a French priest, for striking a sharply anti-Masonic tone, and went so far as to ask that they be replaced. In repeated requests to the GODF to intervene with the French Foreign Ministry at the Quai d'Orsay, Moriah pointed out that not only did the local French officials act in a way that would not be tolerated in secular France, they were also negligent in their duties and were neglecting French interests. In order to convince the GODF, the Moriah members pointed out that French commerce and trade had declined from first place in Palestine ten years prior to fifth place.[105]

The upstart Moriah lodge is the only Palestinian lodge that left a record of its activities and projects, although as they were only proposed to the GODF we have little way of knowing to what extent their plans were actually carried out. At any rate it is interesting to note that among the projects it seriously proposed were the following: the opening of a "scientific, sociological, and philanthropic library" for the use of lodge members; opening a dispensary under the aegis of the French Consulate in Jerusalem to provide free medical care to newly enfranchised Moroccans under French protection; encouraging the establishment of a French society to compete for concessions providing electricity and electric tramways for Jerusalem; and opening a secular school in Jerusalem.[106]

Of all its proposed projects, the most ideologically Masonic was the establishment of a secular (*laïque*) school in Jerusalem. We have already seen that virtually all of the schools in Palestine were private and confessional, and even the Ottoman state school system educated only Muslim students in reality.[107] In an effort to gain popular support, the Moriah lodge published an article in a local newspaper and led a delegation to meet with the French consul in the city to request the establishment of a French secular secondary school. The consul said he would recommend to the ministry that a congregational high school be established instead, a proposition that was not welcomed, according to Moriah, from either the French or Masonic point of view. "From the French point of view," Moriah complained, "the solution of the Consul is not good because all the Greek, Arab, and Jewish elements who are the most numerous will never come to a religious school, and it is precisely this element which is aimed at. From the Masonic point of view, we would lose an excellent occasion to attract with our ideas the rising generation which could bring about a serious blow to religious omnipotence in our city."[108]

The Moriah lodge presented a petition signed by 316 heads of families representing 622 children in support of the establishment of a French lay school.[109] By the next year, however, there had been no progress on the matter of the school, although there were similar Masonic proposals gaining steam in both Beirut and Alexandria. A report in the Arabic press of French plans to establish a scientific school of higher education in Palestine along the lines of the American University in Beirut came to naught, as did Moriah's suggestion that they establish a school for "rational thought" in Jerusalem.[110]

By 1914, the members of the Moriah lodge had modified their initial Francophone elitism and requested permission to establish an Arabic-speaking lodge; while acknowledging they wanted to keep the "homogeneity and brotherhood" of their French-speaking lodge, they recognized that doing so kept out individuals who did not know French well enough to join.[111] The GODF responded that while they did not object to occasional meetings in Arabic, as necessary, they concluded by reminding them to take "the greatest prudence with regard to the initiation of the indigenous laymen."[112]

With the outbreak of the First World War, however, all three Palestinian Masonic lodges ceased activity, so Moriah was unable to carry out its plans for an Arabic-speaking branch. Barkai also was shut down during the war, and its Venerable ʻAraktinji and other lodge members were expelled to Anatolia. In 1919 ʻAraktinji returned home to find the lodge headquarters in shambles. From 1920 to 1924 the lodge was closed down yet again due to Jewish-Arab clashes in the aftermath of the Balfour

Declaration and subsequent establishment of the British Mandate over Palestine, which was predicated on recognizing a "Jewish national home" in Palestine at the expense of its Arab inhabitants. With the 1929 riots in Palestine most of the remaining Arab members of the lodge left to join all-Arab lodges, and by the 1930s mixed Jewish-Arab Freemasonry lodges in Palestine were a thing of the past, another pillar of coexistence toppled by the rising nationalist conflict.[113]

Whereas heterogeneity in the Ottomanist context enabled mixed Masonic lodges to flourish as long as they assumed a shared outlook, the seeds of sectarian and national discord nevertheless infiltrated the supposedly sacred Masonic order. Masonic lodges and individual Masons did not live separate from Ottoman Palestinian society, but rather were deeply integrated into it, and as such were sensitive to the balance between Ottomanism and particularism, Ottoman patriotism and European influence, and the growing intercommunal rivalry which is the subject of the following chapter.

CHAPTER SIX

Ottomans of the Mosaic Faith

In the winter of 1910, the Salonican Judeo-Spanish newspaper *La Tribuna Libera* published a plebiscite in which it asked its readers where the future of Ottoman Jewry lay: assimilation, nationalism, or Zionism. The paper's appeal was an effort to settle the battle that had raged in the Judeo-Spanish press in the preceding eighteen months over the growing clash between Ottomanism and Zionism. According to the paper, the situation was "bordering on fratricide" and threatening to engulf Ottoman Jewry entirely.[1]

In the years between the 1908 revolution and World War I, the Jewish communities of the Ottoman Empire were on the brink of a real communal crisis. For one, questions over changing communal leadership led to a series of power struggles in cities all over the empire, from the capital in Istanbul, to symbolically important Jerusalem, to even relatively small Jewish communities such as Tiberias and Beirut. These power struggles centered on issues related to the modernization of Ottoman Jewry in favor of a younger generation of reformist (*maskilic*) rabbis who were considered reflective of the times as well as more accountable to their flocks.[2]

At the same time, Ottoman Jewry was faced with the same dilemma that confronted their neighbors: what would be their role within the reforming empire, as Ottoman citizens but also as Jews? This chapter focuses on the very complex crossroads at which Sephardi Jews in Palestine found themselves at the end of the Ottoman Empire—straddling Ottoman universalism and Jewish particularism. On the one hand, Ottoman Jews sought to stake a claim in the new Ottoman body politic, embracing the ideological aims of the revolution and seizing the tools of Ottoman citizenship. And yet, this period also coincided with the community's progressive exposure to and reception of the ideas and institutions of European Zionism.

Ottoman Jews throughout the empire responded variously to these contradictory appeals. For many, Zionism was considered a betrayal of the "beloved" Ottoman homeland, particularly unjustifiable coming on the heels of civic enfranchisement and the optimistic new dawn promised by the revolution. Others, however, saw Zionism both as a legitimate expression of Jews' collective cultural aspirations and as a fortuitous boon that would bring tremendous economic and social utility to their beloved empire, consciously divorcing their adoption of Zionism from the territorial-political aspirations of the European Zionist movement.[3] However, both Ottomanism and Zionism were evolving ideologies and practices rather than unchanging beliefs, and the events which took place throughout the empire in those years sharply defined the contours of both. In part, I argue that the increasing appeal of Zionism that emerged after 1908 among the empire's Sephardim was closely related to the perceived failures of Ottomanism and incomplete universalism. Stated differently, Zionism did not gain adherents inasmuch as Ottomanism lost them.

For Palestine's Sephardi (Iberian) and Maghribi (North African) Jewish communities, reconciling the demands of Ottomanism and Zionism was particularly acute. In contrast to their fellow Sephardim in other parts of the empire, the Palestinian Sephardim were surrounded by "practical Zionism," witnessing Jewish immigration, land settlement, and the establishment of Hebraist nationalist cultural institutions firsthand. Some Palestinian Sephardim (including anti-Zionist ideologues) were even quite active as "practical Zionists" themselves, serving as middlemen in land purchases and as intermediaries for the immigrant Zionist community, provincial Ottoman government, and local Palestinians.

Thus, Palestinian Sephardim not only found themselves straddling Ottomanism and Zionism as ideological commitments, but they also had to deal with the visible repercussions of the tension between the two—most notably, the rise of an Arabist movement and a protonational Palestinian consciousness that emerged hand in hand with the altering landscape of the homeland. Intermittent clashes between Arab villagers and immigrant Jewish colonists, increasingly regular anti-Zionism in the Arabic press, and significant pressures to "prove" one's Ottomanism all contributed to the distinct response of the Palestinian Sephardi communities. The complex ways in which Palestinian Sephardi Jews negotiated these tensions alternately put them at odds with the official Zionist movement, Ashkenazi (European) Zionist immigrants in Palestine, fellow Ottoman Sephardim, Christian and Muslim Palestinian neighbors, Ottoman officials, and each other.

"ḤAVIVA 'OTOMANIA"—BELOVED OTTOMANIA

Into the twentieth century, Sephardi Jews by and large regarded the Ottoman Empire with a great deal of gratitude and affection as their historical savior. The Ottoman Sultan Beyazit II's open-arms policy toward the Spanish and Portuguese Jewish refugees in the fifteenth century was an integral part of Ottoman Sephardi collective memory, so much so that attempts by the Spanish government to renew its ties with Sephardi Jews were met with public scorn and disdain.[4] In addition, economic, social, and political competition with the Armenian and Greek communities in Anatolia and the Balkans in the nineteenth century had pushed the Jewish communities of the empire from their earlier privileged position. The consequence of this competition, argues one historian, was that "the Jews saw the best protection of their interests in making common cause with the Muslim elements within a secular and constitutional Ottoman state."[5] Both historic and socioeconomic factors easily translated into enthusiastic support for the Ottoman revolution, and the approximately four hundred thousand Jews of the empire were consistently among the most loyal supporters of the new regime.[6]

According to various accounts, the Sephardi and Maghrebi Jewish communities celebrated alongside the Muslim and Christian Arab communities, while Ashkenazi Jews by and large remained outside the public gatherings.[7] According to Gad Frumkin, the young Ottoman Ashkenazi journalist who observed the celebrations, many Sephardim and Maghrebim mixed with their Arab neighbors, eating sunflower seeds and drinking lemonade together while listening to the military band performing patriotic songs.[8]

As early as the first day of the official celebrations, the Sephardim had projected themselves into the public scene, arriving with a Torah scroll cover, dancing and singing, waving swords and shooting into the air "in the Eastern style." The Torah scroll was decorated with silver and gold ornamentation on top and was followed by youth carrying swordlike lances. When the Jews passed by the army, reports stated that "the soldiers raised their swords and weapons in salute." Jews also participated in the popular speeches that took place in the heady days and nights of August (addressing the crowds in Hebrew, Arabic, and even on occasion, "jargon," i.e., Judeo-Spanish), and the parades through the city's markets and neighborhoods, where they reportedly carried an Ottoman flag as well as the flags of Zion and the Torah.[9]

At one celebration in Galilean Safad, Simha Solomon explained the Jews' support for the empire and for the new constitutional regime. "Sirs and brothers! As a constitutional-Ottoman Jew it is my desire to express the relationship of the Jews to the Turkish constitution. . . . This day is sacred to all the different nations who reside in the lands of the Ottomans . . . holy of holies to us the Israelite people."[10]

At the same time, Solomon pointed out that after the revolution, the traditional "gratitude" for Ottoman government "generosity" had no place in the liberal political spectrum. Instead, a sense of equality and entitlement would come to serve as linchpins of the Jewish Ottomanist agenda as the terms of debate changed dramatically, from that of "tolerated *dhimmi* [non-Muslim]" to "equal partner." On this basis Ottoman Jews were renewing their covenant of loyalty to the Ottoman Empire and its dynastic head, the sultan. In other words, as long as the Jewish community believed in the empire's good will toward upholding the constitution and rule of law, it was committed to participating in the new Ottomanist project.

At one public lecture held to explain the constitution to his coreligionists, the Jewish parliamentary candidate and Galatasaray graduate Yitzhak Levi argued that in the aftermath of the revolution, "we are all citizens of the Ottoman nation and it is incumbent upon us to break out of our special associations." He called on all Jews to learn Ottoman Turkish and Arabic and to participate fully in Ottoman Palestinian public life.[11] Similar faith in the future of Ottomanism was expressed by Levi's political rival and fellow Jewish communal leader Albert Antébi. Although not utopian, Antébi clearly understood the transformative and modernizing potential of the revolution: "We are on a great journey to transform the entire social life of a degenerate and oppressed people, and to unify all these heterogeneous nations which to date have been driven by confessional beliefs made to divide and not to unite. . . . Freedom will undergo convulsions, equality will suffer crises, we will have a Muslim Parliament, moderate, reactionary perhaps, but we will preserve our constitution." Despite the fact that the Ottoman Jewish community was numerically a minority in the empire, "our weapon," Antébi wrote, "will be our principles, a sincere loyalty to the Ottoman homeland, collaboration devoted to political and economic regeneration and remaining true to the historic genius of our Judaism—tolerant, egalitarian, and compassionate."[12]

Jews participated widely in the new institutions established after the revolution—in the branches of the CUP, in Masonic lodges, and in their own civil society organizations. In Istanbul a group of Jewish patriots established the Ligue nationale des juifs de l'Empire Ottoman whose aims were to attain "intellectual and moral perfection and the material and social elevation of the Jewish nation in the empire so it can participate usefully in public life. Its principle preoccupation is to maintain the liberties granted to the people on the 24th of July by the handing-over by force of the constitution of 1876 and the improvement of the latter by legislative means. It strictly recommends to its members to fraternize with all the co-citizens of the other races and religions."[13] Similarly, the Israelite Ottoman Committee, originally founded by Avraham Galante in Cairo as the Israelite Committee of Egypt, aimed to show the Jews the benefits of the constitutional system and to promote faith in equality among all the Ottoman peoples.

In Palestine, in addition to the Society of Ottoman Jews discussed earlier, Shim'on Moyal established the National Israelite Society (NIS) in Jaffa, whose aim was to work to defend the constitution from internal threat and betrayal.[14] At the time, its twenty-seven members sent a telegram to all the high offices in Istanbul demanding that Sultan Abdülhamid II step down, that he be tried in court, and that he return the money he allegedly stole from the imperial coffers. Upon the ascension to the throne of the new sultan, the NIS held a celebration for the reading of the official *ferman*, followed by rousing speeches in Hebrew, Arabic, and Ottoman Turkish; it also sent a telegram congratulating the new sultan and promised to support the government "as long as it upholds the constitution." Since the CUP in Jaffa had moved to establish local civilian militias to keep order, the NIS mobilized eighty Jews from the four main ethnic communities as well as two women to volunteer for the Red Crescent Society. For their loyal efforts the NIS received official thanks from the Jaffa deputy governor and the CUP.

THE ZIONIST CRITIQUE OF OTTOMANISM

The sincere pro-Ottomanist expressions and active participation of the empire's leading Sephardim posed a worrisome development to both the officials and "civilian" ideologues of the Zionist movement. According to Dr. Arthur Ruppin, the local representative of the Zionist Organization (ZO) who headed the Palestine Office in Jaffa, the Sephardi Jews were not expressing sufficient Zionist fervor in the public demonstrations in the weeks after the revolution, but rather were acting as "Ottoman citizens of the Mosaic faith." In fact, Ruppin claimed, several Sephardi community leaders prevented Zionist symbols from being displayed, and one Zionist newspaper complained that they went so far as to tear a Zionist flag from the hands of a parade participant.[15] In the eyes of the Zionist movement, the assimilationist tendencies of Ottoman Jewry should be blamed on the Alliance Israélite Universelle (AIU), the French philanthropic society that had established a network of schools throughout the Middle East in the nineteenth century with the aim of "civilizing" Middle Eastern Jewry.[16] Through the AIU's vocational and primary schools, it had imparted a Francophone cultural outlook at the same time that its philosophy was to keep Ottoman Jewry squarely rooted in their homeland. The official Zionist organ in Hebrew, *Ha-'Olam*, warned about the voices of Ottoman assimilationists who could have potentially dire consequences for the Zionist movement: "They are saying what is familiar to us: Zionism is betrayal of your homeland. The Ashkenazi Zionists are the foreigners, and we are true to our homeland and empire."[17]

This official worry about the political preferences of Ottoman Sephardim was magnified among the radical elements of the Russian socialist Zionists newly arrived in Palestine. Their newspaper, *The Young Worker* (*Ha-Po'el ha-Ẓa'ir*), published a blistering public attack against Yitzhak Levi and his expressions of Ottomanism. Yosef Aharonowitz, the editor, derided Levi's Ottomanism, expressing deep concern that a Zionist official's own Zionism was in doubt. Levi's sins, in their eyes, were numerous. First, Levi had made a distinction within the Jewish community between Ottomans and foreigners. Most disturbing to *The Young Worker*, however, was the fact that in his speech, Levi had claimed that "a new nation [*umah*] has been born in Turkey [*sic*], the Ottoman nation, and we all are sons of the same nation."[18] "We the Jews," he reportedly said, "must leave behind our sectarianism, there is now no difference between Jew, Christian, and Muslim." And yet, as the editor noted, Levi's own campaign to be elected to the Ottoman parliament was inconsistent with his ideology. If we are all part of "the great Ottoman nation," Aharonowitz challenged, why was there a need for a specifically Jewish representative in the Ottoman parliament?

The conflict between Levi and Aharonowitz captured in microcosm the conflict between differing visions of Ottoman public life and its relationship to Jewish communal life in Palestine. For Aharonowitz and the Zionist radicals of the self-proclaimed "New *Yishuv*," participation in the new Ottoman political system was a good strategy, but it was devoid of the inherent value it had for Ottomanist Jews in Palestine.[19] For these instrumentalists, participation in imperial public life was desirable only inasmuch as it would allow Palestinian Jews to push for Zionist separatist aims. Unlike earlier Jewish immigrants, these newcomers rarely took upon themselves Ottoman citizenship, and their outlook toward Jewish nationalism and Zionism was rather dogmatic. In short, they denounced ideological Ottomanism and derided the feelings of brotherhood born of the revolution as one-sided efforts of the Jews—as they saw it, a "tendency to be more Marxist than Marx."[20]

However, these newly arrived immigrants, who numbered less than several thousand of Palestine's approximately fifty thousand to seventy thousand Jews, by no means represented the entire Zionist community.[21] On the contrary, they represented a small faction even within the Palestinian Zionist settlers, a point that the anonymous correspondent "Jaffan/Yafoni" made in the official Zionist newspaper *The Globe* (*Ha-'Olam*). "[*The Young Worker*] wants to present the 'truth from Ereẓ-Israel' but instead it presents truth as it sees it, or rather as it wants it to be," Yafoni complained, highlighting the paper's advocacy of "radical" views on Hebrew labor.[22] Despite their minority status back then, the voices of *The Young Worker* have been magnified in retrospect because of the leading role that the socialist Zionist parties took in the history of (post-Ottoman) prestate Palestine and later, in the leadership of the state of Israel.

Other Ashkenazi Zionist immigrants had a different orientation to the Ottoman state and their role in it. Eli'ezer Ben-Yehuda, a Russian Jew who had immigrated to Palestine in the early 1880s and who would be known as the "father of modern Hebrew" for his linguistic contributions, exhorted his fellow Ashkenazi immigrants to take on Ottoman citizenship—as he urged readers in his newspapers *The Deer* and *The Observation*, "Jews, be Ottomans! [*Yehudim heyu 'Otomanim!*]." This call was echoed by David Yellin, whose father had been a member of the Jerusalem City Council in the second half of the nineteenth century. "We the Jews can enjoy this freedom like the other citizens . . . and we need to do this: every single person will be an Ottoman citizen, and will encourage others to be Ottomans as well."[23]

Ben-Yehuda and his son Itamar Ben-Avi welcomed the revolution and reforms as critical for the development of the empire as a multiethnic and modern entity, strengthened by its diversity if held together by overarching civic bonds. As Jews, the civic identity which they understood as central to the revolution was the very thing which enabled them to feel a part of the changes taking place.

> Turkey [*sic*] is an empire made of many peoples. Every people in Turkey [*sic*] preserves its peoplehood [*'amamut*], speaks its language, knows its culture and nationality that is special to him. But despite that, we all, according to the basic constitution, are Ottomans, sons of one state, equal all of us in the responsibilities and rights in civic and public life. . . . The basic constitution does not demand from anyone to give up his private people-hood, his personal culture or language. But all of us together must from now on participate in the general feeling, the

general good of the state for everyone together, and all work together in peace and quiet for the general good of the state.[24]

Rather than an expression of assimilation, however, Ben-Yehuda explained that this commitment to imperial citizenship allowed him to live out his Hebrew nationalism:

But what is the meaning of the term Ottoman? . . . It is not the name of a nationality, nor of a race, nor of a people in the natural meaning of the word. Ottoman is not a synonym for Turk. No! God forbid! It is a political term, and no more. . . . So the phrase "Jews, be Ottomans" does not mean Jews, be Turks! Or Jews, be Arabs!. . . . In Hebrew the meaning is thus: Jews, be citizens of the state you live in! Jews, enjoy the political rights of the land of freedom in which you live and in which you wish to live national Hebrew lives, without giving up anything of your nationalism! . . . Jews, be like the Arabs, like the Greeks, like the Armenians in the Ottoman Empire! . . . Speak Hebrew, but . . . be citizens of the Ottoman Empire, in order that you can be Hebrews in the land of your fathers.[25]

Ben-Yehuda's attitude was not a radical position, for even before the institutionalization of the Zionist movement, early Zionist settlers were encouraged to take on Ottoman citizenship. This was an outcome of Ottoman government policies which did not favor the settlement of foreign citizens who would push for special privileges and rights accorded to other foreigners under the Capitulation system. As a result, the colonists on the early agricultural colonies (*moshavot*) were required by the sponsoring philanthropist Baron Edmund de Rothschild and his administrators to adopt Ottoman citizenship.[26] After the failure of Jews to elect a candidate or otherwise influence the course of parliamentary elections in the fall of 1908, Ruppin, the leading Zionist official in Palestine, also adopted the position that Zionist immigrants should take Ottoman citizenship.

Indeed, from the early months after the reinstatement of the Ottoman constitution in July 1908, the Zionist movement in Europe placed increased importance on the Ottoman Empire—first, as the object of their diplomatic efforts to secure eventual Jewish autonomy, and a distant second, as the site of Zionist education and mobilization among the Jewish communities in the empire. In 1908, the ZO established an unofficial office in Istanbul under the management of Victor Jacobsohn, with the aim of lobbying the Ottoman government and overseeing Zionist mobilization throughout the empire.[27] In both respects the movement was to make some minor advances, but its overall failures either to win over the government or to mobilize the masses to the Zionist program by the eve of World War I were intimately related.

From the outset, the Hamidian government had been suspicious of the Zionist movement and its intentions toward the territorial integrity of the Ottoman Empire, and rightly so: the Zionist movement operated under the premise that it would seek a charter from the Ottoman sultan for Jewish autonomy in Palestine, known as the Basel Program.[28] The last Hamidian governor of Jerusalem, Ekrem Bey, who left Jerusalem in August 1908, had written to the capital that the Russian Jewish immigrants in Palestine were a "dangerous element," and that Jewish immigration overall was a threat to the empire.[29] Over a thirty-year period, the Ottoman government repeatedly implemented a series of laws aimed at preventing Jewish immigration to the empire and banning land sales to foreign (and occasionally Ottoman) Jews.

With the 1908 revolution, the Zionist movement reevaluated its strategy. In the fall of 1908, the Zionist movement had articulated three main axes from which to operate: (1) to secure a role for the Zionist movement within the Ottoman political spectrum, preferably using Ottoman Jews for this effort; (2) to gain government and Jewish support within the empire, for which it would be necessary to narrow the expressed goals of the movement; and (3) to promote public relations (the press) on behalf of their goals.[30] At the same time, the Zionist movement was struggling with an internal political crisis over the direction of the movement—political-diplomatic ("Herzlian") Zionism or active ("practical") Zionism, in other words creating facts on the ground in Palestine.

Throughout this reevaluation, the proscribed role of Ottoman Jewry in carrying out the Zionist agenda was never clearly defined. On the one hand, some Zionist officials argued that the Jews of the empire should be "awakened" to help the Zionist movement in its diplomatic efforts.[31] Indeed, the Zionist officials in the Istanbul office met with prominent Ottoman Jews, including the four Jewish members of parliament, important Jewish governmental advisors, and Jewish representatives of organizations and communal institutions. The ZO wanted to gauge the individuals' orientation toward Zionism—to enlist friends in the Zionist cause and to try to neutralize the potential damage foes could do to the movement.[32]

In its appeal to high-ranking Ottoman Jews, the Istanbul office carefully spun the goals of the Zionist movement to be more in line with what it perceived to be within the range of acceptability—Zionism within the boundaries of Ottoman patriotism. In its official communication with the Jewish MP Nissim Mazliach and Nissim Russo (secretary to the minister of the interior), the ZO presented its goals as "creating a shelter, a cultural center for the Jewish nation in Palestine, [promoting] their economic, physical, intellectual, and moral rejuvenation."[33] As such, the ZO assured the Ottoman gentlemen that the Zionist movement sought to work within the new Ottoman constitutional parliamentary framework. Ottoman Jews, the ZO assured Mazliach and Russo, had a noble role in the Zionist movement, and would thus serve both the Ottoman homeland and the Jewish people.

Preempting their detractors, the Zionist officials stated:

> If in certain circles Zionism is still considered as a separatist aspiration that could constitute a danger to the Ottoman Empire, this is a monstrous madness, they are only the confused spirits or the slanderers who disfigure and falsify our idea in such a manner. Zionism does not have anything in common with separatist tendencies against the integrity of the Ottoman Empire, which correspond by no means to the real interests of our nation. [We must] reassert the perfect loyalty of our idea and demonstrate that its realization is in harmony with the interests of your beloved homeland.

In order to answer any lingering questions about the matter, the president of the ZO, David Wolffsohn, personally reassured the Ottoman Jewish notables further of Zionism's benign and limited aims. He already had been prepped by Jacobsohn that "the most important thing is the emphasis that we have no separatist aims, no plans for political action in the land."[34] Wolffsohn then wrote to the Ottoman Jews:

> I know that in Turkish circles, even the most enlightened, Zionism is known in the form of a movement that wants to found a Jewish state in Palestine, with separatist aspirations and as a consequence will constitute a danger to the Ottoman Empire. . . . In my capacity as president of the Executive Committee of the ZO, I affirm completely and officially that Zionism does not have anything to do with these tendencies, which from our point of view not only are unrealizable but by no means correspond to the real interests of the Jewish people.[35]

Declaring that "all political aspirations are completely foreign to us," Wolffsohn limited the Zionist movement's concrete aims to increasing Jewish immigration to Palestine and repealing the ban on land sales to Jews there. Through these aims, the Zionists would bring about the "material, intellectual, moral, and social development which will be good for the new Turkey [*sic*]."

Based on this official description of the Zionist movement, both Russo and Mazliach initially informed the ZO that they "consent[ed] to the Zionist idea, in the precise form in which Mr. Jabotinsky presented it to us on December 27 [1908]. We are ready to work for this idea."[36] They agreed to help lobby the Ottoman parliament, the CUP, and the press, in order to spread understanding of the Zionist goals (which they requested in writing, in order to present it to the Young Turks "in an uncontestable manner"). Within a few months, Mazliach and Russo had met with several Ottoman and Jewish officials.[37]

However, despite the Istanbul office's persistent lobbying of prominent

Ottoman Jews, Jacobsohn was indifferent to the Jewish masses of the Ottoman Empire, who he did not think would be "useful" to the Zionist movement.[38] Other Zionist officials, most prominently Wolffsohn, considered the empire's four hundred thousand to five hundred thousand Jews entirely irrelevant to the Zionist program. For his part, Wolffsohn continued to pursue a Herzlian policy of direct diplomacy with the Ottoman state, meeting personally with Ottoman officials.[39] In fact, as public criticism emerged in 1909 over the tensions between Ottomanism and Zionism (as we shall see below), the Zionist leader Max Nordau told Ottoman Jews who voiced criticism to stay out of internal Zionist affairs—in effect disenfranchising them from the very movement which sought to speak and act in their name.[40]

OTTOMAN ZIONISM I: CULTURAL HEBRAISM

Zionism, to the extent that it existed among Ottoman Sephardim, was strongly shaped by cultural Hebraism and a Jewish collective consciousness, and in fact Hebraist clubs and societies formed the bulk of grassroots Zionism in the Ottoman Empire. As early as 1903, the Jerusalem schoolteacher Avraham Elmaliach had founded Ẓe'irei Yerushalayim (Jerusalem Youth) to promote Hebrew as a spoken language among the city's young people. They offered free Hebrew lessons in the evenings and aided in efforts to start the first Hebrew preschool. According to Elmaliach, the organization involved about one hundred Sephardi youth, including the future Ladino and Hebrew publishers, writers and translators Ben-Zion Taragon and Shlomo Cherezli.[41]

These Hebrew-oriented youth were the main leaders of the "renaissance spirit" among the Sephardim. Hebraism was a response to perceived communal stagnation—a call to modernize the Jewish community while at the same time incorporating an authentic element of Jewish culture and identity. In the years after 1908, Zionist-styled clubs like the Jewish sporting association the Maccabis, Hebrew kindergartens and schools, and Hebraic cultural societies spread throughout the Ottoman Empire, especially in large Jewish centers like Istanbul, Salonica, and Izmir.[42] And yet, it is important not to overstate the participation of Ottoman Jews in grassroots Zionist organizations—more frequently, they expressed profound indifference bordering on outright hostility toward the Zionist program, as numerous articles in the Zionist press attest.[43]

To the extent that it did exist, though, Sephardi and Maghrebi Zionism was socially and ideologically distinct from the larger Zionist movement, divorcing Hebraic and Judaic cultural and social renaissance and local communal and economic development on the one hand from Jewish autonomy, anti-Ottoman separatism, and national statehood on the other. Ottoman Jews of Palestine insisted on the absolute compatibility of their Ottomanism and Zionism, and further believed that Zionism was a real contribution to the rest of the Ottoman *umah*. The rebirth of the Jewish people, in its cultural, social, and economic dimensions, would work to the benefit of the empire at large. Hence, the Palestinian Sephardi commitment to Zionism should be characterized as an Ereẓ-Israeli (Land of Israel) commitment within the Ottoman body politic.[44]

According to Elmaliach, Zionism sought to strengthen the Jewish spirit, to widen the study of Hebrew, and to improve the economic and moral situation of the Jews. He called on the Sephardim of the empire to participate in the Zionist movement, consisting of: helping sustain the Jewish colonies in Palestine; founding societies to promote love and solidarity; cultivating Jewish studies (in history, literature, and language); bettering the social and intellectual situation of brother Jews; and paying the shekel to the Zionist movement.[45] In addition to cultural Hebraism, Sephardi Zionism acknowledged the need for immigration to Palestine for persecuted Jews from Russia and Romania at the same time that there was no illusion that this was a necessary or desirable course for Ottoman Jewry itself. In turning to the Ottoman Empire, due to its long tradition of tolerance and hospitality, Zionists were seeking a refuge and in return would bring it utility and material benefits, concurrent with Ottoman interests. "The Zionists do not want to overcome or to conquer," Elmaliach argued, but rather, "they are searching for a shawl, a coat, a place of rest."

As a result, some Ottoman Jews insisted on the absolute compatibility between their Ottomanism and Zionism, claiming that Zionism was a real contribution to the rest of the Ottoman nation. The rebirth of the Jewish people in its cultural, social, and economic dimensions would work to the benefit of the empire at large. This convergence of Ottoman and Jewish interests was duplicated in the language used by the press and was a central component of its outlook. It was not, however, an uncontested or universal claim.

THE OTTOMANIST CRITIQUE OF ZIONISM

There is some evidence that with the regime change in 1908, at least some officials in the Ottoman government supported a Sephardi view of Zionism as cultural Hebraism, emphasizing that as long as the Jews did not carry their Zionism in the political direction, they would continue to be considered loyal Ottomans. As Minister of Education Emrulla Bey reportedly phrased it, "We are truly happy with our Jews. Why shouldn't they learn Hebrew? If the Jews decide to adopt for themselves Hebrew as a national language, the government does not see anything in that which awakens suspicions."[46]

Dr. Rıza Tevfik especially was considered a friend of the movement, and he spoke often to Jewish organizations in the capital. He is reported to have supported Zionism as offering a shelter for persecuted Jews, as well as due to the financial and labor capital it brought into the empire. As he told his Jewish audiences, the Ottoman Empire did not see the Jews as foreigners, and recognized its need for them. In his words, "We are lacking strong workers, honest people who busy themselves more with agricultural labor than with the politics of revolution." In this line of thought, Palestine "will be turned into a rich and fertile province that will lead to the success of Turkey [*sic*]."[47]

According to contemporary scholars, at least in the early years after 1908, Ottoman officials did not consider the Jews a security threat like other minorities, and they did not consider Zionism a nationalist movement along the lines of Balkan nationalism, characterized by its underground committees and armed struggle.[48] Rıza Bey made very clear that the new government's tolerance of cultural Zionism was conditional, and political Zionism would not be tolerated. "If the Jews are moderate," he informed his Ottoman Jewish audiences, "the government will not oppose bringing them into the empire. But we should not forget that if the Jews make out of Zionism a political question . . . then a Jewish question will be created in Turkey [*sic*] and its outcome will be very bitter."[49]

From the point of view of the central Ottoman government, political Zionism was a threat to its central authority and the communitarian status quo in Palestine, but it also did not consider most of its Jewish citizens to be those kinds of Zionists. It viewed political Zionism as a danger imported by European, and largely Russian, Jews, supported by meddling European governments. Even as late as the spring 1911 debate on Zionism instigated in the parliament by the Palestinian Arab delegates, Grand Vezier Ibrahim Hakkı Pasha responded by saying: "Jewish Ottoman citizens who have never deviated even one inch from Ottomanist convictions will not be suspected of sharing views and fantasies of a few witless Zionists whom they themselves consider to be madmen."[50] By that time, however, in the changed context of imperial turmoil, loss of important provinces, and growing ethno-national dissolution, the question of Zionism had taken on a new urgency.

This argument over the nature and aims of Zionism and its subsequent implications for Ottomanism stood at the crux of a series of protracted and bitter debates that took place in the Judeo-Spanish press spanning from Salonica and Anatolia to Palestine and Egypt. On one side stood Sephardi Ottomanist-Zionists who claimed that Ottomanism and Zionism were perfectly or very nearly perfectly compatible. On the other side stood Sephardi Ottomanist anti-Zionists who believed quite simply that "Zionism is contrary to Ottoman patriotism."[51]

The wave of anti-Zionist publishing in the Sephardi press began in May 1909 with a series of articles in the Izmir newspapers of the brothers Alexander and Moshe Ben-Giat. The following month, I. Cohen from Salonica wrote an article in the Istanbul newspaper *Stamboul* against the upcoming Ninth Zionist Congress, saying that Jews should worry about the Ottoman nation and not the Jewish one.[52] Several other prominent Ottoman Jews denounced the Zionist movement in the press. For example the Izmir poet Reuben Qattan wrote to the Jerusalem Judeo-Spanish paper *Liberty* to remind its readers, "Before everything we should live Ottoman lives, cultivate the language of the Ottomans, form an integral part of the Ottoman nation, and sincerely love the Ottoman patria." According to Qattan, "We are Ottomans and nothing else." If the Jews were to turn to work within the Ottoman Empire, they would be a factor for progress and prosperity in the land. "To work and to die for Turkey [*sic*]—that should be our only and sacred duty." But continuing to turn toward Zionism, Qattan warned, would be a "catastrophe" for the Jews, a forecast shared by others.[53] In Qattan's view, Zionism was not like lighting a match on Shabbat but, rather, like working on Yom Kippur—a far more unjustifiable and unpardonable sin.

The aftermath of these articles was swift and nasty. Cohen's article in particular caused a stir in the capital, and the Ottoman Turkish and French press (not to mention the Judeo-Spanish and Hebrew press) covered it extensively.[54] Indeed, the early ease with which the Zionist movement operated in the Ottoman Empire began to change that summer with the Ninth Zionist Congress, which brought to light the contradictions between the benign aims portrayed to and by Ottoman Jews and the separatist aims of many European Zionists. At the congress, the Basel Program of the Zionist movement was only slightly modified, and in an alarming step, the Zionist leadership called for the upcoming congress to be held in Istanbul. Furthermore, the Zionist leadership refused to certify that Zionism had no national aims. In retaliation, the CUP in Salonica took action against its members who participated in the Zionist Congress.[55]

In response to this early wave of anti-Zionism in the Jewish press, the Jerusalem Sephardi press mobilized to defend Zionism. The Judeo-Spanish paper *Liberty* derided Ben-Giat and sarcastically wrote that he "is showing himself more patriotic than Dr. Rıza Tevfik, than Emmanuel

Carasso [Jewish MP from Salonica], than Señor Nissim Mazliach [Jewish MP from Izmir] and others who have all declared themselves in favor of Zionism, and he shows that he understands better than others what Zionism is." Instead, the paper claimed, Zionism had contributed greatly to progress in the Ottoman Empire. Furthermore, the paper asserted that while the Jews in the empire were lucky to have the constitution, they must think of the other Jews who were less fortunate and searching for a safe haven. The new editor of *Liberty*, Haim Ben-'Atar, urged his fellow Jews to show "a little more courage!" by supporting Zionism. Zionism was, in his mind, a commitment to bettering the moral, physical and economic state of the Jews in all lands, as well as a respect for Jewish history and literature. According to Ben-'Atar's view, "every Jew who recognizes himself as a descendant of Israel has declared by this his Zionism! Every Jew who wants to contribute with his time and work to better the situation of the Israelites in Palestine—or outside of it—is with this a Zionist!"[56]

Within weeks a semiorganized campaign had sprung up to boycott the newspaper of the "enemies of Zionism" Alexander and Moshe Ben-Giat. Distributors reportedly refused to sell their newspaper, and even small communities joined in the struggle. "Long live the boycott! Down with the reactionaries!" crowed *Liberty* at the news. "They represented Zionism as a revolutionary organization, with unjust aims against the government. Miserable Ben-Giat brothers!" According to the paper, the consequences of the Ben-Giats' attack was already being felt—Armenian and Greek journals had taken to ridiculing and attacking Jews and Judaism, presumably inspired or emboldened by the internal Jewish feud.[57]

OTTOMAN ZIONISM II: COMMUNAL RIVALRY

Reuben Qattan's article was a heavier, more unexpected blow, for he was a renowned poet who wrote of his love toward Zion. Despite this, Ben-'Atar asserted that Qattan had no real sense of Zionism: "Zionism is in no way a contradiction to Ottomanism. On the contrary, the Jew can, thanks to glorious liberty, be a Jewish-Ottoman nationalist, like one can be Greek-Ottoman, Albanian-Ottoman, and Armenian-Ottoman. Our movement can go together with Ottomanism without Turkish nationalism supporting this." In the end, Ben-'Atar urged Qattan to rethink his opposition and join hands with the Zionists, who will always be "faithful servants to our dear Ottoman *patria*!"[58]

The Jerusalem writer Yehuda Burla also wrote a response to Qattan's piece, saying that Qattan did not realize the harm he was causing the

Jewish people. Because of articles like his, allies in the Ottoman government, like Rıza Tevfik Bey, had declared that they realized their mistake in not considering Zionism a political movement. According to Burla, Qattan did not understand that they proposed *national Zionism, not political Zionism* ("*ha-ẓiyonut ha-le'umit lo ha-medinit*"), and because of that distinction, enemies of Zionism did not see the Jewish people's needs clearly. "In short," Burla wrote, "it will become clear to us how we must be Ottomans, and something more as well."[59]

At the core of Ben-'Atar's and Burla's defense of Zionism was a sense that the cultural and institutional development of the Jewish community, even along Hebraist-Zionist lines, was seen as concurrent with the rights of all Ottomans. Ottoman Zionists were deeply influenced by the other ethnic groups in the empire, and the broader sense of growing rivalry and competition was not far from the surface. For example, after Armenian and Greek students at the prestigious Robert College in Istanbul successfully fought for language courses in their ancestral tongues, Jewish students petitioned to have Hebrew offered as well.[60]

More significant, while seeking to normalize Jews within the Ottoman Empire, the Sephardi Palestinian press sought equality with the other ethnic groups—legal and representative equality, and even the equal right to ethno-national expression. This "race for national rights" in the empire was a subtext of Zionist work among Ottoman Jews as well.[61] Indeed, refusing the Jews the right to express their Zionism was considered unfair if not illegal. As the Hebrew *Liberty* proclaimed:

> Only the Greeks and Bulgarians and Armenians and also the Albanians have the right to be called by the name of "nationalists." . . . Only they can work for their people and their language with their heads held high and openly! Only they can show their origins, declare their nationalism and raise their heads! And because of that no one will raise the call of betrayal of the homeland against them, no one will dare say to them that they want to conquer lands of the empire. . . . But, we the Jews, we have to be different from them, to be denied of that right.[62]

As Elmaliach put it, Zionists want "to establish in Palestine a gathering of citizens as loyal to Turkey [*sic*] as the Armenians and the Greeks," a curious argument considering the fact that the growing national problem within the empire was widely covered in the press (including in Elmaliach's own newspaper).[63]

As well, the disappointing lack of true equality in the Ottoman Empire along with the rise of intercommunal conflict in Palestine led the Judeo-Spanish *Liberty* to link consciously the failure of Ottomanism with the surging popularity of Zionism. Challenging the basic slogans of the 1908 revolution—brotherhood, equality, and liberty—the press upbraided the local administration and fellow Palestinians for pushing the

Jews toward Zionism. "The rise in anti-Semitism in the Arabic press—is this fraternity? The Red Passport for Jewish immigrants into Palestine—is this equality? In fact, if the Jews had known real liberty they would not be turning to the 'mortal enemy'—the Zionist movement."[64] In other words, if Zionism had gained adherents in recent years, it was because Ottomanism was fast losing them.

OTTOMANIST ANTI-ZIONISM, ROUND II

The verbal sparring in the press in early 1909 was only a prelude to the virulent attacks that would follow against David Fresco, labeled by *Liberty* as the "most dangerous internal slanderer."[65] Fresco, who as the editor of the Istanbul Judeo-Spanish mass newspaper *El Tiempo* was extraordinarily influential in the Ottoman Jewish world, came out squarely against the Zionist movement in September 1909. In a series of articles entitled *Is Zionism Compatible with Ottomanism?* Fresco accused Zionism of being primitive, exclusivist, utopian, and exploitative.[66] Fresco's attack was twofold: first, against the basic premise of the Zionist movement, he fiercely denied that the Jews were a nation-people, claiming instead that they were only a religious community. Fresco argued that "assimilation" was not an insult, as the Zionists intended, but rather was a sign of progress. He sought to preserve the Ottoman spirit alongside the Jewish origins of his community.

Fresco also attacked the so-called benign aims of the Zionist movement. He accused the Zionist movement of hiding Wolffsohn's and Nordau's speeches to the Ninth Zionist Congress, where they spoke of concentrating Jews exclusively in Palestine. Fresco called the Zionists "liars and untrustworthy," while their leaders were "crooks and scoundrels," who, he said, were "inciting" the Ottoman Jews against their religion and state.[67]

> I think the central leadership of Zionism is committing a huge crime in its desire to drag the Ottoman Jews after their crazy movement. . . . The Zionist shelter must be in Turkey [*sic*] itself, and because of that Ottoman Jews cannot participate in this movement without being traitors in the eyes of their friends who belong to the other peoples. The heads of Zionism should think a little about the existence of half a million Jews who live quiet and peaceful lives without any pressures, faithful to their homeland.[68]

In order to correct the misinformation the Zionist movement was disseminating, Fresco published his own pamphlet in French about the dangers of the Zionist movement, aimed at a Jewish audience (for the misguided youth following Zionism) as well as at a broader Ottoman audience (so that "our brothers of the other religions will be convinced that the Ottoman Jew, like his brother in all the lands of exile, is loyal to his homeland"). Later, as a defendant in a lawsuit accusing him of libel, Fresco translated the Zionist anthem "Ha-Tivka" to prove his assertion that Zionism was a particularistic and revolutionary movement.[69]

In response, *Liberty* and its allies went on the attack. First, they attempted to discredit Fresco personally, claiming that his anti-Zionist tirade was nothing more than greedy self-interest. Along with several other Jewish and non-Jewish newspapers empire-wide, *El Tiempo* had received regular subsidies from the Zionist movement in exchange for committing to work for the good of the Zionist movement, promoting Jewish entry to the empire and Palestine, the cancellation of Ottoman restrictions, and the revival of Hebrew. According to the Zionist account of the agreement, "Fresco is an energetic man, who can wield great influence, and he can be of great service for winning over this community." He was to "concern himself in his articles—alongside his Turkish-patriotic sentiment—with expressing a nevertheless friendly orientation to the Jewish-national tendencies and to Zionism."[70] In exchange, the Zionist movement was to provide his paper with friendly articles and new subscribers.

Despite *Liberty*'s energetic defense of Zionism, by the winter of 1909 the cumulative effect of the anti-Zionist expressions in the Sephardi Jewish press had borne fruit. At a meeting with the Istanbul rabbinical council, three of the four Jewish members of parliament declared that they "oppose with all their abilities the Zionist movement."[71] According to the account, the three said they were first of all Ottoman representatives whose chief responsibility was to guard the affairs of the Ottoman homeland. Only secondarily were they Jews, but they intended to protect the interests of all Jews and not just those of the Zionist minority. In response, *Liberty* issued "Open Letter to the Honorable Jewish Deputies," decrying them as non-Jews, inhumane, and antinational.[72] They were betraying the values of liberty and the rights of man, as they were turning their backs on thousands of Jews in need. The paper was certain that the deputies were in line with the aims of most Zionists, chief among them which were "revival of the Jewish people and the revival of Turkey [*sic*] itself."

At the outbreak of the Fresco affair, Chief Rabbi Haim Nahum came out clearly on his side, prompting an open letter to the chief rabbi in the Judeo-Spanish *Liberty* from a reader in Istanbul. The reader, David Grasiani, urged the chief rabbi to speak out against Fresco's "calumny" that the Zionists wanted an independent kingdom on Ottoman national territory—arguing that "Señor Fresco must come before

God and the people and tell what Zionist, or what Zionist publications," he gets this from. Instead, promised Grasiani, "We will finally raise our voices and say to our Turkish brothers: we return to Palestine as loyal Ottoman co-citizens. We are ready to give whatever guarantees are demanded of us."[73]

Two months later, however, in February 1910, the French translation of Jacobus Kann's book *Eretz-Israel: Le pays juif* (The Land of Israel: The Jewish Homeland) appeared on the streets of Istanbul and provided further support to the argument of Ottomanist anti-Zionists. The book called for Jewish autonomy in Palestine, complete with a Jewish army and police force. Victor Jacobsohn, the ZO's representative in the Ottoman capital, worried greatly about the impact the book would have, seeing how it directly contradicted the watered-down version of Zionism that he and his colleagues had been peddling among Ottoman Jews and Ottoman officials.

> The publication of the French translation of Kann's book *Eretz-Israel* and the measures that the author proposed to carry out in Turkey [*sic*] have caused a dangerous and unexpected situation for Zionism in this land. The political thoughts of this book stand in direct contradiction to everything we have said about the founding principles of Zionism, contrary to the official explanations given in the press and in the Ninth [Zionist] Congress. Since the author is one of the three members of the Inner Actions Committee, and the translation came out not only after the proclamation of the constitutional regime but even after the congress, this book appears as an official declaration of the Zionist movement. This book will be useful to our enemies . . . and will have difficult political consequences. . . . It is clear that our aims will be seen as "incompatible with the integrity of the Ottoman empire."[74]

Jacobsohn's worries were justified, for immediately after, Chief Rabbi Haim Nahum, not a supporter of the Zionist movement even at that time, had a harsh exchange with one of the ZO's Istanbul officers, "N." According to the report sent to Germany, the chief rabbi stated, "I find that this book is finally a look at the true Zionist views. This is a more sincere Zionism. Now many want to deny this Zionism; that it is the place of Zionism to create a new movement. [But] *this is Zionism* [pointing to the book]."[75] In an attempt at damage control, the Istanbul officer tried to tell Haim Nahum that the book was the product of a "private man"—but the chief rabbi knew better, saying, "Kann is no private person. I don't understand why you are able to give a more correct version of Zionism than is Kann, an official and more deserving man." "N." was concerned with whether Fresco would write about the translation in his newspaper, *El Tiempo*; although Haim Nahum said he thought Fresco was "taking a break" from his attacks on the Zionists, he was clear that "others would write about it."

Indeed, though the Sephardi press quieted down for a few months, Fresco resumed his attacks by the fall of 1910, this time taking aim at the "practical Zionist" program in Palestine:

Not one of our five hundred thousand Ottoman Jews and not a single Ottoman Jewish child that will be born tomorrow [!!—editor's note] will agree to that [Zionist] program. The Ottoman Jews do not have, and will not have, another homeland other than the Ottoman homeland. Every part of the national land must be sacred to him without any difference. . . .

To work against this truth is to betray the homeland [!!], betray the Ottoman Jews, since the land belongs to the Muslims, to the Christians, to the Jews, all of them partners and related in the same social tie, and when one insists on ignoring this truth then not only will he be seen as disregarding the social tie through injustice, but he will also be seen as a rebel against the state and traitor to his partner brothers; he will cause shame and dishonor and provoke an awful hatred against the Jewish people in the empire. All the Ottoman Jews and Arabs are related to each other so it is incumbent upon us to prevent this rebellion, to ban this disgrace, and to take refuge from the catastrophe that can fall on our heads.[76]

A week later, Fresco followed up on this theme in his article "The Great Danger!" where he argued that the struggle in Palestine and Syria expressed in the newspapers "is very dangerous and can bring many troubles, and a real disaster." Fresco argued that the Ereẓ-Israeli delegate to the previous Zionist congress in Hamburg had warned that "even the peasant reads *Die Welt*!" and as such, was aware of the Zionist movement's call for Jews to support the Jewish National Fund's efforts to buy land for Jews in Palestine. According to Fresco, it was only logical that the peasant would want to defend his homeland and organize against the Jewish occupation that would worsen his status. "Today, the peasant defends himself with words, but tomorrow, he can move from words to deeds, and then that will be a great sorrow not only to the Jews of Palestine but also to all Syria and maybe even to the whole empire."[77]

This proved the last straw for Fresco's Sephardi brethren in Jerusalem; from then on, Fresco became a bitter enemy for *Liberty*, someone who not only sought to assimilate but who had become an enemy of the Jewish people. He was attacked for bringing non-Jewish attention to an internal Jewish debate and for inciting Jews and non-Jews against Zionism and the Hebrew community in Palestine. A few days later Betzalel Sa'adi ha-Levi, editor of the Salonica newspaper *La Epoca*, also came out squarely against the Zionist movement, saying that Palestine belonged to the Arabs and all Ottomans should oppose the settlement of Jews there.[78]

It was rumored that Fresco was planning on establishing additional newspapers in Ottoman Turkish and French to battle against Zionism—a plan that threatened to make his influence much stronger. As a result,

Liberty warned its readers, Fresco deserved to be cursed in the pages of history "among the people of Israel." The paper tried to organize public rallies against Fresco in Palestine and Istanbul, but it seems that little came of these efforts other than small rallies in Haifa and Jaffa.[79]

In one of the translations offered by *Liberty* to show its readers the direct damage Fresco was causing, an article from the Istanbul paper *İkdam* was cited, claiming that while the Ottoman Jews were trustworthy the foreign Jews were bringing a new danger to the empire. Unlike the Ottoman Jews, the Ashkenazi immigrants refused to integrate into Ottoman society, did not serve in the army, and caused problems with the locals. "What use will come to our country by immigration of those people?" *İkdam* complained. "We are not enemies of the Jews . . . the Ottoman Jews are wonderful nationalists who love their state with a boundless love, participate in legal commerce, and in the hour of need also take part in battle, and we do not want the Ottoman Jews . . . to follow those delusions. . . . Jerusalem is not of the Jews alone. Jerusalem is a holy place that belongs also to Muslims and to Christians." In conclusion, *İkdam* argued that Zionism "is a new disaster for us, and we hope that Turkey [*sic*] will be preserved from that great tragedy that will come upon her as a holocaust."[80]

By that time, relations between the official Zionist movement and the anti-Zionist Jewish leadership in Istanbul, on the one hand, and Ottoman officialdom, on the other, had deteriorated dramatically. In a meeting attended by Chief Rabbi Haim Nahum, the four Jewish members of parliament, several members of the Istanbul Jewish communal council, and several members of the CUP, it was conveyed that in terms of Zionism, "in the ministry the good will they formerly had for us is completely changed. It is no longer mistrust but something that can be called close to animosity. They do not want to hear any more about Jewish immigration—whether in Jerusalem or Mesopotamia, or even in Konya. The leading circles that before were for us are now against us."[81]

Mazliach stated that he had seen Rıza Tevfik Bey with Ottoman Turkish translations of the Basel Program, which the Arab members of parliament took from him to read. Sasson, the Jewish MP from Baghdad, informed the group that the Arab parliamentarians were under a tremendous amount of pressure from their electorate and notable backers to oppose the Zionists forcefully. According to Fresco, who sent a report of the meeting to the Istanbul Zionist office, the Jewish MP spoke in "meaningfully sharp and pessimistic words." Fresco concluded by saying he hoped this information showed them "that the propaganda of Zionism in Turkey [*sic*], especially as it is now operated, can only be a great misfortune for the Jews of Turkey [*sic*]."

Although no doubt Fresco felt vindicated by the turn of events, the debates between *Liberty* and *El Tiempo* did little to engage the substance of the accusations—*Liberty* was adamant in maintaining that Ottoman Zionists were unstintingly loyal, with great "devotion in spirit and body of the Ottoman Jews to their homeland 'Ottomania." *Liberty* rejected a reader's suggestion to hold an Ottoman Jewish "national meeting" of communal leaders to debate Zionism—rather, it preferred simply to declare opponents "enemies of Israel."[82] Throughout 1911, the fight between the two camps raged on in Istanbul, with press and legal actions going back and forth, but there was little resolution.[83] What was clear, though, was that Zionism was not an intellectual exercise—it was a movement creating facts on the ground. The next front in the battle would move from Istanbul to Palestine.

THE SALE OF PALESTINE AND THE LIMITS OF OTTOMAN ZIONISM

Fresco's outspoken attacks on Zionism found resonance throughout the empire; in Palestine the local spokesman for an Ottomanist anti-Zionism was Albert Antébi. Early after the declaration of the constitution, Antébi had expressed his own concerns about the danger of particularist Jewish interests, especially the foreign Zionist variety. Much like Fresco, Antébi viewed these European Zionists who were resident in Palestine as troublemakers who threatened the communal equilibrium in the Ottoman Empire. A natural response to such provocations, "if I were a Muslim Turkish deputy," he argued, would be to "take the first opportunity to agitate for restrictive measures against Jewish activity in Palestine."[84]

In Antébi's mind, the only path to economic and cultural regeneration was through a broad unity with the Muslims and Christians in Palestine: "I desire to make the conquest of Zion economically and not politically; I want to cherish the historical and spiritual Jerusalem and not the modern temporal one; I want to be a Jewish deputy in the Ottoman parliament and not one in the Hebrew temple on Moriah."[85]

This position earned Antébi the abiding hatred of the radicals of the Zionist movement as well as the suspicion of the more moderate Zionist officials. Damascus-born and Paris-educated, the Francophone Antébi was the prototype of the assimilated Sephardi Jew. The Hebrew newspaper *The Deer* called Antébi "the greatest enemy of Zionism," and the editor of the paper, Itamar Ben-Avi, launched a public campaign to discredit and isolate him.[86] However, the Sephardi press, including the pro-Zionist papers, rallied behind Antébi, arguing not only that he was a significant contributor to the welfare of the Jewish community but that he also expressed a legitimate Ottomanist voice. Instead, the Sephardi press demanded a lawsuit against *The Deer*, arguing that it was a newspaper of anti-Jewish atheists and provocateurs.[87]

Ironically, although Antébi was vigilantly anti-Zionist in ideology and political outlook, in practice he helped the Zionist movement a great deal. As he himself put it, "Without practicing the utopian Zionism, I have consecrated all of my time, all of my faculties, and every beneficial matter for Jewish activity."[88] In addition to his main position as director of the AIU vocational school and beyond his side activities in the Jerusalem Chamber of Commerce and Commercial Society of Palestine, Antébi also served as an intermediary in land sales, mediated between Jewish colonies and Arab villages in periods of clashes, and repeatedly intervened with local Ottoman officials in matters of importance to Jews. He worked for the Jewish Colonization Association (ICA) in an official capacity, and unofficially with the Anglo-Palestine Bank. The Palestine Office also frequently turned to Antébi in requesting aid despite its own misgivings toward him.[89]

Despite his extensive Ottomanist activities, Antébi's aid on behalf of Zionists earned him the opprobrium of his neighbors. As he admitted, "My excommunication by the Zionists is similar to that which the Ottoman government and my Muslim co-citizens direct against my Jewish activities." Indeed, the Arabic-language newspaper *The Crier* referred to him as the "agent of the colonizers [*wakīl rijāl al-istʿimār*]."[90]

Indeed, more than any other issue, it was the sale of land to Ottoman Jews in the service of Zionism that made their Ottomanist commitments suspect to their neighbors. In the first decades of Zionist settlement in Palestine, Zionist settlement companies were able to purchase land frequently due to the intervention and assistance of the local Sephardim. Sephardi and Maghrebi Jews of the most prominent families were active in assisting the Barons de Rothschild and de Hirsch in acquiring lands for Jewish settlement. Avraham Moyal served as the local representative of the Russian society Lovers of Zion (Ḥovevei Ẓion) until his early death in 1885. His brother, Yosef Moyal, assisted the "Bilu" settlers and was considered a "pioneer" in Jewish land purchase, along with Aharon Chelouche, Haim Amzalek, and Yosef Navon. Later generations of Sephardi land agents included the lawyer David Moyal (Yosef's son), Moshe Matalon, David Yellin, and Yitzhak Levi.[91]

In the spring of 1909 two officials of the Ottoman Ministry of Justice were sent to Palestine, and the new governor of Jerusalem, Subhi Bey, was ordered to comply with the 1904 government decision to forbid land sales to foreign Jews, even those residing in Palestine. Antébi blamed the renewed government oversight on Zionists who had insisted on registering land in the names of foreign Jews rather than in the names of Ottoman Jews as had been the custom. On his own initiative, Subhi Bey decided to continue allowing land sales to Ottoman Jews. The new grand vizier, Hilmi Pasha, suggested that if Subhi Bey could devise a plan that would safeguard the rights of Ottoman Jews and yet stop immigration from Romania and Russia, "we shall willingly encourage the economic development of Ottoman Jews and abolish the restrictions." Albert Antébi worked with Subhi Bey to devise a plan to do just that.[92]

However, yet again, in May 1910, the British consul in Palestine reported that foreign Jews were being prevented from purchasing land; the following month, thc Zionist office reported that it was impossible for Ottoman Jews to buy land as well. After the al-Fula land sale controversy in the spring of 1910, 150 Jaffa Arabs sent a telegram to the Ottoman government and various newspapers demanding an end to Zionist immigration and land purchase. As one historian has noted, "they particularly protested against the purchase of land by Ottoman 'men of straw' on behalf of the Zionists."[93] In the aftermath, bans on land sales to foreign Jews were reinforced and land sales to Ottomanized Jews would only be possible after a residence of fifteen to twenty years. *Liberty* responded in the language of citizenship:

> This ban that affected especially the Jews in Ereẓ-Israel saddens us greatly because it comes from the enlightened Ottoman government that always opened her gates to our people and was like a merciful mother to them, like to all the nations. This ban would have caused us great sorrow in the Hamidian period, but in this period of freedom and equality—[how much greater is our sorrow!]. When the rumors of the ban were rife, we did not want to believe it, and even after we received official notice it was difficult for us to believe it, but at any rate, we were forced against our wishes to believe it.[94]

In the spring of 1911, various government officials in the north reinforced existing bans on land sales to Jews, including issuing warnings against the transfer of lands from Ottoman Jewish citizens to foreign Jews.[95] In 1912, the local Jerusalem government announced that it was banning further land purchase by Jews, including those who were Ottoman subjects. Opposition in the Jewish community to the new ban was swift and sharp. Members of the Jewish community's Jaffa General City Council (va'ad ha-'ir ha-klali), including the Sephardi chief rabbi in Jaffa, Ben-Zion 'Uziel, discussed the ban on November 14 and debated a response. The council members were well aware of their position: while they wanted to demand their rights equal to the other Ottoman citizens, the Balkan war in the background was an incentive to prove their loyalty to the empire. Nonetheless, they spoke in the language of "defending the honor of our people," "our national rights," "separating the Jews from the other nations," and "standing ground like the other nations." [96]

The Hebrew newspaper *Liberty* published two interviews held with Muhdi Bey, then governor of Jerusalem, about the new ban. As it turned out, it was the result of local initiative alone and did not originate in Istanbul. When pressed about the ban's applicability to Ottoman Jews, Muhdi Bey cited the role of Sephardi land agents and middlemen in Zionist land purchases as justification for the new policy. "[The law forbids] . . . those Ottomans who buy land in their names for the foreign Jews who arrived in our land to settle here. In recent days such things have taken place . . . which is against the law."[97] Muhdi Bey also informed the paper's editor, Ben-'Atar, that employing foreign Jews on one's own land was against the law.

Ben-'Atar returned to government headquarters two days later to discuss the case of Yosef Elyashar, an Ottoman Jew who had tried to purchase three dunams of land from Fahmi al-Nashashibi, also an Ottoman citizen, but had been prevented by Muhdi Bey. The exchange between Ben-'Atar and Muhdi Bey was heated at times. Why, asked Ben-'Atar, had the paperwork for Elyashar and al-Nashashibi been denied, despite the fact that Elyashar was a member of the city council and an Ottoman Jewish notable? Muhdi Bey's response was as follows:

> We cannot sell to people, despite the fact that they are Ottoman, who sell land to foreigners. . . . The Jews here are not agriculturalists and workers of the land, and most if not all of them are merchants, industrialists, warehouse owners and shopkeepers, writers or clerks in different offices. They do not have any sense of belonging to the land. And because of that [fact], if they purchase land it is not for themselves but for others, for the foreign immigrants who come here or for foreign settlement companies that, according to the old laws, have no authority to settle [here].[98]

But, Ben-'Atar protested, there were a number of Ottoman Jews who were engaged in manual labor; Muslims and Christians were allowed to make investments in land without actually working it themselves; and furthermore, the land restriction violated the equal rights of Ottoman Jews. In the end, the governor asserted that Ottoman Jews were allowed to purchase a courtyard or a warehouse, but that "those Jews . . . have no business with farming."

On November 14, the Jewish City Council sent the following telegram to Istanbul:

> At the moment when our hearts spill blood over the disaster of our homeland and at the hour of unity of all the sons of the homeland it is necessary to increase the honor of the Ottoman Empire—there are officials who differentiate between

brothers through orders and commands against a part of the citizenry, orders that are against the constitutional law and against uprightness. . . . An order like this separates the Jews for the worse and brings a divide between the citizens, which is a dangerous thing, especially in a time like this. We protest against such an injury against the rights of the Ottoman Jewish citizens and request that this illegal order be canceled immediately, and we hope that through this the unity and peace will forever [conquer] our enemies and result in the success of our great government.[99]

In the end, Albert Antébi was again called upon to negotiate with the government. In addition to protesting Muhdi Bey's formulation that Jewish merchants could not speculate in land, Antébi's appeal to the Jerusalem governor emphasized the civic rights of Ottoman Jews, their contribution to the Ottoman state, and the importance of progress for Palestine.

The constitution and its laws accord to all Ottomans absolute equality, and no one can think to withdraw from the Jews the protection accorded by law. Your Excellency, as an Ottoman citizen, native to the land . . . for more than ten generations, I take the liberty of telling you of the profound wound that this restrictive order creates deep in the heart of the Ottoman Jews in a critical moment of zeal for the sacred defense of the homeland. . . . Without speaking of the moral offense done to our Ottomanism . . . , [continuing this ban] will provoke a grave financial retardation from which you will not be able to overcome.[100]

Antébi's appeal must have convinced the governor, for eventually he and Muhdi Bey agreed that land sales could be carried out to Ottoman Jews not known to be working with the Zionist settlers, and Antébi was to submit the names of those Jews in advance for approval.[101] Despite the local government's acquiescence, however, Arab public opinion was being mobilized against Ottoman Jewish land purchase. In November, *The Carmel* revealed that the village lands of Karkur and Beidas had been sold to the Zionist Aharon Eisenberg with the acquiescence of the local administrative council. Weeks later, *Palestine* published an article against the sale, warning that "because of the Zionists the conquest of Palestine in the future will be a second Macedonia, since they do not care about money and they buy village after village. . . . How long will the vulture eat the body of the homeland? If the homeland is lost to us why do we have life?"[102]

In response to the attack, *Liberty* printed the crafted response of the Society for Arabic Printing, which had also been sent to the Reuter's telegraph agency. Aharon Eisenberg had been slandered as a "false" Ottoman. In his defense, *Liberty* claimed: "Mr. Aharon Eisenberg is the father of the Jewish Ottoman army officer Eisenberg, who now stands on the battlefront in Shtalja. The young officer . . . reached the rank of first lieutenant and later yet was honored and achieved the important distinction of *al-ghāzī*. . . . If this gentleman and his father are not considered Ottomans, who, then, are the Ottomans?"[103]

Liberty chose to focus on the contribution to the Ottoman state that the Eisenberg family was making through the active military service of their eldest son, but the truth of the matter was that Eisenberg *was* a Zionist settler as well as a land agent for the Zionist movement—dozens of lands were registered in his name in the last decade before World War I.[104] After another such article appeared in *Ottoman Union* accusing Ottoman Jews of buying lands for foreign settlers, Shlomo Yellin wrote in to defend them, claiming that all of the settlers had Ottoman citizenship, and moreover, that Zionism was a humanitarian movement that would contribute to the greater development of the empire. Neguib Nassar of *The Carmel* wrote back: "Suleiman Effendi says that the farmers in these colonies are all Ottoman subjects, and we believe him, since most of them have identity papers in their hands and foreign passports in their suitcases. . . . [But] how many of them remained Ottomans when they were called up for military service?"[105] In other words, the term *Ottoman* was not only a legal marker of citizenship; it also implied deeply contested elements of civic duty and violations of that duty.

CHAPTER SEVEN

Unscrambling the Omelet

As we saw in the case of *Palestine* and Aharon Eisenberg, the Arabic press played a leading role in stirring up local awareness of and opposition to land sales to Jews, and the fear that Palestine was being bought out from under them was a recurring theme in the years before World War I.[1] In addition to the articles targeting Ottoman Jews for violating the integrity of the Ottoman state, increasingly the Arabic press attacked Palestinian Arab land agents and land sellers on more localist, Palestinianist grounds. The Jerusalem newspaper *The Crier* harshly judged them with these words: "They sell their fathers' patrimony for monetary gain; you can see the treachery in their faces." Following up on an article in *Palestine* that denounced a land sale facilitated by one Salim Mahmud Shahin, *The Crier* demanded that the names of the sellers be made public as well: "We need to know the names of the traitors so the people will know who the liars and occupiers are." After he was denounced in *The Carmel* for reportedly being poised to sell his land near Tiberias to Zionists, Sa'id al-Jaza'iri arrived at the paper's offices to defend himself claiming, "We could never sell the Ottoman homeland, just as we could never sell our own father."[2]

The Crier assumed a preventative role, on the one hand urging people not to sell their land and on the other hand preemptively shaming those who might by publishing lists of landowners and their landholdings.[3] Other newspaper articles blamed the government clerks who were selling Palestine out, "village after village, town after town." One newspaper was even more direct: "To our sorrow we see that even at this time of great crisis for the state like the one we are in now, the governors and deputy governors are selling the state to its enemies. The aims and ambitions of the Zionists [will be revealed] in the near future and the naked truth will be shown to the Arab nation."[4] In the aftermath of the loss of Libya to Italian forces in 1911, in which there was criticism that the

Ottoman state had not done enough to defend the Arab province, the meaning of these articles was unmistakable.

Indeed, the discourse surrounding land sales simultaneously straddled Ottomanism, Palestinism, Arabism, Islamism, and anticolonialism. All of these strands are found in an undated document entitled "A Declaration from Palestinian Personalities to the Ottoman Parliament."[5] The appeal featured a "general call to citizens," but also addressed the "sons of Palestine," "sons of the homeland," and "O nation." While appealing to the parliamentarians' Islamic sensibilities (quoting Qur'anic verses against Jews, against leaving one's home, against angering God and his prophet and the angels, and for commanding good and forbidding evil), the letter also rooted itself in Arab-ness and local-ness. The letter called on the legacy of key Islamic leaders 'Umar bin al-Khattab, who conquered Palestine for Islam the first time in the seventh century, and Salah al-Din al-Ayyubi, who reconquered Palestine for Islam from the hands of the Crusaders—all the while making the historical personal by reminding its audience that "thousands of your fathers died for its walls, the martyrs, and holy warriors." The parallel danger was clear—Palestine, land holy to Islam and fought for by generations of Muslims, Arabs, and Palestinians, was threatened once again by foreign conquest.[6]

The iconic figure of Salah al-Din al-Ayyubi had surfaced in an anonymous article, widely published in 1910 in the regional Arabic press, denouncing the sale of the land of al-Fula, or Afula.[7] As we saw during the Ottoman boycott of Austria-Hungary, Salah al-Din was not only an Islamic hero, but he was also an Arab hero; indeed, the issue of the sale of Palestine would draw Palestinian Christians and Muslims closer together at a critical time. Both *The Carmel* and *Palestine* were Christian-owned, and their own editorials against Zionism emphasized the shared dangers that Muslims and Christians faced in Palestine. The Arabic press proposed that Muslims and Christians unite to establish organizations to purchase land, and Christian Arabs protested the sale vigorously in the fall of 1910 in joint delegations and telegrams. At the same time, Christian and Muslim intellectuals belonged to similar clubs and societies and had joined forces early on to establish a Muslim-Christian society to "battle against the old spirit and to get people to savor the constitution and the new spirit."[8] In other words, Arab Palestinian Muslims and Christians were converging on several different levels, not least of which was in joint opposition to Zionism and the changing Palestinian landscape.

Turning to his Christian and Muslim readers, *The Carmel* editor Neguib Nassar warned them of the danger of private interests and religious

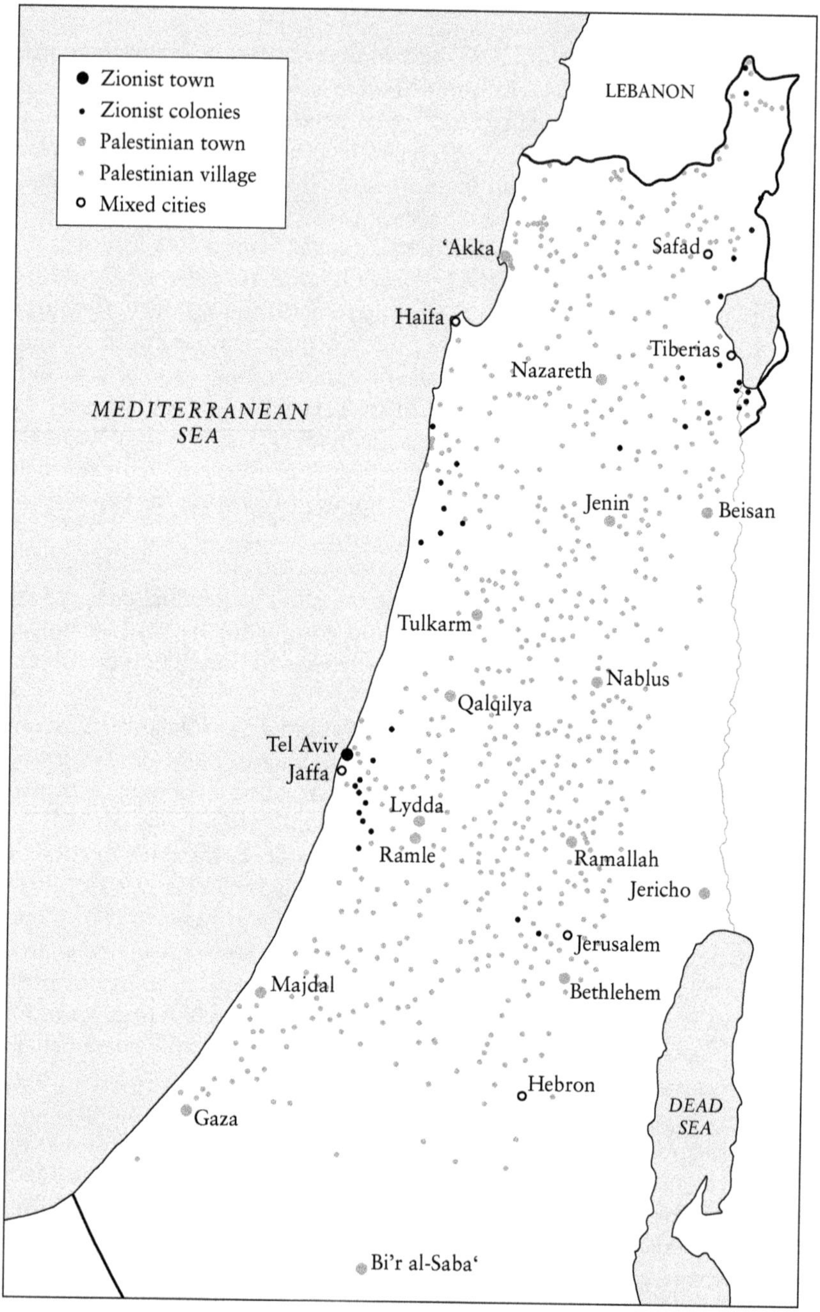

Map 7.1. Jewish settlements and Zionist colonies in Palestine, 1882–1914. Reproduced with permission from Walid Khalidi, *Before Their Diaspora: A Photographic History of the Palestinians, 1876–1948*, Institute for Palestine Studies.

solidarity that came between Muslims and Christians. The time had come to unite. "Our cities which used to be blooming are ruins, our plains which used to be fruitful are deserts. O nation, O people, wake up before your sons or grandsons or grandsons' grandsons are in the same situation. Look around and see how the other peoples have advanced while we have regressed. The Zionists who came to your land and live at your expense did manage to revive their nationalism."[9]

The growing tensions between Arabs and Jews in Palestine were not limited to the pages of the press, and physical clashes took place in the cities as well as in the countryside in Palestine. These physical altercations had taken place even before the 1908 revolution, but they increased in frequency and their political meaning became still more marked after it.[10] From 1909, clashes took place on an intermittent basis between Arab villagers and Zionist colonists and guards. Some of these "clashes" were simply economic in origin, such as thefts and highway robberies, whereas some were personal in nature, such as the case of a drunken brawl between a Jew and a Muslim which left both dead but not before enraging both sides. Undoubtedly, however, whatever their original impetus, virtually all of these clashes became part of the political struggle over Zionism in the land.

In the case of the brawl between the Jew and Muslim, which took place in February 1910, even the facts were disputed by both sides to suit their political interpretation of the event. The only parts of the story that both sides seem to agree on are brief: a Muslim from Gaza named Hashem Saqallah and a North African Jew with French consular protection named Ben-Zion Levi were leaving a house (together? at the same time?) when an argument broke out between them. Reportedly enraged by the argument, Levi pulled out a gun and mortally wounded Saqallah. Within days, the extended Saqallah family hunted down Levi and killed him in revenge. The French and British consuls as well as large numbers of guards were dispatched to Levi's funeral to prevent a wider riot from breaking out.[11]

For the Jewish paper *Liberty*, Levi was an innocent victim, and the paper's editors saw the event as further evidence of the failure of Ottomanism to bring equal rights and protections to Jews, and saw the Jews' failure to protest sufficiently loudly as evidence of their disunity and disorganization. For its part, the Arab newspaper *Success* saw the sad event as another chapter in the Jews' efforts to gain unfair advantage in the country: "People are trying to conceal the facts, but we know that Zion Levi fired first, and we need to preserve the dignity of the homeland. The homeland asks its residents and people without difference to sect or rite if it is just for one sect to rule over them and force its aims and desires on them. . . . And there is not a single person among us who does not know the aims of the other [side], and we are for unity of the nation and service of the homeland."[12]

This article tapped into a certain public discourse about the violence of the Jewish settlers, particularly those who were employed (or self-appointed) as guards on the Jewish colonies, but it also referenced recurring reports that the Zionist settlers were operating outside of the normal Ottoman legal and social setting. Demands for exclusive Hebrew labor, rumors of the violent kidnapping of Arabs found in the "first Hebrew city" Tel Aviv, and myriad other symbols of autonomy and separation disturbed Palestinian and even some Jewish observers.[13] Over three dozen village *mukhtar*s and *imam*s in the area of Daran sent a petition to Istanbul in 1913 in which they complained about the rough contacts villagers between Ramle and Gaza had with neighboring Jewish settlers. According to the petition, Jewish settlers had oppressed and murdered Arab villagers, and would soon force them off the land.[14]

In the Ottoman parliamentary debate over Zionism that took place in the spring of 1911, Jerusalem MP Ruhi al-Khalidi incredulously described the autonomy of the Zionist colonies. "It is quite strange that within these colonies there is no one from the government. They manage themselves; they have courts, they have an apparatus for settling their own affairs. There are absolutely no government representatives among them: no gendarme, no police, no administrative officials. And some of these are even towns of significant size. No one from the government can be found, they get by on their own!"[15] This theme of Zionist separation and autonomy was the topic of a blistering attack in *Palestine* two years later:

> Till ten years ago, the Jews were a fraternal native Ottoman element, living and intermixing with the other elements in harmony, interchanging business relationships, inhabiting the same quarter, sending their children to the same school, and shadowed by one banner and one crescent. Then these accursed Zionists, composed of German revolutionaries, Russian nihilists, and vagabonds of other countries, came with their cry: O Jew, remember you are a nation, and keep yourselves apart. . . . They started in the first place to build special quarters for themselves, to which they gradually attracted their compatriots who were living among Mussulmans and Christians, sifting them out like wheat from bran; then they boycotted the vernacular Arabic tongue, and it is no more heard in their homes and streets; then they confined the teaching in their schools to their own dead language, which is useless to the world except as a weapon for Zionists, and prevents natives from frequenting their schools and mixing [with] their children.[16]

At the same time, it is important to note that the collision course between Jews and Arabs described in such sharp terms on the eve of

World War I was not predetermined or, for that matter, irreversible. We have seen that at various moments different elements of Palestine's citizenry embraced the civic project of a "shared homeland" along Ottomanist lines. Another one of those moments occurred during the period of intense mobilization around the Arab reform movement in 1913–14. During this period, there was a momentary transference of the civic imperative from the Ottoman level to the Arab one. In a way echoing Ben-Yehuda's prorevolutionary calls ("Jews, be Ottomans!"), Palestinian Jews were invited to join the Arab civic nation. The Arabic press called on the Jews to learn Arabic "like the Christian community has done . . . to become part of the Arab nation, and thus this language danger will disappear, [which] brings about a lack of understanding between us."[17]

These calls were not without echo in the Jewish community as well. In the spring of 1913, the Association of Hebrew Teachers of Arabic in Jaffa met at the Alliance Israélite Universelle (AIU) school in an effort to unify teachers countrywide. Their meeting featured "very stormy" debates centered around issues such as amount of time spent teaching the language in the cities as well as in the colonies, methods of teaching the language (as a classical language or as a living one), and the final aim of teaching Arabic (for daily needs or for cultural integration). However, it also reveals the underlying tension between the civic and national visions facing Jews in Palestine and the cultural politics of the times, pitting those Jews fully acculturated to Arab society against others who viewed Arabic as merely instrumental.[18]

On the Arabist side of the debate stood the journalist Nissim Malul, seemingly alone in his cultural-political agenda. For him, "the reason for anti-Semitism in Palestine and Syria is due to the lack of knowledge of Arabic. The masses are guided by this. The association will teach the youth Arabic so that they know how to answer them." In response, Mr. 'Abadi retorted that "we do not need to be patriots to be enthusiastic of Arabic. We are teachers and we need to talk about instruction and that is all!" With this the association declined to define itself as a political organization, instead choosing to serve as a professional one.

Not to be dissuaded, in June 1913 Nissim Malul appealed to his fellow Sephardi Jews in the pages of the Hebrew newspaper *Liberty*, articulating his vision for Jewish-Arab coexistence.[19] In his first article, Malul explained that the study of Arabic was not like other languages, neither in pedagogical terms (Arabic was more difficult, the accent was hard to master) nor in terms of this language's relationship to the Jewish community. According to Malul, if the Jews in Palestine desired to be a people on its own without taking Arabic seriously, they would cut themselves off from the rest of the Ottoman Empire and would not be considered a people who reside in it: "If we desire to root ourselves here in the mode of the land of the past and of the future, then we must learn the language of the land and think in it more than we do in the other languages," Malul warned. According to him, "it is a crime to teach our youth those languages that cause them to leave the land and live in exile and build their futures there. . . . [In that case] it would be better to return to the ways of the ancestors who came just to be buried here."[20]

Malul directly responded to his Ashkenazi Zionist critics who were concerned that by learning Arabic the Jews would assimilate with the Arabs and therefore "lose" their collective identity, or nationalism. However, Malul said,

> those who speak out against learning Arabic or the teachers' association do not understand nationalism other than in name. There is no necessary condition for the nationalist to know his language [*sic*!—editor]—the nationalist is a nationalist in his feelings but not in language [!—from the editor], he is a nationalist according to his nationalist acts. If we say there is no nationalism without language, as Rabinowitz does, then we say to our brothers in Europe who work for the good of the Ereẓ-Israeli community, many good people at the head of whom is Max Nordau, [we say to them] that they are not nationalists because they do not know Hebrew.[21]

Instead, according to Malul, language and nation were not necessarily constitutive of each other.

Malul's concluding remarks offered his readers the most damning evidence to date of his cultural and political commitments to the Arab world that, he believed, coexisted with his equal commitments to the Jewish people. "If we desire to be the inheritors of Rabbi Yehuda Ha-Levi and the Rambam, to follow in their paths," Malul wrote, "then we must know Arabic and mix with the Arabs [?!—editor's note] like they also did [?—editor's note]. In the role of a Semitic nation we must base our nationalism in Semitism and not blur with European culture, and through Arabic we can found a real Hebrew culture. But if we bring into our culture European foundations then we will simply be committing suicide."[22]

Immediately following Malul's third article, the editor of *Liberty*, Haim Ben-'Atar, published his response to the part of Malul's writing that he found objectionable: specifically, his comments on the centrality of Hebrew to Jewish nationalism. Ben-'Atar asserted that while "there is not one of us who does not acknowledge the urgency of studying the Arabic language—the language of the land— . . . or the necessity of teaching it to our sons," Arabic could never replace Hebrew as the primary language of the Palestinian Jews. In fact, the Palestinian Arabs did not want the Jews to assimilate or mix with them.

Ben-ʿAtar invoked the lessons of Jewish history from the Babylonian exile to the modern day to show that "mixing with another people, even if it is also Semitic, endangers the status of the existence of our people." Furthermore, Ben-ʿAtar made the distinction between writing in the contemporary language, as Rabbi Saʿadia Gaon and others did, and mixing with the Arabs, which they did not. The Hebrew language was absolutely critical to the Jewish national renaissance, according to Ben-ʿAtar; besides reviving Hebrew, there was no other method through which to erase the exile and its Tower of Babel. According to Ben-ʿAtar, the Jewish community must manage to teach Arabic as a necessary language while at the same time keeping its culture distinct.

Malul's stand on this question was in the minority, even among the Sephardi community. For the rest of the Sephardi Jews active in the Hebraic public sphere, the "shared homeland" of civic universalism they advocated did not rely on a shared language or nationhood. For Malul, however, the lessons of the growing Arabist movement were clear: to have a place in the civic nation, Jews had to switch their affiliation from Ottomanism to Arabism.[23] As Malul realized, by the time Shimʿon Moyal finally succeeded in establishing the long-awaited Jewish-Arabic newspaper *Voice of Ottomanism* (*Ṣawt al-ʿUthmāniyya*) in 1914, the civic Ottomanist dream was past obsolescence.

The end of the Ottoman era during World War I brought about a widespread "unmixing of peoples," and the formerly heterogeneous, multiethnic, multireligious empire was reshuffled to reflect the prerogatives of the homogenizing nation-state.[24] In Palestine, this process of "unmixing" had already begun as part of the Zionist project since the interdependence of Jews and Arabs threatened the nationalist imperative. In 1914, for example, Zionist functionary Arthur Ruppin complained that the Jews of Jaffa were regrettably less willing to display Jewish national solidarity, an attitude that he blamed on the fact that they lived in mixed neighborhoods with Arabs.[25]

As well, the Balfour Declaration of 1917, which promised British support of a "Jewish national home" in Palestine, was the ultimate undermining of the "shared homeland" ideal, instead inverting the precarious social balance in favor of the minority Jewish community and the Zionist movement's exclusivist Hebraic nationalism. By the 1920s, David Yellin, the former member of the Jerusalem City Council and Ottoman Administrative Council who had given countless patriotic speeches on behalf of civic Ottomanism, proposed the establishment of separate municipalities in Jerusalem along sectarian demographic lines.[26]

THE ARAB NATION AND THE IMPERIAL DIMENSION

> There is still a glamour hanging over the word "Constitution," and public speakers can still move the populace by declaiming high sounding sentences about liberty and union; but under it all there seems to be a growing feeling of resentment against the way the central government is treating the Arabic people, and a feeling that this much talked about liberty and equality is more visionary than real.[27]
>
> Stanley Hollis, U.S. Consul General of Beirut

In 1911 the U.S. Consulate in Beirut made the above assessment of local Arab attitudes toward the Ottoman revolution and the Ottoman central government, indicating that public dissatisfaction with the shortcomings of the revolution stood side by side with a developed Arab ethnic consciousness. As we know from the contemporary press as well as from other historical sources, by this time an Arabist movement had emerged, and the Arabic-language press both documented and exacerbated tensions. While earlier scholars have seen this Arabist movement and mobilized Arabic press as evidence of an Arab nationalism in the Ottoman Empire, a simplification that has been justly critiqued by revisionist historians, it is important to understand the Arabist movement and sentiments within a broader Ottoman imperial politics of multiculturalism as well as against a growing critique of civic Ottomanism.

First, Arabism played up a cultural and ethnic consciousness that tapped into the broader imperial setting and an awareness of—bordering on rivalry with—the other ethnic groups in the empire. The earliest Arabist organization, the Ottoman Arab Brotherhood Society, was founded in Istanbul in the fall of 1908 to defend the constitution, bring together the races, promote equality in the Arab provinces, promote collective and individual aid, and spread education in Arabic. Numerous Arabic language newspapers were supportive of the society's aims, including its namesake in Istanbul, *Al-Mufīd* in Damascus, and *Ottoman Union* in Beirut, and within months there were reports of affiliated committees sprouting up in Jerusalem, Hebron, and Tiberias, as well as in Tripoli, Beirut, Damascus, Basra, and Baghdad. The historian Hasan Kayalı has argued that many of the society's founders were former members of the Hamidian regime who hoped to maintain their position in the new constitutional regime by establishing themselves as protectors of Arab interests, and within the first few months, the brotherhood took on an anti-CUP tone.[28]

Indeed, the society was shut down by the Ottoman government in the spring of 1909 because of alleged ties between the organization and the Damascus branch of the counterrevolutionary Muhammadan Union. And yet, we cannot simply relegate its activities to anti-CUP mobilization, or its membership to ancien régime holdouts. The branches of the Ottoman Arab Brotherhood were engaged in cultural activities and were active in promoting an Arab ethnic consciousness. In Jerusalem the founding members of the branch included the mayor, Faidi al-'Alami, as well as the Christian educators and journalists Nakhla Zurayq, Khalil al-Sakakini, and Hanna al-'Issa.[29] Al-Sakakini, we should note, joined the Ottoman Arab Brotherhood within days of being inducted into the Jerusalem chapter of the CUP.

The following year, the Arab Literary Club was established in Istanbul. Both the Arab Literary Club and the Arab Ottoman Brotherhood framed themselves squarely within the Ottoman Empire. For both groups—as well as for many, and perhaps even most, of the individuals affiliated with them—the Arab nation (*al-umma al-'Arabiyya*) and the Ottoman nation (*al-umma al-'Uthmāniyya*) were perfectly compatible and logical forms of self-identification. A notice in a Jerusalem newspaper in 1911 praised the local chapter of the Literary Club for its national devotion and patriotism, after it held a performance about the love of homeland which benefited injured soldiers and the education of orphans.[30]

In essence, leading Arab Ottomans were promoting themselves as integral constituent elements of, and even vital partners to, the imperial project. In this regard we should look at the activities of many Arab intellectuals in the years before World War I as players in an imperial multicultural politics. Many other ethnic clubs and societies were established in the year immediately following the revolution, such as the Greek Political Club, Serbian-Ottoman Club, Armenian Revolutionary Federation, Bulgarian Club, Jewish Youth Club, Lovers of Anatolia, Albanian Union, and the Kurdish Mutual Aid and Progress Society.[31] While some of these organizations (such as the Greek, Serbian, Bulgarian, and Armenian clubs) aroused the suspicions and concerns of provincial officials, with accusations ranging from support for decentralization to stashing a secret arms cache and promoting ethnic nationalization, the others had clear integrationist purposes. The Kurdish Mutual Aid and Progress Society, for example, proclaimed as its purpose to "consolidate Kurdish ties with the Ottoman state while protecting the constitution as the only way for progress and explaining to those Kurds who are not aware of the virtues of the constitution that it is responsible for the happiness of the people and also compatible with the great rules of Islam." In addition, the society pledged to work to improve Kurdish-Armenian relations and to unite the disparate Kurdish tribes and confederacies.[32]

Language revival and literary expression flourished among all the communities of the empire. Hand in hand with calls for promoting the learning of Ottoman Turkish among many groups that were not sufficiently literate in Ottoman, publication in ethnic languages increased, and in many cases became politicized as a marker of equality in the empire. For example, both Greek and Armenian communities requested that their languages be recognized as official languages alongside Ottoman Turkish, a suggestion which caught the attention of Arabists in the empire. However, the CUP was opposed to language multiculturalism on an official or state level. In the words of the editor of the pro-CUP newspaper *Tanin*, Hüseyin Cahid, "to allow different languages in government would be setting up a Tower of Babel and would lead to decentralization."[33]

Although the CUP actually did little to change the status quo vis-à-vis language, nonetheless there were accusations lodged against it that it was attempting to "Turkify" the various elements of the empire. In fact, defense of the status of the Arabic language became a cause célèbre during this period. Already in 1910, concerns were being expressed about the status of Arabic versus Ottoman Turkish. As the Palestinian paper *Success* wrote, "many people are writing and worrying about the Arabic language these days. . . . There is anger that our brothers the Turks are trying to kill the language by spreading the official language among our notables and public, and in our offices and clubs and schools and groups." Rather than retreating to Arabic purity, however, *Success* decided to publish itself as a bilingual newspaper that would be "a shared service to the two groups—those two languages must be sisters sharing in the service of the nation and the homeland."[34]

These complaints about language Turkification went hand in hand with other complaints about the shortcomings of the revolution. In the public commemorations of the revolution in the summer of 1911, for example, the mood documented in *Palestine* was of a weary cheerleader, criticizing the lack of sufficient reforms while continuing to aspire to the ideals of the revolution. At the same time, among non-Muslims and Muslims alike, faith in civic Ottomanism was tested by a perceived imbalance between the communities, one that found expression and succor in the press of the period. For example, at the official celebrations in 1911 at the CUP headquarters in Gaza, a local religious scholar spoke out, calling on the "sultan of the Muslims and the Islamic kingdom as well as the Muslim forces to reject the other races [*nabdh baqiyat al-'anāṣir*]" of the empire. According to the newspaper account, this caused the reproach of another scholar, a member of the CUP, who instead called for the unity of the races and faithfulness to the Ottoman Empire according to its Ottomanist mission.[35]

On the other hand, it was impossible to ignore the growing tension between Ottomanism and Arabism. A published letter from one of the local youth, Darwish Sakijha, reiterated in many ways the strong emotional attachment to the revolution that was nurtured among the populace. While praising the "beautiful" and "joyous" holiday of the constitution ("a date that should be carved into the breast of every loyal Ottoman"), Sakijha closed with the requisite cries "long live freedom, long live the homeland, long live the people," and then added, "long live the Arabs."[36] Two years earlier, the ending instinctively would have been "long live the Ottoman nation." Even more explicitly, the standard poem included to commemorate the revolution's anniversary opened and closed with articulations of difference and separation between Arab and Turk, again avoiding the previously unanimous appeal to "Ottomans": "To the East on the holiday, oh, what a holiday of joy, on the stage of the two peoples, the Turk and the Arab."[37]

And yet, despite the complex ambivalence toward the empire's current path that found expression in the pages of his newspaper, *Palestine*'s editor Yusuf al-'Issa sought to remind his readers of the proper balance between Ottomanism and criticism. In a stinging article entitled "The Liberals/Freemen of July (Tammuz)," al-'Issa sharply criticized the shortcomings of the revolution. Al-'Issa also, however, lashed out at the indifference and ignorance of the masses and at the self-serving and hypocritical political Arabists in the press who proclaimed themselves to be the inheritors of the revolutionary mandate yet were, according to al-'Issa, complicit in the counterrevolutionary movements. ("Those who call from their high roofs that they are liberals are far from this virtue, as far as the wolf from the blood of the son of Jacob, and I leave it to their [account with] God and their consciences.")[38]

> Then what do we mean by "liberals/freemen of July"? We mean the thousands of students who were set free in the annual [summer] holiday [from school]. We say to them: O new generation, tomorrow you will see your city decorated in flags and your rulers dressed in elaborate clothing—ask your fathers or whoever is older than you the reason and they will respond that this day is the 24th of July upon which the constitution was proclaimed. . . . If you want to know the history of liberty and the constitution then beware of the Arabic newspapers. I am afraid you will understand from them that the constitution is based on [opposition leader] al-'Asali, member of parliament from Damascus, and that its foundations are the officials of Nablus and the notables of Jerusalem and the heroes of Harat al-Maydan in Syria. As we read yesterday: "The homeland will not grow great men until their dust is gathered as one mass to drink from the delicious blood of the martyrs in the cause of justice."
>
> If you ask what they are talking about and who the martyrs in the cause of justice are, they will answer that he is a journalist, the martyr whose blood Istanbul

spilled. If you investigate that martyr you will find that he was a writer who with his writings as a sword caused the destruction of the homeland [*khirāb al-waṭan*] in the days of Abdülhamid and took part in the betrayal of the [constitution].[39]

The critique of an Ottomanism that had fallen far short of expectations as well as of the specific path of centralization chosen by the CUP which held power were at the core of two important movements that emerged in the Arab provinces in 1912–13. The first, the Beirut Reform Committee (al-jami'a al-'umūmiyya al-iṣlāḥiyya), sought to promote increased rights for the provinces. Soon after the BRC was outlawed by the government, the Decentralization Party (ḥizb al-lāmarkaziyya) was established in Cairo to promote federalism in the Ottoman Empire. They both linked their cultural demands on behalf of the Arabic language with political demands of provincial reform.[40]

In many ways, these movements were rearticulations of earlier calls for decentralization that were issued before the revolution as well as immediately after. However, when two Lebanese Christian brothers residing in Paris, Rashid and Nakhla Mutran, had called for Syrian autonomy soon after the revolution, they had been roundly denounced by the head of the Paris Ottoman Commercial Committee, Syrian exiles resident in Cairo in *Al-Ahrām* newspaper, and even their own brother Nadra in the pages of *Istanbul*. When their manifestos surfaced in Damascus and Baghdad, hundreds of notables had signed telegrams to the grand vizier and the Ottoman parliament condemning the pamphlets and reiterating their loyalty to the empire.[41]

By 1911–12, in contrast, the imperial landscape had changed dramatically, and ideas not so far off from the Mutran brothers' earlier proposals for "administrative independence [*istiqlāl idārī*]" were bandied about. It is clear that proposals for administrative reform in the Arab provinces of the empire were rooted in mounting complaints about incomplete Ottomanism and a critique of the CUP, on the one hand, but importantly, they also stemmed from observing ethnic politics in the empire more broadly. Arabs looked to the citizenship claims of other groups in the empire and followed suit. For example, the Haifa-based newspaper *The Carmel* framed the Arab reform movement in the context of the recent gains by Albanians in the empire for decentralization and cultural autonomy. Nejuib Nassar saw the Albanians' demands for local military service, government officials who knew the Albanian language, and primary education in Albanian, as entirely natural. As Nassar saw it, despite the fact that the ethnic Turkish element was a pillar of the empire due to their political and military contributions, the other ethnic groups also had a role to play in the empire and should have complete freedom to live out their national customs, a fact the CUP failed to recognize.[42]

If the Albanians were a positive model for Nassar of a loyal and patriotic ethnic group demanding their rights within the empire, the Balkan nationalists earned his opprobrium. Rather than demanding reform, they had turned to foreign powers and engendered the breakup of the empire. At the same time, however, Nassar also blamed the CUP government for pushing the empire to the brink, and linked a resolution of the Balkan conflict to imperial reform. According to Nassar, the current Ottoman government saw Arab and other lands as mere possessions, and the empire had gone from an "Ottoman nation" ("*al-umma al-'Uthmāniyya*") to its erasure due to the CUP's twin policies of colonization and ethnic nationalism. A recent article in the pro-CUP paper *Tanin* that had called Minister of Interior Talat Pasha the "conqueror of Yemen" ("*fātiḥ al-Yaman*") was evidence of this tendency. As Nassar rhetorically asked his readers, "Do they not realize that Yemen is Ottoman?"[43]

And yet, *The Carmel* remained a deeply patriotic Ottoman newspaper until the very end. Nassar published numerous patriotic poems and letters from readers, such as that by Mikha'il Jirjis Wehbe from Nazareth, whose poem praised Ottoman heroes, denounced foreign occupation, and lauded the empire's various ethnic groups as "brothers walking hand in hand" for the "beloved homeland." In another article *The Carmel* praised the efforts of Labib Effendi, a military officer who taught at an elementary school in 'Akka, drilling students in sports and military education; according to the paper, if every officer volunteered to do this in the schools, "we would be a strong nation." Nassar also took care to emphasize the patriotism of the various opposition figures traveling to and through Palestine, and denounced members of the 'Abd al-Hadi family in Nablus who were rumored to have approached British officials in neighboring Egypt in order to push for the British occupation of Palestine.[44]

In other words, to state the obvious, cultural Arabism and calls for reform in the Arab provinces are not the same thing as Arab nationalism.[45] Instead, Palestinians and other Arabs saw themselves as loyal—even if critical—Ottomans who took on those few Arabs voices who advocated separation from the empire. The fate of one such figure, Neguib Azoury, who is often cited as the "first" Arab nationalist, proves instructive. Azoury was a Lebanese Christian who had worked in the Ottoman provincial government in Jerusalem; after fleeing government employment under shady circumstances, he published a pamphlet in 1905 from Paris calling for the peoples of the Ottoman Empire to abandon the empire and establish independent states. After the revolution, Azoury made his way back to Jerusalem and stood as a candidate for the Ottoman parliament, but he received virtually no public support and disappeared from the historical record shortly thereafter.

The campaign of another parliamentary candidate, Sa'id Abu Khadra', better illustrates the ways in which loyalty and criticism shaped Arab Ottomanism at empire's end. In the spring of 1912, Abu Khadra', a young member of a notable Muslim family from Gaza, published what was likely the first election pamphlet in Palestinian history, attempting to convince his fellow Palestinians to elect him to the Ottoman parliament. Only one of the three standing MPs representing Jerusalem, Ruhi al-Khalidi, was still running as a Unionist; the other two MPs, Sa'id al-Husayni and Hafiz al-Sa'id, were running with the opposition, the Entente Liberale. In response, the CUP endorsed two other candidates: 'Uthman al-Nashashibi, a Jerusalem notable, and Ahmed 'Arif al-Husayni, the mufti of Gaza. The 1912 election season corresponded with the height of Arabist publications and mobilization in the press, a dimension about which other scholars have written. Instead, we will turn to the language of imperial citizenship that Abu Khadra''s campaign revealed.[46]

In his pamphlet, Abu Khadra' outlined his vision of modern politics and an active imperial citizenship. For one, citizenship demanded a dialogue between elected official and constituent, a dialogue based on transparency of aims, means, and results. That is, it was incumbent upon candidates to come to an understanding with the people in order to learn their demands and to prevent misunderstanding between them. Abu Khadra''s pamphlet was therefore the draft of a social contract of mutual understanding between would-be elected official and ostensible constituents.

He addressed his voters: "'What do you promise us?' I'm sure you, dear voter, are thinking of this: 'What do you promise us the people of Palestine [ahālī Filasṭīn] and the residents of the province of Jerusalem?'" With that, Abu Khadra' outlined his ten-point plan for pushing through both imperial reform and local say in that process. Tax reform, much-needed public works like a port for Jaffa and a tramway in Jerusalem, preserving the rights of the religious endowments according to the constitutional proof-text (clause 111), arguing for the modification of the recently enacted censorship laws, all demanded Abu Khadra''s attention, and were all issues that had preoccupied the Palestinian press for months and years beforehand. Abu Khadra' also criticized the elections system and argued for direct elections, argued that land reform would benefit both peasants and the homeland as a whole, and sought a compromise on the language question that would respect the civic mission of Ottoman Turkish while preserving the nobility of Arabic.

Although Abu Khadra' was ultimately unsuccessful in his parliamentary bid, his candidacy was endorsed by *Palestine* and *The Crier*, the most important Arabic newspapers in Jaffa and Jerusalem, respectively.

In his adoption of the language and rationale of the Ottoman reforming classes and in his engagement with the institutions and promises of constitutional liberalism set in place by the 1908 revolution, Abu Khadra' proved himself loyal to the Ottoman imperial project. At the same time, he took issue with the direction of imperial decision making and explicitly demanded more involvement in provincial governance for Palestine and Palestinians on such pressing issues as freedom of the press, public works, and land tenure. In short, Abu Khadra' was neither reflexively loyal to a stagnant empire nor a separatist nationalist, but rather an engaged and empowered imperial citizen. In his words:

> Let me inform you, O brother, that your homeland Palestine is part of great lands claimed by the Ottoman Empire, and as long as the existence of this empire is preserved, if you send me as a deputy on your behalf its stability and its prestige and the preservation of its possessions will be the first order of importance for me. . . . I will not delay in crying out in the face of the Unionists "You are traitors" if they deviate from the law and aim at the Turkification of the elements [tatrīk al-'anāṣir] of the empire, and [likewise] I will not flinch from calling out the baseness of the Liberals if I discern in them the inclination for independence of the elements of the empire [istiqlāl 'anāṣir al-mamlaka], whether Bulgarians, Serbs, Greeks, or Arabs. I will entreat the rest of my colleagues in the parliament in the name of religion, honor, and patriotism to be as one mass uniting this Ottoman Empire either—God forbid—to disappear all together or—God willing—to perpetuate its existence forever and ever.[47]

This loyal-critic role, as we have seen, was also played by others. *Palestine*'s editor, Yusuf al-'Issa, for example, was so against the "Arabist reformers" that he refused to cover the 1913 Paris Congress in his newspaper. That same year the newspaper *Public Opinion* (*Al-Rayy al-'Amm*) published a series of anti-autonomy articles by the Druze emir Shakib Arslan, where he took the decentralists and nationalists to task: "Decentralization means passing an eternity in hell; the [Liberals'] party thinks it is building a palace, but in reality it is digging its own grave."[48]

Despite the harsh criticism they faced by Arslan and the CUP, neither the Beirut Reform Committee nor the Decentralization Party openly sought Arab independence or autonomy from the empire, and even the Arab congress held in Paris in June 1913 upheld the integrity of the empire despite some of the harsh language used there. Attendees at the Arab congress did speak openly on behalf of the "Arab nation" and the "Syrian homeland," but they did so in the context of Arab rights in the Ottoman Empire and decentralization as the basis of political reform.[49] As the general invitation read, "We will explain to the Ottoman state that decentralization is the rule of our life and our life is the holiest right of all our rights, and the Arabs are partners in this empire, partners in war, partners in administration, partners in politics, but inside their lands they are partners [only] to themselves."[50]

At virtually every opportunity, the attendees at the Paris Congress underscored the active participation of Arabs in the life and administration of the Ottoman Empire along the lines of decentralization. The congress also resolved that Arabic should be recognized by the Ottoman parliament as an official language of the empire, that Arab soldiers should fulfill military service locally, and it supported the special privileges secured by Mount Lebanon and Beirut. In addition, the congress expressed its sympathy with the decentralizing demands of Armenian Ottomans. In the words of the president of the congress, former MP from Hama 'Abd al-Hamid al-Zahrawi, "The situation of our Armenian brothers is like our situation: they emigrate like we do, they think like we do, they demand like we do. And we want our victories to be their victories and want to be equal in our demands of decentralization."[51]

The Paris Congress received numerous telegrams of support from the Arab diaspora in the Americas as well as some telegrams from within the Middle East. The seven telegrams that came from Palestine are notable for what they do and do not show us about Palestinian support for the Arab reform movement. Three of the telegrams were from the north of the country, including one from the Jenin region, which supported the "noble cause of progress of the Arab element and the struggle for its rights within the Ottoman Empire." It was signed by twenty village *mukhtars*, a neighborhood *mukhtar* in Jenin city, three Christian notables, and four Muslim notables (two of whom belonged to the 'Abd al-Hadi family—it would not be surprising to learn that the villages listed were all under 'Abd al-Hadi patronage). Another telegram, this time from Nablus, was signed by three 'Abd al-Hadi's as well as three other men. The third telegram from the north was from Haifa and supported the struggle for "Arab public good specifically and Ottoman public good generally"; of the fifty-six signatories, thirty-two were identifiably Christian (including the editor of *The Carmel*, Nejuib Nassar).

The other Palestinian telegrams all came from Jaffa, including one from the Muslim Charitable Association, another from the cultural club "Jaffa Youth," and two more signed by groups of individuals (one of which included several Masons from the Barkai lodge, including the lodge Venerable, Cesar 'Araktinji and failed parliamentary candidate Sa'id Abu Khadra'). In other words, while there was a strong representation of supporters among the 'Abd al-Hadi extended family as well as among Christians in Haifa, the records of the Paris Congress hardly suggest massive or widespread support from Palestine for the Arab reform movement, nor do they suggest that supporters were demanding anything other than imperial reforms.

In the months following the Paris Congress, the central committee of the Decentralization Party based in Cairo, which included many familiar faces among the Syro-Lebanese exile community long resident in Egypt, sought to build up its support and issued a public call to the "Arab nation" in which it clearly laid out its attitude toward demands of the Ottoman government. The call declared: "It is well known that the Arab nation which lives under the flag of the Ottoman crescent is the most devoted of the Ottoman peoples to the high state and is the strongest in loyalty to the bond of Ottoman society," despite the long centuries of suffering under the poor administration of the former authoritarian government. The call requested fairer participation and oversight in local administrative and educational affairs: "a form of self-government which is present in all the advanced states today in Europe and America, which is known as administrative decentralization."[52]

According to the committee, demands for reform would benefit not only the Arab people but the state as a whole. Broad-ranging administrative reforms would also renew the covenant between the Ottoman government and the Arab people and improve trust and relations with their "dear Turkish brothers" in the empire. Underscoring its commitment to the integrity of the empire as well as its appeal for reform, the committee emphasized that it was requesting these reforms in a legal manner congruent to that which is accorded any political party in a constitutional state. Finally, in the era of increased competition and rivalry between the remaining Ottoman peoples, administrative reform was depicted as necessary to saving the empire as well as to continuing its path of advancement and progress.

The practical demands of the committee were based on existing provincial institutions such as the general council, the administrative council, the education council, and the religious endowments council (art. 4), but sought to beef up the autonomy and binding nature of the councils' decisions (art. 5), to standardize election and appointment to the committees (art. 7, 10, and 11), and to enshrine the right of oversight and transparency in provincial administration (art. 6, 8, and 9). In addition, the committee's program called for reforming the land tenure system and ensuring the participation of Bedouin tribes (art. 13), demanded that every province would have two official languages, Ottoman Turkish and the language of the majority of the province's inhabitants (art. 14), insisted that education must be in the language of the province (art. 15), and requested that compulsory military service during peacetime be fulfilled within the home province.

In its principled demand that education and the curriculum be left in the hands of the local education council, as well as in its demand that every province have two official languages, the Decentralization Party reiterated the cultural Arabist resolutions of the Paris Congress. The Paris Congress also had insisted on quotas for Arab representation in all government councils and ministries and demanded that government officials posted in Arab provinces know Arabic. Both groups, however, preserved the role of security and foreign affairs for the central government and did not raise any issue that could be considered separatist nationalist.[53]

At first, the CUP government agreed to several of the Arabs' demands, even making a number of conciliatory gestures toward them. Within months, however, the CUP backpedaled and a sultanic edict was issued that ignored virtually all of their demands for reform. The Decentralization Party sent one more telegram-appeal to the grand vizier in the hopes that their demands would fall on sympathetic ears. Should the reasonable demands of the Arabs not be met, however, the Decentralization Party also issued a veiled threat.

> There is no Arab as far as we know who is devoted to the protection of the flag of the Ottoman crescent who does not want the continuation of the state and life with his brothers the Turks under one flag . . . just as there is no Arab who understands the meaning of life and existence who wishes that his place in this state will be the position of a slave owned by the king . . . nor that of a foreigner among the colonizing occupier. Nay, every thinking Arab who understands the meaning of life demands that his place will be side by side with the Turk in this empire, a position of brother and comrade next to his brother and comrade, where neither of them takes advantage of the other, either in Islamic law or in imperial law, but rather where individuals from each of the two peoples will be preferred according to their knowledge and works. . . . But if our brothers do not want to understand this fact . . . then the Arab people want life and will struggle for it.[54]

FROM WAR TO WAR

If in 1913 the language was still of reform and decentralization, within two years everything would change. The outbreak of the Balkan war in the fall of 1912 was an opportunity for the Arab provinces to show their patriotism and commitment to remaining within the Ottoman Empire. *The Carmel* covered the war extensively as well as the local Palestinian response to it. With the reading of the sultanic declaration of war, large crowds gathered in Haifa and 'Akka, where patriotic poems were read and exhortative speeches were given. Over the coming weeks, numerous patriotic editorials and poems were published in the paper; notices about volunteers heading to the front (including forty-five from Haifa) were welcomed enthusiastically and praised with superlatives; and fundraising performances and donations were duly noted and honored.[55]

However, by the end of the fighting in the Balkans, the demographics of the empire had shifted dramatically as large numbers of Christians were no longer included in the empire's territorial boundaries, leaving the empire the most demographically homogeneous (and the most Muslim) it had ever been in its more than six-hundred-year existence. The impact of the Balkan wars was profound: the trauma of losing Salonica, home to the revolution as well as of many of its leaders, coupled with the temporary loss of Edirne, the capital of the empire until the conquest of Constantinople, was unbearable. At the same time, for many who saw the Christians as a Fifth Column enabling the defeat of the empire to Greece and Bulgaria, Ottomanism as a union of Muslims and Christians was proven to be a delusion.[56]

As a result of this development, the CUP and others in the empire turned to Islamic discourse more openly as a source of Ottoman imperial identity and solidarity. This was apparent in the 1913–14 parliamentary elections, where the *sharīf* of Mecca, the custodian of the holy sites, was paraded throughout the Arab provinces to rally votes for the CUP.[57] The decision of the CUP to enter World War I on the German and Austro-Hungarian side transformed the war effort into a jihad, or holy war. Finally, under the cover of war, the Ottoman government abrogated the Capitulations, which had long been a source of inequality between Europe and the empire, as well as between foreign protégés and Ottoman citizens within.

While the initial entry of the Ottoman Empire into the world war led to a surge in patriotic activity and mobilization, over the course of the war several factors stretched the remaining elements of the Ottoman nation to the breaking point. First, massive conscription from the Arab provinces provided the Ottoman army with up to three hundred thousand recruits, about one-third of the empire's total military forces, but left many homes without breadwinners and workers. The privations of war—famine, disease, locust plagues, poverty—led to great suffering throughout the empire, suffering that would remain seared in the collective memory of the Arab provinces long after the empire ceased to exist. Under the rule of Cemal Pasha, the iron fist of martial law, which included wartime expulsions and imprisonment, further alienated the local population.[58]

Two Palestinians left their impressions of the war years that give the sense of an increased feeling of colonization and subjugation under Ottoman rule. Khalil al-Sakakini, the Christian educator discussed earlier, complained about the labor battalions that conscripted local Christians to work on building roads, cleaning trash, and performing other menial tasks for the local government and army. Al-Sakakini recorded:

> Today a large number of Christians were recruited as garbage collectors to Bethlehem and Bayt Jala. Each was given a broom, a shovel, and a bucket, and they were distributed in the alleys of the town. Conscripts would shout at each home they passed, "send us your garbage." The women of Bethlehem looked out from their windows and wept. No doubt this is the ultimate humiliation. We have gone back to the days of bondage in the Roman and Assyrian days.[59]

A similar sentiment was expressed by al-Sakakini's former student, Ihsan Turjeman, a young Muslim private serving in army headquarters in Jerusalem. According to Turjeman, "We have entered into a compact with this state that can only work if we are treated on equal footing with the Turkish [subjects]. Now, however, the state has chosen to treat us as a colonized possession, and the time has come to break up the partnership."[60]

Only a few months later, dozens of Arab intellectuals were sentenced to death in an Ottoman army court-martial in Aley, north of Beirut. The charge against them was "high treason," and the evidence included a group of papers confiscated from the French Consulate in Beirut, where the men had reportedly asked for French help in securing independence from the Ottomans.[61] Most of those sentenced to death managed to escape or were already out of the country, but eleven were hanged in downtown Beirut; the following year twenty-one additional men went to the gallows in Beirut and Damascus. Among those hanged were several prominent journalists who had been active in the decentralist movement: Shaykh Ahmad Tabbara, editor of *Ottoman Union*; 'Abd al-Ghani al-'Uraisi, editor of *Al-Mufīd*; along with Shukri al-'Asali, the Damascene member of parliament. In addition, four Palestinian men were executed.

For Turjeman and others, these men were martyrs for a new cause, the Arab nation. If most Arabs had been loyal Ottomanists because of their belief in the civic Ottomanist project or their loyalty to the Ottoman state and dynasty, the war years altered that sentiment irrevocably.

Conclusion

On December 9, 1918, the mayor of Jerusalem, Husayn Hashem al-Husayni, surrendered his city to the arriving troops of British General Edmund Allenby, abruptly ending four centuries of Ottoman rule over Palestine. The surrender was signed in the office of the Anglican bishop of Jerusalem; his daughter, who had grown up in Jerusalem, had strong feelings about the divine mission that Great Britain was fulfilling by taking over the Holy Land. In her mind, "Turkish rule is like a cancer, and Palestine was saved only in time."[1] With the benefit of hindsight, of course, we know that British rule over Palestine was itself no paradise, and that exactly thirty years later the governing British high commissioner would pack up the imperial bags, so to speak, leaving behind him a Palestine engulfed in the flames of civil war—the embers of which are still burning today.

This book has sought to undo the view of Ottoman Palestine as a picture of imperial oppression, backwardness, and implacable hatred. Instead, turn-of-the-century Palestine underwent a dynamic and vibrant period of imperial reform and political engagement that was underpinned by an ideological commitment among Muslims, Christians, and Jews to a shared homeland and a shared empire. That the empire in 1914 fell far short of what had been envisioned in the heady days of 1908 was not due to insufficient revolutionary fervor or weak ideological commitment. Rather, we have seen that there were deep structural challenges to that imperial vision, which, combined with a series of wars, territorial contraction, and anxieties over the role of non-Muslims, constrained it even more. In other words, as circumstances changed in the years following the Ottoman revolution, so too did the scope, viability, and desirability of the revolutionary project.

Rather than a battle of competing ethno-nationalist separatist paths, I see late Ottoman political culture as characterized by ultimately irreconcilable imperial citizenship discourses. Looking at the ways which various citizenship discourses and practices coexist within a single state setting has been shown by the social scientists Gershon Shafir and Yoav Peled to be a fruitful and enlightening path of inquiry.[2] Ottomans sought to reconcile the various demands and expectations of new liberal and republican citizenship paradigms with the existing corporate status and shifting political power of the ethno-religious group. Oftentimes, these different understandings of citizenship were simply not compatible.

On the one hand, the liberal basis of citizenship privileged each Ottoman citizen as the bearer of political rights, irrespective of religion or ethnic group, and put forth the expectation of the state as a neutral arbiter with respect to the various ascriptive traits of its citizens. In other words, Ottoman citizenship and its subsequent rights and responsibilities—electoral franchise, conscription—were awarded to the individual Ottoman citizen. Certain aspects of the liberal ideal of citizenship—namely its expansive views of personal liberties—were valorized in the revolutionary period.[3] However, to the extent that Ottoman liberalism was based on erasing political and public roles for other collectivities, it also presented a significant challenge to the existing Ottoman sociopolitical order. Indeed, the words of Ottoman official Hilmi Pasha—that their policy would be "frankly national . . . [knowing] neither Greeks, Bulgarians, nor Albanians, but only Ottomans"—seemed to support such a view.[4] Ottoman liberalism, whether viewed as "fraternity" or "fusion of the peoples," could also bring about—indeed might even be premised on—the obliteration of the distinctiveness of religio-ethno-linguistic collectives.

In fact, the communitarian critique of liberal citizenship centers on this very erasure of ethnic identity at the expense of the civic one. Instead of being attribute-free universal liberal citizens, communitarians argue that individuals are embedded in and have a strong sense of community: "They conceive their identity—the subject and not just the object of their feelings and aspirations—as defined to some extent by the community of which they are a part."[5] As we have seen, a communitarian critique of the Ottoman liberal citizenship project emerged in two directions. First, the loss of an institutionalized role for religious corporate bodies was decried. Before the revolution, the *millet* played a central role as the primary intermediary between the individual subject and imperial state, from cradle to grave, in terms of registering and governing personal life events (birth, marriage, divorce, and death), as well as implementing the collection of taxes, administering conscription, and carrying out other government duties. This political role of the religious leadership to speak for, represent, and implement imperial decisions concerning their co-religionists was directly challenged by a new liberal imperial citizenship. Predictably, officials who had long benefited from this monopoly of political power, such as the patriarchs of the various Christian denominations or the chief rabbis of the empire's Jewish communities, often resented and fought against their demotion in status under the new regime. As the Greek Orthodox patriarch Joachim declared, "What we cannot and will not do is sacrifice one iota of the ecclesiastical autonomy which we have enjoyed since Constantine XI [the last Byzantine emperor] died."[6]

In addition to this real loss of temporal power, the positive aspects of belonging to an ethno-religious corporate body were also powerful factors in terms of the critique of the Ottoman liberal citizenship project, as individuals and groups felt the loss of their privileged (and closed) status as a collective that individual citizenship would impose on them. After all, the nineteenth-century Tanzimat reforms weakened guilds and Sufi brotherhoods as strong nodes of corporate life, while at the same time strengthening the *millet*. As a result, notwithstanding the sincerity and intensity of the ideology of Ottoman brotherhood and the existence of deep cross-confessional social networks, Ottoman Christians, Muslims, and Jews felt a strong affinity to their co-religionists, and their evaluation of the liberal Ottoman project was often filtered through communal lenses.

Furthermore, as the political theorist Jeff Spinner has noted, part of the communitarian critique is rooted in a criticism that the supposed neutrality of the liberal state ignores the reality that members of a certain group often control it.[7] Along those lines, some elements within the larger Muslim community saw the constitutional regime and its view of Ottoman liberal citizenship as threatening their status as the "ruling *millet* [*millet-i hakime*]," and at times sought to reinject neo-*dhimmi* political limitations into the liberal citizenship project, despite consistent attempts by the political and religious leadership to illustrate the congruence of equality with Islamic law. As well, the rise in cultural and ethnic associations among Arabs, Kurds, Turks, and other groups after the revolution indicates that communitarian ethnic identities were taking shape as part and parcel of the Ottoman imperial identity.

Alongside the complex liberal basis of Ottoman citizenship and its communitarian critique, the Ottoman imperial citizenship project was also built on strong elements of republican citizenship, which sees politics both as a communal affair and as the pursuit of the common good. In the best of times, the universal, civic Ottoman nation was protected and strengthened by its members, who all contributed to its welfare. To that end, universal conscription was formally adopted by the Ottoman parliament in 1909, reversing the past exemption of non-Muslims from the Ottoman military. Public discourse embraced universal conscription as sharing the burdens of defending the empire from internal and external threats as well as providing an end to the myriad privileges (and subsequent marginalization) experienced by the non-Muslim communities of the empire. In addition, universal conscription was seen as a tool of social engineering, a universalizing experience that would Ottomanize the empire's polyglot communities.

Increasingly vocal, however, was the awareness that contributions to the (imperial) public good were *not* born equally, and indeed, that certain individuals—and more ominously, entire groups—shirked their duty (conscription most pointedly) at the expense of the nation as a whole. The republican discourse of imperial citizenship, in the name of equality, then, not infrequently promoted rivalries over each group's contribution to the Ottoman nation—in essence, over the relative measure of Ottoman-ness itself.

Perhaps because of this growing, public competition and rivalry between the various ethno-religious groups in the Ottoman Empire, most histories of the Ottoman Empire have attributed its breakup in no small part to ethno-national fragmentation from within. However, the ethnic citizenship discourse that viewed the "nation" as "völkisch, due to membership in a homogeneous descent group,"[8] was highly circumscribed, largely seeing the nation as *also* ethnic and civic. For the vast majority of ethnic and religious groups within the empire, collectively, ethno-religious identity was expressed within the context of Ottoman imperial citizenship, not necessarily outside of or against it.

Even among the most "problematic" ethnic groups within the empire, the Armenians and Greek Orthodox, the historical record is far more equivocal than the historiography. For example, the leading Armenian movement, the Armenian Revolutionary Federation (ARF), or Dashnak, was closely aligned with the CUP until 1912. A joint decision between the CUP headquarters and the ARF Constantinople Responsible Body explains their alliance, "considering that saving the sacred Ottoman fatherland from separation and division is an objective of the two organizations' joint cooperation, they will work to practically dispel within public opinion the false story inherited from the despotic regime that the Armenians strive for independence." When the two parties did finally part ways, the ARF decision was based on their conclusion that the CUP was either unable or unwilling to accede to the Armenians' citizenship demands such as land reform and judicial equality.[9] Likewise, elements of the Greek Orthodox Christian population were split between the irredentism of Greek nationalism's *megali idée* and the claims of Ottoman patriotism and imperial citizenship.[10]

In this regard, then, looking toward multicultural theories of citizenship can be extremely illuminating. Will Kymlicka has theorized a place for group rights within liberal citizenship, along a trajectory he sees of self-government rights, polyethnic rights, and special representation rights.[11] All of these demands were expressed within the late Ottoman Empire as an alternative citizenship discourse within Ottoman imperial citizenship: self-government rights, which "involve the devolution of powers to minorities within the state," hearken back to the Ottoman decentralist movements promoted even before the 1908 revolution; by 1912–13, they were promoted by Albanian and Arab reform groups. Polyethnic rights like cultural autonomy, language, and education rights were also prominent demands in the late empire, in many ways tapping into the communitarian critique of liberalism. Finally, as we have seen, some groups like the Greek Orthodox demanded special representation rights that would guarantee minority representation in imperial bodies such as the parliament.[12] In other words, while the CUP may have complained about the specific demands of the empire's various religious and ethnic groups, there was nothing inherently anti-imperial in any of them—rather, they represented a multicultural vision of an Ottoman imperial citizenship discourse. Given that multicultural citizenship claims still pose significant challenges to twenty-first-century Europe and America, it should come as no surprise that the late Ottoman Empire proved unprepared, unwilling, and ultimately unable to fully deal with them.

A little over a decade after 1908, the Ottoman liberal revolution was a distant if bittersweet memory: a new wave of political authoritarianism had ushered in military rule; ethnic rivalries had exploded in slaughter and population transfer; and the empire had fought three costly wars on three continents, the last of which it did not survive intact. Post–World War I nationalist projects in the Ottoman successor states contributed to an indifference to the Ottoman past bordering on historical distortion. As one recent study has argued about the dominant influence of the war in cementing alienation among Arabs from their Ottoman past, "in the Arabic discourse of what became known as 'the days of the Turks,' the erasure achieved a retrospective replacement of four centuries of relative peace and dynamism . . . by four miserable years of tyranny."[13]

Understanding this key moment of the late Ottoman Empire thus necessarily raises questions about the presumably inevitable historical transition from empire to nation. Rather than a stagnant empire crumbling under its own decay, the Ottoman Empire underwent a dynamic period of political reform and intellectual fermentation in the last decade of its existence. The relationship between empires and their subjects cannot be limited to inequity, coercion, and collaboration; rather, the relationship must be seen as historically contingent and dynamic, and in many cases ties of identification "thicker" than simple cooptation were born.[14]

And yet, this imperial reform that engaged important notions such as liberty, political rights, enfranchisement, and civic belonging did not mesh with the dominant European picture of an Islamic world steeped in "Oriental despotism" and therefore in need of Western enlightenment. Putative adherence to Wilson's principle of self-determination notwithstanding, the League of Nations mandate issued in the aftermath of World War I that awarded Syria and Lebanon to France and awarded Transjordan, Iraq, and Palestine to Britain, illustrates this quite clearly: the mandates were described as in need "of administrative advice and assistance by a Mandatory until such time as they are able to stand alone."[15] It is clear that in the interest of preserving their own political role in the Middle East, the Western mandatory powers had an interest in ignoring and even reversing the developments that had taken place in the last decade of Ottoman rule. Fast forward to the twenty-first century: according to the way that the current American-led regime change and occupation in Iraq is depicted, one would never imagine that Baghdad had ever held parliamentary elections, debated the meanings of "freedom" in the public sphere, or embraced significant political and social reform—although it did all of this a century ago.

In addition, after World War I the Ottoman possibility of a mixed civic political organization was jettisoned in favor of Lord Curzon's "unmixing of peoples" and the colonial powers' promotion of "traditional" tribal and sectarian differences in the Middle East. In Palestine, Great Britain's support for a Jewish National Home (as opposed to Palestine as a state of all its citizens) guaranteed the clash of Zionism and Palestinian nationalism. Ethnic "unmixing" has had a bloody history in the former Ottoman world over the last century—from the League of Nations–sponsored Treaty of Lausanne in 1923, which legitimized and completed the forced transfer of Ottoman Christians to Greece and of Ottoman Muslims to the new Republic of Turkey, through the 1948 and 1967 Israeli-Arab wars, the Lebanese civil war, the ongoing Greek-Turkish battles over the island of Cyprus, and the current dismantling of Iraq.

Moreover, struggles over citizenship continued throughout the post-Ottoman twentieth century, and significant aspects of the particular contours of and struggles over the Ottoman citizenship project echoed into the colonial and postcolonial Middle Eastern successor states: the possibility of a "civic" collectivity and the relationship of religious and ethnic groups to it; the nature of political enfranchisement and representation; and the relationship between secular and religious sources of political legitimacy and mobilization. For all these reasons, this history of a shared civic project and a shared homeland, though short-lived and incomplete, could not be more relevant to the present historical moment.

Reference Matter

Notes

Abbreviations

AAIU	Archive of the Alliance Israélite Universelle
BNR	Bibliothèque Nationale Manuscripts Division, Richelieu
BOA	Başbakanlık Osmanlı Arşivi
CAHJP	Central Archive for the History of the Jewish People
CDGODF	Centre de Documentation du Grand Orient de France
CZA	Central Zionist Archives
ISA	Israel State Archives
JMA	Jerusalem Municipality Archives
JNUL-M	Jewish National and University Library Manuscripts Division
MAEF	Ministère des Affaires Étrangères de France, Quai d'Orsay
NACP	National Archives, College Park
TAMA	Tel Aviv Municipal Archive

Introduction

1. CZA A412/29. In Arabic and Ottoman Turkish documents Shlomo signed his name "Suleiman," the Islamic equivalent of Shlomo or Solomon. *Effendi* denoted men of a certain class, education, and worldview—in other words, gentlemen.

2. CZA A412/13. The pamphlets he wrote were S. Yellin, *Les Capitulations et la juridiction consulaire* and *Une page d'histoire Turque*.

3. CZA A412/21. "Noble Ottoman nation" = *Millet-i Osmaniyye necibe-yi*; "different peoples" = *milel-i muhtelife*; "divide according to race" = *tefrik-i cinsiyet*.

4. "Our beloved nation" = *sevgili milletimiz*; "sacred homeland" = *vatan-ı mukaddes*; "martyrdom" = *fedaya*. On the importance of martyrdom for modern nationalism see Mosse, *Fallen Soldiers*; and Smith, *National Identity*.

5. "New conquest" = *feth-i cedid*. *Feth* in the Ottoman context clearly refers to the conquest of Constantinople, the capital of Byzantium, in 1453 by the Ottoman Sultan Mehmed the Conqueror (known in Turkish as Fatih Mehmet); the word is derived from the Arabic *fatḥ* (sing.), *futūḥ* (pl.) which refer to the

wars of conquest that spread Islam in its earliest centuries. As the CUP "conquered" Istanbul a second time not for Islam but for constitutional liberalism, this is another example of the ways in which religious discourse penetrated Ottoman nationalism. "Holy constitution" = *dustur-ı mukaddes*; "constitutional state" = *devlet-i meşrute*.

6. This was a decade of revolutions: 1905 in the Russian Empire, 1906 in Qajar Iran, 1910 in Mexico, 1911 in Qing China. For a comparative study of revolutions see Sohrabi, "Global Waves"; and Kurzman, *Democracy Denied.*

7. Surprisingly, this active, dynamic process of making an "Ottoman nation" (*millet-i Osmaniyye*, Ott. Tur.; *umma 'Uthmāniyya*, Ara.) remains on the margins of the history of the modern Middle East as well as of the modern history of empires and nations more broadly. Despite the fact that virtually every book on late Ottoman history mentions the nineteenth-century project of fostering imperial loyalty (known as Ottomanism, Osmanlılık or Osmanlıcılık), Ottomanism remains widely underestimated, considered either an official state project alone or as the nucleus of an Islamist or Turkish ethnic nationalism. See Masters, *Christians and Jews*; Karpat, *Politicization of Islam*; Mardin, "Some Consideration"; and Canefe, "Turkish Nationalism." Several important studies on the overlapping Ottoman loyalties of outstanding Arab notables and intellectuals have addressed this gap to some extent, but the spread, content, and power of Ottomanism are still not well understood. For a focus on the intersection of Arabism and imperial loyalty, see Dawn, "Origins of Arab Nationalism"; R. Khalidi, "Ottomanism and Arabism"; Cleveland, *Islam Against the West*; Cleveland, *Making of an Arab Nationalist*; Blake, "Training Arab-Ottoman Bureaucrats"; and the contributions in Jankowski and Gershoni, *Rethinking Nationalism.* Hasan Kayalı rightly argues for a need to focus on the provincial "consent" to the Ottoman imperial system rather than simply the rejection and opposition to it. Kayalı, *Arabs and Young Turks*, 12–13.

8. This last point reflects Hannah Arendt's view of revolution as *both* liberation from oppression *and* freedom to enter into political life. Arendt, *On Revolution*, 25. See the distinction Bryan Turner makes between active and passive citizenship and citizenship from above or below. Turner, "Islam, Civil Society, and Citizenship."

9. To be clear, I mean citizenship in its sociological sense as a "practice through which individuals and groups formulate and claim new rights or struggle to expand or maintain existing rights," rather than simply as a political or legal status or condition of membership. Isin and Wood, eds., *Citizenship and Identity*, 4. See also Turner, "Contemporary Problems in the Theory of Citizenship"; and van Steenbergen, ed., *The Condition of Citizenship*. This book is directly informed by culturalist readings of revolution and anthropological studies of political culture which argue that "publics are not mere passive recipients or consumers of symbols, or mere 'material creatures, but also symbolic [and ritual] producers and symbol users.'" Formisano, "The Concept of Political Culture," 419. For the distinction between a structuralist and culturalist reading of revolution, see Goodwin, "State-Centered Approaches to Social Revolutions"; and Selbin, "Revolution in the Real World." See also Hunt, *Politics, Culture,*

and Class, 72. Some recent works have taken a similar grassroots approach to the Ottoman revolution, such as Kansu, *Revolution of 1908 in Turkey*; Kansu, *Politics in Post-Revolutionary Turkey*; Brummett, *Image and Imperialism in the Ottoman Revolutionary Press*; Frierson, "Unimagined Communities"; and Watenpaugh, *Being Modern in the Middle East*.

10. For critiques of the nationalist literature in the Ottoman case, see the introductions of Gelvin, *Divided Loyalties*; Kayalı, *Arabs and Young Turks*; Todorova, *Imagining the Balkans*; and Reinkowski, "Late Ottoman Rule over Palestine."

11. For an analysis of this argument, see Kasaba, "Dreams of Empire, Dreams of Nations." Andreas Kappeler has written that while Enlightenment scholars wrote often about the multiethnicity of the Russian Empire, by the nineteenth century the history of that empire was nationalized by Russian and Western scholars. Kappeler, *Russian Empire*, 8. See also the critique in King, *Budweisers into Czechs and Germans*, for the Habsburg Empire.

12. As the French intellectual Alan de Benoist writes, "In terms of its birth and foundations, the nation has been an *anti-empire*." De Benoist, "The Idea of Empire," 91. For a discussion of the value-laden character of the empire-nation distinction throughout the twentieth century, see Lieven, *Empire*, xvi.

13. See the introduction to Esherick, Kayalı, and Van Young, eds., *Empire to Nation*. The editors, however, also make the leap from imperial subjects to national citizens (26).

14. My work is clearly influenced by sociological theories that focus on the "rhetoric" and "form" of nationalism. See Calhoun, *Nationalism*; and Brubaker, *Nationalism Reframed*.

15. My thinking has been influenced by the insightful framework offered by Gershon Shafir and Yoav Peled about the interplay of different citizenship discourses within a single state setting. Shafir and Peled, *Being Israeli*. My thoughts on multicultural citizenship have been influenced by Kymlicka, *Multicultural Citizenship*; and Isin and Wood, eds., *Citizenship and Identity*.

16. Abbott, *Turkey in Transition*, 29–30.

17. Aflalo, *Regilding the Crescent*, 31.

18. The sociologist Rogers Brubaker calls this "groupism." Brubaker, "Ethnicity Without Groups," 164. For a more dynamic view of ethnicity see Barth, "Enduring and Emerging Issues in the Analysis of Ethnicity."

19. In the 1774 Treaty of Küçük Kaynarca, Russia earned recognition as protector of the empire's numerous Orthodox Christians; France earned similar recognition over the empire's Maronite and Roman Catholic Christians, and Great Britain sought to stake claim over the empire's Protestants and, at times, its Druze and Jews.

20. I take this term from Aron Rodrigue, in "Interview with Nancy Reynolds." On an everyday basis the Ottoman hierarchy marked non-Muslims' subordination in court documents and through special taxation (*cizye*). Several studies have shown that Islamic courts subordinated non-Muslims textually in several ways. Strauss, "Ottomanisme et 'Ottomanité'"; and al-Qattan, "Litigants and Neighbors."

21. Braude and Lewis, eds., *Christians and Jews in the Ottoman Empire.* Mark Cohen makes a similar point for medieval Islamic civilization as a whole. Cohen, *Under Crescent and Cross.*

22. Issawi, "Transformation of the Economic Position of the Millets."

23. Kasaba, "Dreams of Empire, Dreams of Nations," 204–5.

24. O. Barkan, "Essai sur les données statistiques des Registres de recensement dans l'empire Ottoman aux XVe et XVIe siècles," *Journal of the Economic and Social History of the Orient* 1 (1957): 9–36, cited in Kabadayı, "Inventory for the Ottoman Empire/Turkey, 1500–2000."

25. Population figures for the late Ottoman Empire are notoriously unreliable, as individuals and communities often underreported themselves and their family members in order to avoid taxation and conscription. They are also highly politicized, as later nationalist movements and states used demographic figures to advance their own political claims. These figures are based on the 1906–7 *tahrir.* Karpat, *Ottoman Population,* 167–68. Justin McCarthy has argued that Karpat's figures must be corrected to account for significant undercounting of women and children; Karpat himself suggests that the population figures reflect a 20 percent undercount. Karpat, *Studies on Ottoman Social and Political History.*

26. On ethnic types in the popular Karagöz shadow-puppet theater tradition, see Brummett, *Image and Imperialism,* 434n14.

27. Shaw, "Population of Istanbul in the 19th Century." Unfortunately, the census records did not identify the ethnic origins of Muslims. Also there is significant undercounting of women among all population groups.

28. The census also found 6.7 percent belonged to "others." Rena Molho, *Oi Evraioi tis Thessalonikis: Mia idiaiteri koinotita* [The Jews of Salonica: An Exceptional Community] (Athens: Themelio, 2001), 43. My thanks to Paris Papamichos-Chronakis for this citation.

29. In Salonica, for example, Christian women visited Jewish and Muslim cemeteries to gather dirt to ward off evil spirits, and even decades after the departure of the city's Muslim population, Christian women still went to the tomb of Musa Baba to ask for his help. Mazower, *Salonica,* 80.

30. See for example the first-person accounts in Edib, *House with Wisteria*; and Sciaky, *Farewell to Salonica.* See also Kırlı, "The Struggle over Space."

31. Among other works, see Makdisi, *The Culture of Sectarianism*; Masters, *Christians and Jews in the Ottoman Arab World*; Dumont, "Jews, Muslims, and Cholera"; Braude and Lewis, eds., *Christians and Jews in the Ottoman Empire*; Greene, ed., *Minorities in the Ottoman Empire*; Levy, ed., *Jews of the Ottoman Empire*; and Zandi-Sayek, "Orchestrating Difference, Performing Identity."

32. My figures for the Ottoman population are taken from table 1.4d in McCarthy, *Population of Palestine.* Various Jewish sources have estimated the number of non-Ottoman foreign Jews living in Palestine as between thirty thousand and sixty thousand; given that these sources are impressionistic rather than relying on any actual data or recognized methodology, I have chosen to side with the lower end of the range. On the Zionist colonies, see Shilo, *Nisyonot be-hityashvut*; and Shilony, *Ha-keren ha-kayemet le-Israel.*

33. Schmelz, "The Population of Jerusalem's Urban Neighborhoods."

34. According to Schmelz's figures, twelve of the twenty-six neighborhoods in the New City were homogeneous, while the other fourteen were mixed. Eleven of those twelve homogeneous neighborhoods were Jewish, and the other (Mamilla) was Christian. This unmixing taking place in the New City accelerated after Ottoman rule ended in 1918. For background on the establishment of the extramural neighborhoods see Kark, *Jerusalem Neighborhoods*. Kark writes that of the Jewish extramural neighborhoods, 84 percent were established by philanthropic initiative, building societies, and commercial initiatives.

35. Halper, *Between Redemption and Revival*, 145.

36. Unfortunately we do not have Ottoman census statistics from Jaffa, but German consular figures from 1907 estimated the total Jaffa population at 67,363, which included 51,003 Muslims (76 percent), 12,360 Christians (18 percent), and 4,000 Jews (6 percent). Eliav, *Die Juden Palästinas in der deutschen Politik*. On the establishment of new (exclusively Jewish) neighborhoods in Jaffa starting in the 1880s, see *Ẓaʼaẓaei beit Aharon Chelouche*. Mark LeVine writes that of the sixteen new neighborhoods built in Jaffa from 1881 to 1909, eleven were exclusively Jewish. LeVine, "Overthrowing Geography, Re-Imagining Identities," 76.

37. For memoir sources see: Alami, *Palestine Is My Country*; Chelouche, *Parshat Ḥayai*; Eliachar, *Living with Jews*; Kalvarisky, "Relations Between Jews and Arabs Before the War"; al-Sakakini, *Kadha ana ya dunya*; El'azar, *Ḥaẓarot be-Yerushalayim ha-'atika*; Yehoshu'a, "Neighborhood Relations in the Turkish Period"; Yehoshu'a, *Ha-bayt ve-ha-reḥov bi-Yerushalayim ha-yeshana*; Tamari and Nassar, eds., *Al-Quds al-'Uthmaniyya fil-mudhakkirat al-Jawhariyya*; and Elmaliach, "Me-ḥayei ha-Sfaradim." See also Tamari, "Jerusalem's Ottoman Modernity"; Halper, *Between Redemption and Revival*, 31–35; Cohen, *Yehudim be-veit ha-mishpat ha-Muslimi*; and Yazbak, "Jewish-Muslim Social and Economic Relations in Haifa."

38. See Blyth, *When We Lived in Jerusalem*, 312–13, and Yehoshu'a, *Ha-bayt ve-ha-reḥov bi-Yerushalayim ha-yeshana*. In the aftermath of a blood libel in 1897, the Islamic court removed the Maronite libeler from the neighborhood. Ha-Va'ad le-hoẓa'at kitvei Yellin, *Kitvei David Yellin*, 9.

39. For example, Jewish mourners complained that their funeral processions to the Mount of Olives cemetery were frequently stoned by Muslim children from Silwan village, although it seems this practice was suspended once the appropriate "protection payments" were received. Eliav, *Be-ḥasut mamlekhet Austria*, 399. See also Kark, *Jaffa: A City in Evolution*, 202.

40. Shar'abi, *Ha-yishuv ha-Sfaradi bi-Yerushalayim*, 23; Yehoshu'a, *Ha-bayt ve-ha-reḥov bi-Yerushalayim ha-yeshana*, 222; Y. Yellin, *Zichronot le-ben Yerushalayim*, 20. Other works, however, make clear that the title holder often did rent out to non-Jews, resulting in the mixed courtyards and apartment buildings that were so characteristic of the Old City. See for example El'azar, *Ḥaẓarot be-Yerushalayim ha-'atika*.

41. At the end of the nineteenth century there were nineteen Ashkenazi (European Jewish) religious communities and twelve Sephardi, Maghrebi, and Mizrachi communities. For memoirs on the closeness of Eastern Jews and

Muslims, see Y. Yellin, *Zichronot le-ben Yerushalayim*; Elmaliach, "Me-ḥayei ha-Sfaradim"; Tidhar, *Be-madim ve-lo be-madim*. For a stark and often bitter memoir about intra-Jewish ethnic conflict, see Chelouche, *Parshat Ḥayai*. On the rareness of Ashkenazi-Sephardi intermarriage, see Shar'abi, *Ha-yishuv ha-Sfaradi*, 105; on p. 129 she argues that intermarriage was more common among *maskilim*, or "reformers."

42. Y. Yellin, *Zichronot le-ben Yerushalayim*, 100–106. *Madhhab* (sing.; *madhāhib*, pl.) refers to the four legal schools within Sunni Islam—Hanifi, Hanbali, Maliki, and Shafi'i. See Cohen, *Yehudim be-veit ha-mishpat ha-Muslimi*, on this affair.

43. Ekrem, *Unveiled*.

44. Introduction, Tamari, ed., *Jerusalem 1948*, 2.

45. This relational history approach has emerged in recent years among historians and sociologists. See, for example: Lockman, "Railway Workers and Relational History"; Lockman, *Comrades and Enemies*; Kimmerling, "Be'ayot konẓeptualiot ba-historiografia"; Shafir, *Land, Labor*; and Tamari, "Ishaq al-Shami."

46. For a similar argument see Shafir, *Land, Labor.*

Chapter One: Sacred Liberty

1. Darwaza, *Mudhakkirat*, 181.

2. Frumkin, *Derekh shofet bi-Yerushalayim*, 145. "Bey" was a title used in the Ottoman period for men of high status, lineage, or outstanding personal success.

3. *Ḥavaẓelet*, July 27, 1908; *Ha-Po'el ha-Ẓa'ir*, July–August 1908.

4. Musallam, ed., *Yawmiyat Khalil al-Sakakini*.

5. Henri Franck to Shlomo Yellin, August 10, 1908. CZA, A412/36.

6. For urban histories of these cities see Çelik, *Remaking of Istanbul*; Mazower, *Salonica*; and Hanssen, *Fin de Siècle Beirut*; as well as Eldem, Goffman, and Masters, *Ottoman City Between East and West*.

7. For an internal Ottoman colonial discourse on its "backward" provinces, see Deringil, "'They Live in a State of Nomadism and Savagery'"; Kushner, *Moshel hayiti bi-Yerushalayim*; and Ekrem, *Unveiled*.

8. For example, the well-known Khalidi Library in Jerusalem had holdings of over forty-five hundred printed books (including one thousand in European languages) and several Arabic and Ottoman-Turkish language newspapers in the period before World War I. Ayalon, *Reading Palestine*, 46–49. The library at al-Aqsa Mosque reportedly had an even larger collection of periodicals.

9. For a delightful window onto fin-de-siècle Jerusalem, see Tamari, "Jerusalem's Ottoman Modernity."

10. See Davison, *Reform in the Ottoman Empire*; and Sofuoğlu, *Osmanlı devletinde islahatlar* for an overview of the Tanzimat reforms. See Rogan, *Frontiers of the State*; Hanssen, *Fin de Siècle Beirut*; Makdisi, *Culture of Sectarianism*; and Shareef, "Urban Administration in the Late Ottoman Period" for discussions of the impact of reforms on several Arab provinces.

11. Abu Manneh, "Islamic Roots of the Gülhane Rescript."

12. Rahme, "Namık Kemal's Constitutional Ottomanism and Non-

Muslims." See also Mardin, *Genesis of Young Ottoman Thought*; Kurzman, ed., *Modernist Islam*; Mardin, "Some Consideration"; and Tevfik, *Yeni Osmanlılar.* See also the discussion in Rebhan, *Geschichte und Funktion einiger politischer Termini*, 57–60, for the relationship of constitutionalism and consultation in the writings of al-Tahtawi, al-Afghani, and 'Abduh.

13. Quoted in Kurzman, ed., *Modernist Islam*, 145. In 1873, artisans in Fez, Morocco, insisted on making the oath of allegiance to the Moroccan dynasty contingent on the cancellation of taxes they considered un-Islamic. Eickelman and Salvatore, "Muslim Publics," 4–5.

14. Ali Haydar Midhat Bey, *Life of Midhat Pasha*, 112. For more on this period, see Devereaux, *First Ottoman Constitutional Period*; and Abu Manneh, "Later Tanzimat and the Ottoman Legacy in the Near Eastern Successor States."

15. Ramsauer, *Young Turks*; Lewis, "Idea of Freedom in Modern Islamic Political Thought," 273–75; Ayalon, "O tmura ne'ora." For intellectual histories of leading figures in this period, see Khuri, *Modern Arab Thought*; Sharabi, *Arab Intellectuals and the West*; Mardin, *Genesis of Young Ottoman Thought*; Cole, *Colonialism and Revolution in the Middle East*; and Hourani, *Arabic Thought in the Liberal Age.*

16. See Cole, *Colonialism and Revolution in the Middle East*; and Arjomand, *Shadow of God*, respectively. For an example of the merger of European liberalism and Islamic sacred sources, the late nineteenth-century Persian intellectual Mirza Yusuf Khan Mustashar al-Dawlah propagated the French Declaration of the Rights of Man and Citizen by foregrounding each of its seventeen articles on the Qur'an and hadith. Tavakoli-Targhi, "Refashioning Iran," 94.

17. Quoted in Mango, *Atatürk*, 11.

18. See Hanioğlu, *Preparation for a Revolution*; Hanioğlu, *Young Turks in Opposition*; Ramsauer, *The Young Turks*; Mardin, *Genesis of Young Ottoman Thought*; Kayalı, *Arabs and Young Turks*, 38–48; and Kansu, *Revolution of 1908 in Turkey.*

19. Quoted in Mango, *Atatürk*, 48–49.

20. Donald Quataert writes that the prices of foodstuffs and staples doubled in early 1907, whereas the price of firewood and charcoal increased by 250 percent and 300 percent, respectively. Quataert, "Economic Climate of the 'Young Turk Revolution' in 1908." See also Findley, "Economic Bases of Revolution and Repression"; Kansu, *Revolution of 1908 in Turkey*; Karpat, *Politicization of Islam*; and Quataert, *Social Disintegration and Popular Resistance in the Ottoman Empire* for his analysis of workers' resistance to unequal incorporation into the European world market.

21. For a description of the revolutionary celebrations, see Adivar, *Memoirs of Halide Edip*; Margulies and Manakis, *Manastır'da Ilân-ı Hürriyet*; and Emiroğlu, *Anadolu'da devrim günleri.*

22. Several such letters and reports were republished in *Al-Manār.* See also "Echoes of the Constitution in America," *Al-Ittiḥād al-'Uthmānī*, September 30, 1908.

23. *Al-Manār*, September 25, 1908; *Al-Ittiḥād al-'Uthmānī*, October 3, 1908. See also Kayalı, *Arabs and Young Turks*, 61; and Kansu, "Some Remarks on the 1908 Revolution."

24. Thomas R. Wallace, U.S. Consul in Jerusalem, to the U.S. Department of State, August 12, 1908 (file 10044/60–61); NACP, National Archives microfilm publication M862, roll 717, Jerusalem, numerical file, 1906–10, central files of the Department of State, record group 59.

25. Ibid.

26. Telegram from Ekrem Bey to Rifat Effendi (Istanbul), August 10, 1908 (document 57); based on the Hebrew translation (document 40) in Kushner, *Moshel hayiti bi-Yerushalayim*, 190.

27. Ibid., 190–92.

28. In "To the Minister of Interior," ibid., 194. Ekrem, *Unveiled*, 59 and 73.

29. *Ḥavaẓelet*, August 7, 1908.

30. Unless otherwise noted, details are taken from *Ḥavaẓelet*, August 10, 1908; and *Ha-Hashkafa*, August 9, 1908. *Ha-'Olam* also published a local account of the celebrations on August 14, 1908.

31. Ottoman as well as "Jerusalem" flags. According to 'Izzat Darwaza, each town and village had its own flag which would be carried by pilgrims to the annual Nabī Mūsa (Prophet Moses) festival. Darwaza, *Mudhakkirat*, 112.

32. The U.S. consul reported: "Immense crowds assembled, all races and religions mingling in happy accord." Wallace, August 12, 1908.

33. Given that the official Ottoman census of 1905 had placed Jerusalem's entire Ottoman population at 32,500, although the figure of 40,000 celebrants is statistically unreliable as an actual count, it does offer some glimpse as to the scale of the celebration.

34. Wallace, August 12, 1908. Rıza (Riḍa) Bey, the army commander, hailed from Damascus, and so presumably would have spoken in his native Arabic to the crowd.

35. See Deringil, *The Well-Protected Domains*, 20–24, for a description of the symbolism of the sultanate transmitted in the Hamidian period.

36. For more on this distinction see Ozouf, *Festivals and the French Revolution*.

37. Darwaza, *Mudhakkirat*, 180–81.

38. Saliba, "Wilayat Suriyya," 247–48.

39. *Al-Quds*, November 17, 1908.

40. Telegram from Ekrem Bey to Rifat Effendi (Istanbul), August 10, 1908 (document 57); based on the Hebrew translation (document 40) in Kushner, *Moshel hayiti bi-Yerushalayim*, 190–91.

41. Al-Bustani, *'Ibra wa-dhikra*, 27 and 31.

42. See chapter 4 in Brummett, *Image and Imperialism*, on France and Iran as "revolutionary exemplars"; and Tavakoli-Targhi, "Refashioning Iran," on some discursive elements of the Iranian revolution.

43. Hunt, *Politics, Culture, and Class*, 21–23. For a useful application of "key symbols" and "symbolic actions," see Gelvin, *Divided Loyalties*, 147.

44. The British aristocrat Mark Sykes, who later play a pivotal role in dismantling the Ottoman Empire, made similar observations on his travels throughout the region. Cited in Watenpaugh, "Bourgeois Modernity, Historical Memory, and Imperialism," 35.

45. Quoted in Khuri, *Modern Arab Thought*, 87n48.
46. Quoted in Fargo, "Arab-Turkish Relations," 3.
47. This observation was made as well in Tunaya, *Hürriyetin ilânı*, 5; Brummett, *Image and Imperialism*; and Watenpaugh, *Being Modern in the Middle East.*
48. *Ha-Hashkafa* (The Observation), August 7, 1908.
49. *El Liberal*, January 29, 1909. In the Judeo-Spanish and Hebrew press, "Turkia" and even "Ottomania" were used interchangeably with the Ottoman Empire.
50. "Holiday of the Ottoman Nation," *Al-Manār*, July 28, 1908.
51. See Hobsbawm, *Nations and Nationalism Since 1780*; and Smith, *National Identity*. In the late nineteenth century, Iranian intellectuals also cast Qajar Iran as sickly. Tavakoli-Targhi, "From Patriotism to Matriotism," 225–26.
52. *Al-Quds*, December (date illegible], 1908.
53. This view was already expressed decades earlier by Namık Kemal, when he argued that a consultative regime would force "Europe [to] treat us as a civilized nation, instead of regarding us as a scarecrow planted against Russia, as is now the case." Quoted in Kurzman, ed., *Modernist Islam*, 147.
54. "The Constitution in Turkey [*sic*], Special contribution to *Ha-'Olam*, 26 July, Istanbul," by Y. Farhi, in *Ha-'Olam*, July 29, 1908.
55. *Al-Quds*, November 17, 1908.
56. Brummett, *Image and Imperialism*, 114 and 130–32. A similar process of criticizing and desanctifying the Russian tsar was noted in Figes and Kolonitskii, *Interpreting the Russian Revolution.*
57. Articles on the history of the Ottoman reform movement were published in *Al-Manār*; *Al-Hilāl*, January 1, 1909; *Al-Ittiḥād al-'Uthmānī*, October 1 and 14, 1908. For a fascinating glimpse at the extensive commemorative material culture produced in the aftermath of the revolution, see Öztuncay, *İkinci meşrutiyet'in ilânının 100üncü yılı.*
58. BOA, DH.MKT 2843/5.
59. *Al-Ittiḥād al-'Uthmānī*, September 24, 1908. In 1909 an Arabic translation was published under the title *Khawatir Niyazi.*
60. "Nasıl Oldu," by Kâzim Nâmi Duru. Töre, *II. Meşrutiyet tiyatrosu*, 98–99. My account of the dialogue of the play comes from Buxton, *Turkey in Revolution*, 75–84.
61. For example *Hürriyet kurbanları* and *Hürriyet fedaileri* were the names of two other plays that were performed in Istanbul in 1908. Yalçin, *II. Meşrutiyet'te tiyatro edebiyatı tarihi.*
62. "Muḥarrarei al-waṭan wa-māniḥei al-umma al-ḥaya al-dustūriyya." *Al-Ittiḥād al-'Uthmānī*, October 8, 1908. The newspaper's editor later praised those who had donated money to the cause for their national devotion and patriotic commitment ("al-ghayra al-milliyya wa-al-ḥamiyya al-waṭaniyya"). *Al-Ittiḥād al-'Uthmānī*, October 14, 1908.
63. Aflalo, *Regilding the Crescent*, 114–15; and Buxton, *Turkey in Revolution*, 99.
64. For a report that the Marş-ı Hürriyet was performed before the Marş-ı Hamidiyye at the sultan's weekly *selamlık* (ritual parade and attendance at Friday mosque prayers), see Knight, *Turkey.*

65. For an insightful discussion of this religious source of the sultan's legitimacy, see Karateke, "Legitimizing the Ottoman Sultanate"; Karateke, "Opium for the Subjects?"; and Deringil, "From Ottoman to Turk."

66. Rashid Rida attributed this kind of blind allegiance to the peasants of Anatolia, who were no less faithful to their divine ruler than peasants in Russia to the tsar. *Al-Manār*, July 28, 1908.

67. On the sultanic patriarchal project, see Özbeck, "Philanthropic Activity, Ottoman Patriotism, and the Hamidian Regime," 69–71. The Qajar shah of Iran similarly sought to portray himself as "father" and "shepherd." Tavakoli-Targhi, "From Patriotism to Matriotism."

68. Unowsky, "Reasserting Empire," 34.

69. Wortman, *Scenarios of Power*, 4; Weeks, *Nation and State in Late Imperial Russia*, 11. See also Steinwedel, "To Make a Difference."

70. In "The Constitution in Turkey [*sic*]," *Ha-'Olam*, July 29, 1908.

71. *Al-Manār*, September 25, 1908. For the ritual invocation "Long live the sultan" by the army and at state functions, see Karateke, *Padişahım çok yaşa!*

72. "Māniḥ al-dustūr." On this point I disagree entirely with Kushner, who wrote that in seeing the sultan as the giver of the constitution, the locals did not expect the character of the Ottoman Empire to change. Kushner, *Moshel hayiti bi-Yerushalayim*, 181.

73. *Al-Quds*, December 18, 1908.

74. See Buxton, *Turkey in Revolution*, 93; Al-Bustani, *'Ibra wa-dhikra*, 99.

75. *Al-Manār*, July 28, 1908.

76. Vilified in the foreign press as the "Bloody Sultan" and "Le Sultan Rouge," foreign travelers to the empire seemed to relish in spinning more tales of the sultan's sadism. For an example, see Aflalo, *Regilding the Crescent*, 113.

77. *Al-Manār*, July 28, 1908.

78. Quoted in Saliba, "Wilayat Suriyya," 246–47.

79. "Dawn of Constitutional Era in Turkey [*sic*]," by Ravndal, U.S. Consul in Beirut, August 17, 1908 (file 10044/58–59); NACP, National Archives microfilm publication M862, roll 717, Beirut, numerical file, 1906–10, central files of the Department of State, record group 59.

80. See, for example, Al-Bustani, *'Ibra wa-dhikra*; *Al-Muqtaṭaf*, November 1908.

81. *New York Times*, September 7, 1908.

82. Quoted in Kutlu, "Ideological Currents of the Second Constitutional Era," 57.

83. Al-Khalidi, *(Asbab) al-Inqilab al-'Uthmani wa-Turkiya al-fata*, 3. For biographical details see Kasmieh, "Ruhi al-Khalidi"; and R. Khalidi, *Palestinian Identity*.

84. The essay was entitled "The Ottoman Revolution and Young Turkey," which was published in two Cairene journals—*Al-Hilāl* and *Al-Manār*—and later was published in booklet form. Al-Khalidi, *(Asbab) al-Inqilab al-'Uthmani*. A manuscript version dated October 20, 1908, is preserved in the Jewish National and University Library (JNUL), Jerusalem. Unless otherwise

noted, the page numbers cited are from the manuscript version; the quotation in this paragraph is from page 2.

85. Al-Khalidi only cites the beginning of the first *aya*, which continues to read "and seek their (the people's) counsel in their affairs." This section is cited by the publisher to the book version, Husayn Wasfi Rida.

86. Khuri, *Modern Arab Thought*, 132. Similarly, in late nineteenth-century Iranian political discourse, a split developed between the state (*dawlat*) and the people (*millat*). See Tavakoli-Targhi, "Refashioning Iran."

87. Al-Bustani, *'Ibra wa-dhikra.*

88. As al-Bustani pointed out, constitutional rule (*ḥukm dustūrī*) was not a heretical innovation (*bid'a*); rather, it had significant historical precedents, from ancient Greece and Rome to the rule of the four rightly-guided caliphs (*rāshidūn*) of early Islam.

89. *Al-Manār*, July 28, 1908.

90. *Ha-Ẓvi*, October 26, 1908. For discussion of the Mizanci Murad Bey incident, see İslamoğlu, *İkinci meşrutiyet döneminde siyasal muhalefet*. For the Kör Ali incident, see Akşin, *Jön Türkler ve Ittihat ve Terakki*, 139–42.

91. Buxton, *Turkey in Revolution*, 170.

92. Abbott, *Turkey in Transition*, 164.

93. Commins, *Islamic Reform*, 125–26. *Hilal*, edited by Mustafa Asim, should not be confused with Jurji Zeidan's *Al-Hilāl*. On the CUP chapters see Hanioğlu, *Preparation for a Revolution*. See also Abu Manneh, "Arab Intellectuals' Reaction to the Young Turk Revolution."

94. Ozouf, *Festivals and the French Revolution*, 276.

95. *Ha-Hashkafa*, September 11, 1908. See a similar statement quoted in Aleppo, in Watenpaugh, "Bourgeois Modernity," 37.

96. From Nasif Meshaka, U.S. Consul in Damascus, to Ravndal, U.S. Consul in Beirut, August 10, 1908 (file 10044/58–59); NACP, National Archives microfilm publication M862, roll 717, Beirut, numerical file, 1906–10, central files of the Department of State, record group 59.

97. This is of course directly parallel to "al-Qur'ān al-karīm."

98. Report from Jerusalem, *Ha-'Olam*, September 4, 1908; *Ha-Hashkafa*, August 21, 1908.

99. Monsignor Yusuf al-Mu'allam, in *Al-Quds*, December 18, 1908.

100. "Inti ka'batunā al-thāniyya inti qiblatunā al-ukhra." Emphasis mine. *Al-Quds*, May 11, 1909.

101. See Smith, "'Sacred' Dimensions of Nationalism," 811.

102. In looking at post-Ottoman Syrian nationalism, the historian James Gelvin has similarly argued that "the bonds of Islam came to exemplify, not contravene or replace, the bonds of nation," and that "Islamic symbols did not dislodge nationalist symbols from popular texts; rather, in most texts the two sets of symbols were fully conjoined." Gelvin, *Divided Loyalties*, 187–88.

103. Little is known of the Armenian rebellion other than that the Armenian populace demanded the dismissal of the Armenian patriarch's secretary, which was enforced by the Ottoman government. The struggle over the Patriarchate continued into 1910, and there were several instances of the Armenians tak-

ing over their compound in an effort to block the ecclesiastical leadership. See *Ha-Ẓvi*, November 6, 1908; *Ha-'Olam*, December 22, 1908; and *Ha-Ḥerut*, February 9 and 14, 1910.

104. The Greek Orthodox were by far the most numerous and influential of Palestine's Christians, accounting for 60 percent of Christians in the Jerusalem province. Schmelz, "Population Characteristics of Jerusalem and Hebron Regions," 27–29. According to the Greek Orthodox Patriarchate's official census of the Jerusalem Patriarchate in 1904, the population was 49,596, broken down as follows: Jerusalem, 6,000; Bethlehem, 3,600; Beit Jala, 4,340; Ramallah, 4,500; Jaffa, 2,900; Nazareth, 3,040; 'Akka, 1,500; Housoun 1,600; al-Salt, 3,000; Kerak, 1,600. Housoun, Kerak, and al-Salt were not parts of the Jerusalem province, but rather of the province of Syria. Bertram and Luke, *Report of the Commission Appointed by the Government of Palestine*, 9.

105. Background information can be found in Khuri and Khuri, *Khulasat tarikh kinisat Urshalim al-Urthudhuksiyya*; Qazaqiya, *Tarikh al-kinisa al-rasuliyya al-Urshalimiyya*; Malak, *Ta'ifat al-Rum al-Urthudhuksi 'abr al-tarikh*; Tsimhoni, "Greek Orthodox Patriarchate of Jerusalem"; and Tsimhoni, "British Mandate and the Arab Christians in Palestine."

106. September 30, 1908, and October 11, 1908, entries in al-Sakakini, *Kadha ana ya dunya*, 39–40.

107. "Demands of the Orthodox of Jerusalem [Patriarchate]," no. 11, issued by January 1909. ISA 67, peh/416:32.

108. German Consulate, Jerusalem, to Reichskanzler von Bülow, January 18, 1909. ISA 67, peh/416:32.

109. *Ha-Ẓvi*, December 31, 1908.

110. See J. Falanga (Jaffa) to British Consul Blech (Jerusalem), December 30, 1908; JNUL-M 4°1315/64; and German consular report, January 19, 1909; ISA 67, peh/416:32. As was commented by the German consul in attendance, "It made a strange impression to see a bishop on Holy Night in the Church of the Nativity handing out benedictions right and left with a cross in his hand, attended to only by his armed escort." German Consulate, Jerusalem, to Reichskanzler von Bülow, January 18, 1909. ISA 67, peh/416:32.

111. German consular report, January 19, 1909. ISA 67, peh/416:32; Qazaqiya, *Tarikh al-kinisa al-rasuliyya al-Urshalimiyya*, 192.

112. *Ha-Ẓvi*, February 10, 1909. The editor added a note that the Arab Christians knew how "to fight, to demand their rights." It is likely this was meant to stir up his Jewish readership to act in a similar manner.

113. Albert Antébi to Dizengoff and Saphir, February 26, 1909. AAIU, Israel-IX.E.26.

114. "The Present Conflict Between the Laity and Clergy of the Greek Church of Palestine," Thomas R. Wallace, January 18, 1909; NACP, National Archives microfilm publication M862, roll 102, Jerusalem, numerical file, 1906–10, central files of the Department of State, record group 59. *Filasṭīn* faithfully recorded the minutes of the council meetings in a regular "Orthodox Affairs" column.

115. Al-Sakakini, "Al-Nahda al-Urthudhuksiyya fi Filastin."

116. *Filasṭīn*, July 15, 1911.

117. The American consul in Jerusalem claimed that the rebellion was supported by the other churches in Jerusalem, stating that "every lover of liberty is animated by the hope that the native community will succeed in regaining something of its ancient rights." "The Present Conflict Between the Laity and Clergy of the Greek Church of Palestine," January 18, 1909. In 1909 the Tiberias local council placed a Christian as the representative for the Jewish community, much to their horror. The community appealed to the Beirut-based Jewish attorney Shlomo Yellin for help and demanded to know which clauses of the constitution ensured them what kinds of rights. July 15, 1909 and August 15, 1909. CZA, A412/24.

118. *Ha-Ẓvi*, December 25, 1908.

119. Consulate General of France in Palestine (G. Gueyrand) to M. Pinchon, Minister of Foreign Affairs, Paris; March 3, 1909; MAEF, microfilm roll 132, Correspondence Politique et Commerciale/Nouvelle Série (Turquie). In fact an editorial published months later in *Al-Quds* decried against local Catholics in Bethlehem who insisted that their children be baptized by foreign rather than local priests. Hanania, "Jurji Habib Hanania."

120. See *Ha-'Olam*, October 2, 1908, and October 9, 1908; *Ha-Hashkafa*, September 1, 1908.

121. Hanioğlu, *Preparation for a Revolution*, 310.

122. Ibid., 311.

123. Adivar, *Memoirs of Halide Edip*, 260.

124. Quoted in Saliba, "Wilayat Suriyya," 250–51.

125. Shaykh Muhammad Shakir Diab al-Baytuni, in *Al-Quds*, May 14, 1909. See also "The Holiday of Liberty," by Avraham Elmaliach, *Ha-Hashkafa*, August 9, 1908. The CUP political platform included support for land reforms.

126. See Quataert, "Economic Climate of the 'Young Turk Revolution' in 1908"; December 27, 1908. CZA J15/6342; Saliba, "Wilayat Suriyya", 253; see also the notice that peasants near Haifa were revolting against their Christian and Muslim landowners. Franck to Antébi, November 8, 1908. AAIU, Israel-VIII.E.25.

127. From Ravndal to Leishman, February 23, 1909 (file 10044/130–33); NACP, National Archives microfilm publication M862, roll 102, Jerusalem, numerical file, 1906–10, central files of the Department of State, record group 59. See also *Ha-Ẓvi*, January 6, 1909; Vester, *Our Jerusalem*, 222.

128. Buxton, *Turkey in Revolution*, 101.

129. For a similar argument about the Tanzimat reformers, see Makdisi, "Corrupting the Sublime Sultanate," 196.

130. See Frierson, "Unimagined Communities."

131. "The Constitution in Turkey {*sic*]," *Ha-'Olam*, July 29, 1908.

132. Buxton, *Turkey in Revolution*, 108–9.

133. Commins, *Islamic Reform*, 129; *Al-Ittiḥād al-'Uthmānī*, September 27, 1908.

134. *Al-Manār*, September 25, 1908.

Chapter Two: Brotherhood and Equality

1. *Al-Manār*, September 25, 1908.

2. Ayalon, *Language and Change in the Arab Middle East*, 23.

3. Abu Manneh, "Islamic Roots of the Gülhane Rescript"; Mardin, "Some Consideration."

4. In the language of 1856, it was "Byzantine subjects of the Sublime Porte [Rum tebaa-y devlet-i aliyyem]." Strauss, "Ottomanisme et 'Ottomanité,'" 19.

5. Translation from "Constitution de l'empire Ottoman octroyée par Sa Majeste Imperiale le Sultan le 7 Zilhidjé 1293."

6. Anthony Smith defines the constituent elements of the territorial nation as "historic territory, legal-political community, legal-political equality of members, and common civic culture and identity." Smith, *National Identity*, 11.

7. For the text of the law see [Grégoire], "Législation ottomane." For more on the citizenship law see Osmanağaoğlu, *Tanzimat dönemi itibariyla Osmanlı tabiiyyetinin.*

8. Butenschon, "State, Power, and Citizenship in the Middle East," 26.

9. One historian has estimated that between 1862 and 1882, mass immigration from the Balkans and the Caucasus led to a 40 percent increase in the number of the empire's Muslims. Karpat, *Politicization of Islam*, 97.

10. Kern, "Rethinking Ottoman Frontier Politics."

11. See Deringil, "Some Aspects of Muslim Immigration," 56.

12. ISA 1/123, peh/790:12.

13. AAIU, Israel-I.C.1.

14. Kechriotis, "Greeks of Izmir at the End of the Empire," 60.

15. Karpat lists two hundred thousand foreign citizens resident in the empire in 1906–7, although this is likely a significant undercount. Karpat, *Ottoman Population.*

16. Consular records of citizens and protégés in the province list 1,400–1,600 Americans, 4,000–5,000 Austrians, 500 British, over 1,000 French, and 770 Germans. The number of Russians is unknown. On the United States see: Thomas Wallace, U.S. Consul in Jerusalem, contribution for publication in the daily consular trade reports, October 6, 1908 (file 3943/373); NACP, National Archives microfilm publication M862, roll 359, Jerusalem, numerical file, 1906–10, central files of the Department of State, record group 59. On Great Britain see: Great Britain Diplomatic and Consular Reports, Turkey, report for the year 1909 on the trade of the consular district of Jerusalem, June 1910, ISA 67, peh/455:462; on France see: Jerusalem to Paris, June 2, 1912, MAEF, box 430; on Germany see: Dr. Brode to von Bethmann Hollweg, February 13, 1912, ISA 67, peh/418:77; on Austro-Hungary, see Eliav, *Be-ḥasut mamlekhet Austria.*

17. Dr. Brode to von Bethmann Hollweg, February 5, 1913. ISA 67, peh/418:77.

18. Thomas Wallace, U.S. Consul in Jerusalem, contribution for publication in the daily consular trade reports, October 6, 1908 (file 3943/373); NACP, National Archives microfilm publication M862, roll 359, Jerusalem, numerical file, 1906–10, central files of the Department of State, record group 59.

19. *Ha-Ḥerut*, January 20, 1911.

20. Yellin, *Les Capitulations et la juridiction consulaire*, 10.

21. For an argument that Ottoman citizenship was reactive to the Balkan states' policies, see Iordachi, "The Ottoman Empire." Functionally, after 1869 the state ceased recognizing the Hellenic nationality of Ottoman Greek Orthodox within the empire, instead arguing that though they might remain Hellenic citizens while in the Greek kingdom, they were Ottoman citizens when in the empire and therefore subject to the same taxes and laws as other Ottomans. Kechriotis, "Greeks of Izmir at the End of the Empire," 58–60.

22. Anderson, *Imagined Communities*, 86.

23. Quoted in Ali Haydar Midhat Bey, *Life of Midhat Pasha*, 157–58.

24. Makdisi, "After 1860," 602 and 606.

25. Mardin, "Some Consideration," 175.

26. Deguilheim, "State Civil Education in Late Ottoman Damascus," 222.

27. Petrov, "Everyday Forms of Compliance." Ariel Salzman refers to this as "vernacular political systems" in "Citizens in Search of a State."

28. Rahme, "Namık Kemal's Constitutional Ottomanism and Non-Muslims."

29. Quoted in Heinzelmann, "Die Konstruktion eines osmanischen Patriotismus," 41–42.

30. Quoted in Davison, "Turkish Attitudes Concerning Christian-Muslim Equality," 862.

31. Tevfik, *Yeni Osmanlılar*, 201–5. The hadith also appeared on the masthead of the Beiruti *Nafīr Sūrīyā* in 1860 and *Al-Jinān* in 1870. Zachs, *Making of a Syrian Identity*, 167.

32. Karpat, *Politicization of Islam*, 330–35; quote is on page 331. I have changed Karpat's translation of *vatan* from "fatherland" to "homeland." However, I disagree with Karpat's conclusion that Kemal's Ottomanism was a proto-Turkish nationalism. See also Tavakoli-Targhi, "From Patriotism to Matriotism," for Iranian notions of homeland.

33. Emin, *Development of Modern Turkey*, 73.

34. For example the Greek-Orthodox journalist Theodor Kassap repeatedly embraced the Ottomanist project in his newspapers, declaring that "the whole world knows I am a pure Ottoman [Osmanlıoğlu Osmanlı, lit. 'Ottoman son of an Ottoman'] and that I am proud of my Ottomanism." Quoted in Strauss, "Ottomanisme et 'Ottomanité,'" 36. On the Judeo-Spanish press' role in constructing an Ottoman Jewish loyalty and identity, see Cohen, "Fashioning Imperial Citizens."

35. Abu Manneh, "Christians Between Ottomanism and Syrian Nationalism," 296.

36. *Nafīr Sūrīyā*, November 19, 1860, and *Al-Jinān*, vol. 1, no. 14 (1870), quoted in Zachs, *Making of a Syrian Identity*, 165–66.

37. Quoted in Khuri, *Modern Arab Thought*, 144–45.

38. Cole, *Colonialism and Revolution in the Middle East*.

39. Quoted in Khuri, *Modern Arab Thought*, 48.

40. Quoted in Tavakoli-Targhi, "From Patriotism to Matriotism," 98–99.

41. Strauss, "Ottomanisme et 'Ottomanité,'" 21–23.

42. For a similiar argument, see Dawn, "Origins of Arab Nationalism," 8.

43. Gellner, *Nations and Nationalism.*

44. Fortna, *Imperial Classroom.*

45. Ibid., 64–70 and 99. Fortna reports that many Bulgarian schoolteachers and inspectors in the Bulgarian private schools in Macedonia were political propagandists and revolutionaries.

46. Ibid., 53.

47. Kedourie, *Chatham House Version*, 328; Harshav, *Language in Time of Revolution*; Rodrigue, *Images of Sephardi and Eastern Jewries.*

48. Strohmeier, "Muslim Education in the Vilayet of Beirut." Quotes from 216–17, 219, and 226.

49. See R. Khalidi, *Palestinian Identity*, 49.

50. Deguilheim, "State Civil Education in Late Ottoman Damascus."

51. Fortna, *Imperial Classroom*, 103.

52. Kasmieh, "Ruhi al-Khalidi." The English-run Evelina de Rothschild school in Jerusalem was a prestigious path for girls from good families. In Damascus in 1872 there were twenty-six girls' maktabs with 294 students and six Christian girls' schools with 326 students. Deguilheim, "State Civil Education in Late Ottoman Damascus," 230–31.

53. Salzmann, "Citizens in Search of a State," 49.

54. Erdem, "Recruitment for the 'Victorious Soldiers of Muhammad'."

55. Krikorian, *Armenians in the Service of the Ottoman Empire*, 23; and Fortna, *Imperial Classroom*, 97.

56. See Deringil, "From Ottoman to Turk."

57. Davison, "Turkish Attitudes," 861. See also Devereaux, *First Ottoman Constitutional Period*, for the difficulties that Midhat Pasha had on this question.

58. Davison, "Turkish Attitudes," 23.

59. Kechriotis, "Greeks of Izmir at the End of the Empire," 58–60.

60. Erdem, "Recruitment for the 'Victorious Soldiers of Muhammad.'"

61. Deringil, "From Ottoman to Turk," 328.

62. Quoted in Strauss, "Ottomanisme et 'Ottomanité,'" 39.

63. *Ha-Hashkafa*, August 9, 1908.

64. *Al-Manār*, September 25, 1908.

65. Al-Bustani, *'Ibra wa-dhikra*, 90–104.

66. *Al-Manār*, September 25, 1908.

67. Al-Bustani, *'Ibra wa-dhikra*, 100.

68. *Al-Manār* September 25, 1908.

69. *Al-Manār*, July 28, 1908.

70. "The Constitution in Turkey [*sic*]," *Ha-'Olam*, July 29, 1908.

71. U.S. Consul in Aleppo to Secretary of State, August 5, 1908, quoted in Watenpaugh, "Bourgeois Modernity," 37.

72. Gilbert Bie Ravndal, U.S. Consul in Beirut, to the US Department of State, August 4, 1908 (file 10044/54–55); NACP, National Archives microfilm publication M862, roll 717, Beirut, numerical file, 1906–10, central files of the Department of State, record group 59.

73. Wallace, August 12, 1908. He later corrected the incorrect report that Jews had been allowed inside the Holy Sepulcher; instead, they had been allowed on the street outside of it. For a similar report from Beirut see Ravndal, August 4, 1908.

74. Kemal Karpat cites Ottoman records which stated that the population of Hebron district was forty thousand Muslims and five hundred Jews. Karpat, *Ottoman Population*, 166. Contemporary newspaper accounts list the Jewish population as one thousand.

75. *Ha-Hashkafa*, August 21, 1908.

76. *Ḥavaẓelet*, August 12, 1908.

77. *Ḥavaẓelet*, August 14, 1908.

78. *Ḥavaẓelet*, August 17, 21, and 24, 1908. Thomas R. Wallace, U.S. Consul in Jerusalem, to the U.S. Department of State, August 14, 1908 (file 10044/60–61); NACP, National Archives microfilm publication M862, roll 102, Jerusalem, numerical file, 1906–10, central files of the Department of State, record group 59.

79. *Ha-Hashkafa*, July 31, 1908. My emphasis. "Ottomanized" referred to those Jewish immigrants who took on Ottoman citizenship.

80. Chatterjee reminds us that in colonial India this language of kinship between Muslims and Hindus was contextual and bounded. Chatterjee, *Nation and Its Fragments*, 222. Kinship also was an important trope of the 1906 Iranian constitutional revolution. Tavakoli-Targhi, "From Patriotism to Matriotism," 222–23.

81. Strauss, "Ottomanisme et 'Ottomanité,'" 30.

82. "The Holiday of Liberty," in *Ha-Hashkafa*, August 9, 1908.

83. *Al-Quds*, December 18, 1908.

84. *Al-Quds*, May 14, 1909.

85. *Al-Quds*, May 11, 1909.

86. *Al-Manār*, July 28, 1908.

87. *Al-Hilāl*, October 1, 1908.

88. In 1908–9, for example, *Vatan* was performed by four different theater companies in Istanbul. Yalçin, *II. Meşrutiyet'te tiyatro edebiyatı tarihi*. It was also performed in Manastır in the fall of 1908. Tunçay, *II. Meşrutiyet'in ilk yılı*, 6–7.

89. *Al-Ittiḥād al-'Uthmānī*, October 4, 9, and 14, 1908. According to the report, the army raised money from the performance. Because of the Arabic press's treatment of Kemal generally and his play *Vatan yahut Silestre* in particular, I cannot accept Kemal Karpat's assertion that this was evidence of a Turkish nationalist orientation. Karpat, *Politicization of Islam*, 334.

90. Quoted in ibid., 334.

91. Smith, "'Sacred' Dimensions of Nationalism," 811.

92. *New York Times*, August 14, 1908. See also Kansu, "Souveneir of Liberty," 22–23.

93. *Al-Manār*, September 25, 1908.

94. Denais, *La Turquie nouvelle*, 87.

95. Quoted in McCullagh, *Fall of Abd-ul-hamid*, 172–74. According to Islamic law, martyrs' bodies are treated as already sanctified and therefore are not in need of the ritual washing proscribed by religious law.

96. Pears, *Forty Years in Constantinople*, 282. The names of the martyrs were inscribed on the monument; however, only one Christian has been identified, despite Enver Bey's use of the plural. Kreiser, "Ein Freiheitsdenkmal für Istanbul," 306–7. My thanks to M. Erdem Kabadayı and Kent Schull for the article reference.

97. In 1951 the body of Midhat Pasha, the author of the 1876 constitution and the original "martyr of liberty," was brought from Ta'if and reinterred in a separate grave on the same hill; similarly, the bodies of Talat and Enver Pashas, two of the CUP's final ruling triumvirate, were brought from Berlin and Tajikistan, respectively, and buried in the same complex. Kreiser, "Ein Freiheitsdenkmal für Istanbul," 308–9. Enver Pasha, of course, was formerly Enver Bey, one of the iconic "heroes of liberty."

98. *El Liberal*, May 14, 1909.

99. "The Holiday of Liberty," by Avraham Elmaliach, *Ha-Hashkafa*, August 9, 1908.

100. *Al-Manār*, July 28, 1908.

101. *Al-Manār*, September 25, 1908.

102. The literature on nationalism is enormous, but for the role of the military in sustaining a Habsburg imperial identity, see Deák, *Beyond Nationalism*; on the military and nationalism, see Massad, *Colonial Effects*.

103. *Al-Manār*, September 25, 1908.

104. Ha-Va'ad le-hoẓa'at kitvei David Yellin, *Kitvei David Yellin*, 148.

105. Frumkin, *Derekh shofet bi-Yerushalayim*, 103.

106. For example notices appeared in *Ha-Hashkafa*, September 16, 1908; *Ḥavaẓelet*, November 27, 1908; *Al-Najāḥ*, April 8, 1910; *Ha-Ḥerut* August 22, 1910; *Ha-Ḥerut*, October 28, 1910.

107. Antébi to Meir, February 27, 1910. CAHJP HM2/8644.

108. Schneller School records, January 23, 1907; ISA 67, peh/442:360.

109. *Ha-'Olam*, November 13, 1908.

110. AAIU, Israel-IX.E.26; CZA J41/492. In the matter of Subhi Bey's pressure to admit more Muslim students, see the January 20, 1909, letter from Antébi to the AIU headquarters; AAIU, Israel-IX.E.26.

111. See Harshav, *Language in Time of Revolution*; and Landau, "Educational Impact of Western Culture on Traditional Society."

112. *Al-Manār*, August 27, 1908.

113. Strohmeier, "Muslim Education in the Vilayet of Beirut," 222 and 226.

114. Musallam, ed., *Yawmiyat Khalil al-Sakakini*.

115. Other founders of the school included 'Ali Jarallah, Jamal al-Khalidi, and Eftim Mushabbak. See the entry for January 1, 1911, in al-Sakakini, *Kadha ana ya dunya*, 51–52. Similar projects of pedagogical reform were taking place elsewhere. Tevfik Fikret (Mehmet Tevfik), the director of the prestigious Teachers Academy (Darülmuallimin) in Istanbul from 1909 to 1912, implemented elements of modern pedagogy and published a pedagogical journal. He also took two trips to Europe to study education there and founded a nursery school and a school to train female teachers. Cleveland, *Making of an Arab Nationalist*.

116. See the discussion of al-Sakakini by one of his former pupils, Ihsan Turjeman, in Tamari, "Great War and the Erasure of Palestine's Ottoman Past."

117. "Kalimat khadarat al-za'irin lil-madrasa al-dusturiyya al-wataniyya fil-Quds al-Sharif," Arab Studies Society Collection. The Dusturiyya School was also praised in the local Palestinian newspapers *Filasṭīn* and *Al-Munādī*.

118. Ökay, *Meşrutiyet çocukları*. See also Büssow, "Children of the Revolution."

119. See Gülsoy, *Osmanlı gayrimüslimlerinin askerlik serüveni.*

120. Abbott, *Turkey in Transition*, 96.

121. *Al-Quds*, May 11, 1909.

122. Quoted in Aflalo, *Regilding the Crescent*, 235. He also pointed out that the Armenians could not afford to continue paying the *bedel-i askerî.*

123. *Ha-Ḥerut*, May 18, 1909.

124. *El Liberal*, August 6, 1909.

125. *Tanin*, June 21, 1909. Quoted in Aflalo, *Regilding the Crescent*, 216.

126. Likewise, in Iran, there was a certain degree of religious opposition to the constitutional movement's proclamations of equality. Tavakoli-Targhi, "Refashioning Iran," 99.

127. "The Ottoman Nation and the Constitution," *Al-Manār*, August 27, 1908.

128. Knight, *Turkey*, 221 and 279.

129. *Tanin*, June 13, 1909. Translation from Aflalo, *Regilding the Crescent*, 214–15.

130. Buxton, *Turkey in Revolution*, 79–80.

131. *Ha-Ẓvi*, November 1, 1908. For a historical account of the "lynch" of Todori and Bedriye, see Akşin, *Jön Türkler ve ittihat ve terakki*, 144–45.

132. Kaligian, "Armenian Revolutionary Federation," 144–45. See, for example, *Ha-Ḥerut*, June 22, and July 6, 1909; *El Liberal*, June 29, 1909; *Ha-Ḥerut*, April 6, 1910; *Ha-Ḥerut*, July 6, 1910; *Ha-Ḥerut*, March 7, 1913. On the April 1910 case, see also the letter from the Haifa Jewish community to Chief Rabbi Haim Nahum asking for his intervention, April 18, 1910. CAHJP, HM2/8643. See also Eliav, *Be-ḥasut mamlekhet Austria.*

133. *Al-Ittiḥād al-'Uthmānī*, October 2, 1908.

134. *Ha-Ẓvi*, October 27, 1908.

135. Kaligian, "Armenian Revolutionary Federation," 50–56.

136. See *Ha-Ẓvi*, nos. 163 and 166.

137. Quoted in Ramsay, *Revolution in Constantinople and Turkey*, 179–81.

138. Quoted in Kaligian, "Armenian Revolutionary Federation," 67.

139. Quoted in ibid., 73.

Chapter Three: Of Boycotts and Ballots

1. *Al-Ittiḥād al-'Uthmānī*, September 23, 1908.

2. *Al-Ittiḥād al-'Uthmānī*, September 30, 1908; October 9, 1908; October 15, 1908.

3. *Ha-'Olam*, August 28, 1908. Saliba, "Wilayat Suriyya," 251.

4. Darwaza, *Mudhakkirat*, 182–83.

5. Kushner, *Moshel hayiti bi-Yerushalayim*, 198–202. Shaykh Salim al-Ya'qubi Abu al-Iqbal, *Al-Quds*, May 11, 1909.

6. *Al-Quds*, May 14, 1909.

7. *Al-Ittiḥād al-'Uthmānī*, October 8, 1908.

8. *Al-Ittiḥād al-'Uthmānī*, October 11, 1908.
9. Darwaza, *Mudhakkirat*, 182.
10. *Ha-Hashkafa*, August 9, 1908.
11. *Al-Hilāl*, November 1, 1908; *Ḥavaẓelet*, December 30, 1908; *Ha-Hashkafa*, August 4, 14 and 19, 1908; *Ha-'Olam*, August 21, 1908; *Luaḥ Ereẓ-Israel*, vol. 14 (1909).
12. *Al-Manār*, July 28, 1908.
13. *Al-Hilāl*, October 1, 1908.
14. *Al-Manār*, August 27, 1908.
15. *Al-Ittiḥād al-'Uthmānī*, October 9, 1908.
16. BOA MV. 245/100; BOA I.DUIT. 120/13; BOA MV. 249/201.
17. Hanioğlu, *Preparation for a Revolution*, 288.
18. For an example of a fake announcement see *Al-Ittiḥād al-'Uthmānī*, October 11, 1908. See also Hanioğlu, *Preparation for a Revolution*, 288.
19. Darwaza, *Mudhakkirat*.
20. Among its founders were several Ottomanized Ashkenazi Jews. *Ḥavaẓelet*, October 21, 1908.
21. Hanioğlu, *Preparation for a Revolution*, 282. Other branches were considered dens of political opportunists and closet nationalists, and as a result, the central CUP in Salonica held them at arms' length. See Kushner, *Moshel hayiti bi-Yerushalayim*, 62–64, for a discussion of this.
22. *Ha-Hashkafa*, August 9, 1908.
23. Al-Namura, *Al-Filastiniyun*, 200.
24. Ruppin to the ZAC, August 24, 1908, CZA Z2/632; and Frumkin, *Derekh shofet bi-Yerushalayim*, 147. Apparently in addition to Yellin and Eisenberg, two other Jews affiliated with the Zionist movement, Dr. Yitzhak Levi and Eli'ezer Ben-Yehuda, had proposed their candidacy to the CUP, but were denied admission when they refused to disavow Zionism.
25. October 13, 1908. ISA 67, peh/533:1491–93.
26. Al-Namura, *Al-Filastiniyun*, 200.
27. *Ha-Ḥerut*, September 29, 1909.
28. Al-Sakakini, *Kadha ana ya dunya*, October 8, 1908, entry, 39; and October 23, 1908, entry, 42–43. Al-Sakakini's account is similar in detail to the account given in Mango, *Atatürk*, 68.
29. *Ha-Ḥerut*, March 2 and May 21, 1909. ISA 67, peh/533:1491. ISA 67, peh/415: 26.
30. Darwaza, *Mudhakkirat*, 182; Kayalı, *Arabs and Young Turks*, 63; Wallace, August 12, 1908.
31. Al-Sakakini, *Kadha ana ya dunya*, October 24, 1908, 43. Reported in *Ha-Ẓvi*, cited in *Ha-'Olam*, June 29, 1909. In 1909, Albert Antébi was told by members of the CUP that some new (as well as old) members were increasingly urging the CUP to "not neglect the danger which threatens the country and the peasants by Jewish immigration." He reported that the northern Palestinian branches (Nazareth, Haifa, and Tiberias, along with Beirut) were the most virulent in their attacks. Albert Antébi to Brill, May 12, 1909. AAIU, Israel-IX.E.26.
32. Public demonstrations in Beirut and Damascus appealed to "friends" of

the Ottoman Empire to help it defend its rights. See *Al-Ittiḥād al-ʿUthmānī*, October 14 and 17, 1908.

33. See Quataert, "Ottoman Boycott Against Austria-Hungary," for a discussion of the boycott's development and implementation in Istanbul, Izmir and Trabzon. See also Çetinkaya, "Economic Boycott as a Political Weapon." My thanks to Don Quataert for alerting me to and providing me with access to this unpublished source.

34. Quataert, "Ottoman Boycott Against Austria-Hungary," 125.

35. ISA 67, peh/533: 1491–93. However a notice in *Al-Ittiḥād al-ʿUthmānī* demanding that Beirut's merchants join the boycott shows that the boycott was not yet unanimous among merchants, nor was there a general agreement by the population. *Al-Ittiḥād al-ʿUthmānī*, October 13, 1908. The newspaper did praise the Jaffans' national-patriotic devotion (*ḥamiyya waṭaniyya*). October 15, 1908.

36. Musallam, ed., *Yawmiyat Khalil al-Sakakini*, 309.

37. *Bulletin de la Chambre de commerce d'industrie et d'agriculture de Palestine* (year 1, no. 6, December 1909), 6; JMA, 1779. March 1, 1912, Commerce and Industries—Jerusalem Consular District, calendar year of 1911; NACP, correspondence (January–July 1912), general correspondence, 1912–35, Jerusalem Consulate (350/26/11/1–2), records of the foreign service posts of the Department of State, record group 84. Egypt and the United Kingdom were the only two countries with which Jaffa had a positive trade balance. Gaza port, on the other hand, had an overall positive trade balance (4.5 million francs in imports and 7.8 million francs in exports). *Bulletin de la Chambre de commerce d'industrie et d'agriculture de Palestine* (year 1, no. 6, December 1909), 6. JMA, 1779.

38. ISA 67, peh/533: 1491–93.

39. ISA 67, peh/415: 31. Al-Sakakini mentioned this flyer in his memoirs. Musallam, ed., *Yawmiyat Khalil al-Sakakini*, 314.

40. Rössler (Jaffa) to Marschall von Biebenstern (Istanbul), October 13, 1908. ISA 67, peh/415:31.

41. Wilhelm Steffan to Wenko, October 16, 1908. Document quoted in Eliav, *Be-ḥasut Austria*, and Eliav, *Österreich und das heilige Land*, 448–49. The Austrian post in Jerusalem brought in seven hundred thousand to eight hundred thousand francs every year, a notable sum. Eliav, *Österreich und das heilige Land*, 85.

42. Steffan to Wenko, October 16, 1908; Wenko (vice-consul in Jaffa) to the kaymakam (original in French), October 13, 1908. Original documents found in Eliav, *Österreich und das heilige Land*; and Eliav, *Be-ḥasut Austria*, 350.

43. *Ḥavaẓelet*, October 19, 1908.

44. Al-Husayni and other religious leaders, including the Jewish chief rabbi of the city and Greek Orthodox and Armenian representatives, gave rousing speeches, and telegrams of protest were sent to all the European capitals. *Ḥavaẓelet*, October 19, 1908.

45. November 20, 1908, letter in Eliav, *Be-ḥasut Austria*. The Austro-Hungarian consul complained to the governor and Greek Orthodox patriarch, and received apologies.

46. Salah-al-Din would reemerge on numerous occasions in Palestinian Arab political consciousness, particularly vis-à-vis the emerging conflict with Zionism.

47. Quataert, "Ottoman Boycott Against Austria-Hungary," 145.

48. See *Al-Ittiḥād al-'Uthmānī*, October 15, 1908.

49. Çetinkaya, "Economic Boycott as a Political Weapon," 93.

50. Rössler (Jaffa) to Marschall von Biebenstern (Istanbul), October 14, 1908. ISA 67, peh/415:31.

51. Rössler (Jaffa) to Marschall von Biebenstern (Istanbul), October 15 and 17, 1908. ISA 67, peh/415:31. In periods that the local European and American consuls considered "restless" or detected anti-Christian or anti-European sentiment on the part of the local population or officials, a visit by a European or American warship past the port of Jaffa was requested to pacify the locals and reassert European power.

52. From German Embassy in Istanbul to German chancellor, December 15, 1908. ISA 67, peh/415:31.

53. ISA 67, peh/533: 1491–93.

54. Çetinkaya, "Economic Boycott as a Political Weapon," 88.

55. Rössler to Kaymakam, November 9 and 20, 1908; Rössler to German Embassy, Istanbul, November 24, 1908. ISA 67, peh/415:31.

56. From Jaffa Consulate to Jerusalem Consulate, November 22, 24, and 25, 1908. ISA 67, peh/415:31.

57. The Austrian consul claimed that Jaffa's boatmen were ready to go back to work unloading Austrian ships but were waiting for a signal from the government. See November 20, 1908, letter, December 4, 1908, letter from Austria's Beirut consul to Jerusalem consul, and December 10, 1908, letter, in Eliav, *Be-ḥasut Austria*.

58. Çetinkaya, "Economic Boycott as a Political Weapon," 203–5; Quataert, "Ottoman Boycott Against Austria-Hungary," 130; *and Ha-Ẓvi*, October 30, 1908.

59. *Ha-Ẓvi*, October 27, 1908, and October 29, 1908. Their wish was not granted, for the Ottoman state never declared war on Austria-Hungary over the annexation, preferring instead to pursue diplomacy.

60. Darwaza, *Mudhakkirat*, 185; and Çetinkaya, "Economic Boycott as a Political Weapon," 113.

61. ISA 67, peh/533:1491; Quataert, "Ottoman Boycott Against Austria-Hungary," 142; May 25, 1909, letter, in Eliav, *Be-ḥasut Austria*. Quataert reports that the Austrian shipping line lost 1.8 million Kronen empire-wide.

62. Commercial report of the vice-consulate in Jaffa, 1908 (no date); May 25, 1909, letter; December 10, 1908, letter; in Eliav, *Be-ḥasut Austria*, 360–63.

63. The previous price of 54 francs per roll went up to 140 francs. Wenko to Jerusalem Consulate, May 25, 1909, in ibid., 364–65. See also December 10, 1908, letter, in ibid.

64. Kayalı, "Elections and the Electoral Process in the Ottoman Empire, 269. The 1876 language requirement of reading and "to the extent possible" writing Turkish was not adopted for the 1908 elections; a 1909 amendment which sought to make Turkish an additional requirement for voters failed in parliament. However, Turkish was a requirement for passive election.

65. A. Ruppin to Wolffsohn, October 6, 1908. CZA Z2/632. According to

one press account the province had lost its chance for a fourth member of parliament due to the refusal of the Bedouins of Jericho and the Negev desert to register their numbers accurately. They feared military conscription and increased taxes. *Ha-Hashkafa*, September 26, 1908.

66. *Al-Ittiḥād al-'Uthmānī*, September 29, 1908; *Ha-Hashkafa*, August 14, 1908; *Ha-Hashkafa*, September 26, 1908. The extensive voting laws and procedures were published in the official gazette *Takvim-i Vekayi*, vol. 1, nos. 1–5, starting September 28, 1908. A copy of the election laws was to be sent to every village and region, and there were steep fines and punishments against noncompliance and fraud. *Qanun intikhab majlis al-nawwab al-'Uthmani.*

67. Schmelz, "Population of Jerusalem's Urban Neighborhoods"; letter from Dr. Arthur Ruppin to the president of the Zionist Actions Committee, August 24, 1908, CZA Z2/632; Thomas R. Wallace to Fred Deem, Esq., February 24, 1909 (file 14881/6–7), NACP, National Archives microfilm publication M862, roll 904, Jerusalem, numerical file, 1906–10, central files of the Department of State, record group 59.

68. Ruppin to ZAC, August 24, 1908, CZA Z2/632; Ruppin to ZAC, January 1, 1909, CZA Z2/8.

69. *Ha-Hashkafa*, September 16, 1908.

70. *Vergi* was taxed at 12 percent of the sales price of the home or shop. *Ha-Ḥerut*, January 2, 1911.

71. For example, Greek Orthodox farmers in Epirus protested, arguing that they should receive the franchise since they worked on the lands which were taxed. Knight, *Turkey*, 270. On Jerusalem see: Farhi, "Documents on the Attitude of the Ottoman Government, 200; BOA MV. 120/62, September 16, 1908; Letter from Dr. Arthur Ruppin to the president of the Zionist Actions Committee, August 24, 1908. CZA Z2/632; *Ha-Hashkafa*, September 23, 1908.

72. *Ha-Po'el ha-Ẓa'ir*, September 1908.

73. *Ha-Hashkafa*, September 23, 1908; Y. Levi to A. Ruppin, September 29, 1908. CZA L2/43.

74. Similar claims are made in Makedonski, "La révolution Jeune-Turque"; and Boura, "Greek Millet in Turkish Politics," although neither offer hard data on enfranchisement.

75. Ruppin to Levi, January 1909. CZA L2/43. Although solid demographic data for Jaffa is not available, it seems that Christian enfranchisement may have been slightly higher than their distribution in the population at large. The difference between Christian enfranchisement in Jerusalem and Jaffa is likely explained by the availability of living quarters owned by the church versus privately owned.

76. Cited in Sabato, "On Political Citizenship in Nineteenth-Century Latin America."

77. *Al-Ittiḥād al-'Uthmānī*, October 11, 1908; *Ha-Ẓvi*, September 30, 1908; Also Darwaza, *Mudhakkirat.*

78. *Al-Ittiḥād al-'Uthmānī*, October 9, 1908.

79. *Al-Ittiḥād al-'Uthmānī*, September 25, 1908.

80. *Al-Ittiḥād al-ʿUthmānī*, September 25, 1908; October 1, 1908; October 10, 1908.

81. *Al-Ittiḥād al-ʿUthmānī*, October 1, 1908.

82. *Al-Ittiḥād al-ʿUthmānī*, September 25, 1908.

83. Such was the case in Mecca, Jidda, and the Yemen. Kayalı, *Arabs and Young Turks*, 66.

84. *Al-Ittiḥād al-ʿUthmānī*, October 10, 1908.

85. Consulate General of France in Palestine (G. Gueyrand) to the Directorate of Political and Commercial Affairs, Subdirectorate of the Levant, October 8, 1908; MAEF, microfilm roll 132, Correspondence Politique et Commerciale/Nouvelle Série (Turquie). On the "peasants' party," see *Ha-Poʿel ha-Ẓa'ir*, September 1908; Levi to A. Ruppin, October 14, 1908. CZA L2/43; Antébi to Franck, October 21, 1908. AAIU, Israel-VIII.E.25.

86. Musallam, ed., *Yawmiyat Khalil al-Sakakini*, 306; *Ha-Ẓvi*, October 26, 1908.

87. Knight, *Turkey*, 273.

88. Ibid. See also Kayalı, "Elections and the Electoral Process in the Ottoman Empire"; and Buxton, *Turkey in Revolution*, 187.

89. Abbott, *Turkey in Transition*, 106–7.

90. Knight, *Turkey*, 275–78.

91. *Ḥavaẓelet*, October 19, 1908.

92. One paper reported that only half of the voters at the first level showed up to vote for the second level electors—namely, 40 percent of Jews with voting rights stayed home. *Ha-Poʿel ha-Ẓa'ir*, September 1908. Levi, a former Ottoman government official, was closely identified with the Zionist movement, and considered himself the Zionist candidate for parliament. The local Zionist Palestine Office also supported his candidacy financially. Antébi, on the other hand, was hostile to the expansionist political aims of the European Zionist movement, even though in practice he aided the Zionist settlers. See Levi to Ruppin, September 18, 1908, CZA L2/43; Zionist Centralburo to Ruppin, September 15, 1908, CZA L2/26I; Antébi to Henri Franck, September 7, 1908, AAIU, Israel-VIII.E.25. As it turns out, "Antébi's Yemenites" were split into two electoral districts, ultimately benefiting David Yellin. Levi to Ruppin, October 6, 1908, CZA L2/43. A letter by a leader of the Society of Ottoman Jews, Haim Michlin, indicated that they had little idea how to go about making concrete alliances with village leaderships. H. Michlin to Rabinowitz, Matalon, Abulafia, etc, September 22, 1908. CZA L2/43. On the Christian votes, see: Musallam, ed., *Yawmiyat Khalil al-Sakakini*, 307.

93. Ephraim Cohn to A. Ruppin, September 28, 1908. CZA L2/43.

94. Levi related to the Zionist official Arthur Ruppin that he had been told by Malchiel Mani, a leading Jewish figure in Hebron, that it was possible to purchase votes in his district. Levi to Ruppin, September 18, 1908. CZA L2/43.

95. E. Saphir to Antébi, November 22, 1908. AAIU, Israel-VIII.E.25.; *Ha-Ẓvi*, October 2, 1908. When the governor of Jerusalem, Subhi Bey, was informed about this, he told the press to notify voters in Gaza that such pressure was illegal.

96. See Antébi to Franck, October 21, 1908. AAIU, Israel-VIII.E.25.; Antébi to Dizengoff/Saphir, October 23, 1908. AAIU, Israel-VIII. E.25.; *Ha-Ẓvi*, October 23, 1908; Ruppin to Wolffsohn, November 11, 1908. CZA Z2/632.

97. *Ḥavaẓelet*, October 26, 1908. With his strong base in the coastal region of Jaffa and Gaza, al-Sa'id edged out 'Uthman al-Nashashibi, who had been the third leading candidate in the Jerusalem-area electoral rounds. *Ḥavaẓelet*, vol. 39, nos. 7 and 10.

98. Kayalı, "Elections and the Electoral Process in the Ottoman Empire," 267.

99. For more information, see Manna', *A'lam Filastin*. For further details on al-Khammash, see Darwaza, *Mudhakkirat*, 186.

100. Kayalı, "Elections and the Electoral Process in the Ottoman Empire," 269. For example, another letter from Levi to Ruppin stated that he planned to enter into agreement with Husayn al-Husayni, "who has a great deal of influence with his villagers." Levi to Ruppin, October 6, 1908. CZA L2/43. Within a week, Levi notified Ruppin that Husayni did not want to combine votes, which he considered pointless in a two-tier system, but recommended that the electors agree on two Muslims and one Christian candidate. Levi to Ruppin, October 12, 1908. CZA L2/43.

101. Friman went on to criticize the native Ottoman Jewish communities and accuse them of assimilation, of "trying to be more Turkish than the Turks themselves." *Ha-Ẓvi*, September 30, 1908. This intra-Jewish political tension will be discussed in Chapter Six.

102. *New York Times*, December 20, 1908. And yet, the work of Vangelis Kechriotis shows us that many Greeks were invested in the Ottoman parliamentary and citizenship project. Kechriotis, "Greeks of Izmir at the End of the Empire."

103. Aflalo, *Regilding the Crescent*, 157; and *Al-Hilāl*, January 1, 1909.

104. Denais, *La Turquie nouvelle*, 61.

105. Kayalı, "Elections and the Electoral Process in the Ottoman Empire," 266.

106. *Al-Quds*, November 17, 1908.

107. Ibid.

108. Levi and Yellin to Ruppin, October 18, 1908. CZA L2/43.

109. Levi to Ruppin, October 11, 1908. CZA L2/43.

110. *Ha-Ẓvi*, November 1 and November 17, 1908.

111. See for example, letter from the Society of Ottoman Jews (SOJ) to the Jewish members of parliament ("Monsieur le Deputé"), June 14, 1909, CAHJP, HM2/8640; "Address to Nissim Mazliach," *Ha-Ẓvi*, November 20, 1908; letter from Eli'ezer Ben-Yehuda to the Jewish members of parliament, *Ha-Ẓvi*, January 5, 1909.

112. For discussion of this notion, see Beinin, *Dispersion of Egyptian Jewry*.

113. Sabato, "On Political Citizenship in Nineteenth-Century Latin America," 1304.

114. *Al-Quds*, November 16, 1908.

115. *Al-Quds*, November 17, 1908.

116. See R. Khalidi, *Palestinian Identity*, 76.

117. *Al-Quds*, November 17, 1908.

118. *Al-Hilāl*, November 1, 1908. The December 1 issue of *Al-Hilāl* included a list of all the members of parliament, as well as a photo of the opening session.

119. *Al-Quds al-Sharīf*, December 22, 1908. Description of the Jerusalem and Jaffa events are in: *Al-Quds*, December 18, 1908; *Ḥavaẓelet*, December 18 and 21, 1908; *Ha-Ẓvi*, December 18, 1908; *Ha-'Olam*, December 22, 1908 and January 12, 1909; and *Al-Quds al-Sharīf*, December 22, 1908. Newspapers also covered the reactions in Istanbul and Salonica to the opening of the parliament. See *Al-Quds*, December 18, 1908; *Ha-'Olam*, December 29, 1908; *Ha-Ẓvi*, December 31, 1908.

120. *Al-Quds*, December 18, 1908.

121. Ibid.

122. *Al-Quds al-Sharīf*, December 22, 1908.

123. Ravndal, opening of Ottoman parliament, December 26, 1908 (file 10044/124); NARA, National Archives microfilm publication M862, roll 717, Jerusalem, numerical file, 1906–10, central files of the Department of State, record group 59.

124. *Al-Manār*, "The Opening of the Parliament," v. 11, n. 11.

125. See Abdülhamid's speech to the new parliament, reprinted in *Al-Manār*, and the dinner he held at Yildiz Palace for the new parliamentarians, discussed in Aflalo, *Regilding the Crescent*, 114–15, and Buxton, *Turkey in Revolution*, 163.

126. *Al-Quds*, December 18, 1908.

127. *El Liberal*, May 28, 1909.

128. "Qasida," by Niqula Rizk Allah, *Al-Hilāl*, December 1, 1908.

129. "The Disturbances in Turkey [*sic*] and the Victory of the Constitution," by Sh. Ẓ., in *Ha-'Olam*, April 27, 1909.

130. Arthur Ruppin (Jaffa) to the Zionist Actions Committee, April 22, 1909, CZA, Z2/633; "This Week in the Land of Israel," in *Ha-'Olam*, May 4, 1909; *Ha-Ḥerut*, May 21, 1909; *Al-Quds*, May 11 and 14, 1909.

131. Supplement: "The Impression in Jerusalem," *El Liberal*, April 27, 1909; *Al-Quds*, May 14, 1909.

132. For discussion of the "March events" see Kuran, *Inkilap tarihimiz ve Jön Türkler*, 337–46.

133. Quoted in Khuri, *Modern Arab Thought*, 40.

134. Translation in Pears, *Forty Years in Constantinople.*

135. Quoted in McCullagh, *Fall of Abd-ul-hamid*, 185.

136. *Al-Quds*, May 14, 1909.

137. Ibid.

138. Quoted in Abbott, *Turkey in Transition*, 52–53.

Chapter Four: The Mouthpiece of the People

Chapter Four has been adapted from and expands on "The 'Voice of the People' (Lisan al-Sha'b): The Press and the Public Sphere in Revolutionary Palestine," in *Publics, Politics, and Participation: Locating the Public Sphere in the Middle East and North Africa*, ed. Seteney Shami (New York: SSRC Books and Columbia University Press, 2010).

1. Edib, *House with Wisteria.* A week earlier the opposition newspaper editor Hassan Fehmi had been assassinated, and public rumors in the capital attributed the crime to the CUP itself.

2. "What Is Required of Us After the Constitution," *Al-Ittiḥād al-'Uthmānī,* vol. 1, no. 37.

3. And yet, many of the existing histories of this period ignore the Ottomanist aims of the multilingual press and instead privilege any evidence of Arab "protonationalism." For example, R. Khalidi, "Press as a Source for Modern Arab Political History"; Seikaly, "Damascene Intellectual Life"; Tauber, "Press and the Journalist as a Vehicle." The nationalist reading of the press is dominant in the history of the Zionist-Palestinian conflict as well. See R. Khalidi, *Palestinian Identity*; Mandel, *Arabs and Zionism*; Yehoshu'a, "Tel Aviv in the Image of the Arab Press"; Yehoshu'a, "Yeḥasam shel ha-'itonaim ve-ha-sofrim he-'Aravim"; Roi, "Nisyonoteihem shel ha-mosdot ha-Ẓiyonim"; and Alsberg, "Ha-she'ela he-'Aravit." Beyond the nationalist frame, scholars in recent years have increasingly turned to the press as a rich source for Middle Eastern cultural, gender, and communal history. See, for example: Seikaly, "Christian Contributions to the Nahda"; Frierson, "State, Press, and Gender in the Hamidian Era"; Stein, *Making Jews Modern*; and Sorek, *Arab Soccer in a Jewish State.*

4. See Kırlı, "Coffeehouses"; and Hoexter, Eisenstadt, and Levtzion, eds., *Public Sphere in Muslim Societies.*

5. See Kechriotis, "The Greeks of Izmir at the End of the Empire"; Mardin, "Some Consideration"; Özbeck, "Philanthropic Activity, Ottoman Patriotism, and the Hamidian Regime"; and Frierson, "Gender, Consumption and Patriotism."

6. Emin, *Development of Modern Turkey*, 41. The two Hebrew newspapers the author counted were probably in Judeo-Spanish.

7. Ibid., 52–58; Hanioğlu, *Brief History of the Late Ottoman Empire*, 94–95; Strauss, "Who Read What in the Ottoman Empire," 47.

8. Ayalon, *Reading Palestine*, 50.

9. Between 1875 and 1914, 833 newspapers and periodicals appeared in Egypt. They served as platforms to criticize the *khedive* Isma'il and his aristocracy, to protest against European influence and colonization, and to introduce new ideas to the Egyptian reading public. Ayalon, "Political Journalism and Its Audience in Egypt," 103. Also see Nabavi, "Spreading the Word," for the role of the press in the 1906 Iranian revolution.

10. Ayalon, *Press in the Arab Middle East*, 65.

11. Brummett, *Image and Imperialism*, 25; Yehoshu'a, "Al-Jara'id al-'Arabiyya," 19; Watenpaugh, "Bourgeois Modernity," 50.

12. Khoury, *Al-sihafa al-'Arabiyya.* Sadly, most of these newspapers have been lost, with the exception of *Filasṭīn* (from July 1911 on) and *Al-Munādī* (1912–13), as well as scattered issues of other papers such as *Al-Quds* and *Al-Karmil.* In Palestine on the eve of revolution, only one newspaper had existed to serve its majority Arabic-speaking population: the bilingual official monthly organ of the province, *Al-Quds al-Sharīf/Kudüs-ü Şerif.* As well, a handful of Hebrew newspapers were published in Jerusalem, and Palestine's Jews also read

Ladino newspapers from Istanbul or Salonica, the regional Arabic press, or other Hebrew or Yiddish newspapers imported from Europe.

13. There were eleven newspapers and magazines aimed at children in 1913 Istanbul. Emin, *Development of Modern Turkey*, 14–15.

14. Quoted in Buxton, *Turkey in Revolution*, 88.

15. Quoted in Ayalon, *Reading Palestine*, 106.

16. Emin, *Development of Modern Turkey*, 133–38.

17. Emin cites circulation figures for *İkdam* and *Sabah* post-1908 as sixty thousand and forty thousand, respectively, and wrote that the demand for them was so high that afternoon prices were often raised forty-fold by newspaper boys. Ibid., 87. Emin also wrote that at the height of the counterrevolution the circulation of *Tanin* hit a record high of twenty-eight thousand; for most of its run, however, circulation was in the low thousands. Ibid., 131.

18. *Ha-Ḥerut* claimed it sold out of twelve hundred copies for its first issue, in no. 2, May 14, 1909. Avraham Elmaliach, its one-time editor, claimed they had fifteen hundred to two thousand subscribers and at their high point sold three thousand newspapers. Oral History Program at Hebrew University, interview no. 2 with Avraham Elmaliach. The German Consulate listed the subscription of *Al-Quds* at 300 (220 in the country, 80 to America), and *Ha-Ḥerut*, a Sephardi Jewish organ, at 800 (300 in the country and 500 in Turkey [*sic*]). ISA 67, peh/457:482. In contrast, Khalidi argues that *Al-Quds* was the most important paper of the time, with circulation over fifteen hundred. R. Khalidi, *Palestinian Identity*, 56. A different consular report cited *Filasṭīn*'s subscription rate as 1,600 (465 in Jaffa; 1,200 in Turkey [sic]); *Al-Akhbār*'s circulation of 600 reportedly included 50 subscribers in Egypt, Sudan, and America. ISA 67, peh/533:1493.

19. For information on the cost of basic commodities, wages, and currency, see Luntz, "Luaḥ Ereẓ Israel," 76. Iris Agmon found that a medium level of support in cases of divorce was one *beşlik* (= 3.5 *kuruş*) a day. Food for one adult could be expected to be eighty *kuruş* per month. Agmon, *Family and Court*, 112–13. *Al-Karmil*'s editor complained on a regular basis about subscribers who failed to pay. See *Al-Karmil*, September 7, 1912; September 11, 1912; September 28, 1912; November 27, 1913; and November 30, 1912.

20. Emin, *Development of Modern Turkey*, 135. See also Ayalon, "Political Journalism and Its Audience in Egypt," 116.

21. Yehoshu'a, *Tarikh al-sihafa al-'Arabiyya*, 18–19; *Ha-Ẓvi*, November 17, 1908; ISA 67, peh/533:1491. Membership rates to the reader's library were three *beşliks* per month (approximately nine *kuruş*), or more than a day's wages for laborers. See also Ayalon, *Reading Palestine*, 85, 102, 104, 180n23.

22. Malul, "Ha-'itonut ha-'Aravit."

23. *El Liberal*, January 29, 1909.

24. Permissions for some of these newspapers were granted in: BOA DH.MKT. 2851/64; BOA DH.MKT. 2744/29; BOA DH.MKT. 2689/84.

25. Brummett refers to this as the "self-consciousness" of the Ottoman press. Brummett, *Image and Imperialism*, 28.

26. Travel regulations, in *El Paradizo*, April 20, 1909; and *Ha-Ḥerut*,

August 2, 1909; the closure of nonregistered pharmacies, in *Ḥavaẓelet*, December 16, 1908; *Ha-Ḥerut*, May 25, 1910, November 28, 1910; the procedure on registering a marriage, in *El Liberal*, September 3, 1909; and familiarizing readers with the new court building by Bab al-Zahra, in *Ha-Ḥerut*, October 28, 1910, and January 25 and 30, 1911. The sessions of the general council reportedly were published in the newspaper *Al-Quds al-Sharīf*.

27. *Ha-Ḥerut* and *Filasṭīn* had regular columns covering the capital.

28. For the central role of the press in "imagining community," see Anderson, *Imagined Communities*. However, Sarah Stein cautions us against assuming that print cultures always led to ethno-national identities. Stein, "Permeable Boundaries of Ottoman Jewry," 53.

29. *Ha-Ḥerut*, January 13, 1911.

30. *Al-Quds*, vol. 1, no. 1, September 18, 1908, quoted in Yehoshu'a, *Tarikh al-sihafa al-'Arabiyya*, 10.

31. Yehoshu'a, "Sahifata *al-Taraqqi* wa-*Filasṭīn*."

32. "What Is Required of Us After the Constitution," *Al-Ittiḥād al-'Uthmānī*, vol. 1, no. 37. A similar sentiment was expressed in the Aleppine newspaper *Lisan-i Ahali*. Watenpaugh, *Being Modern in the Middle East*, 54.

33. Yehoshu'a, *Tarikh al-sihafa al-'Arabiyya*, 18–19.

34. *Al-Najāḥ*, April 8, 1910.

35. *Al-Quds al-Sharīf*, December 22, 1908.

36. *Filasṭīn*, December 14, 1911.

37. For example, see *Al-Munādī* to the governor, July 9, 1912; January 14, 1913; February 13, 1913; to the city council: February 12, 1912; to the prosecutors: October 15, 1912. For responses to the paper, see *Al-Munādī*, March 8, 1913; April 3, 1913.

38. *Al-Karmil*, August 24, 1912; August 28, 1912; September 3, 1912; September 7, 1912; September 14, 1912; September 21, 1912.

39. *Al-Karmil*, September 21, 1912.

40. *Ha-Ẓvi*, August 1, 1909. An earlier article on the subject was published on January 20, 1909.

41. *Ha-Ḥerut*, August 4, 1909; August 16, 1909.

42. For example, *Al-Munādī*, July 15, 1912, and April 24, 1913; and *Al-Nafīr*, March 12, 1912.

43. *Ha-Ẓvi*, October 27, 1908.

44. *Al-Munādī*, November 11, 1912.

45. See *El Liberal*, March 12, 1909; *El Paradizo*, March 16, 1909; *Ha-Ḥerut*, May 18, 1909, January 28, 1910, February 2, 1910, April 8, 1910, and April 11, 1910.; *Al-Najāḥ*, April 21, 1910. Notices on fundraising for the Ottoman navy were also published in *Al-Quds*, April 5, 1910.

46. *Ha-Hashkafa*, August 7, 1908.

47. *Ha-Ḥerut*, May 4, 1910.

48. 'Uziel to Palestine Office, December 21, 1913. CZA, L2/43.

49. *El Paradizo*, February 9, 1909; February 12, 1909; March 5, 1909; March 9, 1909; April 20, 1909. See also Albert Antébi to Isaac Fernandez, March 10, 1909. AAIU, Israel-IX.E.26. However in early 1910, when the

interim governor of Jerusalem recommended nominating another Jew to the council, Antébi cautioned that it would provoke Christian opposition. Antébi to Haim Nahum, February 27, 1910. CAHJP, HM2/8644. He later suggested that they wait until the following year to pursue the additional member. Antébi to Haim Nahum, March 7, 1910. CAHJP, HM2/8644. *Ha-Ḥerut* was still agitating for a second council seat a year later. *Ha-Ḥerut*, March 3, 1911.

50. *El Paradizo*, nos. 3, 9, 11, 13, 17; *El Liberal*, nos. 4, 13, etc. Little more is heard from the SOJ until 1913, when it is noted that the organization had closed down in 1910 due to an internal conflict regarding party and ethnicity. *Ha-Ḥerut*, January 6, 1913; Letter from Dr. Arthur Ruppin to the president of the Zionist Actions Committee, August 24, 1908. CZA Z2/632. See letters from the *va'ad ha-zmani* and from David Yellin, September 17, 1908, CZA, A153/140; *Ha-Hashkafa*, September 26, 1908; *Ha-Po'el ha-Ẓa'ir*, May 1909; *Ha-Ḥerut*, July 6, 1909 and June 11, 1909.

51. *El Paradizo*, March 23, 1909.

52. AAIU, Israel-IX.E.26.

53. *El Paradizo*, March 12, 1909. An earlier complaint had been voiced in November 1908, when the band played on Fridays for Muslims and Sundays for Christians, leaving the Jews without musical accompaniment on Saturdays. As the paper put it, "One would think Jerusalem had only Muslims and Christians!" *Ha-Ẓvi*, November 10, 1908. According to a later notice by the paper, the band did play for Purim, a repertoire of the Ottoman anthem and Hebrew and Hasidic melodies. *Ha-Ẓvi*, March 7, 1909.

54. *El Paradizo*, March 16, 1909. Upon their arrival at Jaffa port, Jews were given a red note in exchange for their passport, in essence a visa limiting their stay to three months; however, many Jews (one thousand to two thousand immigrants per month) simply kept the pink slip and never retrieved their passports or paid bribes for their return.

55. Antébi to Franck, November 19, 1909. AAIU, Israel-IX.E.27.

56. Antébi, *L'homme du Sérail*, 371.

57. *Ha-Ḥerut*, February 4, 1910; *Ha-Ḥerut*, August 24, 1910.

58. *Ha-Ḥerut*, June 25, 1909.

59. Brummett, *Image and Imperialism*, 9.

60. Quoted in Yehoshu'a, "Al-sihafa al-'Arabiyya," 38.

61. *El Paradizo*, March 16, 1909.

62. *El Liberal*, October 15, 1909; *El Liberal*, November 15, 1909.

63. "Intolerable!" by Moise Cohen, *El Liberal*, November 5, 1909.

64. *Ha-Ḥerut*, November 5, 1909.

65. Notices in the press about the rise in insecurity abound: *Ḥavaẓelet*, December 11, 1908; *El Liberal*, no. 8 (February 1909); *El Liberal*, July 30, 1909; *Ha-Ḥerut*, August 2, 1909; *Ha-Ḥerut*, August 27, 1909; *Al-Karmil*, September 25, 1912. See also: Antébi to AIU, April 18, 1909, AAIU, Israel-IX.E.26; Antébi to AIU, May 2, 1909, AAIU, Israel-IX.E.26.

66. See Zürcher, "Between Death and Desertion," for a description of the horrors of Ottoman military service.

67. See for example *Ḥavaẓelet*, November 13, 1908.

68. The Jews, in contrast to the Christians, were considered the "most loyal" (*en sadiq*) of the non-Muslim minority groups in this period. See Rodrigue, "Mass Destruction of Armenians and Jews."

69. "Letters from Turkey [*sic*]," *Ha-'Olam*, June 8, 1909.

70. See *Takvim-i Vekayi.*

71. For the figures, see *Ha-Ḥerut*, July 14, 1909, Kushner, "Ha-dor ha-aḥaron," 30; and Ben-Gurion, "Ereẓ-Israel." During this period, non-Muslims were required to continue to pay the *bedel* for the year 1325 (1909–10), and it was not officially canceled until August 1909. *Ha-Ḥerut*, August 2, 1909. In February 1910, however, non-Muslims were still asked to pay up their exemption tax fees for the current year. *Ha-Ḥerut*, February 16, 1910.

72. *Ha-Ḥerut*, May 3, 1910.

73. In theory, all Ottoman men between the ages of twenty to forty, irrespective of religion, were required to serve in the Ottoman military in a combination of active duty, reserves, and provincial or local guard. Published in *El Liberal*, August 27, 1909; *Ha-Ḥerut*, August 25, 1909; November 12, 1909; September 7, 1910; November 23, 1910. Religious leaders, students and teachers were exempted. *El Liberal*, August 6, 1909. Medical exemptions were also detailed in *Ha-Ḥerut*, March 7, 1910; and February 3, 5, 10, 15, and 24, 1911.

74. *El Liberal*, September 3, 1909. See also *Ha-Ḥerut*, December 10, 1909.

75. Antébi to AIU, September 10, 1909. AAIU, Israel-IX.E.27. Early on a satirical play printed in the Hebrew press mocked the process of appeals, where the local officers refused to hear the objections of an old Jewish man (obviously too old to be drafted) as well as a small boy (who was clearly too young). *Ha-Ḥerut*, December 13, 1909.

76. *Ha-Ḥerut*, May 18, 1909; November 1, 1909; December 31, 1909; January 8, 1910; March 29, 1910.

77. "Letters from Turkey [*sic*]," *Ha-'Olam*, June 8, 1909; *El Liberal*, September 24, 1909; *Ha-'Olam*, July 6, 1909; *Ha-Ḥerut*, November 29, 1909 and December 3, 1909. It seems that while Jewish soldiers were initially released to eat kosher food at Jewish homes, in the winter of 1910 the Ministry of War decided that they must eat together with the rest of the soldiers, since it was forbidden to differentiate between Muslim and non-Muslim soldiers. *Ha-Ḥerut*, November 23, 1910. A later article noted that due to the intervention of the military doctors, it was decided that soldiers could bring their own cooking utensils with them rather than eat from the collective pot. *Ha-Ḥerut*, December 14, 1910.

78. *Ha-Ḥerut*, May 18, 1909.

79. *Ha-Ḥerut*, September 29, 1909.

80. "Military Service and the Jews," *Ha-Ḥerut*, October 22, 1909.

81. See *Ha-Ḥerut*, August 18, 1909; August 20, 1909; September 3, 1909; December 8, 1909; September 16, 1910.

82. *Ha-Ḥerut*, March 16, 1910.

83. *Ha-Ḥerut*, November 9, 1910.

84. *El Liberal*, September 10, 1909. At one recruiting session in Jaffa, for example, only three of the seventeen youth called to the *mu'ayyina* showed up. *Ha-Ḥerut*, February 18, 1910. See also *Ha-Ḥerut*, December 1, 1909.

85. See *Ha-Ḥerut*, August 13, 1909; September 29, 1909; July 20, 1910; September 21, 1910, November 21, 1910. British consular documents indicate that at one call-up in 1910, of the sixty Christians summoned twenty paid the tax while another fifteen fled; of the thirty-six Jews called up ten paid the tax and another ten fled. Consul Satow to Foreign Office, September 23, 1910. Cited in Eliav, *Britain and the Holy Land*, 90. The government threatened youth fleeing service and their accomplices with a stiff fines and a double tour of duty (six years instead of three). *Ha-Ḥerut*, February 2, 1910, and January 2, 1911.

86. *Ha-Ḥerut*, March 9, 1910.

87. Ibid.

88. *Ha-Ḥerut*, March 14, 1910.

89. Ibid.

90. *Ha-Ḥerut*, September 21, 1910.

91. See notices in *El Liberal*, September 10, 1909; November 19, 1909; *Ha-Ḥerut*, December 25, 1909; April 22, 1910; August 10, 1910; September 19, 1910; October 10, 1910; October 28, 1910; October 31, 1910; December 10, 1910; January 11, 1911. One society was called the Society for the Pioneers of the Army and Help for the Wives of Soldiers.

92. See, for example, *Ha-Ḥerut*, November 9, 1910; November 25, 1910; December 13, 1910; December 28, 1910.

93. *Ha-Ḥerut*, January 13, 1911; *Ha-Ḥerut*, February 22, 1911. The press complained that 75 percent of Jews did not report for duty. Later reports confirmed that the sons of European Ottomanized Jews were forfeiting their Ottoman citizenship and reclaiming their foreign citizenship. Levontin to Wolffsohn, April 3, 1911. CZA Z2/644; Sokolow to Jacobsohn, October 12, 1912. CZA Z3/43.

94. *Ha-Ḥerut*, October 29, 1912.

95. "The Love of the Jews for their Homeland," *Ha-Ḥerut*, February 24, 1913.

96. "Jews in the Army! Jews in the War!" *Ha-Ḥerut*, November 1, 1912.

97. For example, in the fall of 1910 Shim'on Moyal was fined eight Turkish liras and imprisoned for a month along with the Christian publisher of *Al-Akhbār* for a stinging article he wrote in that paper about the mufti. Translation from *Al-Nafīr* appeared in *Ha-Ḥerut*, November 21, 1910. For another case see *Al-Karmil*, November 16, 1912.

98. *Ha-Ḥerut*, December 26, 1912.

99. R. Khalidi, *Palestinian Identity*, 123; and Mandel, *Arabs and Zionism Before World War I*.

100. "The Beginnings of Anti-Semitism in Palestine," *El Liberal*, March 23, 1909; and *El Paradizo*, March 16, 1909.

101. *El Liberal*, vol. 1, no. 41 (August 1909); *El Liberal*, March 23, 1909.

102. For biographical information on this interesting couple, see Ben-Hanania, "Dr. Shim'on Moyal"; and Ben-Hanania, "Ha-soferet Ester Moyal u-tkufatah."

103. *Ha-Ḥerut*, July 23, 1909.

104. Antébi to Henri Franck, August 2, 1908. AAIU, Israel-VIII.E.25.

105. Antébi to Henri Franck, August 4, 1908. AAIU, Israel-VIII.E.25. The young journalist Gad Frumkin also sought a *ferman* for a trilingual Hebrew-

Arabic-Turkish newspaper, *Ereẓ Avot/al-Waṭan/Vatan* (Homeland), that would articulate a similar Ottomanist agenda. Frumkin, *Derekh shofet bi-Yerushalayim*, 147. Frumkin received permission for the paper, but it never appeared.

106. On this newspaper, see Jacobson, "Sephardim, Ashkenazim, and the 'Arab Question,'"; Efrati, *Ha-'edah ha-Sfaradit*; and Betzalel, "On the Journal 'Ha-Herut.'" In fact, the persistent efforts of *Ha-Ḥerut* to educate the Jewish community about Arab opposition to it earned it the annoyance of Dr. Arthur Ruppin of the Palestine Office, the local branch of the Zionist Organization. Ruppin thought the editorial policy of *Ha-Ḥerut* was unduly alarmist. Roi, "Nisyonoteihem shel ha-mosdot ha-Ẓiyonim," 229–30.

107. *Ha-Ḥerut*, May 25, 1910.

108. *Ha-Ḥerut*, November 8, 1909.

109. *Ha-Ḥerut*, May 21, 1909. See also *Ha-Ḥerut*, July 23, 1909.

110. Thus after Haim Nahum's complaint in mid-February, *Al-Karmil* resumed publication in early April, only to be sued again one month later. See *Ha-Ḥerut*, September 22, 1909; October 22, 1909; February 14, 1910; April 4, 1910; April 6, 1910; May 4, 1910; and May 25, 1910.

111. No date, CZA HM2/8647.

112. *Ha-Ḥerut*, May 25, 1910; September 23, 1912. *Al-Karmil* was blamed for "poisoning" *Al-Muqtabas* and *Al-Najāḥ* against the Jews. *Ha-Ḥerut*, December 19, 21, and 23, 1910.

113. *Ha-Ḥerut*, May 25, 1910.

114. From 'Uziel to Haim Nahum, CAHJP, HM2/9071.1; Roi, "Nisyonoteihem shel ha-mosdot ha-Ẓiyonim," 209. *Al-Karmil*, October 9, 1912; and December 11, 1912. Ruppin to Jacobsohn, May 10, 1914. CZA L2/34II.

115. *Ha-Ḥerut*, January 1, 1913.

116. *Ha-Ḥerut*, December 16 and December 31, 1912.

117. *Ha-Ḥerut*, February 8, 1912. In an interview between Albert Antébi and the editor of *Ha-Ḥerut*, Haim Ben-'Atar, it appears that some officials (of the AIU and ICA at least) pulled their support for Moyal's meeting once Antébi indicated his own disinterest in the meeting. *Ha-Ḥerut*, September 2, 1912.

118. From "Mikhtav ḥozer el ha-adonim ha-yakarim uha-nechbadim" (January–February 1911), quoted in Roi, "Nisyonoteihem shel ha-mosdot ha-Ẓiyonim," 222. *Ha-Ḥerut*, February 8, 1912.

119. *Ha-Ḥerut*, November 18, 1912. See also the society's notices on December 8, 1912; and January 3, 1913.

120. *Ha-Ḥerut*, December 27, 1912.

121. Ram, *Ha-yishuv ha-Yehudi*, 262–63; Elkayam, *Yafo-Neve Ẓedek*.

122. "To the Hebrew Nation in the Lands of Its Dispersion," by Avraham Elmaliach, no date, in Hebrew. TAMA, file 8, folder 729. Nissim Malul is said to have burned all of the group's paperwork while fleeing the iron arm of Cemal Pasha during World War I. This copy survived in the files of the Sephardi chief rabbi for Jaffa, Rabbi 'Uziel.

123. Nissim Malul was the paid translator and main propagandist for the Zionist movement from 1911 to 1914. December 17, 1911, CZA, L2/26I; Yeshivat ha-va'da le-'itonut 'Aravit, January 14, 1912, CZA L2/167.

Chapter Five: Shared Urban Spaces

Part of Chapter Five first appeared in "Freemasonry in Ottoman Palestine," *Jerusalem Quarterly File* 22–23 (Fall–Winter 2005): 37–62.

1. *Ha-Ẓvi*, October 9, 1908.

2. ISA 67, peh/533:1491. Unless otherwise noted, quoted passages come from the pamphlet.

3. Gerber states that the Jerusalem General Council was not actually established until 1913, although al-Namura lists the members of a 1911 council. Gerber, *Ottoman Rule in Jerusalem*, 136; and Al-Namura, *Al-Filastiniyun*, 197. There is evidence that a general council existed in Gaza, Jaffa, Bi'r al-Sab'a, Hebron, and Nablus as well. See Abu Khadra, "Bayan," Arab Studies Society (Jerusalem); and Al-Namura, *Al-Filastiniyun*, 196. For studies of urban civic consciousness in this period in other corners of the empire, see Hanssen, *Fin de Siècle Beirut*; and Alexandra Yerolympos, "Conscience citadine et intérêt municipal."

4. Gerber, *Ottoman Rule in Jerusalem*, 126.

5. Ex officio members included the governor, the *qadi*, the mufti, the provincial treasurer, and official representatives of the Greek Orthodox, Latin, Armenian, and Jewish communities.

6. These were established in: Jerusalem (mid-1860s), Nablus (1867), Nazareth (1875), Haifa (by 1883), Jaffa, 'Akka, Gaza (by 1893), Lydda, Ramle, Hebron, Shefa-'Amr, Safad, Tabaria (Tiberias), Beisan, Tulkarem, Jenin, Majdal, Khan Yunis, Bi'r al-Sab'a, Ramallah, Beit Jala, and Bethlehem. Al-Namura, *Al-Filastiniyun*, 119.

7. The city council had ten seats, five of which were elected every two years for a four-year term. Males over age twenty-five who paid 50 *kuruş* in property taxes were eligible to vote, whereas those who paid over 150 *kuruş* were eligible to run for election. Ha-Va'ad le-hoẓa'at kitvei David Yellin, *Kitvei David Yellin*, 193–94, 222–23. See also Avci, *Değişim sürecinde*.

8. Kark, "Jerusalem Municipality at the End of Ottoman Rule"; and Kark, "P'eilut 'iriyat Yerushalayim," 80. See also Yehoshu'a, *Yerushalayim tmol shilshom*, for interesting cases of municipal involvement; N. Levi, *Prakim be toldot ha-refuah be-Ereẓ Israel*, on the municipal hospital and public health services; and Yazbak, *Haifa in the Late Ottoman Period*, for the municipality in Haifa.

9. For information on the social services projects of the municipality, see Avci, *Değişim sürecinde*, 238–42. On the twins, see *Ha-Ḥerut*, January 21, 1910.

10. Yehoshu'a, *Yerushalayim tmol shilshom*, 20–21.

11. Ibid., 19.

12. Ha-Va'ad le-hoẓa'at kitvei David Yellin, *Kitvei David Yellin*, 103, 224. Also *Ha-Ḥerut*, December 1, 1909.

13. Al-Madani, *Madinat al-Quds*, 43–51. No historical evidence of these neighborhood councils survives.

14. *Filasṭīn* had a regular police blotter column, "akhbār dā'irat al-būlīs." For the context and background of antivagrancy measures in the Ottoman Empire, see Ergut, "Policing the Poor in the Late Ottoman Empire"; *Ha-Ḥerut*, June 22, 29, 1909; *El Liberal*, June 29, 1909.

15. *Ha-Ḥerut*, August 11, 1909; October 25, 1909; January 14, 1910; May 11, 1910; January 20, 1911; January 30, 1911; March 3, 1911; *El Liberal*, October 29, 1909; *Ha-Ẓvi*, October 22, 1908.

16. *Ha-Ḥerut*, November 3, 1909; and November 14, 1910. Another report noted that the government had demanded the chief rabbi notify the Jewish residents of the town not to throw trash in the streets and not to throw water on pedestrian walkways. *Ha-Ḥerut*, October 17, 1910.

17. See, for example, *Ha-Ḥerut*, December 6, 1909; the three-part article "The Economy of Ereẓ-Israel," in *Ha-Ḥerut*, May 18, June 21 and 29, 1909; *Al-Quds*, January 26, 1909; *Filasṭīn*, July 1, 1910; *Ha-Ḥerut*, January 18, 1911.

18. *Ha-Ḥerut*, December 28, 1910; February 25, 1913; *Ha-Ẓvi*, January 21, 1909; "moving pictures" were advertised in *Al-Quds*, November 17 and December 18, 1908; *Ha-Ḥerut*, February 23, 1913. For example the Temperance Society founded by Mitri Damian, reported in *Al-Quds*, November 17, 1908. The establishment of a café at the railroad station was announced in *Ha-Hashkafa*, September 11, 1908. *Al-Quds* praised the establishment of a Society for the Protection of Animals, which purchased thousands of copies of *Al-Jawad al-Adham*, a book that teaches children to be kind to animals, for distribution in the schools. Yehoshu'a, *Yerushalayim tmol shilshom*, 126–27.

19. *Ha-Ḥerut*, January 9, 1911; *Ha-Ḥerut*, July 29, 1910.

20. *Ha-Ẓvi*, November 6, 1908.

21. *Ha-Ḥerut*, December 14, 1910.

22. *Ha-Ḥerut*, August 2, 1909; *Al-Munādī*, July 15, 1912.

23. *Al-Quds*, August 24, 1909, quoted in Yehoshu'a, *Yerushalayim tmol shilshom*, 108–9. Unfortunately I have not been able to locate many of the issues of *Al-Quds* that Yehoshu'a cites.

24. *Filasṭīn*, August 16, 1911, quoted in ibid., 35; *Filasṭīn*, November 11, 1911, quoted in ibid., 56, 59–60.

25. *Ha-Ẓvi*, November 11, 1908; January 20, 1909.

26. See also *Ha-Ḥerut*, July 18, 1910; January 13, 1911.

27. *Ha-Ḥerut*, November 18, 1910.

28. *Al-Munādī*, April 30, 1912, quoted in Yehoshu'a, *Yerushalayim tmol shilshom*, 109.

29. *Al-Munādī*, March 19, 1912.

30. August 10, 1910. CZA A153/143; emphasis mine.

31. Kudüs-ü Şerif tijaret sanaet ve-ziraat odası. Some sources claim that a Chamber of Commerce existed in Jerusalem in 1905, but I have not been able to uncover more information about it. Polus, "Kalkalat Yerushalayim." For information on the early years of the Jaffa chamber, see al-Tawarnah, "Qada Jaffa."

32. Antébi to AIU (Paris), December 24, 1908. AAIU, Israel-IX.E.26. A news report from the time states that half of the members of the Jerusalem branch were Jews, which would have been very possible given the demographic basis of Jerusalem. *Ha-Po'el ha-Ẓa'ir*, December 1908. Unfortunately we have no comprehensive list of the chamber's members, but one issue of the chamber's monthly bulletin listed new members. *Bulletin de la Chambre de commerce d'industrie et d'agriculture de Palestine* (year 1, no. 6, December 1909; Jerusalem). JMA, box

1779. The dues were reportedly four to twelve dollars annually. In local terms this was between 116 and 348 *kuruş*, a sizable sum. J. Hardegg (Jaffa) to S. Edelman (American vice-consul in charge, Jerusalem), December 6, 1913; NACP, correspondence 1913 IV, general correspondence, 1912–35, Jerusalem Consulate (350/26/11/1–2), records of the foreign service posts of the Department of State, record group 84. Brill, an employee of the ICA, paid 42.20 francs for his annual dues in 1909. CZA, J15/6090.

33. The Jerusalem officers of the chamber of commerce were Hajj Yusuf Wafa (president), Albert Antébi (vice-president), Selim Ayoub (secretary), and assessors Isma'il Husayni, David Taher, and Jacob Tagger—three Jews, two Muslims, and one Christian. In Jaffa, the officers were Mahmud al-Bizre (president), Saleh Kinge Ahmet (vice-president), and committee members Darwish Chehab al-Din, George Abu Goss, Nejuib Beiruti, Nassri Talamas, and Daoud Mizrachi—three Muslims, three Christians, and one Jew. J. Hardegg (Jaffa) to S. Edelman (American vice-consul charge, Jerusalem), December 11, 1913; NACP, correspondence 1913 IV, general correspondence, 1912–35, Jerusalem Consulate (350/26/11/1–2), records of the foreign service posts of the Department of State, record group 84.

34. J. Hardegg (Jaffa) to S. Edelman (American vice-consul in charge, Jerusalem), December 6, 1913; NACP, correspondence 1913 IV, general correspondence, 1912–35, Jerusalem Consulate (350/26/11/1–2), records of the foreign service posts of the Department of State, record group 84. See also al-Tawarnah, "Qada Jaffa," 159.

35. Antébi to Aharon Eisenberg (Reḥovot), July 29, 1909. AAIU, Israel-IX.E.27; *Bulletin de la Chambre de commerce d'industrie et d'agriculture de Palestine* (year 1, no. 6, December 1909; Jerusalem). JMA, box 1779.

36. *Bulletin de la Chambre de commerce d'industrie et d'agriculture de Palestine* (year 2, nos. 8–9, August–September 1910; Jerusalem). JMA, box 1779. The chamber noted that the commercial court had been discontinued five to six years prior "for reasons unknown to us."

37. Haifa was linked up to the Hijaz Railroad, but there was public pressure to expand it to provide local transportation to link up 'Akka and Afula via Nazareth, and Afula and Ramle via Nablus. See *Ha-Ḥerut*, November 21, 1910, and letter from Haifa-'Akka French Consulate to Paris, August 16, 1911. Box 430, MAEF. It seems there was also a train between Haifa and 'Akka, which stopped in Balad al-Shaykh—the total trip time was two hours. Letter from Haifa/'Akka French Consulate to Paris, September 23, 1913. Box 430, MAEF. On the intracity trams, see Constantinople Embassy of France to French Foreign Ministry (Paris), May 31, 1909; MAEF, microfilm roll 132, Correspondence Politique et Commerciale/Nouvelle Série (Turquie); September 21, 1909. ISA 67, peh/456:474.

38. See Ben-Arieh, *Jerusalem in the 19th Century*.

39. *Bulletin de la Chambre de commerce d'industrie et d'agriculture de Palestine* (year 1, nos. 3–4, September–October 1909). ISA 67, peh/456:473.

40. Its members consisted of the mufti Kamel al-Husayni; the engineer Nazif al-Khalidi; Wasfi, the city's public works engineer; Mahmud Ragheb al-Husayni, secretary of finances; as well as 'Ali Jaralla, notary; Selim Ayoub, bank director;

and Albert Antébi, director of the AIU vocational school. Committee report reproduced in *Bulletin de la Chambre de commerce d'industrie et d'agriculture de Palestine* (year 1, nos. 3–4, September–October 1909). ISA 67, peh/456:473. The original is in CZA L51/6.

41. Société commerciale de Palestine à Jerusalem, *Statuts*.

42. The bank also had to submit their balance to the grand Vizierate, the Ministry of Commerce, and the local government. Gueyrand to Pichon, July 24, 1909; MAEF, microfilm roll 132, Correspondence Politique et Commerciale/ Nouvelle Série (Turquie). For the political mission of the organization, see also Levontin and Ruppin to Wolffsohn, January 17, 1909. CZA L1/119. For the Young Turks' economic nationalism see Ahmad, "Vanguard of a Nascent Bourgeoisie." However, I disagree with Ahmad's characterization of the non-Muslim bourgeoisie as "compradors" and his assumption that they saw their interests as lying with Europe, not with the Ottoman Empire.

43. Gueyrand to Pichon, July 22, 1909; MAEF, microfilm roll 132, Correspondence Politique et Commerciale/Nouvelle Série (Turquie). See Levontin and Ruppin to Wolffsohn, January 17, 1909. CZA L1/119. See also *Ha-Ḥerut*, *Ha-Po'el ha-Ẓa'ir*, December 1908.

44. For a sample share agreement see file 44/1,57/?/12, Institute for the Revival of Islamic Research and Heritage, Abu Dis (Jerusalem). The BCP aimed to raise 566,750 francs by selling individual and investor shares locally. They reported that the shares were sold at forty-five to fifty francs per share. Letter from David Levontin and Arthur Ruppin (APC) to David Wolffsohn (Cologne), January 17, 1909. CZA L1/119. See also January 6, 1909, Anglo-Palestine Bank report. AAIU, Israel-IX.E.26.

45. Société commerciale de Palestine à Jerusalem, *Statuts*.

46. *Ha-Ḥerut*, September 10, 1909; *El Liberal*, September 24, 1909; Polus, "Kalkalat Yerushalayim"; NACP, May–June 1912 C; general correspondence, 1912–35, Jerusalem Consulate (350/26/11/1–2), records of the foreign service posts of the Department of State, record group 84; NACP, miscellaneous correspondence, January–March 1912 A, general correspondence, 1912–35, Jerusalem Consulate (350/26/11/1–2), records of the foreign service posts of the Department of State, record group 84.

47. Levontin and Ruppin to Wolffsohn, January 17, 1909. CZA L1/119; and Gueyrand to Pichon, July 22, 1909; MAEF, microfilm roll 132, Correspondence Politique et Commerciale/Nouvelle Série (Turquie).

48. Gueyrand to Pichon, July 27, 1909; MAEF, microfilm roll 132, Correspondence Politique et Commerciale/Nouvelle Série (Turquie). "Projet-contrat présenté par la Banque commerciale de Palestine, approuvé par le Conseil administratif avec certains amendements" and "Mazbata du Conseil Administratif," published in the *Bulletin de la Chambre de commerce d'industrie et d'agriculture de Palestine* (year 1, nos. 3–4, September–October 1909). ISA 67, peh/456:473.

49. "Examen du contrat," published in *Bulletin de la Chambre de commerce d'industrie et d'agriculture de Palestine* (year 1, nos. 3–4, September–October 1909). ISA 67, peh/456:473.

50. Ibid.

51. From Sélim Ayoub and Yéroham Elyachar to the Jerusalem governor, in "Réquête-soumission de la Banque-comerciale de Palestine," published in the *Bulletin de la Chambre de commerce d'industrie et d'agriculture de Palestine* (year 1, nos. 3–4, September–October 1909). ISA 67, peh/456:473.

52. For an overview of the exchanges in *La Vérité*, see *Bulletin de la Chambre de commerce d'industrie et d'agriculture de Palestine*, August–September 1910, JMA 1779.

53. A contract was signed between the BCP and the APC in the fall of 1909, outlining the rate of return the APC expected. September 27, 1909. CZA L51/6. In a later memo, representatives of the BCP agreed to the APC's condition of raising the sale price of water to 1.50 francs or at least 1.25 francs, making it competitive with the Franck concession but also undermining the BCP's earlier commitment to low-cost water for the city's residents. CZA L51/6.

54. Letter to Jacobus Kann (the Hague), February 2, 1914. CZA L51/6.

55. Levontin and Ruppin to Wolffsohn, January 17, 1909; and Levontin and Ruppin to Wolfssohn, January 27, 1909. CZA L1/119. Wolfssohn to Ruppin, February 2, 1909. CZA Z2/633.

56. November 13, 1908. CZA L1/119.

57. *Al-Karmil*, September 28, 1912; and October 5, 1912.

58. *Ha-Ẓvi*, March 2, 1909. A rift between Yitzhak Levi, officer of the Jerusalem branch of the APB, and Antébi led to a break between the APB and BCP on personal and political grounds. Antébi to AIU, July 18, 1909. AAIU, Israel-IX.E.27. In public the APB was rejected because of its nature as a Zionist institution, with the Bank of Salonica favored to back the BCP. Gueyrand to Pichon, July 22, 1909; MAEF, microfilm roll 132, Correspondence Politique et Commerciale/Nouvelle Série (Turquie).

59. From APC-Jerusalem to Kann, September 12, 1909. CZA L51/6; *Ha-Ḥerut*, November 2, 1910. By April 1911 the ministry reversed itself and authorized the municipality to seek a tramways concession. April 1911; ISA 67, peh/456:474; CZA A153/143.

60. May 20, 1914. CZA L51/6. The Arabic announcement states "abnā' al-waṭan." The French translation of the announcement describes the reserves for "our co-citizens and friends." February 10, 1914. File 44/1,57/?/12, Institute for the Revival of Islamic Research and Heritage, Abu Dis (Jerusalem). Despite its inability to secure the water concession, the BCP remained busy pursuing concessions for building telephone lines, bringing running water from the Audja River to Jaffa, and mining phosphates from the Dead Sea. APC Memo, November 7, 1913. CZA L51/6.

61. Line 1: through Jaffa Gate to Souk et Allor, the bazaar of the Jewish quarter. Line 2: Jaffa Gate, Me'ah She'arim, Ecole Schneller, Shaykh Badr, Municipal Hospital, Jaffa Gate. Line 3: Jaffa Gate east to Nicofarieh, New Palace. Line 4: Jaffa Gate to Bethlehem. Line 5: Jaffa Gate to the Mount of Olives. Line 6: Jaffa Gate to Saint Croix and Shaykh Badr. President of the city council, CZA, A153/143.

62. Copy of the Arabic conditions for the Jaffa concessions, CZA L51/6.

63. Chelouche, *Parshat Ḥayai*.

64. Landau, "Farmasūniyya." Landau dates the first Freemason lodges in the Middle East to the mid-eighteenth century (in Aleppo, Izmir, and Corfu in 1738, Alexandretta in the 1740s, and Armenian parts of Eastern Anatolia and Istanbul in the 1760s). However, these were small, uncentralized, and short-lived, and little is known about them beyond their existence. For a history of Ottoman Freemasonry, see also Dumont, "La franc-maçonnerie ottomane"; Zarcone, *Mystiques, philosophes et francs-macons*; and Hanioğlu, "Notes on the Young Turks and the Freemasons."

65. See Wissa, "Freemasonry in Egypt from Bonaparte to Zaghloul"; Cole, *Colonialism and Revolution in the Middle East*; Anduze, "La franc-maçonnerie égyptienne"; and Kudsi-Zadeh, "Afghani and Freemasonry in Egypt." Thierry Zarcone argues that Freemasonry and para-Masonic organizations that merged Sufism, politics, and Masonry played a critical role in the 1905–7 Iranian constitutional revolution as well. Zarcone, "Freemasonry and Related Trends."

66. Quoted by Muhammad Pasha al-Makhzumi, author of *Utterances of Jamal al-Din al-Afghani al-Husayni*, cited in Khuri, *Modern Arab Thought*, 30.

67. Hanioğlu, "Notes on the Young Turks and the Freemasons"; and Dumont, "La franc-maçonnerie d'obédience française," 73. In 1908, for example, the lodge Veritas appealed for protection to the GODF, stating that their lodge archives were under attack from the government, and they feared compromising some of their members. The lodge Macedonia Risorta, protected by the Italian consul, provided immunity from police scrutiny for its many Young Turk activists. See also Jessua, *Grand Orient (Gr: Loge) de Turquie.*

68. Jessua, *Grand Orient (Gr: Loge) de Turquie.* For an extensive discussion of the Grand Orient Ottoman, see Anduze, "La franc-maçonnerie coloniale."

69. Also Vefa orientale, Byzantio risorto. Kedourie, "Young Turks, Freemasons, and Jews"; Dumont, "La franc-maçonnerie d'obédience française," 76.

70. I have found extensive evidence from three Masonic lodges in Palestine in the pre–World War I period: Barkai, Temple of Solomon, and Moriah. There was also an irregular (unrecognized) lodge established by Shim'on Moyal in Jaffa in 1910–11, but aside from a complaint issued by Barkai that Moyal was "initiating people right and left" we know little of this lodge. Letter from Barkai to GODF, February 10, 1911. CDGODF, boxes 1126–27. I have also found reference to a lodge in the north, but little evidence survives. Letter from the vice-consul of France in Haifa to the French foreign minister, February 20, 1912; MAEF, microfilm roll 134, Correspondence Politique et Commerciale/Nouvelle Série (Turquie).

71. Letter from Suleiman (Shlomo) Yellin (Beirut), no date. CZA, A412/13.

72. Grand Orient Ottoman, *Instruction pour le premier grade symbolique.* See also Grand Orient de France, Suprême conseil pour la France et les possessions françaises, *Instruction pour le première grade symbolique.*

73. Isaac Rabeno de Botton, Venerable (president) of the Veritas lodge, to the GODF, October 10, 1910; quoted in Dumont, "La franc-maçonnerie d'obédience française," 77.

74. Jessua, *Grand Orient (Gr: Loge) de Turquie*, 12.

75. Landau, "Farmasūniyya."

76. Dumont, "La franc-maçonnerie ottomane et les "Idées Françaises'"; Dumont, "La franc-maçonnerie dans l'empire Ottoman"; and Hivert-Messeca, "France, laïcité et maçonnerie."

77. In Lebanon, Syria, and Egypt, there was widespread participation of the notable classes in Freemasonry. See Safwat, *Freemasonry in the Arab World.* According to Robert Morris's travelogue from 1876, the then-governor of Syria, deputy-governor of Jaffa, and deputy-governor of Nablus were all Freemasons. Morris, *Freemasonry in the Holy Land.* On the middle-class membership of Egyptian lodges, see Cole, *Colonialism and Revolution in the Middle East.* The perceived elite economic networks of Freemasons also stirred up lower-class opposition, according to Landau, "Muslim Opposition to Freemasonry."

78. On the socioeconomics of Masonry see Dumont, "La franc-maçonnerie d'obédience française"; Dumont, "La franc-maçonnerie dans l'empire Ottoman"; Hivert-Messeca, "France, laïcité et maçonnerie"; and Cole, *Colonialism and Revolution in the Middle East.*

79. Kemal al-Din 'Arafat was the mayor of Nablus, and Rafiq and Suleiman Abu Ghazaleh were both civil judges. Sa'id Abu Khadra' served on the General Council of Gaza and he was also a failed candidate for the 1912 Ottoman parliament. 'Umar al-Bitar was the mayor of Jaffa. Eight members of the Jaffan Dajani family were in the Ottoman legal, municipal, bureaucratic, and educational establishment in addition to being Masons. Among the most prominent of Jerusalem's notable families, four members of the al-Khalidi family were Freemasons. One of them, Jamil al-Khalidi, belonged to two lodges. Ragheb al-Nashashibi, elected to the Ottoman parliament in 1912, also belonged to two lodges.

80. The Amzaleks were a wealthy Jewish family. One of the most important Jerusalem Sephardi families, several Elyashars served as chief rabbi of Jerusalem. The Manis were the most important Jewish family in Hebron. David Moyal was an important lawyer dealing in land sales. Three members of the wealthy Valero banking family were Masons.

81. Nathans, "Habermas's Public Sphere in the Era of the French Revolution," 633.

82. Freemasonry in the colonies and beyond was another face of "humanistic colonialism" which aimed to spread Western ideas of progress, public health, secular education, justice, social laws, solidarity, freedom of opinion, press, and association, and economic and technological development. Among other things, colonial Freemasonry created a social and cultural elite and sought to assimilate the "native" Freemasons to Francophone and European values and culture. See Odo, "Les réseaux coloniaux." On the new middle class, see R. Khalidi, "Society and Ideology in Late Ottoman Syria," 126.

83. Based on those who shared a last name and place of birth; clearly this does not cover matrilineal or marital family ties.

84. *Who's Who: Alumni Association, AUB, 1870–1923.*

85. From the files of various Egyptian Masonic lodges we know that there were periodic Masonic assemblies for networking purposes, and Masons who moved or traveled from one locale to another had a ready network awaiting them. See CZA A192/812.

86. Chelouche, *Parshat Ḥayai*, 194.

87. Garcea later tried to establish another Masonic lodge in Egypt, passing himself off as a Jew and compromising the daughter of a respectable rabbinical family in the process. Frigere to GODF, February 12, 1917. BNR, RES FM2–142.

88. The Barkai lodge secretary in 2000 refused to disclose whether or not the lodge was in possession of archival material from the Ottoman period, but the long-time lodge Venerable Cesar ʿAraktinji reported to the GODF central office after World War I that his home, the former lodge headquarters, had been destroyed during the war. Letter from ʿAraktinji (in Konya) to GODF, January 8, 1919. CDGODF, boxes 1126–27.

89. Letter from ʿAraktinji, July 1913. CDGODF, boxes 1126–27.

90. January 11, 1910. CDGODF, boxes 1126–27.

91. Hafiz Saʿid. ʿAraktinji wrote in a postscript: "We have already written to the Grand Orient Ottoman of all his wretched qualities, especially his election which was by the despotic ways." Letter from Barkai to GODF, November 8, 1909. CDGODF, boxes 1126–27.

92. Letter from ʿAraktinji to GODF, April 7, 1913. CDGODF, boxes 1126–27.

93. March 11, 1913. BNR, RES FM2–142.

94. April 29, 1913. BNR, RES FM2–142.

95. Ibid.

96. They were called "foreigners" despite the fact that all of the Jewish members had been born in Ottoman territories (two in Jerusalem, one in Istanbul, and two in Ottoman Sofia). BNR, RES FM2–142.

97. ʿAraktinji to GODF, April 7, 1913. CDGODF, boxes 1126–27.

98. GODF to ʿAraktinji, April 24, 1913. CDGODF, boxes 1126–27.

99. Although French was the official "liturgical language" of the GODF lodges, Barkai in Jaffa informed Paris headquarters that they were using Arabic for substantive lodge activities, since many members did not know French well enough. A lodge in Egypt (*Les amis du progrès*, Mansura) had translated GODF rites into Arabic, and Barkai was using these translations in their work along with a summary in French. Letter from ʿAraktinji to GODF, May 19, 1911. CDGODF, boxes 1126–27.

100. ʿAraktinji to GODF, June 24, 1913. CDGODF, boxes 1126–27. Frigere was an employee of the Ottoman Imperial Bank, which was partly French-owned. ʿAraktinji seems to have assumed that the GODF Paris headquarters could intervene with the central bank administration to have Frigere transferred.

101. Frigere to GODF, June 27, 1913. BNR, RES FM2–142. This letter quoted in Sabah, "La loge Moriah," 70–74.

102. Ibid.

103. ʿAraktinji to GODF, July 24, 1914. CDGODF, boxes 1126–27.

104. Ibid.

105. Sabah, "La loge Moriah."

106. According to Moriah, "this [concessionary society], which appears at first to be commercial, is on the contrary a primarily secular work and we greatly await it. It should be known indeed that the secular French population is excessively restricted in Jerusalem," most of them being Freemasons. "The

rest of the population is composed of religious of all orders." Moriah to GODF, October 2, 1913. BNR, RES FM2–142. In 1912 Henry Frigere had written to the French government proposing the establishment of a French concessionary society along the model of the Société commerciale de Palestine, established by Jerusalem's notables of all three religions. See Frigere letter of May 17, 1912. BNR, RES FM2–142.

107. In the study submitted by Moriah lodge member Nissim Farhi (director of the AIU primary school in Jerusalem), there were twenty schools from six religions or denominations and five different nationalities serving ten thousand children in Jerusalem. June 19, 1913. BNR, RES FM2–142. A report in *El Liberal* claimed there were seventy-three schools in Jerusalem, no doubt including in their count the many traditional religious schools. *El Liberal*, April 23, 1909.

108. Quoted in Sabah, "La loge Moriah."

109. October 18, 1913. BNR, RES FM2–142.

110. February 10, 1914. BNR, RES FM2–142. On the Alexandrian Masons, see the file CZA, A192/812. See also CZA, A192/816, in particular the November 1910 meeting of the L'Assemblée maçonique de la neutralité scolaire et des études laïques. In Lebanon the Freemasons of Le Liban lodge argued that confessional education promoted the "division of the country, intolerance, and the perpetuation of religious hatred."

111. Moriah to GODF, May 25, 1914. BNR, RES FM2–142.

112. GODF to Frigere, June 11, 1914. BNR, RES FM2–142. This statement was crossed out in the original letter, perhaps considered too brash or stating the obvious.

113. See David Tidhar, *Barkai*; and Tidhar, *Sefer he-aḥim.*

Chapter Six: Ottomans of the Mosaic Faith

An earlier version of Chapter Six was published as "Between 'Beloved Ottomania' and 'The Land of Israel': The Struggle over Ottomanism and Zionism Among Palestine's Sephardi Jews, 1908–13," *International Journal of Middle East Studies*, 37, no. 4 (November 2005): 461–83. Copyright Cambridge University Press. Reprinted with permission.

1. *La Tribuna Libera*, November 11, 1910; and November 25, 1910. The newspaper published the various responses it received from Jewish leaders and laymen alike over the next several months. The initial poll was republished in *Ha-Ḥerut*, December 2, 1910.

2. See Benbassa, "Zionism and Local Politics"; Rodrigue, *French Jews, Turkish Jews*; and Stein, *Making Jews Modern.*

3. Much of the scholarship of Sephardi and Middle Eastern Jewry has been nationalized and mobilized for the Zionist movement and sees Middle Eastern Jews as "strangers" in their countries of origin. See Stillman, *Sephardi Responses to Modernity*; and Betzalel, "Prolegomena to Sephardi and Oriental Zionism"; see also Benbassa's sharp critique in the same issue.

4. For example, see *Ha-Ḥerut*, August 19, 1910.

5. Kayalı, "Jewish Representation in the Ottoman Parliaments," 511.

6. For an account of the reaction of the Jews in Istanbul, see Benbassa, "Les 'Jeunes Turcs' et les Juifs."

7. In the 1905 Ottoman census in Jerusalem, 5,500 Ashkenazi Jews were counted as Ottoman nationals (41 percent of the 13,687 Ottoman Jews of Jerusalem). Schmelz, "Population of Jerusalem's Urban Neighborhoods."

8. Frumkin, *Derekh shofet bi-Yerushalayim*, 146. See also *Ha-Po'el ha-Ẓa'ir*, July–August 1908.

9. *Ha-'Olam*, September 4, 1909; *Ha-Hashkafa*, August 9, 1908.

10. CAHJP, IL/Sa/IX/14.

11. *Ha-Po'el ha-Ẓa'ir*, July–August 1908.

12. Antébi to Henri Franck, September 28, 1908. AAIU IX.E.25.

13. CZA, A412/41.

14. *Ha-Ḥerut*, May 21, 1909. The journalist reporting on the society complained that its protocols were kept in Arabic.

15. Ruppin, August 8, 1908. CZA L2/49I; *Ha-Po'el ha-Ẓa'ir*, July–August 1908.

16. Such was the sentiment expressed in numerous articles in the Zionist press; for example, "The Current Situation in Turkey [*sic*] and the Jews," by Dr. D. Pasmiak, *Ha-'Olam*, September 7, 1909.

17. "Assimilation in Turkey [*sic*]," *Ha-'Olam*, December 4, 1908. A later assessment by Dr. Shim'on Bernfeld sought to reassure the readers (and leadership) that Ottoman Jews would not "sell their Judaism" by participating in Ottoman life; instead, he saw them as "natural nationalists." "Sephardi Jews in the East," in *Ha-'Olam*, March 10, 1909. An article in the Sephardi journal *Ha-Ḥerut* denounced Bernfeld's study as "superficial." *Ha-Ḥerut*, December 22, 1912.

18. *Ha-Po'el ha-Ẓa'ir*, July–August 1908. Levi was the head of the Anglo-Palestine Bank branch in Jerusalem.

19. Kolatt, "Organization of the Jewish Population." Kolatt mistakenly argues that the entire pro-Zionist *yishuv* in this period was "strategically" Ottoman, choosing to conceal their Zionist aims for a long-term strategy. This was certainly the strategy adopted by the WZO, as detailed in Weiner, "Ha-mediniyut ha-Ẓiyonit be-Turkiya," but it does not accurately apply to the Sephardi and Maghrebi communities, even the Zionists among them.

20. *Ha-Po'el ha-Ẓa'ir*, July–August 1908. On the problems with the immigrants' foreign citizenship, see: Jacobsohn to Wolffsohn, November 8, 1909. CZA Z2/8.

21. While there are no reliable statistics for Jewish immigration and settlement in this period, it seems that annually approximately two thousand Jews arrived in Palestine intending to stay. According to the German Consulate in Jaffa, in 1907 there were 1,746 immigrants, while in 1908 there were 2,097, half of whom were from Lithuania and south Russia. The consulate claimed that only 247 of these immigrants went to the Jewish colonies. See Rössler report, no date. ISA 67, peh/455:462. *Ha-Ḥerut* published similar statistics, with a sizable increase in immigrants in 1909 (2,459), of whom only 88 went to the Jewish colonies. See *Ha-Ḥerut*, February 23, 1910. According to Ḥovevei Ẓion (the Odessa-based Zionist organization), the number of Zionist immigrants (cumulative) was

10,986. Ḥovevei Ẓion figures also estimate that around 20 percent of immigrants turned around and went back home annually. *Ha-Ḥerut*, May 30, 1910.

22. *Ha-'Olam*, July 29, 1908.

23. *Ha-Hashkafa*, August 9, 1908. See also the appeals in *Ha-Ẓvi*, January 12 and 18, 1909, as well as the rebuttal by Barzilai that he was keeping his foreign citizenship. *Ha-Ẓvi*, January 21, 1909.

24. *Ha-Hashkafa*, August 7, 1908.

25. *Ha-Ẓvi*, January 21, 1909.

26. By the eve of World War I, the Palestine Office did not have complete statistics on the citizenship of Zionist settlers, but it used the number of eligible voters in the Ottoman elections as a standard of measurement: approximately 250 Ottoman citizens in six Judean colonies, another 50 Yemenites in five colonies, and virtually all of the ICA (Rothschild-funded) settlers in the Galilee. PO to Jacobus Kann, April 30, 1913. CZA Z3/1449.

27. By 1909, two more figures who would become central in Zionist (and Israeli) history—Menachem Ussishkin and Vladimir Jabotinsky—were sent to work in the Istanbul office. *Ha-Ḥerut*, August 23, 1909.

28. By 1907, however, an internal memorandum indicated that the Zionist movement felt this was unrealistic given the demographics of Palestine; the best they could hope for would be partial autonomy, preferably over part of Judea and Tiberias. Memorandum of the Future Zionist Work in Palestine, November 1907. CZA H148/34.

29. Zionist Central Office to Ruppin, September 15, 1908. CZA L2/26I. For more on Ekrem Bey's report and attitudes toward the Zionist movement, see Kushner, *Moshel hayiti bi-Yerushalayim*.

30. August 8, 1909. CZA Z2/1.

31. "The New Situation in Turkey [*sic*]," by Vladimir Jabotinsky, *Ha-'Olam*, February 2, 1909.

32. One of these important figures in the capital was Isaac Fernandez, the AIU and ICA representative in Istanbul said to have good ties with high-ranking Muslims and Christians. Jacobsohn to Wolffsohn, September 10, 1908. CZA A19/7. Another prominent Jew was Nachmias Bey, the dragoman of the Ottoman Imperial Bank who was a close friend of the Minister of Interior Hakkı Pasha; in the case of Nachmias Bey it was a lost cause, for he was adamantly against Zionism. Jacobsohn to Wolffsohn, October 6, 1908. CZA Z2/7.

33. Zionistische Zentralburo to Mazliach and Russo, January 24, 1909. CZA Z2/7. As Weiner affirms, this was a deliberate "camouflaging" of the long-term ambitions of the Zionist movement. Weiner, "Ha-mediniyut ha-Ẓiyonit be-Turkiya," 268 and 274.

34. Jacobsohn to Wolffsohn, January 14, 1909. CZA Z2/7.

35. Wolffsohn to Mazliach and Russo, early 1909. CZA A19/7.

36. December 31, 1908. CZA Z2/7.

37. Rıza Tevfik Bey and Enver Bey were deemed to be sympathetic, whereas Nâzım Bey was very nervous about the idea of concentrating Jews in Palestine. Jacobsohn to Wolffsohn, February 12, 1909. Jacobsohn to Wolffsohn, February 15, 1909. CZA Z2/7. In a meeting with the Baghdad MP Ezekiel Sasson,

Mazliach ascertained that he was anti-Zionist. "The difficulty with Mr. Sasson is that he seems to be to be an Arab patriot." Cited in Jacobsohn to Wolffsohn, February 22, 1909. CZA Z2/7.

38. Jacobsohn to Wolffsohn, March 10, 1909. CZA A19/7.

39. Weiner, "Ha-mediniyut ha-Ẓiyonit be-Turkiya," 276. For example in 1909 Wolffsohn met with Ahmed Rıza. *Ha-Ḥerut*, August 25, 1909.

40. *El Liberal*, July 30, 1909. Also see Nahum Sokolow, "The Jews of Turkey [*sic*] and Zionism," *Ha-Ḥerut*, January 17, 1910, for European Zionism's official expectations of Ottoman Jewry.

41. Interview with Avraham Elmaliach, Oral History Project, Institute for Contemporary Jewry, Hebrew University of Jerusalem, December 17, 1963. For early discussion in the Sephardi press about the possibility and desirability of reviving Hebrew, see Romero, *La creación literaria en lengua sefardí.*

42. In addition to the extensive work of Esther Benbassa on Istanbul, see also reports in *Ha-Ḥerut*, August 11, 1909, and September 3, 1909; on Salonica: *Ha-Ḥerut*, May 25, 1909, and June 8, 1909; on Izmir: *El Liberal*, May 7, 1909, and June 11, 1909; *Ha-Ḥerut*, July 14, 1909. In addition see "The Hebrew Renaissance in Damascus," *Ha-Ḥerut*, April 13, 1913. Benbassa argues elsewhere that the Zionist focus on populist themes contributed to its appeal in the Balkans. Benbassa, "Zionism in the Ottoman Empire."

43. For example, a complaint that there was only a single Sephardi present at a conference of Hebrew culture. *Ha-Ḥerut*, February 9, 1910. Complaints also abounded that Hebrew (national) life in Beirut, Damascus, Aleppo, and Egypt was nonexistent; see Ruppin to ZAC, May 30, 1913. CZA Z3/1449; *Ha-Po'el ha-Ẓa'ir*, December 1909. As a corrective measure Nissim Malul envisioned translating Theodor Herzl's Zionist utopian novel *Altneuland* into Arabic, and the Palestine Office sent the Sephardi chief rabbi of Jaffa on a propaganda tour in greater Syria in 1913. Thon to ZAC, August 21, 1913, CZA Z3/1450; Ruppin to ZAC, June 6, 1912, CZA, Z3/1448. See also Bessemer, "Ottoman Jewry and the 1908 Revolution."

44. Michael Laskier has referred to the local commitment of Albert Antébi as "pro-palestinienne." See Laskier, "Avraham Albert 'Antebi."

45. *El Liberal*, February 5, 1909.

46. Lecture by Celal Nuri Bey, editor of *Jeune Turc*, to the Young Jews' club in Istanbul. *Ha-Ḥerut*, November 19, 1909. On Imrulla Bey, see *Ha-Ḥerut*, March 21, 1910. For an overview of Ottoman officials' attitudes toward Zionism, see Landau, "He'arot 'al yeḥasam shel ha-Turkim ha-Ẓe'irim la-Ẓiyonut." See also Olson, "Young Turks and the Jews"; and Reinkowski, "Late Ottoman Rule over Palestine" for historiographic comments.

47. *Ha-Ḥerut*, July 30, 1909 and June 8, 1909. Rıza Tevfik studied at the Alliance Israélite Universelle in Edirne and was said to speak Judeo-Spanish like a Sephardi Jew. *Ha-'Olam*, March 3, 1909; March 17, 1909; and May 4, 1909, for a sympathetic account.

48. Hanioğlu, "Jews in the Young Turk Movement to the 1908 Revolution," 523; and Ortayli, "Ottomanism and Zionism During the Second Constitutional Period, 532. However, Neville Mandel quotes an internal Zionist report from

the fall of 1908 that worried the opposite: "[The Young Turks] consider us as separatists, if not today, then at any rate tomorrow. And they do not wish to let people enter [Palestine] who 'will create a new Armenian question' for them." Quoted in Mandel, *Arabs and Zionism Before World War I*, 60.

49. *Ha-Ḥerut*, July 30, 1909.

50. Quoted in Kayalı, "Jewish Representation in the Ottoman Parliaments," 513.

51. *El Liberal*, May 14, 1909.

52. *Ha-Ḥerut*, June 25, 1909.

53. *El Liberal*, August 27, 1909 and September 3, 1909.

54. *Ha-Ḥerut*, July 6, 1909.

55. As early as March 1909 the Zionist movement had sought to schedule the Ninth Zionist Congress in Istanbul, but it had been told that it was "not advisable" and that the sultan would be very opposed. Jacobsohn to Wolffsohn, March 2, 1909. CZA A19/7. On the CUP's retaliation, see Farhi, "Documents on the Attitude of the Ottoman Government," 198. Jacob Landau wrote that one delegate from Salonica, Moshe Cohen, gave a speech at the congress more in favor of Ottomanism than Zionism; by 1910–11, Cohen, fearing that Zionism would harm Ottomanism and bring anti-Semitism in its wake, had moved further from Zionist tenets. Landau, "He'arot 'al yeḥasam shel ha-Turkim ha-Ẓe'irim la-Ẓiyonut."

56. *El Liberal*, May 28, 1909.

57. *El Liberal*, June 11, 1909, and no. 32 (June 1909).

58. "First Know, Then Speak," *El Liberal*, September 10, 1909. See Qattan, "Himnos a Zion" in *El Liberal*, June 11, 1909.

59. *Ha-Ḥerut*, September 28, 1909.

60. *Ha-Ḥerut*, January 5, 1910.

61. *Ha-Po'el ha-Ẓa'ir*, November 1908. See also "On the Agenda/'Al haperek" in *Ha-Po'el ha-Ẓa'ir*, July–August 1908.

62. *Ha-Ḥerut*, December 30, 1910.

63. *El Liberal*, February 5, 1909.

64. "We Are Waiting," by Haim Ben-'Atar, *El Liberal*, October 22, 1909.

65. *Ha-Ḥerut*, December 26, 1910.

66. Stein, "Creation of Yiddish and Judeo-Spanish Newspaper Cultures," 117–18.

67. *Ha-Ḥerut*, November 19, 1909.

68. "*El Tiempo* and Zionism: Part A," in *Ha-Ḥerut*, January 19, 1910.

69. Fresco, *Le Sionisme*. Fresco had accused the Zionist youth group in Istanbul, the Ancient Maccabeans, of being "traitors" to the empire. In response, the Maccabeans sued Fresco in Ottoman court for defamation and incitement. *Ha-Ḥerut*, November 21, 1910. After appearing in court in Pera, the judge decided that since Fresco had not signed the article in question and since he was not the editor responsible for the newspaper, he could not be tried for libel. From *Ha-Mevasser*, cited in *Ha-Ḥerut*, November 25, 1910.

70. He agreed to print all articles he received provided they were "suitable to the unity of Turkey [*sic*]." *Ha-Ḥerut*, November 26, 1909. Jacobsohn to

Wolffsohn, November 7, 1908. CZA A19/7; Jacobsohn to Wolffsohn, October 30, 1908. CZA Z2/7.

71. *Ha-Ḥerut*, December 1, 1909. This account was taken from *El Tiempo*. In the three parliaments of the Second Constitutional Period, there were five Jewish members cumulative, all members of the CUP: Emmanuel Carasso (Salonica), Vitaly Faraji (Istanbul), Victor Corbasi (Istanbul), Ezekiel Sasson (Baghdad), and Nissim Mazliach (Izmir).

72. *Ha-Ḥerut*, December 27, 1909.

73. *El Liberal*, November 19, 1909. On the Chief Rabbi's position, see Victor Jacobsohn to Wolffsohn, November 10, 1909. CZA A19/7. In September 1910, Jacobson asked the chief rabbi to publicly declare that Zionism had no separatist tendencies, but he refused.

74. Istanbul Zionist Office to Wolffsohn, February 15, 1910. CZA Z2/9. According to Weiner, Wolffsohn rebuffed Jacobsohn's demands to recall the book and publicly denounce Kann. See Weiner, "Ha-mediniyut ha-Ẓiyonit be-Turkiya," 288.

75. Istanbul Zionist Office to Wolffsohn, February 15, 1910. CZA Z2/9. Emphasis mine.

76. *Ha-Ḥerut*, November 23, 1910.

77. *Ha-Ḥerut*, November 30, 1910.

78. *Ha-Ḥerut*'s answer was "to spit in their faces." *Ha-Ḥerut*, December 9, 1910. See also "Echoes of Fresco's Slander in Tunis," *Ha-Ḥerut*, February 27, 1911.

79. *Ha-Ḥerut*, December 7 and December 21, 1910.

80. "The Turkish Press and Zionism," *Ha-Ḥerut*, January 21, 1910. The paper cited articles against Zionism that had appeared in the past week in the Turkish language papers *İkdam*, *İtilaf*, and *Sabah*.

81. From Fresco to Jacobsohn, January 5, 1911. CZA Z2/10.

82. *Ha-Ḥerut*, December 7 and December 30, 1910. Similar calls in 1909 by *La Nacion* for an Ottoman Jewish congress were never realized. *Ha-Ḥerut*, September 28, 1909.

83. See *Ha-Ḥerut*, especially in February 1911.

84. Antébi to Franck, November 17, 1908, AAIU, Israel-VIII.E.25.

85. Antébi to Henri Franck, August 4, 1908. AAIU, Israel-VIII.E.25.

86. A. S. Yahuda to Wolffsohn, June 16, 1909, CZA L1/29, based on *Ha-Ẓvi*, nos. 183–88. See *Ha-Ẓvi* May 24, 1909, *Ha-Ẓvi*, November 6, 1908.

87. June 1909, AAIU, Israel-IX.E26. Antébi referred to Beit ha-'Am as a "Russian Zionist-anarchist club." Antébi to AIU, March 11, 1909. AAIU, Israel-IX.E.26.

88. Antébi to Dizengoff, June 11, 1909. CZA, CM434/13.

89. See for example letters from the Hartuf colony (*Ha-Ḥerut*, May 28, 1909), and from Yitzhak Malchiel Mani (*Ha-Ḥerut*, June 8, 1909), defending Antébi from his detractors. See also the interview with Avraham Elmaliach, no. 2, February 23, 1964, Oral History Program at Hebrew University. Antébi later intervened with the governor to secure the release of his main detractor, Itamar Ben-Avi, from prison. Ben-Avi, *'Im shaḥar aẓma'utenu*, 202. For the Palestine Office's de-

liberations on Antébi as a difficult but indispensable partner, see: letter from July 15, 1912, in CZA, L2/26II; and P.O. to Jacobsohn, June 2, 1914, in CZA, L51/96.

90. Antébi to AIU president, June 24, 1909. CZA CM434/13. *Al-Munādī*, July 16, 1912.

91. Glass and Kark, *Sephardi Entrepreneurs in Eretz Israel*, 126; Efrati, *Ha-'edah ha-Sfaradit bi-Yerushalayim*; Rokeach, *Vetikim Mesaprim*; and Y. Levi, "Dr Yitzhak Levy."

92. Mandel, *Arabs and Zionism Before World War I*, 62–63; and Antébi to AIU, March 12, 1909. AAIU, Israel-IX.E.26.

93. Mandel, *Arabs and Zionism Before World War I*, 104 and 107. However the following month *Ha-Ḥerut* published a notice saying that those reports were baseless, and Ottomans could bring their birth certificates with them to register their land purchases. *Ha-Ḥerut*, July 6, 1910. Albert Antébi complained that the years 1910–11 took their toll on the support of the local population for the local Jews. "In all eyes the Jew is becoming an antipatriot, the traitor prepared to plunder his neighbor to take possession of his goods. The Christian excels in these accusations, but the Muslim follows on his heels." Quoted in Mandel, *Arabs and Zionism Before World War I*, 121.

94. *Ha-Ḥerut*, December 2, 1910; see also November 23, 25, 28, 1910.

95. See Tabu, March 21, 1911, ISA 83, tet/87/6; June 4, 1911, ISA 83, tet/87/5; from the Mutasarrıf of 'Akka, June 5, 1911, ISA 83, tet/87/5; Tabu, July 26, 1911, ISA 83, tet/87/6; Tabu, August 10, 1911, ISA 83, tet/87/6.

96. Information on this meeting is taken from Va'ad ha-'ir ha-klali, October 27 and 28, 1912. TAMA 423-008-076a; and Yodfat, "Va'ad ha-'ir ha-klali li-Yehudei Yafo," 240–47.

97. *Ha-Ḥerut*, November 12, 1912.

98. *Ha-Ḥerut*, November 14, 1912.

99. Quoted in Yodfat, "Va'ad ha-'ir ha-klali li-Yehudei Yafo," 246–47.

100. Antébi to Jerusalem governor (draft), n.d., CZA L2/615.

101. Laskier, "Sephardim and the Yishuv in Palestine, 115–16.

102. *Al-Karmil*, November 27, 1912; and December 7, 1912. Hebrew translation of the *Filasṭīn* original published in *Ha-Ḥerut*, December 24, 1912.

103. "Mi bno ha-'Otomani?" *Ha-Ḥerut*, December 26, 1912. "Al-Ghāzī"—literally "warrior," though often used for a religiously inspired battle. On Ben-Carmi Eisenberg, see Markovitsky, *Be-kaf ha-kel'a shel ha-ne'emaniyut*.

104. "Mr. Eisenberg gave his name for Zionist purposes according to the decision of the Zionist congress." Ruppin to Zionist Zentralburo, April 14, 1912. CZA, Z3/1448. Lands in Eisenberg's name: Kafrurie (4,800 dunams), Karkur Beidas (11,400 dunams), CZA, L18/272; land on the Carmel near Haifa, CZA L18/7/1; 1,932 dunams near Jaffa, CZA L18/7/1; Talpiot, Caesaria, in CZA L51/100; Ben Shemen, Hulda, in land registered to Ottoman Jews, CZA L5/70. See also a complaint in *Al-Mufīd* (Beirut) about Eisenberg's land purchases; *Ha-Ḥerut*, February 5, 1913; and *Al-Karmil* in CZA Z3/1447.

105. Quoted in R. Khalidi, *Palestinian Identity*, 138. In fact, the land purchase organization that Yellin worked for, the ICA, did require its settlers to adopt Ottoman citizenship.

Chapter Seven: Unscrambling the Omelet

1. By 1914, Jews had purchased 420,587 dunams of land in northern and southern Palestine, a quarter of which was owned by the Zionist Organization and the Jewish National Fund. The majority of the land, 54 percent, was owned by the ICA, the non-Zionist Jewish Colonization Association. Penslar, *Zionism and Technocracy*, 4.

2. *Al-Munādī*, October 12, 1912 and March 22, 1913. *Al-Karmil*, September 25, 1912. Other people wrote in to defend the ʿAbd al-Hadi family from charges that it was selling land to Zionists, but *Al-Karmil* awaited their personal response to no avail. *Al-Karmil*, September 3, 1912.

3. *Al-Munādī*, June 17, 1912; and September 17, 1912.

4. Quoted in *Ha-Ḥerut*, February 6, 1913. See also: letter to the editor in Beirut's *Al-Mufīd*, translated in *Ha-Ḥerut*, February 5, 1913; the critique of Muhammad ʿAbd al-Rahman al-ʿAlami published in April 1914, quoted in R. Khalidi, *Palestinian Identity*, 132; and *Al-Karmil*, September 7, 1912; October 13, 1912; December 11, 1912.

5. Arab Studies Society (Orient House). The Arab Studies Society archivist, Qasim Harb, believes that it was written in 1908, but I think it must have appeared at least two years later, around 1910 or 1911.

6. This foreign danger came not only from the Zionists, but also from European countries. For a discussion of the furor which emerged after a British archaeological team was accused of stealing antiquities from the Dome of the Rock complex, see Fishman, "Palestine Revisited."

7. The author was later revealed to be Shukri al-ʿAsali, a former deputy governor in Nazareth and future member of parliament representing Damascus.

8. *Ha-Ḥerut*, May 23, 1910; November 7, 1910. See also the report in CZA Z3/116, and September 21, 1908, entry in al-Sakakini, *Kadha ana ya dunya*, 38.

9. *Al-Karmil*, September 7, 1912.

10. For a discussion of the earliest clashes between Palestinian peasants and Zionist colonists, see R. Khalidi, *Palestinian Identity*. Also on the Purim 1908 fight in Jaffa, see Eliav, *Be-ḥasut Austria*, 339.

11. On the fight between Ben-Zion Levi and Hashem Saqallah, see *Ha-Ḥerut*, February 21 and 23, 1910; *Al-Najāḥ* April 8, 1910; H. Calmy to AIU president, February 15, 1910, CZA,CM434/4;H. Calmy to AIU president, February 27, 1910, AAIU, I.C.2. The local AIU official conveyed his opinion to his superiors that the French vice-consul in the city had been admirably energetic in hunting for the killer, and that the general prosecutor of Jerusalem, Celal Bey, was handling the investigation with perfect impartiality.

12. *Al-Najāḥ* April 8, 1910.

13. Zionist officials also considered the idea of Hebrew labor dangerous, and they agreed the Jewish guards needed to be controlled. Report by Dyk, n.d., CZA L1/70; Ruppin to Zentralburo, July 28, 1912, CZA L5/70; Thon to Zionist Actions Committee, August 25, 1913, CZA Z3/1450.

14. See Fishman, "Palestine Revisited," 71.

15. Quoted in ibid., 247.

16. *Filasṭīn*, April 29, 1914; translated in Public Record Office FO 195/2459; quoted in ibid.

17. See the report to the Zionist Actions Committee, May 28, 1914. CZA, L2/31II. See also Roi, "Zionist Attitude to the Arabs." For example, Haqqi al-'Azm demanded that the Jewish schools teach Arabic side-by-side with Hebrew (article in June 1914, *Al-Muqattam*). Cited in Mandel, "Attempts at an Arab-Zionist Entente." *Al-Ahram*'s correspondent Ibrahim Salim Najjar demanded that the Jewish community learn Arabic and merge with Arab culture. Cited in Yehoshu'a, "Tel Aviv in the Image of the Arab Press," 222.

18. *Ha-Ḥerut*, April 20, 1913.

19. Malul's articles were a response to Ya'kov Rabinowitz's attack against him in *Ha-Po'el ha-Ẓa'ir. Ha-Ḥerut*, June 17, 18, and 19, 1913.

20. Ibid.

21. Ibid.

22. Ibid.

23. Malul was one of the few (or only?) Jewish members of the Decentralist Movement documented to date.

24. See Rogers Brubaker, "Aftermaths of Empire and the Unmixing of Peoples."

25. Cited in Kark, *Jaffa*, 109. Of course the establishment of Tel Aviv to the north of Jaffa was intended to establish a "modern Hebrew" city far away from Levantine Jaffa. In 1913, the Palestine Office also drew up plans to establish a Jewish commercial center in Jaffa, to draw Jewish merchants and customers away from the central commercial street, Butrus Street. CZA, L51/4. For more on the relationship between Jaffa and Tel Aviv, see LeVine, *Overthrowing Geography*.

26. He proposed the Muslim municipality be in the north, the Jewish one in the center, and the Christian one in the south; the Old City would be a shared municipality. Nevertheless, even the New City was not hermetically divided, although neighborhoods were certainly more homogeneous. CZA, A153/1212.

27. Letter from Stanley Hollis, U.S. Consul General of Beirut, August 16, 1911 (file 867.00/349); NACP, National Archives microfilm publication M353, roll 4, internal affairs of Turkey, central files of the Department of State, record group 59.

28. Kayalı, *Arabs and Young Turks*, 68–69.

29. *El-Destour*, October 11, 1908; *Ha-Ẓvi*, November 15, 1908. Khalil al-Sakakini documents the establishment of the brotherhood in Jerusalem in al-Sakakini, *Kadha ana ya dunya*, October 21, 1908, entry. He says the ten founding members included himself, Musa Shafik al-Khalidi, Mayor Faidi al-'Alami, Hanna al-'Issa, and Nakhla Zurayq. See also Saab, *Arab Federalists of the Ottoman Empire*, for background information on these organizations.

30. The chapter was under the leadership of Shukri al-Husayni. *Al-Nafīr*, October 24, 1911.

31. Kayalı, *Arabs and Young Turks*, 75.

32. Özoğlu, *Kurdish Notables and the Ottoman State*, 78.

33. *Tanin*, April 19, 1910. Quoted in Kayalı, *Arabs and Young Turks*, 88.

34. *Al-Najāḥ*, April 8, 1910.

35. *Filasṭīn*, August 2, 1911.

36. *Filasṭīn*, July 29, 1911.

37. "Holiday of the Homeland," by Salim Abu al-Aqbal al-Ya'qubi, *Filasṭīn*, July 26, 1911.

38. The reference is to the biblical tale of Joseph, the favored of Jacob's twelve sons, sold into slavery by his jealous brothers who then lied to their father saying their brother had been killed by a wolf. The story is also recounted in the Qur'an, and hence is well known by Muslims, Christians, and Jews.

39. This is a reference to the 1909 coup, instigated by the former sultan, conservative religious scholars, and according to some critics, the conservative Arab notables as well. *Filasṭīn*, July 22, 1911. Shukri al-'Asali, the target of al-'Issa's wrath, was strongly affiliated with the opposition Entente Liberale political party.

40. See some of their demands in "We Want to Live," *Al-Mufīd*, December 17, 1912, quoted in CZA A19/3. However the two organizations took a different approach to the question of whether or not foreign power aid should be requested.

41. Tauber, "Four Syrian Manifestos."

42. *Al-Karmil*, August 24, 1912, and August 28, 1912.

43. *Al-Karmil*, August 28, 1912; September 14, 1912; October 5, 1912; December 11, 1912.

44. *Al Karmil*, August 24, 1912; September 25, 1912; October 13, 1912; November 6, 1912. Nassar called Kurd 'Ali a "*mujāhid* (holy warrior) in the cause of liberty and reform," *Al-Karmil*, September 21, 1912; the head of the Arab Literary Club was termed a "zealous patriot", November 16, 1912.

45. In fact, several scholars have shown that Arab nationalism as a separatist, anti-Ottoman ideology was quite marginal before World War I. See Dawn, *From Ottomanism to Arabism*; Haddad, "Nationalism in the Ottoman Empire"; Blake, "Training Arab-Ottoman Bureaucrats"; and Kayalı, *Arabs and Young Turks*. Only two secret societies (al-Fatat and al-'Ahd) were established that could be considered as properly nationalist in that they advocated Arab self-determination and separation from the empire, but their reach was quite limited. According to Dawn's research, no more than 126 men were known to be public advocates of Arab nationalism or members of Arab nationalist societies before 1914, 80 percent of whom were from Damascus.

46. "Appeal," by Sa'id Abu Khadra', Jerusalem 1912, Arab Studies Society. On the general election see Kayalı, "Elections and the Electoral Process," R. Khalidi, "The 1912 Election Campaign," and Yazbak, "Elections in Palestine."

47. "Appeal," 3–4.

48. Quoted in Cleveland, *Islam Against the West*, 25.

49. Kawtharani, ed., *Watha'iq al-mu'atamar al-'Arabi al-awal 1913*. The congress also concerned itself with the status of emigration from and immigration to Syria.

50. *Al-mu'atamar al-'Arabi al-awal* (1913 booklet), republished in ibid., 10.

51. Ibid., 117.

52. Decentralization Party (Ḥizb al-lāmarkaziyya), *Bayan lil umma al-'Arabiyya min hizb al-lamarkaziyya*, 5.

53. Tauber has shown that several leaders within the Decentralization Party were engaged in talks with both British and French officials, but there is no evidence that this turn to foreign powers had broader support. Tauber, "Ha-elmerkaziut."

54. Decentralization Party, *Bayan lil umma al-'Arabiyya*, 19–20.

55. *Al-Karmil*, September 28, 1912; October 2, 1912; October 5, 1912; October 9, 1912; October 17, 1912; October 20, 1912; October 30, 1912; November 6, 1912.

56. Edib, *House with Wisteria*; and Ginio, "Mobilizing the Ottoman Nation During the Balkan Wars."

57. Kayalı, *Arabs and Young Turks*.

58. About eleven hundred Beirutis were exiled to Anatolia and Jerusalem under Cemal Pasha. Cleveland, *Islam Against the West*, 33. Around ten thousand "enemy aliens" resident in Palestine were expelled to Alexandria, and several hundred Ottoman Jews and Christians from Jaffa–Tel Aviv and Jerusalem were exiled to Damascus and Anatolia. Several thousand Jews did Ottomanize in the months after the outbreak of the war. Elmaliach, *Ereẓ Israel ve-Suriya be-milḥemet ha-'olam ha-rishona*.

59. Quoted in Tamari, "Great War and the Erasure of Palestine's Ottoman Past," 116. For a study of Jerusalem during the war, see Jacobson, "From Empire to Empire."

60. April 28, 1915; quoted in Tamari, "Great War and the Erasure of Palestine's Ottoman Past," 123.

61. Their "secret plots" included replacing the khedivate in Egypt with a caliphate under British protection; turning the eastern coast of the Mediterranean over to the French; and declaring Muslim independence in interior Syria. Le Commandement de la IVme Armée, *La vérité sur la question syrienne*.

Conclusion

1. Blyth, *When We Lived in Jerusalem*, 88.

2. Shafir and Peled, *Israeli Citizenship*.

3. See for example the list in Al-Bustani, *'Ibra wa-dhikra*.

4. Quoted in Abbott, *Turkey in Transition*, 102.

5. Quoted in Isin and Wood, eds., *Citizenship and Identity*, 8. For the communitarian critique of liberal citizenship see Faulks, *Citizenship*.

6. Interview with the *Daily Telegraph*, October 31, 1908. Quoted in Ilıcak, "Unknown 'Freedom' Tales of Ottoman Greeks," 28.

7. Spinner, *Boundaries of Citizenship*.

8. Shafir and Peled, *Being Israeli*, 6.

9. Kaligian, "Armenian Revolutionary Federation," 73.

10. Kechriotis, "Greeks of Izmir at the End of the Empire."

11. Kymlicka, *Multicultural Citizenship*.

12. Faulks, *Citizenship*, 89.

13. Tamari, "Great War and the Erasure of Palestine's Ottoman Past," 107.

14. This understanding was eloquently expressed by Reinhold Niebuhr as the presence of "dominion" *and* "community" in empires as well as nations. Niebuhr, *Structure of Nations and Empires.*

15. Article 22 of the Covenant of the League of Nations.

Bibliography

Archival Collections

Arab Studies Society (Orient House) (Jerusalem)
Archive of the Alliance Israélite Universelle (Paris)
Başbakanlık Osmanlı Arşivi (Istanbul)
Bibliothèque Nationale Manuscripts Division, Richelieu (Paris)
Central Archive for the History of the Jewish People (Jerusalem)
Central Zionist Archives (Jerusalem)
Centre de Documentation du Grand Orient de France et de la Franc-Maçonnerie Européenne (Paris)
Institute for the Revival of Islamic Research and Heritage (Abu Dis, Jerusalem)
Israel State Archives (Jerusalem)
Jerusalem Municipality Archives (Jerusalem)
Jewish National and University Library Manuscripts Division (Jerusalem)
Khalidi Library (Jerusalem)
Ministère des Affaires Étrangères de France, Quai d'Orsay (Paris)
National Archives (College Park)
Oral History Program, Institute of Contemporary Jewry, Hebrew University (Jerusalem)
Tel Aviv Municipal Archive (Tel Aviv)
Türkiye Büyük Logesi (Grand Lodge of Turkey)(Istanbul)
Yeshiva University Archives, Israeli Broadside Collection (New York)

Newspapers

El-Destour (Constitution; Istanbul)
Filasṭīn (Palestine; Jaffa)
Ha-Hashkafa (The Observation; Jerusalem)
Ḥavaẓelet (Lily; Jerusalem)
Ha-Ḥerut (Liberty; Jerusalem)
Al-Hilāl (The Crescent; Cairo)
Al-Ittiḥād al-'Uthmānī (Ottoman Union; Beirut)
Al-Karmil (The Carmel; Haifa)
El Liberal (Liberty; Jerusalem)

Luaḥ Ereẓ-Israel (Eretz-Israel Almanac; Jerusalem)
Al-Manār (The Lighthouse; Cairo)
Al-Munādī (The Crier; Jerusalem)
Al-Muqtaṭaf (The Digest; Cairo)
Al-Nafīr al-ʿUthmānī (The Ottoman Clarion; Jerusalem)
Al-Najāḥ (Success; Jerusalem)
New York Times
Ha-ʿOlam (The Globe; Cologne)
El Paradizo (Paradise; Jerusalem)
Ha-Poʿel ha-Ẓaʾir (The Young Worker; Jaffa)
Al-Quds (Jerusalem)
Al-Quds al-Sharīf/Kudüs-ü şerif (Noble Jerusalem; Jerusalem)
Ṣawt al-ʿUthmāniyya (The Voice of Ottomanism; Jaffa)
Takvim-i Vekayi (Register of Events; Istanbul)
La Tribuna Libera (The Free Tribune; Salonica)
Ha-Ẓvi (The Deer; Jerusalem)

Other Works

Abbott, G. F. *Turkey in Transition*. London: Edward Arnold, 1909.

Abedi, Mehdi, and Michael M. J. Fischer. "Thinking a Public Sphere in Arabic and Persian." *Public Culture* 6 (1993): 219–30.

Abu Manneh, Butrus. "Arab Intellectuals' Reaction to the Young Turk Revolution." In *Rethinking Late Ottoman Palestine: The Young Turk Rule, 1908–1918*, ed. Yuval Ben-Bassat and Eyal Ginio. London: I. B. Tauris, forthcoming.

———. "The Christians Between Ottomanism and Syrian Nationalism: The Ideas of Butrus al-Bustani." *International Journal of Middle East Studies* 11, no. 3 (1980): 287–304.

———. "The Islamic Roots of the Gülhane Rescript." *Die Welt des Islams* 34, no. 2 (1994): 173–203.

———. "The Later Tanzimat and the Ottoman Legacy in the Near Eastern Successor States." In *Transformed Landscapes: Essays on Palestine and the Middle East in Honor of Walid Khalidi*, ed. Camille Mansour and Leila Fawaz, 61–81. Cairo: American University in Cairo Press, 2009.

Adivar, Halide Edib. *Memoirs of Halide Edip*. New York: Arno Press, 1972.

Aflalo, F. G. *Regilding the Crescent*. London: Martin Secker, 1911.

Agmon, Iris. *Family and Court: Legal Culture and Modernity in Late Ottoman Palestine*. Syracuse, NY: Syracuse University Press, 2006.

Aharonsohn, Alexander. *With the Turks in Palestine*. Boston: Houghton Mifflin, 1916.

Ahmad, Feroz. "Unionist Relations with the Greek, Armenian, and Jewish Communities of the Ottoman Empire, 1908–1914." In *Christians and Jews in the Ottoman Empire*, ed. Benjamin Braude and Bernard Lewis, 1: 401–34. New York: Holmes and Meiers, 1982.

———. "Vanguard of a Nascent Bourgeoisie: The Social and Economic Policy of the Young Turks, 1908–1918." In *Türkiye'nin Sosyal ve Ekonomik Tarihi*

(1071–1920), ed. Osman Okyar and Halil Inalcik, 329–50. Ankara: Meteksan, 1980.

———. *The Young Turks: The Committee of Union and Progress in Turkish Politics, 1908–14*. Oxford: Oxford University Press, 1969.

Akşin, Sina. *Jön Türkler ve Ittihat ve Terakki* (Young Turks and Union and Progress). 4th ed. Istanbul: Imge Kitabevi, 2006.

Alami, Musa. *Palestine Is My Country*. New York: Praeger, 1969.

Alexandris, Alexis. "The Greek Census of Anatolia and Thrace, 1910–12: A Contribution to Ottoman Historical Geography." In *Ottoman Greeks in the Age of Nationalism: Politics, Economy, and Society in the Nineteenth Century*, ed. Dimitri Gondicas and Charles Issawi, 45–76. Princeton, NJ: Darwin Press, 1999.

Ali Haydar Midhat Bey. *The Life of Midhat Pasha*. London: John Murray, 1903.

Alsberg, P. A. "Ha-she'ela he-'Aravit be-mediniyut ha-hanhala ha-Ẓiyonit lifnei milḥemet ha-'olam ha-rishona" (The Arab Question in the Policy of the Zionist Leadership Before the First World War). *Shivat Ẓion* 4 (1954), 161–209.

Anderson, Benedict. *Imagined Communities*. London: Verso, 1991.

Anduze, Éric. "La franc-maçonnerie coloniale au Maghreb et au Moyen Orient (1876–1924): Un partenaire colonial et un facteur d'èducation politique dans la genèse des mouvements nationalistes et révolutionnaires." Ph.D. diss., Universités des sciences humanes de Strasbourg, 1996.

———. "La franc-maçonnerie égyptienne (1882–1908)." *Chroniques d'Histoire Maçonnique*, no. 50 (1999): 69–88.

Antébi, Elizabeth. *L'homme du Sérail*. Paris: Nil Éditions, 1996.

Arendt, Hannah. *On Revolution*. New York: Viking Press, 1963.

Al-'Arif, 'Arif. *Al-Mufassal fi tarikh al-Quds* (Chapters in the History of Jerusalem). Vol. 1. Jerusalem: al-Ma'rif, 1961.

Arjomand, Said. *Shadow of God*. Chicago: University of Chicago Press, 1984.

Arnon, Adar. "Mifkedei ha-ukhlusiya bi-Yerushalayim be-shalhei ha-tkufa ha-'Otomanit" (Population Censuses in Jerusalem at the End of the Ottoman Period). *Katedra* 6 (1977): 95–107.

———. "The Quarters of Jerusalem in the Ottoman Period." *Middle Eastern Studies* 28, no. 1 (1992): 1–65.

Avci, Yasemin. *Değişim sürecinde bir Osmanlı Kenti: Kudüs (1890–1914)*(An Ottoman City in the Process of Change: Jerusalem, 1890–1914). Ankara: Phoenix, 2004.

'Awadat, Ya'qub. *Min 'ulama' al-fikr wal-adab* (Scholars of Thought and Literature). Jerusalem: Dar al-Usra, 1992.

Ayalon, Ami. *Language and Change in the Arab Middle East: The Evolution of Modern Political Discourse*. New York: Oxford University Press, 1987.

———. "O tmura ne'ora: Dmut ha-mahapekha be-'einei he-'Aravim" (O Enlightened Change: The Image of the Revolution in the Eyes of the Arabs). *Zmanim* 30 (1989): 151–59.

———. "Political Journalism and Its Audience in Egypt, 1875–1914." *Culture and History* 16 (1995): 100–121.

———. *The Press in the Arab Middle East.* Oxford: Oxford University Press, 1995.

———. *Reading Palestine: Printing and Literacy, 1900–1948.* Austin: University of Texas Press, 2004.

Ayyad, Abdelaziz A. *Arab Nationalism and the Palestinians, 1850–1939.* Jerusalem: PASSIA, 1999.

Barkey, Karen, and Mark Von Hagen, eds. *After Empire: Multi-Ethnic Societies and Nation-Building: The Soviet Union and the Russian, Ottoman, and Hapsburg Empires.* Boulder, CO: Westview Press, 1997.

Bartal, Israel. "On the Multiethnic Nature of Jewish Society in Jerusalem in the Nineteenth Century" (in Hebrew). *Pe'amim* 57 (1993): 114–24.

Barth, Fredrik. "Enduring and Emerging Issues in the Analysis of Ethnicity." In *The Anthropology of Ethnicity: Beyond "Ethnic Groups and Boundaries,"* ed. Hans Vermeulen and Cora Govers, 11–32. The Hague: Het Spinhuis, 1994.

Beinin, Joel. *The Dispersion of Egyptian Jewry: Culture, Politics, and the Formation of a Modern Diaspora.* Berkeley: University of California, 1998.

———. "The Jewish Business Elite in 20th Century Egypt: Pillars of the National Economy or Compradors?" *Bulletin of the Royal Institute for Inter-Faith Studies* 1, no. 2 (1999): 113–38.

Ben-Arieh, Yehoshua. *Jerusalem in the 19th Century: The Old City.* New York: St. Martin's Press, 1984.

———. *Jerusalem in the 19th Century: Emergence of the New City.* Jerusalem: Yad Ben-Zvi, 1986.

Ben-Avi, Itamar. *'Im shaḥar atzma'utenu* (In the Dawn of Our Independence). Tel Aviv: Magen Press, 1961.

Benbassa, Esther. *Ha-Yahadut ha-'Otomanit bayn hitma'arevut la-Ẓiyonut, 1908–1920* (Ottoman Jewry Between Westernization and Zionism, 1908–1920). Jerusalem: Shazar Center, 1996.

———. "Les 'Jeunes Turcs' et les Juifs, 1908–1914." In *Mélanges offerts à Louis Bazin par ses disciples, collègues et amis,* ed. Jean-Louis Bacqué-Grammont and Rémy Dor, 311–19. Paris: L'Harmattan, 1992.

———. "Zionism and Local Politics in Oriental Jewish Communities" (in Hebrew). *Pe'amim* 73 (1997): 36–40.

———. "Zionism in the Ottoman Empire at the End of the 19th and Beginning of the 20th Century." *Studies in Zionism* 11, no. 2 (1990): 127–40.

Ben-Gurion, David. "Ereẓ-Israel ba-tkufah ha-'Otomanit: Mosdot ha-mishpat" (The Land of Israel in the Ottoman Period: Legal Institutions). In *Ereẓ-Israel ba-'avar u-ve-hove,* ed. Yitzhak Ben-Zvi. New York, 1918.

Ben-Hanania, Yehoshu'a [Ya'kov Yehoshu'a]. "Dr. Shim'on Moyal ve-ha-be'aya ha-Yehudit-ha-'Aravit" (Dr. Shimon Moyal and the Jewish-Arab Problem). *Hed ha-Mizraḥ,* October 10, 1944.

———. "Ha-soferet Ester Moyal u-tkufatah" (The Author Esther Moyal and Her Era). *Hed ha-Mizraḥ,* September 17, 1944.

Berkes, Niyazi. *Secularism in Turkey.* Montreal: McGill University Press, 1964.

Bertram, Sir Anton, and Harry Charles Luke. *Report of the Commission Appointed by the Government of Palestine to Inquire into the Affairs of the*

Orthodox Patriarchate of Jerusalem. London: Oxford University Press, 1921.

Bessemer, Paul. "Ottoman Jewry and the 1908 Revolution." In *İkinci meşrutiyet'in ilânının 100üncü yılı* (Hundredth Anniversary of the Declaration of the Second Constitution), ed. Bahattin Öztuncay. Istanbul: Sadberk Hanım Müzesi, 2008.

Betzalel, Yitzhak. "On the Journal 'Ha-Herut' (1909–1917) and on Haim Ben 'Atar as Its Editor" (in Hebrew). *Pe'amim* 40 (1989): 121–47.

———. "Prolegomena to Sephardi and Oriental Zionism" (in Hebrew). *Pe'amim* 73 (1997): 5–35.

Blake, Corinne Lee. "Training Arab-Ottoman Bureaucrats: Syrian graduates of the Mülkiye Mektebi, 1890–1920." Ph.D. diss., Princeton University, 1991.

Blyth, Estelle. *When We Lived in Jerusalem*. London: John Murray, 1927.

Boura, Catherine. "The Greek Millet in Turkish Politics: Greeks in the Ottoman Parliament (1908–18)." In *Ottoman Greeks in the Age of Nationalism: Politics, Economy, and Society in the Nineteenth Century*, ed. Dimitri Gondicas and Charles Issawi, 193–206. Princeton, NJ: Darwin Press, 1999.

Bozkurt, Gülnihal. *Gayrimüslim Osmanlı Vatandaşlarının Hukuki Durumu (1839–1914)* (Non-Muslim Ottoman Citizenship Laws, 1839–1914). Ankara: Türk Tarih Kurumu, 1996.

Braude, Benjamin, and Bernard Lewis, eds. *Christians and Jews in the Ottoman Empire: The Functioning of a Plural Society*. Vols. 1–2. New York: Holmes and Meier, 1982.

Brown, L. Carl, ed. *Imperial Legacy: The Ottoman Imprint on the Balkans and the Middle East*. New York: Columbia University Press, 1996.

Brubaker, Rogers. "Aftermaths of Empire and the Unmixing of Peoples." In *After Empire: Multi-Ethnic Societies and Nation-Building: The Soviet Union and the Russian, Ottoman, and Hapsburg Empires*, ed. Karen Barkey and Mark Von Hagen, 155–80. Boulder, CO: Westview Press, 1997.

———. "Ethnicity Without Groups." *Archives Européennes de Sociologie* 43, no. 2 (2002): 163–89.

———. *Nationalism Reframed: Nationhood and the National Question in the New Europe*. Cambridge: Cambridge University Press, 1996.

Brummett, Palmira. *Image and Imperialism in the Ottoman Revolutionary Press, 1908–1911*. Albany: State University of New York Press, 2000.

Büssow, Johann. "Children of the Revolution: Youth in Palestinian Public Life, 1908–1914." In *Rethinking Late Ottoman Palestine: The Young Turk Rule, 1908–1918*, ed. Yuval Ben-Bassat and Eyal Ginio. London: I. B. Tauris, forthcoming.

Al-Bustani, Suleiman. *'Ibra wa-dhikra, aw al-dawla al-'Uthmaniyya qabl al-dustur wa-ba'dihi* (Admonition and Remembrance; or, The Ottoman State Before the Constitution and After It). Beirut: al-Akhbar, 1908.

Butenschon, Nils A. "State, Power, and Citizenship in the Middle East: A Theoretical Introduction." In *Citizenship and the State in the Middle East: Approaches and Applications*, ed. Nils A. Butenschon, Uri Davis, et al., 3–27. Syracuse, NY: Syracuse University Press, 2000.

Buxton, Charles Roden. *Turkey in Revolution.* London: T. Fisher Unwin, 1909.

Calhoun, Craig. "Imagining Solidarity: Cosmopolitanism, Constitutional Patriotism, and the Public Sphere." *Public Culture* 14, no. 1 (2002): 147–71.

———. *Nationalism.* Minneapolis: University of Minnesota Press, 1997.

Campos, Michelle U. "Between 'Beloved Ottomania' and 'The Land of Israel': The Struggle over Ottomanism and Zionism Among Palestine's Sephardi Jews, 1908–13." *International Journal of Middle East Studies* 37, no. 4 (November 2005): 461–83.

———. "Freemasonry in Ottoman Palestine." *Jerusalem Quarterly File* 22–23 (Fall–Winter 2005): 37–62.

———. "Remembering Jewish-Arab Contact and Conflict." In *Reapproaching Borders: New Perspectives on the Study of Israel/Palestine*, ed. Mark LeVine and Sandy Sufian, 41–65. Lanham, MD: Rowman and Littlefield, 2007.

———. "The 'Voice of the People' (*Lisan al-Sha'b*): The Press and the Public Sphere in Revolutionary Palestine." In *Publics, Politics, and Participation: Locating the Public Sphere in the Middle East and North Africa*, ed. Seteney Shami. New York: SSRC Books and Columbia University Press, 2010.

Canefe, Nergis. "Turkish Nationalism and Ethno-Symbolic Analysis: The Rules of Exception." *Nations and Nationalism* 8, no. 2 (2002): 133–55.

Çelik, Zeynep. *The Remaking of Istanbul: Portrait of an Ottoman City in the Nineteenth Century.* Berkeley: University of California Press, 1993.

Çetinkaya, Yusuf Doğan. "Economic Boycott as a Political Weapon: The 1908 Boycott in the Ottoman Empire." M.A. thesis, Boğaziçi University, 2002.

Chatterjee, Partha. *The Nation and Its Fragments: Colonial and Postcolonial Histories.* Princeton, NJ: Princeton University Press, 1993.

Chelouche, Gila. *Ẓ'aẓ'aei beit Aharon Chelouche, 1838–1971* (Descendants from the House of Aharon Chelouche, 1838–1971). Tel Aviv: G. Chelouche, 1970-71.

Chelouche, Yosef Eliyahu. *Parshat Ḥayai, 1870–1930* (My Life, 1870–1930). Tel Aviv: Stroud, 1930.

Cleveland, William L. *Islam Against the West: Shakib Arslan and the Campaign for Islamic Nationalism.* Austin: University of Texas, 1985.

———. *The Making of an Arab Nationalist: Ottomanism and Arabism in the Life and Thought of Sati' al-Husri.* Princeton, NJ: Princeton University Press, 1971.

Cohen, Amnon. *Yehudim be-veit ha-mishpat ha-Muslimi: Ḥevrah, kalkala ve-irgun kehilati bi-Yerushalayim he-'Otomanit* (Jews in the Muslim Court: Society, Economy, and Communal Organization in Ottoman Jerusalem). Jerusalem: Yad Ben-Zvi, 2003.

Cohen, Julia Philipps. "Fashioning Imperial Citizens: Sephardi Jews and the Ottoman State, 1856–1912." Ph.D. diss., Stanford University, 2008.

Cohen, Mark. *Under Crescent and Cross.* Princeton, NJ: Princeton University Press, 1995.

Cole, Juan. *Colonialism and Revolution in the Middle East.* Princeton, NJ: Princeton University Press, 1993.

Combes, André. "Le Grand Orient de France en Palestine." *Chroniques d'Histoire Maçonnique*, no. 52 (2001): 31–46.

Commins, David Dean. *Islamic Reform: Politics and Social Change in Late Ottoman Syria*. New York: Oxford University Press, 1990.

"Constitution de l'empire Ottoman octroyée par Sa Majeste Imperiale le Sultan le 7 Zilhidjé 1293." Constantinople: Levant Herald, 1908.

Darwaza, Muhammad 'Izzat. *Mudhakkirat Muhammad 'Izzat Darwaza: Sijjil hafil bi-masirat al-haraka al-'Arabiyya wal-qadayya al-Filastiniyya khilal qarn min al-zaman, 1887–1984* (Memoirs of Muhammad 'Izzat Darwaza: A Record of Service to the Arab Movement and to the Palestinian Cause Throughout a Century, 1887–1984). Beirut: Dar al-gharb al-Islami, 1993.

Davison, Roderic H. *Reform in the Ottoman Empire, 1856–1876*. Princeton, NJ: Princeton University Press, 1963.

———. "Turkish Attitudes Concerning Christian-Muslim Equality in the Nineteenth Century." *American Historical Review* 55, no. 4 (1954): 844–64.

Dawn, C. Ernest. *From Ottomanism to Arabism: Essays on the Origins of Arab Nationalism*. Urbana, IL: University of Illinois Press, 1973.

———. "The Origins of Arab Nationalism." In *The Origins of Arab Nationalism*, ed. Rashid Khalidi, Lisa Anderson, et al., 3–30. New York: Columbia University Press, 1991.

de Benoist, Alain. "The Idea of Empire." *Telos*, nos. 98–99 (Winter 1993–Spring 1994): 81–98.

Deák, István. *Beyond Nationalism: A Social and Political History of the Habsburg Officer Corps, 1848–1918*. New York: Oxford University Press, 1990.

Decentralization Party (Ḥizb al-lāmarkaziyya), *Bayān lil-umma al-'Arabiyya min ḥizb al-lāmarkaziyya*. Cairo: Ḥizb al-lāmarkaziyya, 1913.

Deguilheim, Randi. "State Civil Education in Late Ottoman Damascus." In *The Syrian Land: Process of Integration and Fragmentation: Bilad al-Sham from the 18th to the 20th century*, ed. Thomas Philipp and Birgit Schaebler, 221–50. Stuttgart: Franz Steiner Verlag, 1998.

Denais, Joseph. *La Turquie nouvelle et l'ancien régime*. Paris: Marcel Rivière, Librairie des Sciences Politiques et Sociales, 1909.

Deringil, Selim. "From Ottoman to Turk: Self-Image and Social Engineering in Turkey." In *Making Majorities: Constituting the Nation in Japan, Korea, China, Malaysia, Fiji, Turkey, and the United States*, ed. Dru C. Gladney, 217–26. Stanford, CA: Stanford University Press, 1998.

———. "Some Aspects of Muslim Immigration into the Ottoman Empire in the Late 19th Century." *Al-Abhath* 38 (1990): 37–41.

———. "'They Live in a State of Nomadism and Savagery': The Late Ottoman Empire and the Post-Colonial Debate." *Comparative Studies in Society and History* 45, no. 2 (2003): 311–42.

———. *The Well-Protected Domains: Ideology and the Legitimation of Power in the Ottoman Empire, 1876–1909*. London,: I. B. Tauris, 1998.

Devereaux, Robert. *The First Ottoman Constitutional Period: A Study of the Midhat Constitution and Parliament*. Baltimore: Johns Hopkins University Press, 1963.

Doganalp-Votzi, Heidemarie. "The State and Its Subjects According to the 1876 Ottoman Constitution: Some Lexicographic Aspects." In *Aspects of the Po-*

litical Language in Turkey (19th–20th Centuries), ed. Hans-Lukas Kieser, 61–70. Istanbul: Isis Press, 2002.

Doumani, Beshara. “Rediscovering Ottoman Palestine: Writing Palestinians into History.” *Journal of Palestine Studies* 21, no. 2 (1992): 5–28.

Dumont, Paul. “La franc-maçonnerie dans l’empire Ottoman: La loge grecque Prométhée à Jannina.” In *Les villes dans l’empire Ottoman: Activités et sociétés*, ed. Daniel Panzac, 105–12. Paris: Presses du CNRS, 1991.

———. “La franc-maçonnerie d’obédience française à Salonique au début du XXe siècle.” *Turcica* 16 (1984): 65–94.

———. “La franc-maçonnerie ottomane et les ‘Idées Françaises’ à l’époque des Tanzimat.” *Revue du Monde Musulman et de la Méditerranée* 52–53, nos. 2–3 (1989): 150–59.

———. “Jews, Muslims, and Cholera: Intercommunal Relations in Baghdad at the End of the 19th Century.” In *The Jews of the Ottoman Empire*, ed. Avigdor Levy, 353–72. Princeton, NJ: Darwin Press, 1994.

Edib, Halide. *House with Wisteria: Memoirs of Halidé Edib*. Charlottesville, VA: Leopolis Press, 2003.

Efrati, Natan. *Ha-‘edah ha-Sfaradit bi-Yerushalayim, 1840–1917* (The Sephardi Community in Jerusalem, 1840–1917). Jerusalem: Mossad Bialik, 1999.

Eickelman, Dale F., and Armando Salvatore. “Muslim Publics.” In *Public Islam and the Common Good*, ed. Armando Salvatore and Dale F. Eickelman, 3–27. Leiden: Brill, 2004.

Ekrem, Selma. *Unveiled: The Autobiography of a Turkish Girl*. New York: Ives Washburn, 1930.

El‘azar, Ya‘kov. *Ḥaẓarot be-Yerushalayim ha-‘atika* (Courtyards in Old Jerusalem). Jerusalem: Galor.

Eldem, Edhem, Daniel Goffman, and Bruce Masters. *The Ottoman City Between East and West: Aleppo, Izmir, and Istanbul*. New York: Cambridge University Press, 1999.

Eliachar, Elie. *Living with Jews*. London: Weidenfeld and Nicolson, 1983.

Eliav, Mordechai. *Be-ḥasut mamlekhet Austria, 1849–1917* (Under Protection of the Austrian Empire, 1849–1917). Jerusalem: Yad Ben-Zvi, 1985.

———. *Britain and the Holy Land, 1838–1914: Selected Documents from the British Consulate in Jerusalem*. Jerusalem: Yad Ben-Zvi, 1997.

———. *Die Juden Palästinas in der deutschen Politik: Dokumente aus dem Archiv des deutschen Konsulats in Jerusalem, 1842–1914* (The Jews of Palestine in German Policy: Documents from the Archive of the German Consulate in Jerusalem, 1842–1914). Tel Aviv: Ha-kibbutz ha-meuḥad, 1973.

———. *Österreich und das heilige Land: Ausgewählte Konsulatsdokumente aus Jerusalem, 1849–1917* (Austria and the Holy Land: Selected Consular Documents from Jerusalem, 1849–1917). Vienna: Österreichischen Akademie der Wissenschaften, 2000.

Elkayam, Mordechai. *Yafo-Neve Ẓedek* (Jaffa-Neveh Tzedek). Tel Aviv: Misrad ha-Bitaḥon, 1990.

Elmaliach, Avraham. *Ereẓ Israel ve-Suriya be-milḥemet ha-‘olam ha-rishona*

(The Land of Israel and Syria During the First World War). Vols. 1 and 2. Jerusalem: Ha-Solel, 1927.
———. "Me-ḥayei ha-Sfaradim" (From the Life of the Sephardim). *Ha-Shiloaḥ*, no. 24 (1910): 260–69, 348–59.
Emin, Ahmed. *The Development of Modern Turkey as Measured by Its Press*. New York: AMS Press, 1968.
Emiroğlu, Kudret. *Anadolu'da devrim günleri: İkinci meşrutiyet'in ilânı, Temmuz-Ağustos 1908* (Days Gone by in Anatolia: The Proclamation of the Second Constitution, July–August 1908). Ankara: Imge Kitabevi, 1999.
Ener, Mine. "Prohibitions on Begging and Loitering in Nineteenth-Century Egypt." *Die Welt des Islams* 39, no. 3 (1999): 319–39.
Erdem, Hakan. "Recruitment for the 'Victorious Soldiers of Muhammad' in the Arab Provinces, 1826–1828." In *Histories of the Modern Middle East: New Directions*, ed. Israel Gershoni, Hakan Erdem, and Ursula Woköck, 189–206. Boulder, CO: Lynne Rienner, 2002.
Ergut, Ferdan. "Policing the Poor in the Late Ottoman Empire." *Middle Eastern Studies* 38, no. 2 (2002): 149–64.
———. "The State and Civil Rights in the Late Ottoman Empire." *Journal of Mediterranean Studies* 13, no. 1 (2003): 53–74.
Esherick, Joseph W., Hasan Kayalı, and Eric Van Young, eds. *Empire to Nation: Historical Perspectives on the Making of the Modern World*. Lanham, MD: Rowman and Littlefield, 2006.
Fargo, Mumtaz Ayoub. "Arab-Turkish Relations from the Emergence of Arab Nationalism to the Arab Revolt, 1848–1916." Ph.D. diss., University of Utah, 1969.
Farhi, David. "Documents on the Attitude of the Ottoman Government Towards the Jewish Settlement in Palestine After the Revolution of the Young Turks, 1908–09." In *Studies on Palestine in the Ottoman Period*, ed. Moshe Ma'oz, 190–210. Jerusalem: Magnes Press, 1975.
Faulks, Keith. *Citizenship*. London: Routledge, 2000.
Fawaz, Leila. *Merchants and Migrants in 19th Century Beirut*. Cambridge, MA: Harvard University Press, 1983.
Figes, Orlando, and Boris Kolonitskii. *Interpreting the Russian Revolution: The Language and Symbols of 1917*. New Haven, CT: Yale University Press, 1999.
Findley, Carter Vaughn. "The Advent of Ideology in the Islamic Middle East." *Studia Islamica* 55 (1982): 143–69.
———. "The Advent of Ideology in the Islamic Middle East (Part II)." *Studia Islamica* 56 (1982): 147–80.
———. "Economic Bases of Revolution and Repression in the Late Ottoman Empire." *Comparative Studies in Society and History* 28, no. 1 (1986): 81–106.
Fishman, Louis. "Palestine Revisited: Reassessing the Jewish and Arab National Movements, 1908–14." Ph.D. diss., University of Chicago, 2007.
Formisano, Ronald P. "The Concept of Political Culture." *Journal of Interdisciplinary History* 31, no. 3 (2001): 393–426.

Fortna, Benjamin C. *Imperial Classroom: Islam, the State, and Education in the Late Ottoman Empire.* New York: Oxford University Press, 2002.

Frankel, Jonathan. "The 'Yizkor' Book of 1911: A Note on National Myths in the Second Aliya." In *Religion, Ideology and Nationalism in Europe and America: Essays Presented in Honor of Yehoshua Arieli*, ed. Moshe Zimmerman, 355–84. Jerusalem: Graph Chen Press, 1986.

Fresco, David. *Le Sionisme.* Istanbul: Fresco, 1909.

Frierson, Elizabeth B. "Gender, Consumption and Patriotism: The Emergence of an Ottoman Public Sphere." In *Public Islam and the Common Good*, ed. Armando Salvatore and Dale F. Eickelman, 99–126. Leiden: Brill, 2004.

———. "Unimagined Communities: State, Press, and Gender in the Hamidian Era." Ph.D. diss., Princeton University, 1996.

———. "Unimagined Communities: Women and Education in the Late-Ottoman Empire, 1876–1909." *Critical Matrix* 9, no. 2 (1995): 55–90.

Frumkin, Gad. *Derekh shofet bi-Yerushalayim* (The Way of a Judge in Jerusalem). Tel Aviv: Dvir, 1954.

Gellner, Ernest. *Nations and Nationalism.* Ithaca, NY: Cornell University Press, 1983.

Gelvin, James L. *Divided Loyalties: Nationalism and Mass Politics in Syria at the Close of Empire.* Berkeley: University of California Press, 1998.

Gerber, Haim. *Ottoman Rule in Jerusalem, 1890–1914.* Berlin: K. Schwarz, 1995.

Gilbar, Gad, ed. *Ottoman Palestine in the 19th Century.* Leiden: Brill, 1990.

Ginio, Eyal. "Mobilizing the Ottoman Nation During the Balkan Wars (1912–1913): Awakening from the Ottoman Dream." *War in History* 12, no. 2 (2005): 156–77.

Glass, Joseph, and Ruth Kark. *Sephardi Entrepreneurs in Eretz Israel: The Amzalak Family, 1816–1918.* Jerusalem: Magnes Press, 1991.

Göçek, Fatma Müge. "Decline of the Ottoman Empire and the Emergence of Greek, Armenian, Turkish, and Arab Nationalisms." In *Social Constructions of Nationalism in the Middle East*, ed. Fatma Müge Göçek, 15–83. Albany: State University of New York Press, 2002.

Goodwin, Jeff. "State-Centered Approaches to Social Revolutions." In *Theorizing Revolutions*, ed. John Foran, 11–37. London: Routledge, 1997.

Gorni, Yosef. *Zionism and the Arabs, 1882–1948: A Study of Ideology.* New York: Oxford University Press, 1987.

Grand Orient de France. Suprême conseil pour la France et les possessions françaises. *Instruction pour le première grade symbolique (apprenti).* Paris: Secretariat General du GODF, 1893.

Grand Orient Ottoman. *Instruction pour le premier grade symbolique: Apprenti.* Constantinople: n.p., 1910.

———. *Règlement général du Grand Orient Ottoman pour les ateliers du 1er au 3me degré.* Constantinople, 1910.

Greene, Molly, ed. *Minorities in the Ottoman Empire.* Princeton, NJ: Markus Weiner, 2005.

[Grégoire], Aristarchi Bey. *Législation Ottomane*. Constantinople: Fréres Nicolaïdes, 1873.

Groiss, Arnon. "Religious Particularism and National Integration: Changing Perceptions of the Political Self-Identity Among the Greek-Orthodox Christians of Greater Syria, 1840–1914." Ph.D. diss., Princeton University, 1986.

Gülsoy, Ufuk. *Osmanlı Gayrimüslimlerinin askerlik serüveni* (Ottoman Non-Muslims' Military Service). Istanbul: Simurg, 2000.

Habermas, Jürgen. "Citizenship and National Identity." In *The Condition of Citizenship*, ed. Bart van Steenbergen, 20–35. London: Sage Publications, 1994.

———. "The Public Sphere." In *Jurgen Habermas on Society and Politics: A Reader*, ed. Steven Seidman, 231–36. Boston: Beacon Press, 1989.

Haddad, Mahmoud. "Iraq Before World War I: A Case of Anti-European Arab Ottomanism." In *The Origins of Arab Nationalism*, ed. Rashid Khalidi, Lisa Anderson, et al., 120–50. New York: Columbia University Press, 1991.

Haddad, William W. "Nationalism in the Ottoman Empire." In *Nationalism in a Non-National State: The Dissolution of the Ottoman Empire*, ed. William W. Haddad and William Ochsenwald, 3–24. Columbus: Ohio State University Press, 1977.

Halper, Jeff. *Between Redemption and Revival: The Jewish Yishuv of Jerusalem in the Nineteenth Century*. Boulder, CO: Westview Press, 1991.

Hanania, Mary. "Jurji Habib Hanania: History of the Earliest Press in Palestine, 1908–14." *Jerusalem Quarterly*, no. 32 (2007): 51–69.

Hanioğlu, M. Şükrü. *A Brief History of the Late Ottoman Empire*. Princeton, NJ: Princeton University Press, 2008.

———. "Jews in the Young Turk Movement to the 1908 Revolution." In *Jews of the Ottoman Empire*, ed. Avigdor Levy, 519–26. Princeton, NJ: Darwin Press, 1994.

———. "Notes on the Young Turks and the Freemasons, 1875–1908." *Middle Eastern Studies* 25, no. 2 (1989), 186–97.

———. *Preparation for a Revolution: The Young Turks, 1902–1908*. New York: Oxford University Press, 2001.

———. *The Young Turks in Opposition*. New York: Oxford University Press, 1995.

Hanssen, Jens. *Fin de Siècle Beirut: The Making of an Ottoman Provincial Capital*. Oxford: Oxford University Press, 2006.

Harshav, Benjamin. *Language in Time of Revolution*. Berkeley: University of California Press, 1993.

Ha-Va'ad le-hoza'at kitvei David Yellin. *Kitvei David Yellin*. Vols. 1–2. Jerusalem: Reuven Mass, 1972.

Heinzelmann, Tobias. "Die Konstruktion eines osmanischen Patriotismus und die Entwicklung des Begriffs *Vatan* in der ersten hälfte des 19. Jahrhunderts." In *Aspects of the Political Language in Turkey (19th–20th Centuries)*, ed. Hans-Lukas Kieser, 41–51. Istanbul: Isis Press, 2002.

Heater, Derek. *What Is Citizenship?* Cambridge: Polity Press, 1999.

Hivert-Messeca, Yves. "France, laïcité et maçonnerie dans l'empire Ottoman: La loge 'Prométhée' à l'Orient de Janina (Epire)." *Chroniques d'Histoire Maçonnique* 45 (1992): 119–29.

Hobsbawm, Eric. *Nations and Nationalism Since 1780: Programme, Myth, Reality.* 2nd ed. Cambridge: Cambridge University Press, 1992.

Hoexter, Miriam, Shmuel N. Eisenstadt, and Nehemia Levtzion, eds. *The Public Sphere in Muslim Societies.* Albany: State University of New York Press, 2002.

Hourani, Albert. *Arabic Thought in the Liberal Age, 1798–1939.* London: Oxford University Press, 1962.

Hunt, Lynn. *Politics, Culture, and Class in the French Revolution.* Twentieth-anniversary ed. Berkeley: University of California Press, 2004.

Ilıcak, H. Şükrü. "Unknown 'Freedom' Tales of Ottoman Greeks." In *İkinci meşrutiyet'in ilânının 100üncü yılı* (100th Anniversary of the Declaration of the Second Constitution), ed. Bahattin Öztuncay. Istanbul: Vehbi Koç Foundation, 2008.

Instituto de cultura Juan Gil-abert. *Exposición: La masoneria española, 1728–1939.* Alicante: Instituto de cultura Juan Gil-abert, 1989.

Iordachi, Constantin. "The Ottoman Empire." In *What Is a Nation? Europe, 1879–1914*, ed. Timothy Baycroft and Mark Hewitson, 120–51. Oxford: Oxford University Press, 2006.

Isin, Engin F. "Citizenship After Orientalism: Ottoman Citizenship." In *Citizenship in a Global World: European Questions and Turkish Experiences*, ed. E. Fuat Keyman and Ahmet Iduygu, 31–51. London: Routledge, 2005.

Isin, Engin F., and Patricia K. Wood, eds. *Citizenship and Identity.* London: Sage Publications, 1999.

İslamoğlu, Abdullah. *İkinci meşrutiyet döneminde siyasal muhalefet, 1908–13 (Political Opposition in the Second Constitutional Period, 1908–13).* Istanbul: Gökkubbe, 2004.

Issawi, Charles. "The Transformation of the Economic Position of the Millets in the 19th Century." In *Christians and Jews in the Ottoman Empire: The Functioning of a Plural Society*, ed. Benjamin Braude and Bernard Lewis, vol. 1, 261–85. New York: Holmes and Meier, 1982.

Jacobson, Abigail. "From Empire to Empire: Jerusalem in the Transition from Ottoman to British Rule, 1912–1920." Ph.D. diss., University of Chicago, 2006.

———. "Sephardim, Ashkenazim, and the 'Arab Question' in Pre–First World War Palestine: A Reading of Three Zionist Newspapers." *Middle Eastern Studies* 39, no. 2 (2003): 105–30.

Jankowski, James, and Israel Gershoni, eds. *Rethinking Nationalism in the Arab Middle East.* New York: Columbia University Press, 1997.

Jessua, Is. *Grand Orient (Gr: Loge) de Turquie: Exposé historique sommaire de la maçonnerie en Turquie.* Constantinople: Francaise L. Mourkides, 1922.

Kabadayı, M. Erdem. "Inventory for the Ottoman Empire/Turkey, 1500–2000." Unpublished paper, History Department, Bilgi University, Istanbul.

Kaligian, Dikran Mesob. "The Armenian Revolutionary Federation Under Ottoman Constitutional Rule, 1908–14." Ph.D. diss., Boston College, 1993.

Kalvarisky, H. M. "Relations Between Jews and Arabs Before the War." *Sheifoteinu* 2, nos. 2–3 (1930): 50–55.
Kansu, Aykut. *Politics in Post-Revolutionary Turkey, 1908–1913*. Leiden: Brill, 2000.
———. *The Revolution of 1908 in Turkey*. Leiden: Brill, 1997.
———. "Some Remarks on the 1908 Revolution" (Yadigâr-ı Hürriyet: Orlando Carlo Calumeno Koleksiyonu'ndan Meşrutiyet Kartpostalları ve Madalyaları). In *Souvenir of Liberty: Postcards and Medals from the Collection of Orlando Carlo Calumeno*, ed. Osman Köker, 10–37. Istanbul: Birzamanlar Yayincilik, 2008.
Kappeler, Andreas. *The Russian Empire: A Multiethnic History*. Harlow, England: Pearson Education, 2001.
Karateke, Hakan T. "Legitimizing the Ottoman Sultanate: A Framework for Historical Analysis." In *Legitimizing the Order: The Ottoman Rhetoric of State Power*, ed. Hakan T. Karateke and Maurus Reinkowski, 13–54. Leiden: Brill, 2005.
———. "Opium for the Subjects? Religiosity as a Legitimizing Factor for the Ottoman Sultan." In *Legitimizing the Order: The Ottoman Rhetoric of State Power*, ed. Hakan T. Karateke and Maurus Reinkowski, 111–29. Leiden: Brill, 2005.
———. *Padişahım çok yaşa! Osmanlı devletinin son yüzyılında merasimler* (Long Live the Sultan! Festivals in the Last Century of the Ottoman State). Istanbul: Kitap Yayinevi, 2004.
Kark, Ruth. *Jaffa: A City in Evolution, 1799–1917*. Jerusalem: Yad Ben-Zvi, 1990.
———. "The Jerusalem Municipality at the End of Ottoman Rule." *Asian and African Studies* 14 (1980): 117–41.
———. *Jerusalem Neighborhoods: Planning and By-Laws, 1855–1930*. Jerusalem: Magnes Press, 1991.
———. "Pe'ilut 'iriyat Yerushalayim be-sof ha-tkufah ha-'Otomanit" (Activities of the Jerusalem Municipality at the End of the Ottoman Era). *Katedra* 6 (1977): 74–94.
Karpat, Kemal H. *Ottoman Population, 1830–1914: Demographic and Social Characteristics*. Madison: University of Wisconsin Press, 1985.
———. *The Politicization of Islam: Reconstructing Identity, State, Faith, and Community in the Late Ottoman State*. New York: Oxford University Press, 2001.
———. *Studies on Ottoman Social and Political History*. Leiden: Brill, 2002.
Kasaba, Reşat. "Dreams of Empire, Dreams of Nations." In *Empire to Nation: Historical Perspectives on the Making of the Modern World*, ed. Joseph Esherick, Hasan Kayalı, et al, 198–225. Boulder, CO: Rowman and Littlefield, 2006.
———. "Economic Foundations of a Civil Society: Greeks in the Trade of Western Anatolia, 1840–1876." In *Ottoman Greeks in the Age of Nationalism: Politics, Economy, and Society in the Nineteenth Century*, ed. Dimitri Gondicas and Charles Issawi, 77–87. Princeton, NJ: Darwin Press, 1999.
Kasmieh, Khairieh. "Ruhi al-Khalidi, 1864–1913: A Symbol of the Cultural

Movement in Palestine Towards the End of the Ottoman Rule." In *The Syrian Land in the 18th and 19th Century: The Common and the Specific in the Historical Experience*, ed. Thomas Philipp, 123–46. Stuttgart: Franz Steiner Verlag, 1992.

Kawtharani, Wajih, ed. *Watha'iq al-mu'atamar al-'Arabi al-awal 1913: Kitab al-mu'atamar wal-murasalat al-diblumasiyya al-Faransiyya al-muta'aliqa bihi* (Documents from the First Arab Congress 1913: Book of the Congress and the French Diplomatic Telegrams Relating to It). Beirut: Dar al-hadatha, 1980.

Kayalı, Hasan. *Arabs and Young Turks: Ottomanism, Arabism and Islamism in the Ottoman Empire, 1908–18*. Berkeley: University of California, 1997.

———. "Elections and the Electoral Process in the Ottoman Empire, 1896–1919." *International Journal of Middle East Studies* 27 (1995): 265–86.

———. "Jewish Representation in the Ottoman Parliaments." In *Jews of the Ottoman Empire*, ed. Avigdor Levy, 507–18. Princeton, NJ: Darwin Press, 1994.

Kechriotis, Vangelis Constantinos. "The Greeks of Izmir at the End of the Empire: A Non-Muslim Ottoman Community Between Autonomy and Patriotism." Ph.D. diss., Leiden University, 2005.

Kedourie, Elie. *The Chatham House Version and Other Middle-Eastern Studies*. New York: Praeger, 1970.

———. "Young Turks, Freemasons, and Jews." *Middle Eastern Studies* 7, no. 1 (1971): 89–104.

Kern, Karen M. "Rethinking Ottoman Frontier Politics: Marriage and Citizenship in the Province of Iraq." *Arab Studies Journal* 15, no. 1 (2007): 8–29.

Khalid, Adeeb. "Ottoman Islamism between the Ümmet and the Nation." *Archivum Ottomanicum* 19 (2001): 197–211.

Al-Khalidi, Muhammad Ruhi. *(Asbab) al-Inqilab al-'Uthmani wa-Turkiya al-fata* ([Reasons for] The Ottoman Revolution and Young Turkey). Cairo: al-Manar, 1908.

Khalidi, Rashid. "The 1912 Election Campaign in the Cities of Bilad al-Sham." *International Journal of Middle Eastern Studies* 16 (1984): 461–74.

———. "Ottomanism and Arabism in Syria Before 1914: A Reassessment." In *The Origins of Arab Nationalism*, ed. Rashid Khalidi, Lisa Anderson, Muhammad Muslih, and Reeva S. Simon, 50–69. New York: Columbia University Press, 1991.

———. *Palestinian Identity: The Construction of Modern National Consciousness*. New York: Columbia University Press, 1997.

———. "The Press as a Source for Modern Arab Political History: 'Abd al-Ghani al-'Uraisi and *al-Mufid*." *Arab Studies Quarterly* 3, no. 1 (1981): 22–42.

———. "Society and Ideology in Late Ottoman Syria: Class, Education, Profession, and Confession." In *Problems of the Modern Middle East in Historical Perspective: Essays in Honor of Albert Hourani*, ed. John P. Spagnolo, 119–32. Ithaca, NY: Reading, 1992.

Khalidi, Walid. *Before Their Diaspora: A Photographic History of the Palestinians, 1876–1948*. Washington, DC: Institute for Palestine Studies, 1991.

Khoury, Yusuf. *Al-Sihafa al-'Arabiyya fi Filastin, 1876–1948* (The Arabic Press in Palestine, 1876–1948). 2nd ed. Beirut: Institute for Palestine Studies, 1986.

Khuri, Ra'if. *Modern Arab Thought: Channels of the French Revolution to the Arab East*. Princeton, NJ: Kingston Press, 1983.

Khuri, Shihada, and Niqola Khuri. *Khulasat tarikh kinisat Urshalim al-Urthudhuksiyya* (Excerpts from the History of the Jerusalem Orthodox Church). Jerusalem: Beit al-Maqdis, 1925.

Kimmerling, Baruch. "Be'ayot konẓeptualiot ba-historiografia shel ereẓ u-vashnei 'amim" (Conceptual Problems in the Historiography of the Land of Two Peoples). In *Ereẓ ahat u-shnei 'amim ba* (One Land, Two Peoples), ed. Danny Ya'kobi, 11–22. Jerusalem: Magnes Press, 1999.

King, Jeremy. *Budweisers into Czechs and Germans: A Local History of Bohemian Politics, 1848–1948*. Princeton, NJ: Princeton University Press, 2002.

Kırlı, Cengiz. "Coffeehouses: Public Opinion in the Nineteenth-Century Ottoman Empire." *Public Islam and the Common Good*, ed. Armando Salvatore and Dale F. Eickelman, 75–97. Leiden: Brill, 2004.

———. "The Struggle over Space: Coffeehouses of Ottoman Istanbul, 1780–1845." Ph.D. diss., State University of New York, Binghamton, 2000.

Knight, E. F. *Turkey: The Awakening of Turkey; The Turkish Revolution of 1908*. Boston: J. B. Millet, 1910.

Köker, Osman. *Yadigâr-ı hürriyet: Orlando Carlo Calumeno koleksiyonu'ndan meşrutiyet kartpostalları ve madalyaları* (Souvenir of Liberty: Postcards and Medals from the Collection of Orlando Carlo Calumeno). Istanbul: Birzamanlar Yayincilik, 2008.

Kolatt, Israel. "The Organization of the Jewish Population." In *Studies on Palestine in the Ottoman period*, ed. Moshe Ma'oz, 211–45. Jerusalem: Magnes Press, 1975.

Kreiser, Klaus. "Ein Freiheitsdenkmal für Istanbul" (A Freedom Monument for Istanbul). In *Istanbul: Vom imperialen Herrschersitz zur Megapolis*, ed. Yavuz Köse, 183–201. Munich: Martin Meidenbauer, 2006.

Krikorian, Mesrob K. *Armenians in the Service of the Ottoman Empire, 1860–1908*. London: Routledge and Keagan Paul, 1977.

Kudsi-Zadeh, A. Albert. "Afghani and Freemasonry in Egypt." *Journal of the American Oriental Society* 92 (1972): 25–35.

Kuran, Ahmet Bedevi. *Inkilap Tarihimiz ve Jön Türkler* (Our Revolutionary History and the Young Turks). Istanbul: Kaynak, 2000.

Kurzman, Charles. *Democracy Denied, 1905–1915: Intellectuals and the Fate of Democracy*. Cambridge, MA: Harvard University Press, 2008.

———, ed. *Modernist Islam, 1840–1940: A Sourcebook*. New York: Oxford University Press, 2002.

Kushner, David. "Ha-dor ha-aḥaron le-shilton ha-'Othmanim be-Ereẓ Israel, 1882–1914" (The Last Generation of Ottoman Rule in Eretz-Israel, 1882–1914). In *Toldot ha-yishuv ha-Yehudi be-Ereẓ Israel me'az ha-'aliya ha-rishona: Ha-tkufah ha-'Otomanit* (History of the Jewish Community in the Land of Israel from the First Aliya: The Ottoman Era), ed. Israel Kolatt, 1–74. Jerusalem: Mossad Bialik, 1989.

———. *Moshel hayiti bi-Yerushalayim: Ha-'ir ve-ha-meḥoz be-'eynav shel 'Ali*

Ekrem Bey, 1906–1908 (A Governor in Jerusalem: The City and the Province in the Eyes of Ali Ekrem Bey, 1906–1908). Jerusalem: Yad Ben-Zvi, 1995.

Kutlu, Sacit. *Didâr-i hürriyet: Kartapostallarla ikinci meşrutiyet, 1908–13* (The Face of Freedom: Postcards of the Second Constitutional Period). Istanbul: Bilgi University, 2004.

———. "Ideological Currents of the Second Constitutional Era." In *İkinci meşrutiyet'in ilânının 100üncü yılı* (Hundredth Anniversary of the Declaration of the Second Constitution), ed. Bahattin Öztuncay. Istanbul: Sadberk Hanım Müzesi, 2008.

Kymlicka, Will. *Multicultural Citizenship*. New York: Oxford University Press, 1995.

Landau, Jacob. "The Educational Impact of Western Culture on Traditional Society in 19th Century Palestine." In *Jews, Arabs, Turks*, ed. Jacob Landau, 60–67. Jerusalem: Magnes Press, 1993.

———. S.v. "Farmasuniyya." *The Encyclopedia of Islam*. New ed. Supplement, 1982.

———. "He'arot 'al yeḥasam shel ha-Turkim ha-Ẓe'irim la-Ẓiyonut" (Notes on the Attitudes of the Young Turks toward Zionism). *Ha-Ẓiyonut* 9 (1984): 195–205.

———. "Muslim Opposition to Freemasonry." *Die Welt des Islams* 36, no. 2 (1996), 186–203.

———. "The Young Turks and Zionism: Some Comments." *Jews, Arabs, Turks*, ed. Jacob Landau, 167–77. Jerusalem: Magnes Press, 1993.

Laskier, Michael. "Avraham Albert 'Antebi: Prakim be-fo'alo bi-shnot 1897–1914" (Avraham Albert 'Antebi: Chapters in His Activities in the Years 1897–1914). *Pe'amim* 21 (1984): 50–82.

———. "The Sephardim and the Yishuv in Palestine: The Role of Avraham Albert Antébi, 1897–1916." *Shofar* 10, no. 3 (1992): 113–26.

Le Commandement de la IVme Armée. *La vérité sur la question syrienne*. Istanbul: Tanine, 1916.

Levi, Nissim. *Prakim be toldot ha-refuah be-ereẓ Israel, 1799–1948* (Chapters in the History of Medicine in Eretz Israel, 1799–1948). Tel Aviv: Ha-Kibbutz ha-Meuḥad, 1998.

Levi, Yitzhak. *Dr Yitzhak Levi: The Man and His Work from His Arrival in the Country to the Beginning of World War I*. Jerusalem: Institute for Contemporary Jewry, 1984.

LeVine, Mark. *Overthrowing Geography: Jaffa, Tel Aviv, and the Struggle for Palestine, 1880–1948*. Berkeley: University of California Press, 2005.

———. "Overthrowing Geography, Re-Imagining Identities: A History of Jaffa and Tel Aviv, 1880 to the Present." Ph.D. diss., New York University, 1999.

Levy, Avigdor, ed. *Jews of the Ottoman Empire*. Princeton, NJ: Princeton University Press, 1994.

Lewis, Bernard. "The Idea of Freedom in Modern Islamic Political Thought." In *Islam in History: Ideas, Men and Events in the Middle East*, ed. Bernard Lewis, 323–336. London: Alcove Press, 1973.

Lieven, Dominic. *Empire: The Russian Empire and Its Rivals*. New Haven, CT: Yale University Press, 2000.

Lockman, Zachary. *Comrades and Enemies: Arab and Jewish Workers in Palestine, 1906–48*. Berkeley: University of California Press, 1996.

———. "Railway Workers and Relational History: Arabs and Jews in British-Ruled Palestine." *Comparative Studies in Society and History* 35, no. 3 (1993): 601–27.

Luntz, Avraham Moshe. *Luaḥ ereẓ Israel* (Eretz Israel Almanac). Jerusalem: Avraham Moshe Luntz, 1909.

Lybyer, Albert H. "The Turkish Parliament." *Proceedings of the American Political Science Association* 7, no. 7 (1910): 65–77.

Al-Madani, Ziyad 'Abd al-'Aziz. *Madinat al-Quds wa-jawarha fi awakhir al-'ahd al-'Uthmani, 1831–1918* (Jerusalem and Its Surroundings in the Late Ottoman Period, 1831–1918). Amman: Ziyad 'Abd al-'Aziz Al-Madani, 2004.

Mah, Harold. "Phantasies of the Public Sphere: Rethinking the Habermas of Historians." *Journal of Modern History* 72 (2000): 153–82.

Makdisi, Ussama. "After 1860: Debating Religion, Reform, and Nationalism in the Ottoman Empire." *International Journal of Middle East Studies* 34, no. 4 (2002): 601–17.

———. "Corrupting the Sublime Sultanate: The Revolt of Tanyus Shahin in Nineteenth Century Ottoman Lebanon." *Comparative Studies in Society and History* 42, no. 1 (2000): 180–208.

———. *The Culture of Sectarianism: Community, History, and Violence in Nineteenth-Century Ottoman Lebanon*. Berkeley: University of California Press, 2000.

Makedonski, Stojan. "La révolution Jeune-Turque et les premières élections parlementaires de 1908 en Macedoine et en Thrace orientale." *Études Balkaniques* 10, no. 4 (1974): 133–46.

Malak, Hanna 'Isa. *Ta'ifat al-Rum al-Urthudhuksi 'abr al-tarikh* (The Greek Orthodox Sect through History). Jerusalem: Hanna Malak, 2000.

Malul, Nissim. "Ha-'itonut ha-'Aravit" (The Arabic Press). *Ha-Shiloaḥ* 31 (1913): 364–74, 439–50.

———. *Kitab Suriya wa-Masr: majmu'at maqalat udrijat fi jaridat al-Nasir al-Bayruti wa-jama't khidma lil-dawla wal-watan al-'Uthmani*. (The Book of Syria and Egypt: A Collection of Articles Published in the Beiruti Newspaper al-Nasir as a Service to the Ottoman State and Homeland). Beirut: Al-Nasir, n.d.

Mandel, Neville. *The Arabs and Zionism Before World War I*. Berkeley: University of California Press, 1976.

———. "Attempts at an Arab-Zionist Entente, 1913–1914." *Middle Eastern Studies* 1 (1965): 238–67.

———. "Ottoman Policy and Restrictions on Jewish Settlement in Palestine, 1881–1908." *Middle Eastern Studies* 10, no. 3 (1974): 312–32.

———. "Ottoman Practice as Regards Jewish Settlement in Palestine, 1881–1908." *Middle Eastern Studies* 11, no. 1 (1975): 33–46.

———. *Turks, Arabs and Jewish Immigration into Palestine, 1882–1914*. St. Antony's Papers, 17. *Middle Eastern Affairs* 4 (1965).

Mango, Andrew. *Atatürk: The Biography of the Founder of Modern Turkey*. Woodstock, NY: Overlook Press, 2002.

Manna', 'Adil. *A'lam Filastin fi awakhir al-'ahd al-'Uthmani, 1880–1918* (Scholars of Palestine at the End of the Ottoman Period, 1880–1918). Beirut: Muassasat al-dirasat al-Filastiniyya, 1995.

———. *Tarikh Filastin fi awakhir al-'ahd al-'Uthmani, 1700–1918 (qira' jadida)* (The History of Palestine at the End of the Ottoman Period, 1700–1918 [A New Reading]). Beirut: Mu'assasat al-dirasat al-Filastiniyya, 1999.

Ma'oz, Moshe, ed. *Palestine During the Ottoman Period: Documents from Archives and Collections in Israel*. Jerusalem: Hebrew University Press, 1970.

Mardin, Şerif. *The Genesis of Young Ottoman Thought: A Study in the Modernization of Turkish Political Ideas*. Princeton, NJ: Princeton University Press, 1962.

———. "Some Consideration on the Building of an Ottoman Public Identity in the Nineteenth Century." In *Converting Cultures: Religion, Ideology and Transformations of Modernity*, ed. Dennis Washburn and A. Kevin Reinhart, 167–82. Leiden: Brill, 2007.

Margulies, Roni, and Yanakis Manakis. *Manastır'da Ilân-ı Hürriyet, 1908–1909* (The Proclamation of Freedom in Manastir, 1908–1909). Istanbul: Yapi Kredi Yayinlari, 1997.

Markovitsky, Ya'kov. *Be-kaf ha-kel'a shel ha-ne'emaniyut: Bnei ha-yishuv ba-ẓava ha-Turki, 1908–18* (Entangled Loyalties: Sons of the Community in the Turkish Army, 1908–18). Ramat Efal: Yad Tabenkin, 1995.

Massad, Joseph A. *Colonial Effects: The Making of National Identity in Jordan*. New York: Columbia University Press, 2001.

Masters, Bruce. *Christians and Jews in the Ottoman Arab World: The Roots of Sectarianism*. New York: Cambridge University Press, 2001.

Mazower, Mark. *Salonica, City of Ghosts: Christians, Muslims, and Jews, 1430–1950*. New York: Vintage Books, 2004.

McCarthy, Justin. *The Population of Palestine: Population History and Statistics of the Late Ottoman Period and the Mandate*. New York: Columbia University Press, 1990.

McCullagh, Francis. *The Fall of Abd-ul-hamid*. London: Methuen, 1910.

Migdal, Joel S. "Mental Maps and Virtual Checkpoints: Struggles to Construct and Maintain State and Social Boundaries." In *Boundaries and Belonging: States and Societies in the Struggle to Shape Identities and Local Practices*, ed. Joel S. Migdal, 3–23. New York: Cambridge University Press, 2004.

Miller, Alexei, and Alfred J. Rieber, eds. *Imperial Rule*. Budapest: Central European University, 2004.

Morris, Robert. *Freemasonry in the Holy Land; or, Handmarks of Hiram's Builders*. Chicago: Knight and Leonard, 1876.

Mosse, George. *Fallen Soldiers: Reshaping the Memory of the World Wars*. Oxford: Oxford University Press, 1991.

Musallam, Akram, ed. *Yawmiyat Khalil al-Sakakini* (The Diaries of Khalil al-Sakakini). Vol. 1. Ramallah: Khalil Sakakini Culture Centre and the Institute of Jerusalem Studies, 2003.

Muslih, Muhammad. *The Origins of Palestinian Nationalism*. New York: Columbia University Press, 1988.

Nabavi, Negin. "Spreading the Word: Iran's First Constitutional Press and the Shaping of a 'New Era.'" *Critique: Critical Middle Eastern Studies* 14, no. 3 (2005): 307–21.

Al-Namura, Mahmud Taleb. *Al-Filastiniyun wa-mu'assassat al-hukm al-mahali bayn al-hukm al-dhati wal-ihtilal wa-haq taqrir al-masir min al-'ahd al-'Uthmani ila al-intifada* (The Palestinians and Local Government Between Self-Rule and Occupation . . . from the Ottoman Era to the Intifada). Dura (Palestine): Mahmud al-Namura, 1994.

Nathans, Benjamin. "Habermas's Public Sphere in the Era of the French Revolution." *French Historical Studies* 16, no. 3 (1990): 620–44.

Niebuhr, Reinhold. *The Structure of Nations and Empires: A Study of the Recurring Patterns and Problems of the Political Order in Relation to the Unique Problems of the Nuclear Age*. New York: Charles Scribner's Sons, 1959.

Odo, Georges. "Les réseaux coloniaux ou la 'magie des Blancs.'" *L'Histoire*, no. 256, special issue, *Les Francs-Maçons* (2001): 46–49.

Ökay, Cüneyd. *Meşrutiyet çocukları* (Children of the Constitution). Istanbul: Bordo Kitaplar, 2000.

Olson, Robert. "The Young Turks and the Jews: A Historiographical Revision." *Turcica* 18 (1986): 219–35.

Ortaylı, İlber. "Ottomanism and Zionism During the Second Constitutional Period, 1908–1915." In *Jews of the Ottoman Empire*, ed. Avigdor Levy, 527–36. Princeton, NJ: Darwin Press, 1994.

Osmanağaoğlu, Cihan. *Tanzimat dönemi itibarıyla Osmanlı tabiiyyetinin (vatandaşlığının) gelışımı* (The Development of Ottoman Citizenship Beginning with the Tanzimat). Istanbul: Legal, 2004.

Osmanlı Mebusları, 1324–1328 (Ottoman Representatives, 1908–1912). Istanbul: Ahmet Ihsân, 1908.

Özbeck, Nadir. "Philanthropic Activity, Ottoman Patriotism, and the Hamidian Regime, 1876–1909." *International Journal of Middle East Studies* 37 (2005): 59–81.

Özoğlu, Hakan. *Kurdish Notables and the Ottoman State: Evolving Identities, Competing Loyalties, and Shifting Boundaries*. Albany: State University of New York Press, 2004.

Ozouf, Mona. *Festivals and the French Revolution*. Cambridge, MA: Harvard University Press, 1988.

Öztuncay, Bahattin. *İkinci meşrutiyet'in ilânının 100üncü yılı* (Hundredth Anniversary of the Restoration of the Constitution). Istanbul: Sadberk Hanım Müzesi, 2008.

Pandey, Gyanendra. "Can a Muslim Be an Indian?" *Comparative Studies in Society and History* 41 (1999): 608–629.

Pears, Sir Edwin. *Forty Years in Constantinople.* 1916. Repr., Freeport, NY: Books for Libraries Press, 1971.
Penslar, Derek J. *Zionism and Technocracy: The Engineering of Jewish Settlement in Palestine, 1870–1918.* Bloomington: Indiana University Press, 1991.
Petrov, Milen V. "Everyday Forms of Compliance: Subaltern Commentaries on Ottoman Reform, 1864–1868." *Comparative Studies in Society and History* (2004): 730–59.
Polus, P. "Kalkalat Yerushalayim 'erev milḥemet ha-'olam" (The Economy of Jerusalem on the Eve of the World War). *Bulletin lishkat ha-misḥar Yerushalayim* (1964): 45–48.
Porath, Yehoshua. *The Palestinian Arab Nationalist Movement.* London: Frank Cass, 1977.
Qanun intikhab majlis al-nawwab al-'Uthmani (Election Laws for the Ottoman Parliament). Vol. 5. N.p: n.p., n.d.
Al-Qattan, Najwa. "Litigants and Neighbors: The Communal Topography of Ottoman Damascus." *Comparative Studies in Society and History* 44, no. 3 (2002): 511–33.
Qazaqiya, Khalil Ibrahim. *Tarikh al-kinisa al-rasuliyya al-Urshalimiyya* (History of the Jerusalem Apostolic Church). Jerusalem: Al-Muqtataf wal-Muqtasim, 1924.
Quataert, Donald. "The Economic Climate of the 'Young Turk Revolution' in 1908." *Journal of Modern History* 51, no. 3 (1979): D1147–61.
———. "The Ottoman Boycott Against Austria-Hungary." *Social Disintegration and Popular Resistance in the Ottoman Empire, 1881–1908: Reactions to European Economic Penetration*, ed. Donald Quataert, 121–45. New York: New York University Press, 1983.
———. *Social Disintegration and Popular Resistance in the Ottoman Empire, 1881–1908: Reactions to European Economic Penetration.* New York: New York University Press, 1983.
Rahme, Joseph G. "Namık Kemal's Constitutional Ottomanism and Non-Muslims." *Islam and Christian-Muslim Relations* 10, no. 1 (1999): 23–39.
Ram, Hanna. *Ha-yishuv ha-Yehudi be-Yafo: mi-kehila Sfaradit le-merkaz Ẓioni, 1839–1939* (The Jewish Community in Jaffa: From Sephardi Congregation to Zionist Center, 1839–1939). Jerusalem: Hoẓa'at Carmel, 1996.
Ramsauer, Ernest Edmonson, Jr. *The Young Turks: Prelude to the Revolution of 1908.* Princeton, NJ: Princeton University Press, 1957.
Ramsay, Sir W[illiam] M[itchell]. *The Revolution in Constantinople and Turkey: A Diary.* London: Hodder and Stoughton, 1909.
Rebhan, Helga. *Geschichte und Funktion einiger politischer Termini im Arabischen des 19. Jahrhunderts (1798–1882)* (The History and Function of Some Political Terms in Arabic in the Nineteenth Century [1798–1882]). Wiesbaden: Otto Harrassowitz, 1986.
Reinkowski, Maurus. "Late Ottoman Rule over Palestine: Its Evaluation in Arab, Turkish and Israeli Histories, 1970–90." *Middle Eastern Studies* 35 (1999): 66–97.
Rodrigue, Aron. *French Jews, Turkish Jews: The Alliance Israélite Universelle*

and the Politics of Jewish Schooling in Turkey, 1860–1925. Bloomington: Indiana University Press, 1990.

———. *Images of Sephardi and Eastern Jewries in Transition: The Teachers of the Alliance Israélite Universelle, 1860–1939*. Seattle: University of Washington Press, 1993.

———. "Interview with Nancy Reynolds." *Stanford Humanities Review* 5, no. 1 (1996): 81–92.

———. "The Mass Destruction of Armenians and Jews in the 20th Century in Historical Perspective." In *Der Völkermord an den Armeniern und die Shoah*, ed. Hans-Lukas Kieser and Dominik J. Schaller, 303–16. Zurich: Chronos Verlag, 2002.

Rogan, Eugene. *Frontiers of the State in the Late Ottoman Empire: Transjordan, 1850–1921*. Cambridge: Cambridge University Press, 1999.

Roi, Ya'kov. "Nisyonoteihem shel ha-mosdot ha-Ẓiyonim lehashpi'a 'al ha-'itonut he-'Aravit be-Ereẓ Israel ba-shanim, 1908–1914" (Attempts of the Zionist Institutions to Influence the Arabic Press in the Land of Israel in the Years 1908–1914). *Ẓion* 3–4 (1967): 201–27.

———. "The Zionist Attitude to the Arabs, 1908–1914." *Middle Eastern Studies* 4, no. 3 (1968): 198–242.

Rokeach, Yitzhak. *Vetikim Mesaprim* (Old-Timers Speak). Ramat Gan: Hoẓa'at Meẓada, 1972.

Romero, Elena. *La creación literaria en lengua sefardí*. Madrid: Editorial MAPFRE, 1992.

Rubin, Avi. "Bahjat and Tamimi in Wilayat Beirut: A Journey into the Worldviews of Two Ottoman Travelers at the Turn of the 20th Century" (in Hebrew). Master's thesis, Ben Gurion University of the Negev, 2000.

Saab, Hassan. *The Arab Federalists of the Ottoman Empire*. Amsterdam: Djambatan, 1958.

Sabah, Lucien. "La loge Moriah à l'Or: De Jérusalem, 1913–14." *Chroniques d'Histoire Maçonnique*, no. 35 (1985): 65–78.

Sabato, Hilda. "On Political Citizenship in Nineteenth-Century Latin America." *American Historical Review* 106, no. 4 (2001): 1290–1315.

Safwat, Najdat Safwat. *Freemasonry in the Arab World*. London: Arab Research Centre, 1980.

Al-Sakakini, Khalil. *Al-Nahda al-Urthudhuksiyya fi Filastin* (The Orthodox Renaissance in Palestine). Jerusalem: n.p., 1913.

———. *Kadha ana ya dunya* (Such Am I, O World). Jerusalem: al-Matba'a al-tijariyya, 1955.

———. *Kazeh ani, rabotai!* (Such Am I, O World). Jerusalem: Keter, 1990.

Salam, Nawaf A. "The Emergence of Citizenship in Islamdom." *Arab Law Quarterly* 12, no. 2 (1997): 125–47.

Saliba, Najib Elias. "Wilayat Suriyya, 1876–1909." Ph.D. diss., University of Michigan, 1971.

Salibi, Kamal S. "Beirut Under the Young Turks, as Depicted in the Political Memoirs of Salim 'Ali Salam (1868–1938)." In *Les Arabes par leurs Archives*

(XVIe–XXe siècles), ed. Jacques Berque and Dominique Chevallier, 193–216. Paris: Éditions du Centre National de la Recherche Scientifique, 1976.

Salnâme-i devlet-i âliye-i Osmâniye. (Ottoman Imperial Yearbook). Istanbul: Ahmed Ihsan, 1908.

Salzmann, Ariel. "Citizens in Search of a State: The Limits of Political Participation in the Late Ottoman Empire." In *Extending Citizenship, Reconfiguring States*, ed. Michael and Charles Tilly Hanagan, 37–66. Lanham, MD: Rowman and Littlefield, 1999.

Schmelz, Uziel O. "Population Characteristics of Jerusalem and Hebron Regions According to Ottoman Census of 1905." In *Ottoman Palestine in the 19th Century*, ed. Gad Gilbar, 15–68. Leiden: Brill, 1990.

———. "The Population of Jerusalem's Urban Neighborhoods According to the Ottoman Census of 1905." In *Aspects of Ottoman History*, ed. Amy Singer and Amnon Cohen, 93–113. Jerusalem: Magnes Press, 1994.

Sciaky, Leon. *Farewell to Salonica: Portrait of an Era.* New York: Current Books, 1946.

Seikaly, Samir. "Christian Contributions to the Nahda in Palestine Prior to World War I." *Bulletin of the Royal Institute for Inter-Faith Studies* 2, no. 2 (2000): 49–61.

———. "Damascene Intellectual Life in the Opening Years of the 20th Century: Muhammad Kurd 'Ali and *al-Muqtabas*." In *Intellectual Life in the Arab East, 1890–1939*, ed. Marwan R. Buheiry, 129–53. Beirut: American University of Beirut Press, 1981.

Selbin, Eric. "Revolution in the Real World: Bringing Agency Back In." In *Theorizing Revolutions*, ed. John Foran, 118–32. London: Routledge, 1997.

Shabani, Omid A Payrow. "Who's Afraid of Constitutional Patriotism? The Binding Source of Citizenship in Constitutional States." *Social Theory and Practice* 28, no. 3 (2002): 419–43.

Shafir, Gershon. *Land, Labor, and the Origins of the Israeli-Palestinian Conflict, 1882–1914*. Berkeley: University of California Press, 1996.

Shafir, Gershon, and Yoav Peled. *Being Israeli: The Dynamics of Multiple Citizenship*. Cambridge: Cambridge University Press, 2002.

Sharabi, Hisham. *Arab Intellectuals and the West: The Formative Years, 1875–1914*. Baltimore: Johns Hopkins University Press, 1970.

Shar'abi, Rachel. *Ha-yishuv ha-Sfaradi bi-Yerushalayim be-shalhei ha-tkufah ha-'Otomanit* (The Sephardi Community in Jerusalem at the End of the Ottoman Period). Tel Aviv: Misrad ha-Bitaḥon, 1989.

Shareef, Malek Ali. "Urban Administration in the Late Ottoman Period: The Beirut Municipality as a Case Study, 1867–1908." M.A. thesis, American University in Beirut, 1998.

Shaw, Stanford. "The Population of Istanbul in the 19th Century." *International Journal of Middle East Studies* 10, no. 2 (1979): 265–77.

Shilo, Margalit. *Nisyonot be-hityashvut: Ha-misrad ha-Arẓ-Israeli, 1908–14* (Experiments in Settlement: The Eretz-Israeli Office, 1908–14). Jerusalem: Yad Ben-Zvi, 1988.

Shilony, Zvi. *Ha-keren ha-kayemet le-Israel ve-ha-hityashvut ha-Ẓiyonit, 1903–*

14 (The Jewish National Fund and Zionist Settlement, 1903–14). Jerusalem: Yad Ben-Zvi, 1990.

Singer, Brian C. J. "Cultural Versus Contractual Nations: Rethinking Their Opposition." *History and Theory* 35, no. 3 (1996): 309–37.

Smith, Anthony D. *National Identity*. London: Penguin Books, 1991.

———. "The 'Sacred' Dimensions of Nationalism." *Millennium: Journal of International Studies* 29, no. 3 (2000): 791–814.

Société commerciale de Palestine à Jerusalem. *Statuts de la Société commerciale de Palestine à Jerusalem*. Jerusalem: A. M. Luncz, 1908.

Sofuoğlu, Ebubekir. *Osmanlı devletinde islahatlar ve I. meşrutiyet* (Reforms and the First Constitution in the Ottoman Empire). Istanbul: Gökkubbe, 2004.

Sohrabi, Nader. "Global Waves, Local Actors: What the Young Turks Knew About Other Revolutions and Why It Mattered." *Comparative Studies in Society and History* 44, no. 1 (2002): 45–79.

———. "Historicizing Revolutions: Constitutional Revolutions in the Ottoman Empire, Iran, and Russia, 1905–8." *American Journal of Sociology* 100, no. 6 (1995): 1383–1447.

Sorek, Tamir. *Arab Soccer in a Jewish State: The Integrative Enclave*. Cambridge: Cambridge University Press, 2007.

Sosevsky, Chana. "Attitudes of Zionist Intellectuals to the Arab Population in Palestine as Expressed in the Literature Before the Young Turk Revolution of 1908." Ph.D. diss., New York University, 1980.

Spinner, Jeff. *The Boundaries of Citizenship: Race, Ethnicity, and Nationality in the Liberal State*. Baltimore: Johns Hopkins University Press, 1994.

Stein, Sarah Abrevaya. "The Creation of Yiddish and Judeo-Spanish Newspaper Cultures in the Russian and Ottoman Empires." Ph.D. diss., Stanford University, 1999.

———. *Making Jews Modern: The Yiddish and Ladino Press in the Russian and Ottoman Empires*. Bloomington: Indiana University Press, 2003.

———. "The Permeable Boundaries of Ottoman Jewry." In *Boundaries and Belonging: States and Societies in the Struggle to Shape Identities and Local Practices*, ed. Joel S. Migdal, 49–70. Cambridge: Cambridge University Press, 2004.

Steinwedel, Charles. "To Make a Difference: The Category of Ethnicity in Late Imperial Russian Politics, 1861–1917." In *Russian Modernity: Politics, Knowledge, Practices*, ed. David L. Hoffman and Yanni Kotsonis, 67–86. New York: St. Martin's Press, 1999.

Stillman, Norman. *Sephardi Responses to Modernity*. Camberwell, Victoria, Australia: Harwood Academic Publishers, 1995.

Stoddard, Philip Hendrick. "The Ottoman Government and the Arabs, 1911–1918: A Preliminary Study of the Teşkilati Mahsusa." Ph.D. diss., Princeton University, 1963.

Strauss, Johann. "Ottomanisme et 'Ottomanité': Le Témoignage Linguistique." In *Aspects of the Political Language in Turkey (19th–20th Centuries)*, ed. Hans-Lukas Kieser, 15–39. Istanbul: Isis Press, 2002.

———. "Who Read What in the Ottoman Empire (19th–20th Centuries)?" *Arabic Middle Eatern Literatures* 6, no. 1 (2003): 39–76.

Strohmeier, Martin. "Muslim Education in the Vilayet of Beirut, 1880–1918." In *Decision Making and Change in the Ottoman Empire*, ed. Cesar E. Farah, 215–41. Kirkville, MO: Thomas Jeffferson University Press, 1993.

Suny, Ronald Grigor. "Religion, Ethnicity, and Nationalism: Armenians, Turks, and the End of the Ottoman Empire." In *In God's Name: Genocide and Religion in the Twentieth Century*, ed. Omer Bartov and Phyllis Mack, 23–61. New York: Berghahn Books, 2001.

Tamari, Salim. "The Great War and the Erasure of Palestine's Ottoman Past." In *Transformed Landscapes: Essays on Palestine and the Middle East in Honor of Walid Khalidi*, ed. Camille Mansour and Leila Fawaz, 105–35. Cairo: American University in Cairo Press, 2009.

———. "Ishaq al-Shami and the Predicament of the Arab Jew in Palestine." *Jerusalem Quarterly*, no. 21 (2004): 10–26.

———. "Jerusalem's Ottoman Modernity: The Times and Lives of Wasif Jawhariyyeh." *Jerusalem Quarterly File* 9 (2000): 5–27.

———, ed. *Jerusalem 1948: The Arab Neighborhoods and Their Fate in the War.* Jerusalem: Institute for Jerusalem Studies, 1999.

Tamari, Salim, and Issam Nassar, eds. *Al-Quds al-'Uthmaniyya fil-mudhakkirat al-Jawhariyya: Al-kitab al-awwal min mudhakkirat al-musiqi Wasif Jawhariyya, 1904–1917* (Ottoman Jerusalem in the Jawhariyya Memoirs: Book One of the Memoirs of the Musician Wasif Jawhariyya). Vol. 1. Beirut: Mu'assasat al-dirasat al-Filastiniyya, 2003.

Tauber, Eli'ezer. "Ha-elmarkaziut: Ha-miflaga ha-Surit ha-rishona" (The Decentralization: The First Syrian Party). *Ha-mizraḥ he-ḥadash* 39 (1997–98): 55–66.

———. "Four Syrian Manifestos After the Young Turk Revolution." *Turcica* 19 (1987): 195–213.

———. "The Press and the Journalist as a Vehicle in Spreading National Ideas in Syria in the Late Ottoman Period." *Die Welt des Islams* 30 (1990): 163–77.

Tavakoli-Targhi, Mohamad. "From Patriotism to Matriotism: A Tropological Study of Iranian Nationalism, 1870–1909." *International Journal of Middle East Studies* 34, no. 2 (2002): 217–38.

———. "Refashioning Iran: Language and Culture During the Constitutional Revolution." *Iranian Studies* 23, no. 1 (1990): 77–101.

Al-Tawarnah, Muhammad Salem. "Qada Jaffa During the Period 1864–1914" (in Arabic). Ph.D. diss., University of Jordan, 1997.

Tevfik, Ebuzziya. *Yeni Osmanlılar: Imparatorluğun son dönemindeki Genç Türkler* (Young Ottomans: Young Turks in the Empire's Final Days). Istanbul: Pegasus, 2006.

Tidhar, David. *Barkai: Album ha-yovel* (Barkai: Album of Its 50th Anniversary).

———. *Be-madim ve-lo be-madim* (In and Out of Uniform). Tel Aviv: Yadidim, 1937.

———., ed. *Enẓiklopedia le-ḥaluẓei ha-yishuv u-vonav* (Encyclopedia of the Yishuv and Its Founders). Tel Aviv: Sifriat Rishonim, 1947.

———. *Sefer he-aḥim: 60 shana le-hivasdah shel ha-lishka* (Book of Brothers: 60 Years of Barkai). Tel Aviv: Lishkat Barkai, 1966.

Todorova, Maria. *Imagining the Balkans*. New York: Oxford University Press, 1997.
Töre, Enver. *II. Meşrutiyet tiyatrosu: Yazarlar-piyeseler* (Second Constitutional Theater: Writers and Plays). Istanbul: Duyap, 2006.
Tsimhoni, Daphne. "The British Mandate and the Arab Christians in Palestine, 1920–25." D.Phil. thesis, School for African and Oriental Studies, University of London, 1976.
———. "The Greek Orthodox Patriarchate of Jerusalem During the Formative Years of the British Mandate." *Asian and African Studies* 2 (1978): 77–121.
Tunaya, Tarik Zafer. *Hürriyetin ilânı: İkinci meşrutiyet'in siyasi hayatına bakışlar* (Declaration of Freedom: Glances at Political Life in the Second Constitutional Period). Istanbul: Bilgi University, 2004.
Tunçay, Mete. *II. Meşrutiyet'in ilk yılı: 23 Temmuz 1908–23 Temmuz 1909* (The First Year of the Second Constitution). Istanbul: Yapi Kredi, 2008.
Turner, Bryan S. "Contemporary Problems in the Theory of Citizenship." In *Citizenship and Social Theory*, ed. Bryan S. Turner, 1–18. London: Sage Publications, 1993.
———. "Islam, Civil Society, and Citizenship: Reflections on the Sociology of Citizenship and Islamic Studies." In *Citizenship and the State in the Middle East: Approaches and Applications*, ed. Nils A. Butenschon, Uri Davis, and Manuel Hassassian, 28–48. Syracuse, NY: Syracuse University Press, 2000.
Unowsky, Daniel. "Reasserting Empire: Habsburg Imperial Celebrations After the Revolutions of 1848–9." In *Staging the Past: The Politics of Commemoration in Habsburg Central Europe, 1848 to the Present*, ed. Maria Bucur and Nancy M. Wingfield, 13–45. West Lafayette, IN: Purdue University Press, 2001.
van Steenbergen, Bart, ed. *The Condition of Citizenship*. London: Sage Publications, 1994.
Vester, Bertha Spafford. *Our Jerusalem: An American Family in the Holy City, 1881–1949*. Jerusalem: Ariel Publishing House, 1988.
Vogel, Ursula, and Michael Moran, eds. *The Frontiers of Citizenship*. London: MacMillan, 1991.
Wallerstein, Immanuel. "Citizens All? Citizens Some! The Making of the Citizen." *Comparative Studies in Society and History* (2003): 650–79.
Wasserman, Stanley, and Katherine Faust. *Social Network Analysis: Methods and Applications*. Cambridge: Cambridge University Press, 1994.
Watenpaugh, Keith David. *Being Modern in the Middle East: Revolution, Nationalism, Colonialism, and the Arab Middle Class*. Princeton, NJ: Princeton University Press, 2006.
———. "Bourgeois Modernity, Historical Memory, and Imperialism: The Emergence of an Urban Middle Class in the Late Ottoman and Inter-War Middle East, Aleppo, 1908–1939." Ph.D. diss., University of California, Los Angeles, 1999.
Weeks, Theodore R. *Nation and State in Late Imperial Russia: Nationalism and Russification on the Western Frontier, 1863–1914*. DeKalb: Northern Illinois University Press, 1996.
Weiner, Chana. "Ha-mediniyut ha-Ẓiyonit be-Turkiya 'ad 1914" (Zionist Policy

in Turkey Until 1914). In *Toldot ha-yishuv ha-Yehudi be-Erez Israel me'az ha-'aliya ha-rishona: Ha-tkufah ha-'Otomanit, helek 1* (The History of the Jewish Community in the Land of Israel from the First Aliyah: The Ottoman Period, part 1), ed. Israel Kolatt, 257–349. Jerusalem: Mossad Bialik, 2000.

Who's Who: Alumni Association, AUB, 1870–1923. Beirut: American Press, 1924.

Wild, Stefan. "Ottomanism Versus Arabism: The Case of Farid Kassab (1884–1970)." *Die Welt des Islams* 28 (1988): 607–27.

Wissa, Karim. "Freemasonry in Egypt from Bonaparte to Zaghloul." *Turcica* 24 (1992): 109–32.

Worringer, Renee. "'Sick Man of Europe' or 'Japan of the Near East'? Constructing Ottoman Modernity in the Hamidian and Young Turk Eras." *International Journal of Middle East Studies* 36 (2004): 207–30.

Wortman, Richard S. *Scenarios of Power: Myth and Ceremony in Russian Monarchy*. Princeton, NJ: Princeton University Press, 1995.

Yahuda, Avraham Shalom. "Le-zikhron David Yellin" (In Memory of David Yellin). In *'Ever ve-'Arav: Osef mekhkarim ve-ma'amarim, shirat he-'Aravim, zikhronot u-reshamim* (Hebrew and Arab: Collection of Research and Articles, Poems of the Arabs, Memories and Documents). New York: Ha-Histadrut ha-'Ivrit be-Amerika/Shulsinger, 1946.

Yalçin, Alemdar. *II. Meşrutiyet'te tiyatro edebiyatı tarihi* (The Literary History of the Theater in the Second Constitutional Period). Ankara: Gazi Universitesi Yayin, 1985.

Yazbak, Mahmud. "Elections in Palestine During the Late Ottoman Period." In *Rethinking Late Ottoman Palestine: The Young-Turk Rule, 1908–1918*, ed. Yuval Ben-Bassat and Eyal Ginio. London: I. B. Tauris, forthcoming.

———. *Haifa in the Late Ottoman Period, 1864–1914: A Muslim Town in Transition*. Leiden: Brill, 1998.

———. "Jewish-Muslim Social and Economic Relations in Haifa (1870–1914), According to Sijill Registers." In *Aspects of Ottoman History*, ed. Amy Singer and Amnon Cohen, 114–23. Jerusalem: Magnes Press, 1994.

Yehoshu'a, Ya'kov. "Al-Jara'id al-'Arabiyya allati sudirat fi Filastin: 1908–1918" (Arabic Newspapers Published in Palestine, 1908–1918). *Al-Sharq* 2, no. 8 (1972): 18–21.

———. "Al-sahafa al-'Arabiyya fi Yafa, 1908–1914" (The Arabic Press in Jaffa, 1908–1914). *Al-Sharq* 3, no. 7 (1973): 36–38.

———. *Ha-bayt ve-ha-reḥov bi-Yerushalayim ha-yeshana* (House and Street in Old Jerusalem). Jerusalem: Reuven Mass, 1966.

———. *Neighborhood Relations in the Turkish Period*. Unpublished pamphlet.

———. "Sahifata *al-Taraqqi* wa-*Filastin*" (The Newspapers *Al-Taraqqi* and *Filastin*). *Al-Sharq* 3, no. 8 (1973): 37–42.

———. *Tarikh al-sihafa al-'Arabiyya fi Filastin fil-'ahd al-'Uthmani, 1908–1918* (History of the Arabic Press in Palestine in the Ottoman Period, 1908–1918). Jerusalem: Matb'a al-ma'rif, 1978.

———. "Tel Aviv in the Image of the Arab Press in the Five Years After Its

Founding, 1909–14" (in Hebrew). *Ha-Mizraḥ he-ḥadash* 19, no. 4 (1969): 218–22.

———. "Yeḥasam shel ha-'itonaim ve-ha-sofrim he-'Aravim le-teḥiata shel ha-safa ha-'Ivrit be-dorenu" (The Attitudes of Arab Journalists and Writers to the Revival of the Hebrew Language in Our Times). *Ba-ma'aracha: Bitaon ha-ẓibur ha-Sefaradi ve-'edot ha-Mizraḥ*, no. 279 (1974).

———. *Yerushalayim tmol shilshom* (Jerusalem in Days of Old). 2 vols. Jerusalem: Reuven Mass, 1979.

Yellin, S. *Les Capitulations et la juridiction consulaire*. Beirut: Selim E. Mann, 1909.

———. *Une page d'histoire Turque: Conference tenue en decembre 1908*. n.p.: n.p., 1911.

Yellin, Yehoshu'a bar David. *Zichronot le-ben Yerushalayim* (Memories of a Son of Jerusalem). Jerusalem: Zion Press-Ruhold Brothers, 1923.

Yerolympos, Alexandra. "Conscience citadine et intérét municipal à Salonique à la fin du XIXe siècle." In *Vivre dans l'empire Ottoman: Sociabilités et relations intercommunautaires (XVIIIe–XXe siècles)*, ed. François Georgeon and Paul Dumont, 123–44. Paris: L'Harmattan, 1997.

Yodfat, Arieh. "Va'ad ha-'ir ha-klali li-Yehudei Yafo u-p'eulotav ba-shanim 1912–1915" (The General City Council of the Jews of Jaffa and Its Activities in the Years 1912–1915). In *Vatikin: Meḥkarim be-toldot ha-yishuv*, ed. H. Z. Hirschberg, 233–55. Ramat Gan: Bar Ilan University Press, 1975.

Young, Iris Marion. "Polity and Group Difference: A Critique of the Ideal of Universal Citizenship." In *Theorizing Citizenship*, ed. Ronald Beiner, 175–208. Albany: State University of New York Press, 1995.

Zachs, Fruma. *The Making of a Syrian Identity: Intellectuals and Merchants in Nineteenth Century Beirut*. Leiden: Brill, 2005.

Zachs, Fruma, and Basilius Bawardi. "Ottomanism and Syrian Patriotism in Salim al-Bustani's Thought." In *Ottoman Reform and Muslim Regeneration*, ed. Itzhack Weismann and Fruma Zachs, 111–26. London: I. B. Tauris, 2005.

Zandi-Sayek, Sibel. "Orchestrating Difference, Performing Identity: Urban Space and Public Rituals in 19th c. Izmir." In *Hybrid Urbanism: On the Identity Discourse and the Built Environment*, ed. Nazar al-Sayyad, 42–66. Westport, CT: Praeger, 2001.

Zarcone, Thierry. "Freemasonry and Related Trends in Muslim Reformist Thought in the Turko-Persian Area." Unpublished article.

———. *Mystiques, philosophes et Francs-maçons en Islam: Riza Tevfik, penseur Ottoman (1868–1949)* (Mystics, Philosophers, and Freemasons in Islam: Riza Tevfik, Ottoman Thinker). Paris: Librairie d'Amérique et d'Orient Jean Maisonneuve, 1993.

Zecharia, Shabtai. *Jerusalem Neighborhoods: Jaffa Road, Buildings and Sites* (in Hebrew). Jerusalem: Shabtai Zecharia, 1998.

Zürcher, Erik Jan. "Between Death and Desertion: The Experience of the Ottoman Soldiers in World War I." *Turcica* 28 (1996): 235–58.

Index

CPSIA information can be obtained
at www.ICGtesting.com
Printed in the USA
LVHW03s1434050818
586022LV00003B/534/P